CW00504153

THE ECONOMIC DEVELOPMENT
OF THE BRITISH COAL INDUSTRY
*From Industrial Revolution
to the Present Day*

THE ECONOMIC DEVELOPMENT
OF THE
BRITISH COAL INDUSTRY

From Industrial Revolution
to the Present Day

BY

NEIL K. BUXTON

Department of Economics,
Heriot-Watt University,
Edinburgh

BATSFORD ACADEMIC

First published 1978
© N.K. Buxton 1978
ISBN 0 7134 1994 6

To my Mother, Janet Anne Buxton —
who set me on the right path.

Printed and bound in Great Britain by
Redwood Burn Ltd, Trowbridge & Esher

for the Publishers, B.T. Batsford Ltd.
4 Fitzhardinge Street, London, W1H 0AH

CONTENTS

PREFACE

Note: Unless otherwise indicated, Table numbers quoted refer to tables in the chapter in which the reference occurs.

PREFACE

Coalmining has played an extremely important part in the modern development of Britain. It typified the growth and general prosperity experienced by the heavy staple industries for much of the 18th and 19th centuries, the social costs incurred during the growth to maturity of these industries and the economic difficulties subsequently encountered in the 20th century. The loss of markets, surplus capacity and heavy unemployment which characterised the interwar years were nowhere better illustrated than in the case of coal. Again in the modern era, the problems of coalmining are archetypal of those which the traditional sectors were forced to tackle, once the brief prosperity following the second world war had come to an end. Since, in so many respects, it represents the 'typical case', coalmining may be used as a yardstick against which to measure the performance and prosperity of British industry as a whole. Conclusions of general significance may be drawn about the rate of innovation, attitudes to new technology, the use of, and returns to, labour and the levels of efficiency and competence achieved in good times and bad.

Despite the fact that it has occupied a central position on the industrial stage in Britain for the best part of three centuries, the role of coalmining has consistently been under-estimated. No comprehensive history of the industry's progress, incorporating the findings of recent research, presently exists. Parts of the story are to be found scattered across a wide range of articles, theses and monographs; but as Baron Duckham has pointed out in his introduction to Galloway's *Annals of Coalmining,* 'no one, as yet, has appeared willing to master the secondary sources of the day ... to give us the balanced general history which is needed'. The present study, based on both primary and secondary materials, is an attempt to fill this gap in existing knowledge. However, to cover fully all aspects of the industry's development, both at national and at regional level, is simply not possible. Necessarily, limits have been imposed by time-constraints, the space permitted by publishing economics and the need to preserve a balance between breadth and depth.

Above all, two considerations have largely determined the scope of the study. First, the need to emphasise only the important issues at particular periods, whether at national or at regional level. Second, a desire to take as dispassionate a view as possible of the industry's performance and problems. Because of the nature of work below ground, and the qualities of the men who have undertaken it, problems in coalmining have evoked passionate responses and a wealth of

7

emotional and heartfelt surveys, reports and pamphlets. But too often more heat than light has been generated. To some, the present study will appear too clinical and lacking in 'human appeal'. I can only reply that this was a deliberate and conscious decision, taken at the outset, in an attempt to provide as balanced and unbiased a judgement of the industry's development as possible.

As always in the searching out and sifting of material, a large number of debts of gratitude have been incurred. Particularly, I should like to thank the Carnegie Trust for the Universities of Scotland which generously financed the study. Without the help of the Trust, the book could never have been completed. I am also grateful for the kind and patient assistance offered in several libraries, especially the North of England Institute of Mining and Mechanical Engineers, the PRO and SRO, the NCB library at Hobart House and various University libraries. To Mrs Susan Sinclair who endured the time spent 'down the pits' by typing successive drafts with cheerfulness and fortitude my heartfelt thanks. I am also indebted to Mrs. Anne Torrance for so conscientiously compiling the index and to my former head of department, Professor Tom Johnston, who not only provided me with much useful material but also the encouragement to 'stay with it'. Above all my thanks to my wife and family who alone know, and suffered with me, the many ups and downs encountered during the period of research and writing.

Heriot-Watt University   NEIL K. BUXTON

8

PART ONE
CHANGES IN RESOURCE USE: THE TYRANNY OF COAL

1 Demand and Supply before 1750

1 THE DEMAND FOR COAL

According to Nef there was virtually a revolution in the consumption and uses made of coal between 1550 and 1700, this being part of an alleged first 'Industrial Revolution' that was only slightly less dramatic than that originating in the second half of the 18th century. This overstates the case since the scale of development in pre-industrialised Britain did not deserve such a label. On the other hand, it does seem that relatively high rates of growth of coal output and trade were achieved during most of the 16th century due, it was claimed, to nothing less than a complete 'change in the habits with respect to fuel of the entire British people'.[1] Prior to the accession of Elizabeth I, it is probable that less than 1 cwt of coal was consumed annually per head of population. Before it could become widely adopted, the mineral had to overcome the prejudices and objections of potential consumers. Initially, it was regarded as inferior to wood in terms of heat and an 'intolerable nuisance'[2] due to the smoke and grime it exuded into the atmosphere. Queen Elizabeth herself, although the owner of a number of collieries, strongly objected to coal smoke and the use of the mineral is said to have been severely restricted in London during her reign.[3] However, the general adoption of chimneys and growing realisation that coal was more efficient both as a source of heat in the home and as a fuel in industry were sufficient to overcome most aesthetic objections.

By the start of the 18th century, annual consumption per head had reached some 9 cwts, coal output having expanded in absolute terms from an estimated 0.2 million tons per annum in the 1550's to 3 million tons by 1700. Evidence of the sustained growth in demand is presented in Table 1.

Concern has been expressed about the validity of the estimates in Table 1, particularly those relating to the earlier years. It has been alleged that since data defects make these 'guesstimates' rather than estimates, the fourteen-fold increase in output shown between 1551/60 and 1681/90 is less than statistically meaningful.[4] What can be asserted with greater confidence is first, that the rate of growth of output was relatively high about the middle of the 16th century

Changes in Resource Use: The Tyranny of Coal

Table 1

*Estimates of (i) Average Annual Output of Coal (000 tons)
and (ii) Proportion of Total U.K. Output Produced in the Principal
Mining Districts, Selected Periods, 1551/60-1781/90*[1]

District	1551-60 (i)	(ii)	1681-90 (i)	(ii)	1781-90 (i)	(ii)
Durham & Northumberland	65	31	1,225	41	3,000	29
Scotland	40	19	475	16	1,600	15
Wales	20	10	200	7	800	8
Midland[2]	65	31	850	29	4,000	39
Cumberland	6	3	100	3	500	5
Kingswood Chase	6	3			140	
			100	3		4
Somerset	4				140	
Forest of Dean	3	3	25		90	
				1		
Devon and Ireland	1		7		25	
Total	210	100	2,982	100	10,295	100

SOURCE:
Nef, op. cit., I, pp. 19-20.
NOTES:
1. Volume figures have been converted from their original weights. Since in the 16th and 17th centuries measurement of weight was notoriously inaccurate the figures should be regarded as denoting trends rather than as precise measurements.
2. Includes Yorkshire, Lancashire, Cheshire, Derbyshire, Shropshire, Staffordshire, Nottinghamshire, Warwickshire, Leicestershire and Worcestershire.

and second, that the greater part of the overall increase in output between mid-Tudor and later Stuart times was concentrated in the earlier rather than later part of the period. For much of the 17th century there is evidence of surplus capacity in the Northern Coalfield. A large number of new sinkings were made and over-investment became a characteristic of the mining industry as owners struggled for a share of southern markets.[5]

The outstanding feature of Table 1 is the early predominance of the Northern Coalfield, a position based on the relative ease with which it could distribute coal by sea. Throughout the period specified in the Table, the great bulk of output was destined for the home market, exports generally accounting for less than 5% of total output. Yet more than 40% of output in 1700 was carried by water, reflecting

12

the inadequacy of overland transport and the relatively wide geographical separation between demand and supply within Britain. Since
the principal sources of supply were to be found in the north while
markets had developed mainly in the south, the mineral was shipped
coastwise. Hence, the coastal shipping industry thrived largely on
a diet of coal: in 1750, as in 1850 and 1950, the tonnage of coal
carried coastwise exceeded the weight of all other cargoes combined.[6]
At the heart of this trade were Newcastle and the river Tyne in the
north, London and the river Thames in the south.

The Tyne valley had established itself from the 13th century as
the principal source of supply, developing routes, both coastal and
foreign, to carry the coal of the district by sea. It enjoyed a virtual
monopoly of the coal trade until about the 1630's when its position
began to weaken. The best-situated shallow mines were worked out,
necessitating either sinking to greater depths, at increased costs and
with greater attendant risks in working, or moving inland, away
from the coast and river to exploit fresh deposits. In addition, a
series of random shocks dislocated the Tyne's trade, including raids
by the Dunkirk pirates, war with France and Spain and, most serious
of all, the Civil War during which Newcastle fell into Royalist hands.[7]
Of greater importance in the long term was the development of
collieries in the Wear district using Sunderland as an outlet for
shipments to London and other east coast ports. During the 17th
century, shipments from the Wear grew from humble beginnings to
average between one-fifth and one-quarter of those from the Tyne.
The process continued in the following century with Sunderland
accounting for an increasingly large proportion of northern shipments.
The position is outlined in Table 2.

Table 2 shows total shipments from the Tyne and Wear during
the 18th century. The trade was dominated by Newcastle and
Sunderland but smaller ports in the north-east such as Whitley, Blyth
and Hartley earned some share of the southern coal trade. Throughout,
London and the South-East of England remained by far the most
important markets, both served by the river Thames. Coal imports
into London increased from 265.6 thousand tons in 1660 to 395.4
thousand in 1690: by the start of the 18th century consumption per
head in the capital was 16 cwts, far higher than the national average
noted earlier of 9 cwts.[8] By 1750, coastwise shipments to London
from Northumberland and Durham exceeded half a million tons.
The extent of the northern monopoly is shown by the fact that in
the following twenty years London absorbed an average of only 7,000
tons from all other ports. Only after 1800 did the Northern Coalfield's
overwhelming dominance of the British coal trade begin to weaken.
The development of canals and early railways enabled previously
land-locked collieries in the Midlands to compete for markets.

Although in certain regions this posed a serious threat to northern sales, penetration of the London market via these routes was slight before 1850. In that year, a mere 85,000 tons of inland coal were sent to London, 55,000 tons of which were delivered by railways. This was insignificant compared with the total of 3.5 million tons delivered to the metropolis by sea (see Chapter 2, Table 2 below).

On the other hand, improvements in inland distribution allowed collieries in Yorkshire and the Midland counties to serve more efficiently neighbouring industrial and domestic consumers. It was this, together with the growing concentration of industry in the

Table 2

Total Shipments from Tyne & Wear at Decade Intervals during the Eighteenth Century (000 tons)[1]

	Shipments from Tyne	Shipments from Wear
1700	543	111
10	445	175
22[2]	697	_[3]
30	734	_[3]
40	848	_[3]
50	763	429
60	755	477
70	986	564
80	970	596
90	1,081	750
1800	1,638	853

SOURCES:

Calculated from *Grand Allies Minute Book, Partnership Minutes, Memorandums etc. with Colliery Views, Computations etc; Royal Commission on Coal, 1871, Committee E;* British Association, *The Industrial Resources of the District of the Three Northern Rivers, the Tyne, the Wear and Tees, including Reports on the Local Manufacturers* (1863); T. S. Ashton and J. Sykes, *The Coal Industry of the Eighteenth Century* (1929, revised edition 1964), appendix E, pp. 249-51.

NOTES:

1. Converted for purposes of the Table from Newcastle chaldrons to tons. In the 17th century, the Newcastle chaldron varied according to type and quality of coal being shipped but the weight was officially settled at 53 cwts in 1695.
2. Details of shipments from the Tyne are not available between 1711 and 1721.
3. Details not available.

Midlands, which accounted for a rapid increase in the production of coal by these districts and a corresponding decline in the north's share of total U.K. output. In absolute terms, Northumberland and Durham remained by far the most important coalfield throughout the Industrial Revolution, increasing output from just over one million tons at the end of the 17th century to an average of 3 million in 1781-90 and to 15.5 million in 1854-58. Yet the coalfield's share of total production over the corresponding period fell from 41 to 29 to 24%.

The rapid growth of output about the mid-16th century (see Table 1) can largely be attributed to the relatively rapid development of the British economy. The very fact that there was no parallel economic expansion abroad before 1700 meant that there was no comparable increase in the use of coal. Initially, the industry depended heavily on demand from domestic users but increasingly coal was harnessed to a variety of industrial pursuits. It was, for instance, in Britain that developments in the manufacture of salt, glass and metals were particularly rapid, these being closely followed by expansion in shipbuilding and shipping. At the same time, several new specialisms emerged such as the production of saltpetre and gunpowder, soap-making and the alum and copperas industries. Industrial techniques were borrowed heavily from abroad, resulting in greater diversification of the economy. Expansion in the 'new' trades together with the steady, yet continuous, growth of established sectors such as textiles, iron and brewing produced a wider industrial base from which subsequent development could be launched.[10] Although they were not worth calling an Industrial Revolution, these changes could not have taken place at all had it not been for the ready response of the coal industry. By 1700, England had almost certainly become the largest coal-producing and consuming country in Europe. Increasingly coal was used to replace timber as a fuel in the boiling of soap, refining of sugar and manufacture of starch and candles. It was also needed in large quantities to heat the salt pans,[11] evaporating the brine to produce salt. In addition, by 1700, both brewing and textiles ranked in the top half-dozen of coal-using industries.

Yet one of the most significant technical breakthroughs, resulting in a much increased demand for coal, has received surprisingly little attention. Due acknowledgement has not been made of the fact that coal and coke were successfully used in the smelting of non-ferrous metals long before they were found viable in the manufacture of iron. As early as the 1620's, coke had been tried and approved for the smelting of copper and successful experiments followed in the smelting of tin and lead. This application of coal fuel to the manufacture of non-ferrous metals was associated with the introduction to England of the reverberatory furnace, one of the most important technical developments of the 17th century. It was part of a general movement to improve furnaces or kilns in order to protect the material which was being burned from the noxious properties of coal. As one observer has pointed out, by the 1680's this type of furnace was the key to successful English breakthroughs in the smelting of lead, copper and tin and by 1700 increasing success was being obtained with brass.[12]

Neglect in the literature of this early success in using coal to smelt non-ferrous metals can be attributed to the amount of time and space devoted to the problems of smelting iron with mineral fuel. In a sense this emphasis is inevitable in view of the vital part played in the Industrial Revolution by the developing inter-dependency between coal and iron. Dud Dudley alleged in his *Mettallum Martis*[13] that he had successfully discovered how to smelt iron ore with coal fuel before the outbreak of the Civil War. His pamphlet was, in essence, a plea for adequate financial backing to allow him to prove the commercial viability of his discovery. Although overstating his achievement, Dudley in all likelihood did succeed in smelting iron ore with mineral fuel. Almost certainly it would have been of inferior quality to charcoal iron and the furnace which he specially designed was capable of producing only seven tons of iron per week, about one-third to one-half of the output of the average charcoal furnace.[14] Several other attempts followed from the 1650's to smelt iron with peat and coal, some of which achieved partial success,[15] but it was left to Abraham Darby I to make the important breakthrough at his Coalbrookdale furnace in Shropshire in 1709. Coal, in the form of coke, was used to provide significant quantities of pig iron, albeit of poor quality. The argument that coke-smelted pig yielded bar iron that was too 'cold-short' (i.e. brittle when cold) has now largely been discounted: it was no more brittle than if charcoal iron had been used in the process of conversion. What was important was the higher silicon content of coke pig iron which made it difficult to convert into bar iron in the forge. In comparison to charcoal iron, increased quantities of coke-smelted pig and charcoal were required per ton of bar iron, driving up forgemasters' total costs by as much as 30%.[16]

Although the process was discovered in 1709, its use did not become widespread in Britain until the 1750's. Indeed, charcoal-smelting capacity even increased between 1720 and 1750. At first sight, this lag between invention and innovation is difficult to understand in view of the alleged chronic shortage of wood that existed for conversion into charcoal. It has been explained by a variety of factors, ranging from the deliberate efforts of the Darbys to keep their process secret to the unique characteristics of the coal used at Coalbrookdale and the inferior quality of the pig iron produced by the new technology.[17] None of these stand up to critical examination.

It is certain that other iron-masters knew of the Darby process in the first half of the 18th century and that knowledge of it must have spread both from partners and from workers employed in the Coalbrookdale works. Equally, although the sulphur content of the coal used by Darby in Shropshire was indeed low, it was not significantly lower than that available in, for instance, S. Staffordshire. Yet the new process was adopted neither in that region nor elsewhere in Shropshire where iron-masters had access to the same type of coal as employed in Coalbrookdale. As observed, there was a quality difference between charcoal and coke-smelted pig iron but this did not effectively prevent more rapid adoption of the latter process. The quality difference remained relatively constant throughout the entire 18th century, yet coke smelting was, after all, rapidly innovated from the 1750's.

Had Darby's process been more rapidly innovated, clearly the demand for coal would have been very much larger over the early decades of the 18th century than it actually was. Recently a further explanation of the slow rate of take-up of the new technology has been advanced. It has been argued[18] that since a critical shortage of wood never in fact existed in Britain, insufficient pressure was exerted on iron-masters to effect the change from charcoal to coke-smelting techniques during the first half of the 18th century. It was precisely because coke smelting did not enjoy a clear cost advantage over the charcoal-based process until the 1750's that the former was not innovated during the first half of the 18th century. The costs of making pig iron with mineral fuel fell significantly after 1709, yet smelting with charcoal remained the less costly technique until the early 1750's.[19] During that decade the relative costs of production of the two techniques significantly changed: the costs of producing charcoal pig iron rapidly increased due to rising raw material costs, while coke pig iron costs dramatically fell. Only now did the adoption of coke-smelting technology make sound economic sense. By the later 1750's the superiority of mineral fuel smelting was established and iron-masters rapidly effected the change-over.

Hence at the outset of the Industrial Revolution, the crucial relationship between coal and iron had been confirmed and an even more rapid increase in the demand for coal was assured. But the long struggle to unite the two sectors should not obscure two important issues. First, for some considerable time before Darby's discovery, coal had been successfully employed in the smelting of non-ferrous metals and second, a constantly growing number of other industrial uses for coal was being found during the course of the 17th century. From being originally confined to such domestic functions as cooking and heating, by 1700 about one million tons of coal were being burned annually in British manufacturing industry.

This represented approximately one-third of all coal being mined in the country at that time.

2 THE SUPPLY OF COAL

In response to the growing pressure of demand, the supply side of the industry was jolted out of its previous equilibrium during the latter part of the 16th century. The success achieved in substantially raising output from the 1550's meant not only that the supply of coal was sufficient but, indeed, that it was more than sufficient to cater for the needs of an expanding economy. Therefore, as noted earlier, a condition of surplus capacity existed in coalmining for much of the 17th century. This ability to bring supply up to, and beyond, the level of a steadily increasing demand depended upon forces 'external' to coalmining as well as on major developments within the industry itself.

A Factors 'External' to the Industry

Without doubt British coalmining greatly benefited from general economic and social changes taking place during and after the 16th century. The case of *Queen* v. *Northumberland* in 1568 had established that only mines of gold and silver belonged to the Crown. All baser metals and other minerals belonged to the proprietor of the land; generally, to the owner of the surface of the land. However, this decision was not as serious for the State as it might have been since 'the Dissolution of the Monasteries' in the reign of Henry VIII had effectively transferred extensive mineral properties from the Church to Crown ownership. Whereas the former had been unwilling to invest heavily itself in coalmining and was sometimes reluctant to grant leases on reasonable terms to allow others to work the coal, a totally different attitude was adopted by the State. From the outset, the State was prepared to grant leases to mine for coal on highly favourable terms to 'adventurers' prepared to risk their capital. Long leases on easy terms, low royalties and usually no limit placed on the output which the leaseholder could extract from the property remained standard over the second half of the 16th and early 17th centuries. Royalty payments were covered by, or merged in, the rent as far as the latter extended, but there were no standard criteria for determining such royalties. They might consist of a fixed sum per ton raised, a fixed sum per acre worked or, as was to be the case in Scotland during the 18th century, be determined by a sliding scale, varying with the selling price of coal raised. The first type was probably the most common but even within this category significant differences occurred. The royalty was sometimes based simply on total tonnage raised, sometimes on total *sales* and occasionally varied according to the different descriptions of coal worked.[20]

With the steady increase in demand for coal during the second half of the 16th century, large discrepancies began to appear between the fixed rent paid by the lessee for the right to work the mineral and the value of the output obtained.[21] Moreover these sizeable differences between revenues accruing to the lessee and to the proprietor of land could continue over an extended period in view of the lengthy leases of between 21 and 63 years usually conferred. Lessees were therefore in a position to make substantial profits, a factor which encouraged capital to pour into the coalmining industry up to the first quarter of the 17th century. At the same time, the advancing Enclosure Movement was reducing the number of small landholders and encouraging the promotion of large-scale colliery enterprise. Indeed, increasingly between 1550 and 1700 enclosure was effected specifically for the purpose of consolidating mineral property and to restrict the mineral rights of smallholders. In short, the transfer of mineral property from the Church and small farmers by means of the Reformation and developing Enclosure Movement contributed directly to the rapid expansion of the coal industry during the later 16th century and early part of the 17th.

Another 'external' factor traditionally regarded as vital to the development of coalmining was the acute scarcity of wood in Britain which, it was argued, became apparent during the reign of Queen Elizabeth and persisted throughout the following century. This scarcity was allegedly due to inadequate initial reserves, expanding domestic demand and above all, rapidly increasing industrial requirements. In particular, the manufacture of charcoal iron was regarded as having taken a savage toll of British woodlands.

Seen in this light the expansion of coalmining owed much to an inadequate endowment, and subsequent scarcity, of timber. Although this is an attractively simple hypothesis, the true situation was rather different. It is now clear that the iron industry was not, after all, the villain of the piece, responsible for creating a serious wood shortage. At peak production, the highest rate of consumption of the charcoal iron industry was under 60 million cubic ft of solid wood per year.[22] Although the full extent of woodlands in the 17th and 18th centuries is indeterminate, their remnants in England and Wales by the 1950's occupied some 2.3 million acres. This could have maintained the charcoal iron industry in peak production for about 100 years. Moreover, due to tree growth, an acre of woodland can gain up to 100 cubic ft in a year. Thus 650,000 acres of woodland, less than 2% of the land surface of England and Wales, could have sustained the maximum output of the British charcoal iron industry for ever.

Indeed, there appears to have been little absolute shortage of timber in Britain during the critical period 1550-1750, when coal allegedly benefited from just such a shortage. It is true that transport costs and the relative fragility of charcoal limited the distances that it could be carried to particular iron works. Thus, *sustained* production of iron on any one site could become increasingly difficult, especially where concentration of plant developed in relatively desirable locations. However, this is far removed from the argument advanced by Nef, Ashton and others that the substitution of coal for wood on a national scale was 'urgent', 'vital' and accomplished out of sheer necessity. In fact, the continued availability of charcoal supplies largely explains why charcoal smelting remained the least-cost method of producing pig iron before the 1750's. Simply, the cost of wood as a fuel was not yet sufficiently high to induce iron-masters to change to smelting with mineral fuel, particularly in view of the relatively high costs incurred in converting coke-smelted pig into finished bar iron.

Yet, on balance the forces at work in British society from at least the reign of Queen Elizabeth were conducive to a more rapid expansion of coalmining. The transfer of mineral properties, the generous terms granted to early lessees, the resultant inflow of capital into mining, and those forces which encouraged a growth in scale of colliery enterprise all had a formative influence on the development of the young coal industry. But it would be wrong to regard these general influences as solely responsible for the expansion of output. The industry itself was far from passive.

B Technological Advance in Coalmining

Increasingly before 1750 the coal industry practised a degree of 'self-help' in bringing supply into line with expanding demand. Important in this context was the gradual innovation in several districts of the longwall system of coalmining. Before the mid-17th century, the use of 'pillar and stall' ('stoop and room' in Scotland) had been general, with headways driven along the grain of the coal from which the stalls of the hewer were cut out. It was an individualistic type of mining, with each hewer working alone in his stall. By the start of the 18th century these stalls were some three yards wide and were separated from each other by pillars of coal, usually four yards in breadth, which were left standing to support the roof. The intention was, therefore, that at least half the coal would be left in the pit in the form of roof supports although there was a constant temptation for miners to whittle away at these pillars as a means of readily increasing their individual outputs.

About the middle of the 17th century, longwall mining was introduced into Shropshire. Regarded as particularly suitable for thin seams and more economical than 'pillar and stall', the method involved removing the whole seam in a single operation. The workings advanced in a continuous line, the space (goaf) previously occupied by coal being filled in with stone and refuse upon which the superincumbent strata settled down. During the first half of the 18th century the new system made steady progress in both the Midlands and South of England allowing more economical working and easing the problem of ventilation. Where air currents could be introduced they were able to sweep along the entire face where the miners worked. Although its invasion of other coalfields during the 18th and 19th centuries has been described as 'one of the most outstanding developments in the technical history of coal-mining'[23] longwall signally failed to gain a foothold in one principal area, the Northern Coalfield. It was considered that longwall mining required roof and floor to be of hard, stable material not given to frequent subsidence. In the north, where workings were near, or even under rivers and sea, pillars were regarded as essential to provide adequate support.

Gradual changes in the system of mining were accompanied by an expansion in the number of pits and important improvements in the technology of the industry before 1750. The latter were responsible not only for a greater efficiency in the production and distribution of coal from the pit-head to the staithes but also allowed the mineral to be worked at much greater depths. In this way, the productive capacity of the industry was significantly expanded. It was here that the early application of steam power had such a vital role to play.

The problem which dwarfed all others in importance up to the 18th century was that of securing adequate drainage. By 1700, mines of at least 20 fathoms, or over one hundred feet, were common in almost all British coalfields, with depths of between 300 and 400 feet being reached in the Tyne and Wear districts.[24] But as mines grew deeper, so the problem of the steady accumulation of water underground became more difficult to solve, not only in the mining of coal but also in copper, tin and lead mining. Hence the most serious, and urgent, technical difficulty facing mining engineers was to devise more powerful drainage systems; specifically to find more effective means of pumping water out of mines. Hitherto, drainage had generally been accomplished by employing a variety of different methods. In earlier years, adits, or soughs, had commonly been used: these were tunnels driven from the seams (generally situated on high ground) down to an adjacent valley. Since the pit-bottoms were above the level of free drainage, unwanted water would flow away through the adits to the side of the hill. Mining at constantly greater depths, however, meant that adits became increasingly insufficient; simply, the depth of working was such that free drainage of this type was no longer adequate.

Where adits could not be used, or were becoming inadequate, various types of pumps were employed to rid the pits of water. The early hand-pump and endless chain of pots, although still used to supplement drainage systems, had generally given way during the

17th century to the use of horse-power. The horse-gin, drawing buckets or tubs up the shaft was sometimes supplemented, particularly in Scotland, by windmills but these were found to be most unreliable. In certain districts, water-wheels were used for drainage but as one observer pointed out, 'there is not that conveniency of water everywhere.'[25] Since most of these devices were capable only of forcing water up some 15-20 fathoms at a single flight, drainage had become, by the late 17th century, the great engineering problem of the age. J. C. in his *Compleat Collier* pointed out that by the start of the 18th century there were many flooded collieries in the north where all known methods had proved incapable of handling the frequent inrushes of water. Could any invention be discovered that would make these pits commercial again, it would 'be most lucrative to the inventor.'[26]

He was, of course, correct. The solution to the critical problem of adequate drainage was to be found in the application of steam power to pumping devices. It was indeed to prove extremely lucrative but, as is often the way, rather for those who added necessary refinements to the steam pumps to make them commercially viable than for the early pioneers. More lucrative, in fact, than was once thought since it is now apparent that steam was much more extensively applied during the course of the 18th century than earlier authorities such as Lord had supposed.[27] As early as 1631, David Ramsay had attempted to raise water by 'fire'. In 1663, the Marquis of Worcester claimed to have raised water 40 feet by means of steam pressure[28] and in this early experimental work he was followed by several others, most notably, perhaps, Sir Samuel Morland. These early engine-builders, of whom James Watt may for present purposes be considered the last in a long and distinguished line, benefited greatly from parallel advances in the frontiers of scientific knowledge and the application of scientific principles. Indeed the increasing use of steam power, regarded as 'the greatest gift from science to industry,'[29] was wholly dependent upon the emergence of greater efficiency and precision in engineering; the new iron-founding techniques developed by the Darbys who initially supplied most of the engine parts; and perhaps above all upon individuals acquiring an education in, and maintaining close links with, the developing streams of scientific knowledge.[30]

Yet, ironically, neither Savery nor Newcomen, the most famous of the early pioneers, can be included directly within this educated scientific tradition.[31] Thomas Savery's engine, patented in 1698, was of little practical use in the early years of the 18th century. Popularly known as the 'Miner's Friend' it was clumsy, dangerous to use and is unlikely to have produced an effective lift of water of much more than 40 feet. It was therefore extremely expensive, given the large number of such engines that would be needed to drain pits of any considerable depth. Nonetheless, engines constructed upon Savery's principles by the engineer Joshua Wrigley and others were to enjoy something of an 'Indian Summer' later in the century.[32] The first steam engine of major practical significance was that produced by Thomas Newcomen. His 'fire', or 'atmospheric', engine was probably first built about 1705, and first erected at a colliery around 1712. Much has been written elsewhere about this pioneer effort[33] and although details vary,[34] it is clear that while heat-loss from the engine was considerable and it was highly extravagant in the use of fuel,[35] it had the over-riding advantage that it could lift water from considerable depths. In 1713 at Griff colliery in Warwickshire it was already said to have reduced pumping costs from £900, using horses, to only £150 per annum.

For a coal industry that had become increasingly desperate for just such an effective pumping machine and for which heavy fuel consumption was relatively unimportant,[36] this new piece of technology represented a major breakthrough. Sold at first under Savery's patent which monopolised the marketing of steam engines until 1733, it would seem that by that date over 60 Newcomen engines had been built, more than 50 of which found employment within Great Britain.[37] By 1769, according to Matthias Dunn there were 99 that he knew of in operation,[38] and by 1781 when rotative motion was introduced, it is likely that at least 360 Newcomen engines had been built in Britain.

It would be difficult, therefore, to accept the view advanced by some observers[39] that the rate of take-up of the engine in the various mining regions of the country was slow and sporadic. What can be accepted is that only deep mines, operated on a large scale, could justify the use of the engine. During the first 30 years of its life, the Newcomen engine with pumping equipment generally cost between £1,000 and £1,500. *The Minute Book of the Grand Allies* shows in a 'Computation of the Expenses of Winning Long Benton out of the Workings of the Wheat Pit' in 1739 that the cost of erecting one 'fire' engine amounted to £1,200, more than half the total cost involved of £2,032.6s (see Table 3 below).[40] It may have been these relatively high costs and the practicality of using the engine only at large-scale pits which persuaded earlier writers that diffusion of the new technology must have been slow. The evidence now available of experience in different mining districts suggests a different picture. Continuing research has meant that even quite recent estimates of the extent of engine-use have had to be substantially revised. Harris, for instance, estimated in 1967 that a minimum of 1,300 steam engines of all types had been employed in Britain by 1800. More recently, the same author has accepted that this was far too low a figure and that a total in excess of 2,000 should be substituted, with at least half the steam power by that date being employed at coal mines.[41]

The great value of the Newcomen engine lay in its ability to perform tasks which neither horses nor water-powered machinery were capable of accomplishing. In this sense, it removed bottlenecks which had held back development in deeper and larger-scale mining, so permitting a breakthrough into an era of relatively high profits. But more than that, deeper pits immediately required *technical* breakthroughs in other directions. The increasing scale of mining operations meant a greater complexity of processes and layout. In turn, this demanded improvements in underground ventilation, haulage, winding techniques and numerous other operations involved in winning the coal.

An immediate consequence of deeper shafts was the increased danger of fatal accidents due to suffocation and explosions in the mine caused by sparks or flame coming into contact with gas. Chokedamp (carbonic acid gas) had been an important early enemy of the miner in that it could cause suffocation. However, a brief warning of its presence was usually afforded since it first extinguished the miner's candle. The chief danger as mines grew deeper became firedamp (methane gas) which, being lighter than air, tended to gather near the roof of the pit. It was capable of giving rise to instant explosions, and its existence in the workings was commonly detected before the 18th century by slowly raising a lighted candle. A bluish tint at the tip of the flame was evidence of the presence of firedamp. It was common practice in the 17th century for 'firemen' to dispel the gas by causing a deliberate explosion ('firing the gas'). Where possible safer and more straightforward methods were used to remove the gas. In the best mines, the importance of adequate ventilation was realised. Physical conditions permitting, it was customary to sink vertical air-shafts to the workings. If air still did not circulate within the pit, the expedient of deliberate face-airing was adopted. Viewers were well aware by the late 17th century that the foul air in the mine had to be heated to allow it to rise upwards and enable cold air to enter to take its place. In this way, a current of air through the mine was obtained. The roads were deliberately stopped to direct the fresh air to the coal face and baskets of burnings coals, or fire-lamps, were hung in the upcast shaft. The foul air, on being heated, was carried upwards, fresh air entered the pit through the downcast shaft, passed round the faces and, in turn, passed out of the pit through the upcast shaft. A refinement of this practice was the introduction of a constantly burning furnace, located at the foot of the upcast shaft, to set in motion a current of air.[42]

The danger inherent in the naked flame of the miner's candle was readily appreciated,[43] but other forms of illumination in the pits were found to be seriously deficient. Various expedients were tried, notably Carlisle Spedding's steel and flint mill to provide a continuous stream of sparks, thereby affording light for the face workers; mirrors were strategically placed at the surface to reflect sunlight down into the workings; and on the Tyne even the use of phosphorous and putrescent fish to shed a glow of light on mining operations was tried. None proved an effective or permanent substitute for the miner's candle.

Above all, it was essential that a more efficient form of ventilation be found to remove, as far as possible, the danger of gas and allow the use of the candle below-ground to be retained. Only on the threshold of the Industrial Revolution was a degree of success achieved. Around 1760, James Spedding, son of Carlisle Spedding, introduced his new method of 'air-coursing' by which the air-current was made to travel throughout the entire pit, including all the underground roads, before passing into the upcast shaft. The air was regulated by doors and stoppings, 'coursing it up and down each division of work, sweeping and ventilating the dead waste in the interior'.[44] How readily this, or indeed the standing furnace at the foot of the upcast shaft, were taken up is open to question. According to Dunn, in the Northern Coalfield during the second half of the 18th century, 'ventilation was ill-undertaken in regard to coursing the air ... and furnaces were rare.'[45]

The first succinct account of the state of mining technology and of the improvements which had been effected by the start of the 18th century is provided by *The Compleat Collier.* Boring and sinking were already highly skilled operations, the former, as with so many of the early improvements in British mining, having been introduced to this country from the metalliferous mines of Germany. Boring as a hand process, involving the employment of boring rods, developed rapidly in the north of England from the early 17th century.[46] The practice was warmly commended by the author of *The Compleat Collier* who pointed out that, without prior testing, sinking shafts to determine the existence of coal could become rather an expensive pastime: 'it saves a great deal of moneys in sinking, so deep as 30, 40 or 60 fathoms to no purpose, for you will not be at above 15 or 20s. per fathom boring, when perhaps it may cost 50s. or £3 per fathom to sink at least.'[47]

Equally the raising of hewn coal had made some progress from being borne on human backs or lifted by the simple windlass.[48] In the latter part of the 17th century the whim gin had been introduced, utilising horse power, to wind coal to the surface.[49] Yet there can be little doubt that this remained one of the most backward areas of mining technology up to the Industrial Revolution. Winding gear of the whim type also doubled as a 'lift' by means of which men and boys were raised from, or lowered into, the mine. Either they made use of the coal baskets attached to the winding rope, sat astride crude wooden 'horses', or simply inserted their feet into a loop formed at the end of the rope. Not surprisingly, accidents were frequent due to falling debris, losing a footing on the rope or falling off the 'horse'. Once again, it was only by the mid-18th century that some improvement was effected to this primitive form of winding appliance. Attempts were made to apply the steam engine directly to winding but were generally unsuccessful. Nonetheless a system was devised which indirectly secured the benefits of steam power. By the 1750's water-wheels had been applied to winding and where a natural head of water was not available, Newcomen engines were used to pump mine water to the surface. This water could be used to turn a water-wheel, so actuating the winding drum.

Finally, mention should be made of the steady but considerable progress made before the Industrial Revolution in both surface and underground transport. By the opening decades of the 17th century, many of the larger collieries in the north of England owned several hundred carts or wagons which carried the coal from pit-head to staithes for shipment. This incessant traffic of both empty and laden wagons must have contributed significantly to the wear and tear of the roads. Hence between 1620 and 1650, 'railways' or, more accurately, 'wagon-ways' began to develop on a significant scale in the north and in Shropshire.[50] Although wagon-ways had first been employed in the German metalliferous mines, the early examples on Tyneside were more advanced than those on the Continent in that the wheels of the wagons were provided with flanges. Constructed wholly of wood, railways in the North of England were designed by the early 18th century to travel on long inclined planes so that loaded wagons could run from pit-heads to staith by means of their own gravity. The return journey was accomplished by horses hauling the empty carts up again to the shaft.[51]

Below ground, the carriage of coal emerged as a problem during the course of the 17th century only in the large, rapidly developing collieries of the North of England. In the smaller Scottish pits, for instance, transport caused little difficulty because of the simple practice of using women and children to carry, or 'bear', the coal along the relatively short roadways. At first, attempts to improve underground haulage on Tyneside consisted of repeatedly sinking new shafts as the distance of the workings from the pit-bottom increased. However, this practice died out in view of the prohibitive costs involved, leaving the putter to travel ever longer distances below ground, hauling sledges from the face. Since his wages were deter-mined by the length of the haul, even this involved a relatively heavy cost to the coalowner. It is doubtful whether wheeled vehicles were being used at all underground in the Northern Coalfield until the early 18th century.[52] The general practice was for the coal to be hauled in corves, placed on sledges, to the pit-bottom where the corves were attached to the winding rope to be raised to the surface.

Ironically, it was precisely in those coalfields where expansion and technical progress were most marked that the increase in use of child-labour was greatest. The gradual introduction, where the floor of mines permitted, of the wheeled corf was later followed by the laying of planks underground to reduce friction between wheel and road. The widespread use of these underground wagon-ways from the early 18th century gave rise to the employment of the horse below the surface. Here was a faster, cheaper and more efficient means of drawing sledges along the underground roads.[53] Moreover, horses could be led and tended to by children, particularly where wheeled carts were used. This, along with the need to tend to doors and stoppings in the pit in order to secure better ventilation, ensured a significant expansion in the use of boys below ground. Where seams were narrow, with insufficient room or height for horses, boys had to crawl along on hands and knees, dragging the laden sledges behind them by means of a girdle and chain (the guss). Where circumstances permitted, another important device that could be used for underground haulage was the self-acting inclined plane. Patented by Michael Menzies in 1750, the principle involved was simplicity itself, but depended on the seams running on a gradient. Using ropes, the laden wagons, in descending gradually from the face to the pit-bottom, were made to haul up the empty carts, in reverse direction on a parallel track.

By the opening decades of the 18th century, it is evident that important improvements had been made in most branches of mining technology. The growing use of the steam engine, improved forms of ventilation, advances in the smelting of minerals and the progress made in such diverse activities as boring, sinking and transport both above and below ground were certainly not accomplished overnight. Yet, during the later 17th and early decades of the 18th century, the growing and cumulative effect of these improvements meant that the supply of coal was more than capable of matching a steadily mounting demand. On balance therefore, one can agree with Nef that by 1715 most of the technical changes upon which the Industrial Revolution was to be based had been worked out.

3 CAPITAL COSTS AND PROFITS

In view of the steadily increasing use of more capital-intensive techniques and the constantly developing scale and depth of mining operations, the industry required much larger inputs of capital throughout the 17th century than the country yeoman or husbandman could generally muster. Formerly important, along with the clergy, in financing mineral exploitation, the influence of this rural middle class rapidly declined as the capital requirements of mining expanded. In common with most of British industry, there is little evidence that coalmining suffered to any significant extent from capital shortage. Rather, as the scale of operations grew larger, the sources of finance available to the industry changed. Increasingly, the supply of capital to coalmining narrowed to depend largely on two groups in society. First, landed families had traditionally been important in financing mineral exploitation. There is a large literature on the part played by landowners and members of the aristocracy in developing mineral deposits on their estates.[54] Until the early decades of the 19th century, they played a vital role in promoting the growth of the coal industry. Second, the merchant classes particularly in such towns as Newcastle and Sunderland, Bristol, Coventry, Manchester and Glasgow became increasingly concerned in coalmining. By the start of the 18th century, merchant capital was prominent in virtually every mining district of Great Britain.[55] Hence, while individual ownership by the landowner remained important, there was a long-term tendency towards abdication of his managerial function in coalmining.

The growth in scale of operations meant that the landowner was reluctant to risk such a large proportion of his assets in mining enterprise. Therefore the practice developed of leasing the right to work his mineral properties to interested merchant adventurers. Of growing significance, too, was the financial partnership with trans-ferable shares. Buying and selling 'part-ownerships' of collieries, depending on the anticipated worth and reserves of particular enterprises, became a common means of financing mining activity, especially in the North of England. As a speculation, it was relatively attractive since the element of risk was obviously much smaller than that implied by full ownership of the colliery. Equally important was the developing practice in both 17th and 18th centuries of money loans being advanced by merchant capitalists to owners in financial difficulties. Usually negotiated at relatively high rates of interest, these loans often had the effect of 'delivering owners into the hands of the merchant.'[56] Several owners became increasingly, or even wholly, reliant upon this method of financing and could no longer pursue independent policies with regard to their collieries. In diverse ways, therefore, merchant capitalists secured 'control' of a large part of coalmining development during the course of the 17th century. This was achieved at substantially less risk to themselves than if they had owned all, or even major parts of, individual colliery enterprises.

These methods of financing reflected, of course, the relatively heavy cost of mining exploration, development and working. Some indication of the magnitudes involved can be derived from Table 3 below which shows the cost of sinking and installing the necessary fixed capital at individual colliery enterprises in the Northern Coalfield during the early 18th century.

Table 3

Costs of Sinking and Winning (a) Kibblesworth and South Blackburn Collieries and (b) Long Benton out of the Workings of the Wheat Pit

Kibblesworth and South Blackburn (1728)	£	Long Benton (1733)	£
Bringing up the River (Wear) to where the engines are to be fixed	200	Driving 210 yds. of drift at approx. 6/- per yd.	60
Sinking 2 engine pits at 28 fathoms each (timber included)	560	Sinking one pit and Boring	400
		Erecting one Fire Engine	1,200
Sinking a halfshaft at 16 fathoms	120	Driving upper stone drift 20 yds.	30
		Sinking a stapple 29 fathoms to the main coal	87
Sinking 3 pits to hasten the winning of Blackburn	360	Slope pumps, 750 yds. at 6/- per yd.	225
Driving 1,160 yds. of coal drift at 5/- per yd.	290	Laying the same and preparing the way	30
Two Bob Engines and fixing	250		
Three Coal Gins	130		
Total	1,910	Total	2,032

SOURCE:
Grand Allies Minute Book, Partnership Minutes, Memorandums etc., op. cit.

The initial capital costs involved in mining were relatively heavy when viewed alongside the capital requirements of manufacturing industry over a comparable period. Comparatively small amounts of fixed capital were needed to set up in business in most forms of manufacturing.[57] The major requirement in both cotton and woollen textiles, and even in iron manufacture, was for circulating capital. In extractive industry, while the need for circulating capital was at least as heavy as in these branches of manufacturing,[58] the input of fixed capital was considerably greater. Coalmining, particularly, was one of the first industries to be 'transformed' in the sense that it adopted capitalistic lines of production at a comparatively early stage of its development.

Table 4

A Computation of the Expense of Working and Profit per Ten of the Collieries Specified, 1738, with Estimated Future Total Profits of these Collieries

	Long Benton £ s. d.			Gateshead Park £ s. d.			Salt Meadows £ s. d.		
Charges:									
Sinking and Working	2	17	6	2	10	9	2	5	
Leading	1	7	6		5	6		5	6
Way and Wagons		12			4			4	
Colliery Rent		13	8		15			15	
Water Charges		12			8			8	
Contingents		2	6		2	6		2	6
Staith Charges		1	8		1	8		1	8
Rents of Lying Collieries		2	4½		2	6		2	6
Winning Charges		3	6		5	7½			
Wayleaves and Staith Room		7	7		1	3½		1	3½
Total	7	0	3½	4	16	10	4	5	5½

PROFIT:

Average Selling Price per chaldron of coal, All specified Collieries=11s. 4½d.

Average Revenue per ten of coal, All specified collieries=£10.16s.1½d.

	Long Benton			Gateshead Park			Salt Meadows		
Profit per ten (Receipts minus Costs)	3	15	10	5	19	3½	6	10	8

ESTIMATED FUTURE TOTAL PROFIT:

a) At Gateshead Park, there is computed to be 260 acres of unwrought colliery which yield 140 tens to every acre=36,400 tens. Profit per ten=£5.19s.3½d. Therefore total profitability of colliery, at present level of profit= £217,110.16s.7d.

b) At Salt Meadows there is computed to be 45 acres of unwrought colliery which will yield 140 tens to every acre=6,300 tens. Profit per ten= £6.10s.8d. Therefore total profitability of colliery, at present level of profit=£41,160.0s.0d.

c) At Long Benton, approx. the same quantity of tens will be yielded as in Gateshead Park and Salt Meadows together=43,200 tens. Profit per ten= £3.15s.10d. Therefore total profitability of colliery, at present level of profit=£163,200.0s.0d.

Therefore aggregate profit gained by working unwrought areas of these collieries at present level of profits=£421,470.16s.7d.

SOURCE:

Grand Allies Minute Book, Partnership Minutes, Memorandum etc., op. cit.

In districts like South Wales and the West Midlands many under-takings remained small, owning a few tiny pits which employed fewer than a dozen men each. But already by the start of the 18th century, the number of large units in the industry, with advanced forms of organisation, was relatively high, especially in the North of England. Indeed in terms of the larger colliery enterprises, the totals specified in Table 3 as being necessary to start a coal mine were nothing untoward. Although information is limited, at an even earlier date more than £6,500 had been spent trying to develop coalmining at Cowpen in Northumberland during the reign of James I. In 1660-7, over £8,000 had been spent in opening a new mine in Fife and it is certain that the amounts spent in developing the largest collieries in the North of England would have been in excess of that figure. It has, for instance, been estimated that by the end of the 17th century reserves of at least £15,000-20,000 were required for undertaking any of the large sea-sale colliery enterprises, almost as much for the river-sale collieries of the Midlands and some £3,000-5,000 for the larger land-sale collieries.[59]

These were relatively high sums, particularly when viewed along-side the capital required to finance the principal joint-stock enterprises of the age. An analysis of 140 companies operating in 1695 showed that in only five[60] was capital significantly in excess of that probably invested in the largest colliery on the Tyne. Moreover, excluding the 27 chief companies, the average capital of a joint-stock enterprise (other than in mining) in 1695 was about £5,000 in England and £3,000 in Scotland, no more than the amounts invested in the more important land-sale mines of the Midlands.

During the course of the 18th century, costs of sinking and winning escalated further as mines became deeper[61] and the processes of working and moving the coal more complex. By 1787, Lord Ravens-worth's Friar's Goose pit was estimated to have cost £20,000 to sink, with tramways which he installed costing some £450 per mile. Yet mounting costs could generally be accommodated without much difficulty due to the rapidly rising demand for the industry's product. Taking into account sinking and other capital costs, plus the costs involved in working the coal, the level of profit was still relatively attractive. An indication of the costs of production and profits per ten of coals[62] which, it was estimated, would follow from the winning of certain northern collieries in 1738 is provided in Table 4 above. Despite the high levels of profits which were forecast, the collieries were not in fact won until several years later.

It was on the basis of the type of calculation shown in Table 4 that investment was undertaken in the coal industry before 1750. In fact, of course, the level of profits did not remain stable after 1738 but fluctuated in line with general economic activity. However, the secular increase in demand for coal during the second half of the 18th century, the result of advancing industrialisation and steady population growth, inevitably attracted fresh capital into mining. In addition, output regulation by northern mines, by offering the coalowners some degree of monopoly profits, further encouraged investment in the hope of realising these profits.[63] Capital, therefore, continued to flow into the coal industry, John Buddle providing the following estimates of the total amount invested on the Tyne alone by 1807:[64]

	£(000)
In the Above Bridge Collieries	290
In the Below Bridge Collieries	593
	883

The aggregate profit made by these collieries in 1807 was given as £150,000, representing almost 17% on the capital invested. However this is to look rather ahead. It is sufficient to note here that coalmining, an expanding and relatively prosperous industry in the decades before 1750, was on the verge of breaking through into a yet more profitable era in the period known as 'The Industrial Revolution'.

2 Organisation and Distribution

The significance of the coastwise trade in coal was early recognised by employers in the Northern Coalfield, merchants and middlemen engaged in the trade and by the Crown. Each sought to protect what they considered to be their vital interests in the constantly developing traffic between north and south. Employers attempted to exploit their monopoly position by periodically regulating output to determine selling-price and levels of profit; merchants and middlemen conducted, or manipulated, the trade in coal in an effort to secure windfall gains; and finally the Crown, almost permanently short of funds, imposed taxes, or duties, on coal shipped coastwise as a means of raising revenue. The interests of these groups tended to conflict, each achieving at different times a greater or lesser degree of success. But none achieved a lasting control over the coal trade since in the final analysis faith in the freedom of enterprise proved too strong.

In the early regulation of output and in industrial management generally, the coal industry became something of a model for other sectors of the economy. In essence this virtually means the coal industry of the North of England since this region maintained an overwhelming superiority over all other districts before the 19th century. Scotland was its only serious rival in the export trade to Europe; South Wales dominated the coal trade in South-West England; and Cumberland and later Lancashire served the Irish market. The land-sale collieries were largely dependent on pack-horses for the local distribution of their coal since in the winter months the state of the roads made them impassable even for carts. Only Warwickshire enjoyed relatively wide land-sale distribution: elsewhere little coal was carried more than 10 miles by road until well into the 18th century.[1] These instances apart, the favourable position of collieries in the north allowed them to monopolise the market. This chapter concentrates, therefore, mainly on the Northern Coalfield, the heart of the British coal industry during the formative stages of its development.

1 EMPLOYERS' ORGANISATIONS

At a relatively early stage in the industry's development northern employers formed associations both to exploit their market position and to protect themselves against the efforts of middlemen in the coal trade to reduce pit-head prices to a minimum. The most significant of the early combinations was that formed by the Hostmen of Newcastle. The origins of the Hostmen are uncertain but it seems clear that by 1517 they had organised themselves into a company. Their influence grew with the expansion of the coal trade during the 16th century, the larger coalowners dominating not only the policy of the company but also occupying important positions in the town government. The power of the Hostmen was confirmed when the Grand Lease came into their possession during the latter part of the century.[2] Opposition to the Lease and the restrictive practices which it encouraged came from both consumers in London and the smaller northern owners excluded from the advantages which the powerful Hostmen now enjoyed. The ensuing struggle was bitter, but the wealth and influence of the larger owners was sufficient to carry the day.[3] Having overcome all resistance, they were in a position to request a new charter for the city of Newcastle.

Accordingly, the Hostmen were incorporated by Queen Elizabeth in 1600, promising support and revenue to the Crown in return for privileges and protection in the selling of coal. The combine consisted of 44 coal-owning partners who between them monopolised the principal mines of Newcastle and district.[4] Between 1600 and 1640 no fewer than six agreements were reached within the Company of Hostmen under which owners agreed to pool the coal produced for coastwise shipment from the Tyne. The intention was to maintain prices by regulating output and restricting competition. Not all Hostmen were signatories of these agreements, only those owning significant parts of local collieries.[5] Nor were these agreements ever intended to be permanent. For the most part, they were designed to last for only one year or even less. Yet, brief as they were, these attempts at collusion once again aroused fierce opposition. They were alleged to be virtual monopolies and, to the extent that they affected prices by limiting output, contrary to the public interest.

Opposition to these restrictive practices came from two main sources. First, the attack was led by rival colliery owners in areas such as the Wear Valley and along the Northumberland coast. With output rapidly growing in these regions during the first half of the 17th century, competition with owners on the Tyne became increasingly fierce. Such competition exposed the precarious nature of the Hostmen's agreements, all the more so in view of the difficulty of effectively disciplining disobedient members of the combine. Particularly when selling prices rose, the more progressive collieries moved to exploit improved market conditions and rebelled against output-restriction. Second, traders in coal bitterly fought the Hostmen's agreements since they meant that a much larger share of the proceeds

Table 1

Prices of Best Coal Recorded in Northern Ports & in London,
Specified Years, 1655-1800[1]

Year	Price in the North per Newcastle chaldron	Price in London per Imperial chaldron
1655	11/-	—
1665	13/-	30/-
1674	14/-	20/-
1699	10/-	42-44/-
1703	11/6	40/-
1729	12/-	32/-
1731	9/6	23/6
1739	13/-	28/-
1744	11/-	29/-
1750	11/6	29/-
1761	15/-	36/-
1763	—	55/-
1771	12-15/-	41-47/-
1785	—	40/-
1794	19/-	44/-
1800	26/6	60-70/-

SOURCES:
Royal Commission on Coal, 1871, Committee E; House of Commons, Select Committee on the Coal Trade, 1830; Ashton & Sykes, op. cit., Appendix F, pp. 252-3; Sweezy, op. cit., pp. 143-4, 157-65.
NOTE:
1. Prices are given per chaldron. According to Nef, op.cit., pp. 367-70, the Newcastle chaldron varied between 52 and 53 cwts from the 1650's to the 1690's before being fixed by statute at the latter figure in 1695. The Imperial chaldron contained about 26 cwts.

of sales to London would be retained by the owners. Although conducted under the guise of protecting the public interest, these campaigns were generated largely by self-interest. There is little evidence that shippers and wholesalers, when successful in dissolving producers' combines, passed on the advantages in the form of lower prices to the consumer. On the contrary, their main purpose in attacking producers was probably to divert public attention from their own, more oppressive, restrictive practices.

The disruption caused to the Newcastle trade by the Civil War, together with the scale of opposition from competing owners, merchants and public resulted in the disintegration of producers' combines during the second half of the 17th century.[6] However, this was by no means the end of the Hostmen. Already by mid-century, the emphasis within the organisation had shifted from monopolising the ownership of large parts of collieries to the function of fittage. The Hostmen increasingly began to act as 'middlemen', buying up the coal of mine-owners and negotiating its sale to shippers for eventual distribution in the South of England. By the 1700's, the majority of leading Hostmen were actively engaged in organising fitters' vends.

However, output-restriction by the owners was rarely absent for long in the north. On the one hand, the district represented what was virtually the only effective source of supply for markets in the south. On the other, surviving evidence of coal prices shows that these, rising rapidly in the London market at the turn of the century, fell sharply thereafter before stabilising between the 1730's and 1750's. Although far from comprehensive, Table 1 provides some indication of the trend in prices of best coal in the north and in the London market.

It is probable that the revival of combination by northern owners in the early 18th century was mainly for defensive purposes. Once the temporary revival of the London market had come to an end in the opening years of the century, there was strong incentive for owners to seek the protective strength of an association. By regulating supply, they could maintain prices and better defend themselves from the increasingly doubtful practices of shippers and traders. For precisely these reasons, a new employers' organisation, the Grand Allies, was formed in the north during the 1720's. Although rather neglected in the literature of the industry this association of leading owners became a real force during the two decades which followed. A measure of the strength of the new combine is the fact that it brought together the powerful Ravensworth, Strathmore and Wortley families who used their wealth and influence to buy up wayleave rights in the districts of both Tyne and Wear. Minutes of the partnership reveal that in the years following the first recorded meeting in Newcastle in September, 1726, a large number of mines were acquired on a lease, or licence, basis.[7] Moreover, the rapid purchase of wayleaves conferred upon the Allies control of a large share of the north's potential production. In many instances, dead rents[8] were paid for the rights to land, the intention being less to use the land than to prevent potential competitors from securing a right of way. As a result, the Allies gained 'so large a share of all lands adjoining to the river Tyne that they have almost totally debarred all other persons from access to it with coals, especially on the south side where the best coals lie, and the like has been done with respect to the River Wear.'[9] Many northern owners with no access to the rivers were obliged to leave their collieries unworked or lease them to the Grand Allies on the latter's terms. Less frequently, the combine would simply pay owners not in the association to leave their collieries unworked.

These activities provoked opposition and resentment. It was bitterly pointed out at the end of the 1730's that while an effort had been made to secure fair trading by laying various restrictions on merchants and dealers in coal, and the price had been regulated in London by the Lord Mayor and Aldermen, all this was to no purpose since 'a monopoly of the commodity at the fountainhead has been forming undisturbed; and is now so thoroughly established as almost to defy opposition.'[10] There is also evidence that the Allies indulged in other unfair practices. It is clear that best coals were often mixed with inferior grades, the whole being sold as best grade, and that they gave 'underhand premiums to lightermen or other vendors of coals in order to retain them steady in their interest.'[11]

It is difficult to determine precisely the influence of this quasi-monopoly on the course of coal prices. In addition to output-restriction, the latter were obviously affected by the vagaries of demand, the influence of random shocks on the coal trade and the activities of middlemen as described in section 2 below. Critics of the Allies and the several petitions presented to Parliament were in no doubt that the effect of the combine had been to keep coal prices at levels appreciably higher than they would otherwise have been.[12] There was probably some substance in this argument since legislation periodically passed to condemn, and move against, the restraint of trade was generally followed by sharp price-falls. It has been noted that following legislation in 1730, the price of coal at Newcastle fell from 12/- to 9/6d. per chaldron. By 1739, it had risen once more to about 13/- before a further Act in 1744 again reduced the price of best coal to 11/-.[13] In the short term, there seems little doubt that the Grand Allies, by influencing the amount supplied to the south, benefited considerably from the scale of their operations. But in the long term, heavy costs were incurred. It is true that the Allies controlled the working of a significant number of northern collieries. Since rising coal prices were a feature of the 18th century (see Table 1), the value of the right to work productive pits tended to increase *pari passu*. But as Dunn has pointed out, many of the pits acquired by the Allies were subsequently to prove a serious liability. Technical improvements during the course of the 18th century enabled new, deeper and more profitable mines to be sunk in the north, particularly below Newcastle and in the neighbourhood of the Wear. The increased competition generated by these new sources of supply meant that the Allies were saddled with long and costly leases of the older pits of which they were unable to divest themselves.[14]

The ability of the Allies to control output, and hence prices, depended largely on restricting the entry of fresh interests and capital into mining. In the event, several factors played a part in weakening their hold over the coal trade after 1749. First, technical progress enabled new and deeper sinkings to be made thus making possible precisely that type of competition which the Allies had gone to such lengths to prevent. Second, the emergence of a banking system on Tyneside provided new entrepreneurs with a wider access to capital than had previously been available.[15] Finally, strict control over the supply of coal became increasingly difficult in face of rapid changes in market conditions. After a period of wildly fluctuating demand in the 1750's, the London market for coal steadily expanded in the following decade. Relatively high prices in the early 1760's induced new entrants into the industry and resulted in a rapid expansion of investment. As the quantity of coal placed on the market increased, prices declined to less profitable levels.[16]

Largely for this reason, renewed agitation began in the north for a combination of coalowners. Capacity had once again been raised to a level which enabled supply to run ahead of demand, promoting fierce competition as collieries fought to hold their respective shares of the market. Moreover, owners were becoming increasingly concerned about irregularities in the coastwise trade, particularly with regard to the methods used to measure coal. The Limitation of the Vend was therefore established in 1771, becoming operative a year or two later.[17] Coalowners on the Tyne and Wear agreed, for specified periods, to fix the price at which coastwise coal of various grades might be sold in southern markets. Each colliery within the Vend was assigned a 'basis', representing the quantity which it could contribute to the general supply. This was constantly amended in light of prices prevailing in London. Output control did not extend to coal shipped abroad, owners remaining free to expand their share of overseas markets by all means at their disposal. The result was that prices of northern coal in foreign markets were frequently lower than levels prevailing in London, sometimes by more than 40 per cent.[18]

The total vend of both rivers was initially divided in the ratio three parts supplied by the Tyne to two parts by the Wear. But regulation was far from continuous: for a number of years between 1771 and its final abolition in 1845, the Vend did not operate.[19] Despite its patchy existence the Vend encountered growing opposition during the early decades of the 19th century. Northern owners tried to justify their activities on several grounds. The Vend assured them of a fair, remunerative price to cover the expense of working their coal and compensate for the heavy investment and degree of risk involved. John Buddle assured the Lords' Select Committee of 1830 that northern employers did not charge monopolistic prices. Indeed, he argued, the average price they obtained to cover all expenses and risks of working and delivering the coal on board ship at Newcastle or Sunderland had never exceeded the cost of merely taking the coal out of the ship on the Thames and distributing it to the London consumer.[20] In addition, the Vend enabled owners to adjust capacity according to the quota granted to them, so over the long term reducing uncertainty and violent fluctuations in output. By maintaining capacity at a steady level a greater regularity of employment was possible. Miners were therefore shielded from the free play of market forces which could reduce employment and money wages to a minimum.

However, the main argument used to justify the Vend was that the interests of the public were best served by an agreement between colliery owners to share the market. In the short term, an open coal trade would cause prices to fall: unable to compete at low unremunerative prices, the less profitable collieries would be forced out of business. In the long term, fewer supply-points would mean shortages and rising prices in periods of expanding demand. Indeed inelasticities on the supply side would cause prices to rise to levels higher than those fixed by the Vend. Buddle in his evidence to the 1830 Commons' Select Committee cited as an example the activities of the previous year. Between January and August, 1829, regulation of output had been discontinued by northern owners. Subsequent competitive pressures had forced coal prices down to levels at which many collieries operated at a loss. Had trade remained open, these would have been forced to close,[21] leaving a few large producers to monopolise the market. Hence an agreed form of output-sharing, by keeping collieries in production, saved the public 'from much distress from want of a proper supply of coals.'[22]

Although not in sympathy with the arguments used in defence of the Vend, the Commons' Select Committee of 1830 was prepared to tolerate the continued existence of the combine. First, it recognised that the main responsibility for relatively high coal prices in London lay less with the activities of owners than with the restrictive practices of those engaged in the distribution of the coal (see section 2 below). Second, it believed that any attempt to charge monopolistic prices would attract greater competition from those collieries in the north, particularly in the Tees district, Yorkshire and Scotland, that were not in the regulation. The existence of such collieries would force the Vend to pursue a policy of moderation and act as the principal safeguard of consumers in London. That this faith was misplaced was demonstrated in 1834 when coalowners in the Tees district joined with their counterparts of the Tyne and Wear to form an even more formidable regulation. Of the allotted vend of 1¾ million Newcastle chaldrons in 1835, collieries on the Tyne were asked to provide 54%, the Wear 33% and the Tees 9%. The remainder came from the smaller mines of Hartly, Cowpen and Netherton.[23]

The added strength of the Vend convinced the 1836 Commons' Select Committee on the Coal Trade that its predecessor had been wrong and that the combination of owners in the north 'cannot successfully be maintained without prejudice to the public'.[24] It condemned output-regulation on several counts. First, it had led northern mining interests to oppose all new sources of supply where marketing costs in London might be lower than those of collieries situated on the Tyne and Wear (for a discussion of this point see chapter 3, section 4 below). Second, the Vend had forced on the market a large proportion of inferior coal at prices which could not have been secured in the absence of regulation.[25] Finally, it was clear that the removal of government duty on coastwise coal in 1831 had led to a consolidation, rather than the anticipated disintegration, of the Vend. W. Brandling, chairman of the Committee of Coal Owners on the Tyne, had testified before the Commons' Select Committee of 1830 that the removal of duty would lead to such an increase in demand that no form of output-restriction would be necessary. His forecast that 'demand would be nearly equal to the power of supply'[26] had not been fulfilled.

The recommendation of the Commons' Committee of 1836 that all existing restrictions on the free supply of coal should be removed was in keeping with measures already taken to promote greater freedom of the coal trade. Duties on coal shipped coastwise had been removed along with other restrictions on deliveries to London. In the event, legislation to force the dissolution of the Vend was not necessary.[27] Improvements in transport had enabled competitors steadily to erode the north's monopoly of the London market. Collieries in the Tees district had become enough of a threat with the opening of the Stockton to Darlington railway in 1825 that their inclusion within the Vend a few years later had been a matter of necessity. But this, and continued opposition to the opening of new railway lines, was not sufficient to stem the tide of competition. During the 1840's, the railway began to revolutionise the fabric of the coal industry. From that decade, the volume of coal brought to London from inland sources increased at a spectacular rate. It came from as far afield as Scotland, but more especially from South Wales and the Midlands. Table 2 shows the quantity of coal and coke carried to London by different forms of transport.

During the decade 1845-55, inland collieries recognised the potential of the railways as a means of carrying coal to London. Between 1850 and 1855 alone, the tonnage brought by rail into London increased 20 times. By 1870, railways had become the principal means of conveying coal to the capital. The amount they carried exceeded that shipped coastwise by one-quarter. The Vend was in no position to withstand the resultant increase in competition. By

Table 2
*Volume of Coal and Coke Brought into London Coastwise,
and by Railways and Canals, 1840-70 (000 tons)*

	Coastwise	Railways	Canals
1840	2,567	—	22
1845	3,403	8	60
1850	3,553	55	30
1855	3,017	1,138	32[1]
1860	3,573	1,478	20
1865	3,162	2,733	8
1870	2,994	3,758	7

SOURCES:
Royal Commission on Coal, 1871, Committee E; B. R. Mitchell and P. Deane,
Abstract of British Historical Statistics (1971), p. 113.
NOTE:
1. Relates to 1854.

enabling inland-sale collieries to supply coal to southern markets at
relatively low cost, the railways had effectively cracked open the
northern monopoly. New collieries, opened as a result of the railways,
joined the Vend at a faster rate than its sales increased. To maintain
high coal prices in London, the market-share of each colliery within
the combine had to be reduced. Between 1828 and 1844 the old
mines had to surrender approximately 50% of their allocated quotas
to accommodate more recent entrants.[28] In consequence, northern
collieries had to tolerate a greater degree of excess capacity. The
incentive to sell more than the allocated quota was strong and the
larger, more progressive mines yielded to temptation. Under these
conditions, preservation of the Vend became impossible and the
organisation was dissolved in 1845. In the short run, London prices
fell but this trend was reversed in the 1850's due to a steady rise in
demand for coal.[29] The lack of an organised supply from the north
allowed the inland coalfields to break fully into the London market.
An end to the northern monopoly had been achieved, not by the
State, but by technological development in the form of the railways.
Even so, the demand for coal was rising so rapidly that output and
sales from the north continued to increase sharply during the 1840's
and 1850's.

2   THE DISTRIBUTION OF COAL

It was ironic that the main attack on the efforts of northern owners
to regulate coal prices in London should come from merchants,

41

dealers and those employed in the coastwise distribution of the mineral. It was precisely in the activities of the latter group that the most glaring examples of inefficiency, doubtful and fraudulent practices can be found. So many different tasks were involved between the actual production of coal in the north and its eventual consumption in the south that countless opportunities existed for different groups to manipulate the trade to their own advantage. Nor were they slow to seize their chance, the rights of each group in the many stages along the way being jealously guarded against encroachment from outsiders. As was plaintively recorded in a pamphlet of 1747, 'It has ever been the reproach as well as the misfortune of trade that persons have been found in every branch of it who have acted as if their profession was but a licence to cheat with impunity.'[30]

Abuses can indeed be found at each stage of the coal trade, from the loading of the mineral on board ship at the staithes in Newcastle and Sunderland to its arrival in the Pool of London and its subsequent weighing and measuring at the port. Repeated complaints against 'false weights and measures, and all those innumerable devices with which the crafty deceive the credulous'[31] were of little avail until the authorities were at last goaded into action in the 19th century. Not until 1831 were effective measures taken by Parliament to regulate 'the vend and delivery of coals in the city of London and Westminster.'[32] To appreciate the need for such measures and the extent to which unfair practices could raise the final selling-price of coal, some indication of the main activities involved in the distribution of coal is necessary.

Even in producing saleable coal, restrictions were immediately in evidence. First, as observed above, owners commonly limited output according to a pre-determined 'size of vend'. Second, once raised from the pit a sizeable proportion of output was wasted due to regulations governing screening. Only the large pieces of coal which failed to pass through a screen half-an-inch wide were regarded as suitable for sale in the London market. The remainder, amounting to between 25-30% of the total, was screened again using a three-eighths-of-an-inch mesh to separate out the very smallest pieces. By the 1820's, the latter were being shipped coastwise at a duty of only 1/- per London chaldron. Yet the coal which passed through the first but not the second screen was *not* entitled to any reduction of duty. By 1829, the duty on best coal shipped coastwise amounted to 6/- per London chaldron. Although considered to be perhaps the finest parts of the coal, owners could find no market for the intermediate grade at a price which would compensate for duty, costs and effort involved. As a result such coal was often wasted.[33] John Buddle, for instance, testified before the Select Committee of the House of Lords in 1830 that he had known times when this small coal could not be given away; further, that he had seen at one colliery in the north 'as many as from 90-100 chaldrons a day destroyed, because there was no market'.[34] The discriminatory nature of these duties was not removed until all coal duties were finally repealed under the provisions of the 1831 Act.

Once the coal suitable for sale in **southern** markets had been determined, the owner commissioned a fitter to negotiate its sale to a shipowner, convey it to the ship's side and obtain a clearance certificate from the Customs House enabling the ship to sail. Shipmasters were entitled to receive from the fitter a loading of their chosen grade of coal in the order in which their ships arrived in port. In practice, for a variety of reasons, there were often lengthy delays in the 'turn-around' of colliery vessels. For instance, until the 1770's it was the practice to lay ships up during the winter months of December and January. With ships out of commission for 6-8 weeks, the number of trips made per year was immediately restricted to an average of between 8 and 11.[35] Second, a common complaint was 'queue-jumping' by ships on the Tyne and Wear. A favoured master might secure an immediate 'turn-around', leaving his unfortunate counterparts to wait, possibly for weeks, for a loading. Finally, in periods when 'regulation' by the owners was practised, the limitation of output sometimes involved ships waiting for weeks for best coals. This became particularly common with the creation of the Limitation of the Vend in the 1770's. When the stipulated monthly vend of a grade which the shipmaster was to receive had been reached, the ship had no recourse but to wait for a share of the ensuing month's vend.[36] These delays in sailing could significantly affect the quantity and hence the price of coal available on the London market.

Abuses were even more common once the mineral had arrived in the Pool of London. The sale of all coal in the London market was transacted through factors who cleared the different duties charged on the cargo and received from Customs a certificate enabling them to offer the coal for sale. Before 1769, the cargo was sold in the open market but thereafter all deals were conducted in the Coal Exchange. During the later 18th century, this institution developed as a 'closed shop', all negotiations being confined to a small number of factors and a select band of recognised coal buyers.[37] Should an 'outsider' wish to negotiate with this exclusive group he had first to pay a commission for the privilege. Hence, for consumers obtaining their coal in this way, a premium on the price of coal had to be paid to cover the commission. Once a buyer had purchased the coal, a meter was appointed to measure the cargo from the ship and ostensibly to ensure fair play between buyer and seller. Here lay one of the major causes of grievance. Coal was measured rather than weighed, so permitting numerous opportunities for false dealing. According to

Buddle, selling by the measure was a direct incentive at each round of the marketing process to break the coals into even smaller pieces since 'coals, as they become decreased in size are increased in measure'. He further pointed out that in the north it had been discovered that the chaldron wagon of 53 cwts of round coals could only carry 46.48 cwts when filled with small coals.[38]

Moreover, the number of meters was extremely small,[39] a problem made more acute by the habit of appointing them *before* the arrival of ships in the port of London to ensure a speedy turn-around. According to Thomas Smith, a Brentford corn distiller, it frequently happened that those ships which obtained an early meter had been cleared, returned to Newcastle and arrived *back* in London with coal before some of the ships of the same fleet had been unloaded.[40] Once appointed, meters were not allowed to offer their services to other shipmasters. As a result, they frequently spent much of their time simply waiting for their ships to arrive, so aggravating delays in supplying coal to London. Along with the meter, an undertaker was employed to provide the labour necessary to unload the cargo. When measuring the coal from ship to lighter the meter and his men were subject to the discretion of the lighterman, operating on behalf of the buyer. Frequently, ingrain was withheld[41] or in supposedly unloading a score of 21 London chaldrons, often as few as 17.5 chaldrons were actually put on board the lighter.[42] Lightermen were also accused of passing from one ship to the next, loading different qualities of coal. Best grades were mixed with inferior qualities, yet the whole was sold as best coal at the top price. This defeated the whole purpose of the meter's certificate, the intention of which was to show the quality, price and source of each shipload of coal sold in port.

From the lighter, coal was either distributed directly to the larger consumers, or stored by the buyer to be sold at some future date to smaller customers and domestic users. Here lay the last, but possibly one of the easiest chances of swindling the customer. Two methods of measurement were employed. The pool measure was that used when distributing directly to the large industrial consumers and important retailers. It was a measure of the coal, direct from the ship, which the consumer ought to receive, although he was dependent entirely upon the honesty of the first buyer. The wharf measure, on the other hand, involved remeasuring the coal by the bushel once it had reached the warehouse of the first buyer. This was the method employed in selling the coal to householders and smaller consumers. The process was allegedly supervised by land-meters who were, however, notorious for their ability either to ignore or bend the regulations.[43] Sacks were often filled without measurement of any description. In 1815 one observer considered it unlikely that during

44

the preceding five years as much as one-third of 'wharf' coal had been put into the bushel measure at all.[44] Alternatively sacks were often smaller in size than required by Act of Parliament: despite this, a certain number of sacks were considered 'equal' to a London chaldron.[45] Fortunately, perhaps, some five-sixths of the coal arriving in the Pool of London was sold according to the pool measure, directly to the larger consumers. The remainder was distributed after 'remeasurement' to domestic customers.

Not surprisingly in view of the frauds and abuses which could be perpetrated in the process of delivering the coal from the north to cellars in London, the 'spread' between pit-head prices and those finally paid by the southern consumer was extremely high. During the Industrial Revolution this 'mark-up' in prices could raise the final retail value of sales by between three and five times the original pit-head value.[46] Table 3 below shows the average revenue accruing to the owner per chaldron of best coal and the charges made on the shipowner at the start of the 19th century.

Table 3

Average Revenue received by Coalowner on the Tyne per Chaldron of Best Coals and Costs Incurred by the Shipowner, 1800

Revenue of Coalowner	Per Newcastle Chaldron		
	£	s.	d.
As sold to shipowner	1	2	0
Less fittage		1	6
	1	0	6
Costs of Shipowner			
As paid to Coalowner	1	2	0
Charges at Newcastle:			
Real dues		2	1¾
Duke of Richmond duty		1	0
Lights, Cocket etc.			8¾
Trimming			4½
Town's House			2
	1	6	5

SOURCE:
House of Commons, Select Committee on the Coal Trade, 1800.

45

The figures in Table 3 are quoted in terms of the Newcastle chaldron, a measure which was approximately double the London chaldron. Hence for best coal, the coalowner would receive only about 10s. 3d. per London chaldron, the return being even lower for other grades. In 1800, for second, or medium, grade coal the northern owner received an average of 9s. 0.1d. per London chaldron and for third or inferior grade, 7s. 6.1d.[47] Yet in the same year, the selling-price of best coal in London reached between 60/- and 70/- per London chaldron (see Table 1).[48] There was therefore a huge discrepancy between the northern owner's return and the price finally paid by the consumer in the south. These figures were inflated by wartime scarcities and the mounting demand for coal from both industry and a rapidly expanding number of domestic consumers. Even so, it is apparent that the final selling-price bore little resemblance to the actual costs of winning the coal. In part this was, of course, inevitable in view of the costs of transporting and retrading a bulky, low-value commodity such as coal. Nor is it the intention to suggest that all middlemen engaged in the coal trade habitually deceived their customers. To the extent that opportunities for fraudulent dealing existed and were seized upon by some, the gap between pit-head and market prices was frequently wider than that determined by normal trading conditions.

Evidence that this 'spread' between owners' receipts and prices finally charged in London was a permanent feature, having little to do with wartime inflation, can be gathered from the large number of petitions to Parliament and contemporary pamphlets complaining about the abuses perpetrated by middlemen in the coastal trade. The Marquis of Londonderry pointed out in the House of Lords in 1830 that the average price of best coals at the pit-head in the Tyne and Wear had never exceeded 14/- per London chaldron. It cost 2/- per chaldron to put on board ship and a further 11/- to 12/- for freight to London, making a maximum cost in the Pool of 28/- per chaldron. Yet the price of best coal into the cellars of London consumers amounted to over 50/- per chaldron. Hence, about half the final price was taken up with King's duty, imposts, metage, tenderage 'and in short all the extravagant, shameful charges in the port of London ... levied in the most oppressive manner.'[49] Evidence of these 'shameful' charges was provided in more detailed form by John Buddle before the Select Committee of the House of Lords in 1830.[50] Buddle's estimates of charges levied in the Pool of London again showed that it apparently cost as much to put on board in the north and freight the coal from Tyne or Wear to London as it did simply to unload the coal in the Pool and deliver to the waiting consumers.

Efforts to control the coal trade during the 18th and early 19th centuries proved unsuccessful largely because the Government was

simply not prepared to enforce laws against restrictive practices. Legislation had been passed in 1710 and again in 1731[51] but had not materially affected the conduct of the trade. At the end of the 1780's, bills were introduced to the House of Commons designed to ensure a steady supply of coal to the metropolis at a reasonable price. These were rejected due to the 'lateness of the session', although powerful vested interests played no small part in the failure of these measures.[52]
The House of Commons' Select Committee of 1800 also recommended that measures should be taken to correct misconduct in the coastwise trade and that inland supplies of coal should be brought to London as a means of breaking the northern monopoly.[53] Despite these stipulations, little effective action was taken for a further 30 years. An Act passed in 1807 attempted to regulate the distribution of coal from the arrival of vessels in the Thames to the ultimate delivery of coal to the consumer in London, Westminster and the home counties. In the event, careful specifications as to what constituted 'proper practice' in the coal trade were largely ignored since the Act was incapable of being enforced.

Passing legislation was nonetheless a useful way of appearing to do something to safeguard consumers while in fact doing nothing that would harm organised interests in the trade. Abuses were so common that consumers accepted them as part and parcel of the trade and preferred not to report them. Even if reported, the guilty parties were rarely brought to justice and the likelihood was of even greater discrimination being practised in future against the complainant. In 1830 two further select committees, one appointed by the Commons and one by the Lords, showed in unequivocal terms that corruption had reached such an extent that meaningful legislation was imperative.

The 1831 Act, regulating the vend and delivery of coals in London and the home counties, at last proved an effective piece of legislation bringing about significant changes in the conduct of the coal trade. It repealed previous Acts passed since the reign of Queen Anne and released the coastwise trade from the burden of restrictions.[54] In particular, the Act confirmed that coal delivered from any ship in London or within a radius of 25 miles was to be sold by weight, not measure.[55] The office of meter was therefore abolished along with City of London regulations involving certificates, entries and re-measurements. The Coal Exchange was to continue, vested in the Corporation of London, but was to be an open market. To maintain it and provide compensation for meters and others discharged by the Act, a duty of 1d. per ton was to be paid by the master of every coal vessel arriving in the Port of London. The levy on coastwise coal was therefore to consist of 12d. per ton payable to the Corporation of London, plus 1d. per ton for the Coal Market.[56] All duties on coastwise coal payable to the national exchequer were abolished, including the King's duty of 6/- per London chaldron and the 'Richmond shilling'. The Act also reduced City Corporation dues on inland coal brought by canal or river to London from 15d. to the same figure of 13d. per ton. This coal had, of course, always been free of government duty. In total this represented a substantial reduction in charges made on coal shipments. Moreover, duties charged on shipments sent overseas were significantly relaxed in 1834 and again in the 1840's, before being finally abolished in 1850.

Although generally successful, the 1831 Act proved something of a disappointment in certain important respects. A Select Committee of the House of Commons in 1836, reviewing progress since the passage of the Act, provided the following figures of coal shipments:

Table 4

Tonnage of Coal Shipped Abroad and Coastwise to London,
1828-35 (000 tons)

	Exports	Coastwise Shipments
1828	357.9	1,960.6
1830	514.4	2,079.3
1835	736.1	2,298.8

SOURCE:
As in text.

On the credit side, the reduction in export duty was regarded as primarily responsible for a much fuller use of British shipping and for the fact that exports doubled in terms of volume between 1828 and 1835. In addition, before the Act between one-quarter and one-third of total output, in the form of small coal, had been wasted due to screening. Since it often could not be sold at a price that covered transport and delivery charges, including the payment of duty, the practice developed in some collieries of burning it at the pit-head. The relaxation of duties from 1831 brought this practice to an end, with very little being wasted. Finally, since the coastwise trade was much less exposed to malpractice a substantial fall in the cost of delivering coal from on board ship to the London consumer had resulted. In 1830, the average delivery charge per ton amounted to 11/-; by 1836, it had fallen to 7/-, a reduction of 36%. Due to this and other economies effected under the Act, the average selling-price per ton in London varied between 30/- and 35/- during the period 1831-6. This represented a significant decline from the average of 50/- per London chaldron (=26 cwts) charged in 1830.

Yet not all was gain. The removal of government duty did not result in the major expansion of demand that had been anticipated. As Table 4 indicates, coastwise shipments increased by only some 10% between 1830 and 1835. This was far short of expectations. It had been hoped that the increase in demand would be sufficient to make output-regulation by northern owners unnecessary (see p. 40 above). In fact, the control of output was not only maintained but further extended by owners on the Tees joining with their counterparts on the Tyne and Wear in the Limitation of the Vend.

Nor were restrictions wholly eliminated in the Pool of London: rather a new form of 'control' developed from 1834. In an effort to placate northern owners who complained about severe price fluctuations in London, factors operating in the port agreed not to bring to the market the cargoes of more than 40 ships per day unless the price of best coal rose to 20/- or more per ton (revised in 1835 to 21/- or above). Ships arriving in the Thames were compelled to wait strictly in turn before discharging their cargoes. Any coalowner or shipmaster refusing to employ factors, or discharging cargo out of turn, was reported to the Committee of Coalowners in the north. Factors therefore enjoyed a monopoly position in the port of London. All dealings were conducted under their auspices and the free market envisaged by the 1831 Act did not materialise. To free the London coal trade and counteract the monopoly of owners in the north and factors in the south, the House of Commons Select Committee of 1836 strongly urged that every means of promoting new sources of supply in the Midlands and West of England should be encouraged. It was the railways that provided the source of encouragement.

3 CROWN REVENUE

The Crown recognised at an early stage in the development of the coal industry that in the production and distribution of the mineral lay a new and important source of revenue. Over time, therefore, there emerged a complex system of taxes, duties and other levies on coal which had the effect of discriminating between land-sale coal and that shipped coastwise. Although government duty was the most important, it was by no means the only charge made on the coal trade. Charges were imposed both at the port of shipment and in London, the principal market. In Newcastle, town dues levied on coal remained at 2d. per chaldron throughout the 18th century but in Sunderland rose from 2d. to 6d. over the same period. The City of London imposed various charges on coal entering the city, including the right of metage until 1831 and city dues which were only abolished in 1890. It is possible here to emphasise only the most significant of these levies, those that indicated new departures in policy or important landmarks in the development of the industry.[57]

Changes in Resource Use: The Tyranny of Coal

The origins of State interest can be traced back to the 14th century, the first tax on coal probably being imposed in 1379. This was followed in the 1420's by Henry V's demand that the King should henceforth have two pence for every chaldron of coal shipped from Newcastle as a customs duty. Moreover, it was stipulated that all keels, or boats, which carried coal to ships should bear a load of 20 chaldrons. By fixing the burden to be carried by these keels the levying of customs duty, it was hoped, would become a comparatively simple task. Hence the practice had already developed of concentrating on seaborne coal. The sea was the main means of distributing the mineral and it was thought that revenue could be siphoned off without damaging the long-term prospects of the trade.

Increasingly, the actual organisation of the coastwise trade in coal became inextricably bound up with the imposition of levies and duties. The Crown was fully aware that its power to grant monopolies in the distribution of coal conferred upon it an effective bargaining weapon, not only to demand financial recompense in return but also to determine selling-price in London. Important steps were taken during the reign of Queen Elizabeth that were to have an enduring influence on the coal industry. In 1600, a Royal Charter gave to the Society of Free Hostmen in Newcastle the exclusive right to trade in coal from the city.[58] In return, since Crown tax had not been paid for many years, the Hostmen agreed that henceforth all coals shipped from Newcastle to domestic ports would be levied at the rate of 1/- per chaldron and those shipped abroad at the rate of 5/- per chaldron. The former became the famous 'Richmond Shilling' since Charles II in 1677 granted the revenue to his son, the Duke of Richmond and his successors. The tax on Newcastle shipments endured in this form until 1799 when it was bought by the Government for the sum of £400,000, but was not finally abolished until 1831.[59]

By the later 17th century, another new departure in policy involved the imposition of the first significant import duty charged on coal. The mineral was being so heavily consumed in London that its import via the Thames provided an excellent opportunity to raise revenue for improvement schemes being effected within the city. In 1670, an import duty was imposed, the revenue from which was specifically intended to rebuild St Paul's and other churches destroyed by the 1666 Great Fire of London. Subsequently increased so that additional churches could be built, the duty was finally made perpetual in 1719 and assigned to the City of London. Such duties were, of course, bitterly resented. It was pointed out that the 1710 Act, outlining the need for additional revenue from the coal trade for the purpose of building fifty new churches in and about the cities of London and Westminster, had imposed only a temporary duty on all coals brought coastwise. Converting duties on to a perpetual basis

50

was regarded as 'unnecessary, unjust, partial and oppressive because the purpose for which they were originally imposed had been fully answered'.[60] To complete a complex network of taxes and duties, heavy export dues were periodically imposed on shipments to foreign countries. During the 18th century these were successively increased from 3/- per chaldron on coal sent in British ships and 5/- on that sent by foreign vessels in 1714 to no less than £1 per chaldron in 1795. Charges on coal were also made for 'extraordinary purposes', principally to finance war-time expenditure. For instance war levies raised the duty on foreign shipments to a peak of £1 5s. 2d. in 1809.

Hence long before the Industrial Revolution of the 18th century, the coal industry was making an important contribution to regional and national finances. English governments, perpetually in need of revenue, found in the taxation of the mineral a tempting means of raising it. The reverse side of the coin was, of course, that such charges represented a burden on both customers and producers that periodically became difficult to bear. The incidence of tax was most unevenly distributed over different parts of the country, consumers in London where duties were generally higher than elsewhere, being particularly unfortunate. During the 18th century as a whole, the increase in price occasioned by duties to London buyers can rarely have been below $33^1/_3\%$ per chaldron of coal.[61] For producers, too, the burden of tax on the production of coal could have serious implications for particular collieries. By raising the price to the consumer, demand was not allowed to rise by as much as might otherwise have been possible. This was especially important during the last three-quarters of the 17th century when, as observed above, supply consistently outstripped demand, resulting in cut-throat competition in the scramble to acquire markets.

Regarded as most inequitable for both producers and consumers was the fact that land-sale coal carried no government duty. Initially coal carried inland, emanating mainly from the Midlands, served only local demand. The collieries in Yorkshire and the North Midlands, for instance, supplied much of the fuel required by the rapidly growing industry of the West Riding and Sheffield district. However, with the gradual improvement in transport facilities, northern owners became aware that land-sale coal, with no government duty, might successfully compete for markets in London and the South-East. They campaigned vigorously against unfair competition and the discrimination practised against seaborne coal.[62] In the event, they had little to fear in the context of the London market. Not until the 1840's did railways successfully open up the metropolis to land-sale coal (see Table 2). By that time, government duty on coastwise coal had been swept away and, along with it, any discrimination practised against northern coal. Hence throughout the 'Canal Age',

51

the greater cost of road and canal, as opposed to coastwise, transport guaranteed the north's continued domination of the London market. For consumers, too, equity was hardly the guiding principle of policy with regard to land-sale collieries. Those served by land-sale enter-prises did not carry the burden of government duty levied on seaborne coal. In contrast those dependent upon the latter type of coal, particularly in the home counties, were hit hard. Here, in addition to government tax, consumers had to contend with the relatively high cost of carriage on the Thames. In such areas, fuel was generally expensive, all the more so since, unlike London, they received no part of the revenue raised by taxes on coal.

Expenditure during the Napoleonic Wars resulted in several increases in government duty on coal shipped coastwise. As a result, duty per London chaldron reached a peak of 12s. 6d. between 1809 and 1814, fell to 9s. 4d. until 1824 and finally settled at 6/- before being abolished altogether in 1831. However, as observed in section 2, coastwise coal entering London was still subject to City Corporation dues, these being rationalised along with those on land-sale coal to 13d. per ton. The removal of discriminatory government duties on seaborne coal resulted in the disintegration neither of the Vend nor of the north's hold of the London market. Both were to yield only with the advance of railway technology from the 1840's.

At the same time the opportunity was taken successively to relax duties on coal sent overseas. Between 1830 and 1834, duties had ranged from 3/4d. to 5/9d. per ton on coal carried in British ships and from 6/8d. to 12/2d. per ton on coal shipped in foreign vessels. Gradual reductions in these rates over the next few years meant that by 1845, coal sent overseas in British ships was free of duty while that in foreign ships was levied at 4/- per ton. Finally in 1850, all duties on exported coal were repealed, this being associated with a rapid increase in overseas demand. British coal exports rose from over 600 thousand tons in 1834 to 2.8 million in 1849 to 10.6 million in 1869.[63] Although contemporaries regarded this as a prime example of cause and effect, it is likely that natural market forces, unrelated to the abolition of duties, were at least as important. Population growth and industrialisation in Europe inevitably resulted in a rapid increase in demand for British coal, a situation facilitated, rather than created, by the relaxation and final abolition of duties on foreign shipments.

3 'King Coal'
The Basis of the Industrial Revolution

1   OUTPUT AND SHIPMENTS

By the middle of the 18th century coalmining in Britain was poised to take advantage of the decisive changes which were to follow in the technology and organisation of manufacturing industry. These changes were to have such an influence on the course of economic development between 1760 and 1840 that the term 'Industrial Revolution' has commonly been applied to the period. Although 18th-century estimates are necessarily tentative, Deane and Cole have constructed an index of total real output,[1] based on decennial averages, which provides some indication of the nature and extent of economic growth. The index shows that real output expanded by 25% between 1700 and 1750 and by over 200% between 1750 and 1800. The rate of development of industry and commerce was even faster than these figures suggest. While total real output in the economy as a whole more than doubled during the course of the century, that of industry and commerce roughly quadrupled.

Expansion on this scale owed much to the 'new' forms of fuel and power introduced during the second half of the century. The tyranny which wood and water had exercised over the economy gradually gave way after 1750 to that of coal, largely in the form of steam, and iron. Indeed the achievement of the Industrial Revolution was the forging of the vital link between coal and iron upon which Britain's subsequent prosperity came so heavily to depend. Coal became the lifeblood of British industry with developments in coalmining lying 'somewhere near the centre of the driving motor of the Industrial Revolution'.[2] As is well known, the transformation was not accomplished overnight. Watt's refinements to the steam engine and his success in adapting it to rotary motion during the 1780's did not entail the sudden disappearance of water as a source of power for industry. By 1800, water-power was still much more widely used than steam and long after that water-wheels were still being constructed and used to generate power.[3] The more widespread acceptance of Darby's coke-smelting techniques in the 1750's and the advances in iron-making associated with Henry Cort in the 1780's did not immediately result in the replacement of wooden machinery or even wooden rails by substitutes made of iron. Nor did the growing

53

advantages of locating on, or near, the coalfields produce a rash of newly constructed factories. On the contrary, the factory as a form of organisation became commonplace only by the middle of the 19th century.

It is appropriate therefore to emphasise the need for caution: to avoid overstating the rapidity of change in the economy and particularly the rate of take-up of the 'new' coal-using techniques after 1760. In the same way, the extent to which the coal industry itself was transformed during the Industrial Revolution is a matter of debate. It is customary to argue that the forces at work in the economy as a whole did not call for, or evoke, a dramatic response from the coal industry.[4] The frequently long period of gestation between invention and innovation, the stubborn survival of the domestic system of industry and the persistence of water-power imply no sudden or immediate impact on the coal industry.[5] In general the process of discovery and improvement in extractive industry is a continuous and gradual one, the result of long and often bitter experience. In the 18th century there was the further problem of lack of adequate communications. New ideas spread only slowly from pit to pit and from coalfield to coalfield. Hence progress was regarded as evolutionary rather than revolutionary: 'no flash of genius of a Crompton or a Watt could transform coal-mining'.[6] It was, apparently, a sector which could safely be ignored when looking for instances of the new ideas and far-reaching changes in technique which characterised other, more dynamic, branches of industry during the first half of the 19th century.

Not all would accept this interpretation, but the question of whether the rate of change of output and technique in coalmining amounted to a 'revolution' is largely a matter of semantics. It is true that the industry experienced a derived demand, depending on the prior expansion of other sectors and the emergence of new uses of coal. Yet, it is difficult to accept the argument advanced by Ashton and Sykes that development was gradual since, in relation to the century which followed, the market for coal during the 18th century showed 'no vast expansion'.[7] The adjective 'vast' is suitably vague and is used because statistics of the coal industry are most uncertain before 1854. Only in that year, following the Reports of the Committees of Inquiry into Public Offices, were arrangements made to gather and publish data on minerals on an annual basis.[8] Since no precise measurement of the rate of growth of output is possible before the middle of the 19th century, recourse must be made to contemporary sources and statistics of coal shipments. The former vary widely in their likely degree of accuracy due principally to the obscurities of domestic consumption. The latter can be used with greater confidence since by order of the House of Commons detailed returns of seaborne coal had to be published on a regular basis. On the basis of the evidence available, there are plausible grounds for assuming that the expansion of demand during the 18th century was indeed significant. Statistics relating to output, exports and coastwise shipments are presented in Table 1.

Table 1
*UK Coal Output, Exports and Shipments to London,
Selected Years 1750-1860*

Year	Output (m. tons)	Exports (000 tons)	Shipments to London By Sea (000 tons)	By Rail (000 tons)
1750	4.9	164[1]	584	–
70	6.2	289[1]	782	–
1800	10.1	579[2]	1,289	–
16	15.9	238	1,553	–
30	22.4	504	2,079	–
45	45.9	2,443	3,403	8[3]
50	49.4	3.212	3,553	55
54	64.7	4,120	3,400	945
60	80.0	7,050	3,573	1,478

SOURCES:
Royal Commission on Coal, 1871; Finlay A. Gibson, *The Coalmining Industry of the United Kingdom, the Various Coalfields thereof, and the Principal Foreign Countries of the World* (1922); B. R. Mitchell and P. Deane, *Abstract of British Historical Statistics* (1971), pp. 108-21; Deane and Cole, op. cit., p. 216.
NOTES:
1. Relates to England and Wales only.
2. Relates to Great Britain.
3. 1845 was the first year in which London received coal shipments by rail.

The estimates provided in Table 1 show that during the 18th century as a whole output increased by a factor of four, rising from about 2.6 million tons to 10.1 million tons. This was a relatively modest rate of development when compared to that achieved in the following century.[9] But this is hardly the correct yardstick to use since the whole environment within which the industry operated changed during the two periods. Development must essentially be viewed within its proper historical context. It can best be evaluated by comparing the standards achieved by one industry over a given time-period with those of other sectors over the same period. On this basis, the expansion of the coal industry was relatively rapid during the course of the 18th century. It was certainly inferior to that of certain branches of the textile industry but was considerably faster than several other important lines of activity. In volume terms, the output of soap and candles only doubled during the 18th century; strong-beer production rose by three-fifths; and both meat and corn output increased by two-fifths.[10]

As noted in Chapter 1, Northumberland and Durham gradually lost their position of absolute dominance of the British coal industry after 1800 due to the development of coalfields in South Wales, Yorkshire and the Midlands. Clear evidence of the scale of development during the early decades of the 19th century is provided in Table 1 of this chapter. All indicators show a rapid expansion of the industry as transport improvements opened up new sources of supply and coal was increasingly adapted to a wide range of industrial uses. Output doubled between 1800 and 1830, doubled once more between 1830 and 1845 and had almost doubled again between 1845 and 1860.

2 INDUSTRIAL INTER-RELATEDNESS AND THE EXPANDING MARKET FOR COAL

During the 19th century, coal came to occupy a position of central importance in the British economy. In the short term, it had a dynamic effect on the technology of the period, underpinning the development of the steam engine and later the railways. In the longer term, it became the indispensable raw material of British manufacturing industry, vitally influencing the nature and rate of growth in the economy as a whole. In turn, changes in the rate of growth of coal output can largely be attributed to changes in the character of the market which it served. In 1800 by far the greatest share of output was still being used for cooking and heating purposes in the home. Indeed, in Table 2 below it is likely that the proportion absorbed by households tended in that year towards the higher of the estimates provided for domestic consumption. This supports the view that the application of steam power throughout the economy was making steady rather than spectacular progress. Even in cotton spinning which was generally well ahead of other sectors in adopting new techniques, steam did not predominate as a source of power until the 1830's.[11] Over the early decades of the 19th century, Table 2 shows that the most important single factor in the expanding demand for coal was the development of the iron industry.

The outstanding feature of the Industrial Revolution was the extent to which the consumption of coal became so intimately bound up at all points with that of iron. Due in part to this inter-relationship coalmining, which accounted for rather less than one per cent of British national income at the start of the 19th century, steadily

Table 2

Distribution of Coal Output in the UK, Selected Years, 1800-1869[1]
(as % of Total Tonnage Raised)

1800 (Tonnage Raised=10.1m)	%	1840 (Tonnage Raised=33.7m)	%	1855 (Tonnage Raised=58.2m)	%	1869 (Tonnage Raised=107.4m)	%
Iron Industry	10-15	Iron Industry	25	Iron Industry	26[2]	Iron Industry	30
Other Industrial Consumers (principally brickmakers, brewers, distillers, bakers, potteries, copper and tin smelters)	17-38	General Manufacturing	32.5	General Manufacturing: Copper smelting, Iron and Brass manufacture	17	General Manufacturing	26
Domestic Consumption	50-66	Mines	3	Salt & Glass Works	1.5	Mines	6.5
		Steam Navigation	1.5	Lime and Brick works	1.5	Steam Navigation and Railways	5
		Gas & Electricity	1.5	Railway Carriages, Steamboats	5	Gas and Electricity	6
		Domestic Consumption	31.5	Domestic Consumption and Small Manufacturers	36	Domestic consumption	17
		Exports	5	Exports	7.5	Exports	9
	100		100		100		100

57

SOURCES:

Royal Commission on Coal, 1871, Committee E: figures based on J. R. McCulloch, *Dictionary of Commerce* (several editions from 1832); Deane and Cole, op. cit., pp. 218-19.

NOTES:

1. No allowance made for stocks.
2. This understates the consumption of the iron industry since some part of the coal normally attributed to the manufacture of iron has been included in the category Copper Smelting etc. A more accurate figure would probably be about 30%. See Table 3 below.

expanded to reach almost two per cent for most of the second quarter of the century. In absolute terms, the volume of coal output rose more than ten times over the 70-year period specified in Table 2. Over the same period the tonnage of coal consumed by the iron industry increased by over 20 times. As might be expected in view of the rapid industrial expansion after 1800, general manufacturing also absorbed a relatively high share of the coal industry's output. If, as seems probable, the proportion of output taken by 'Other Industrial Consumers' in 1800 leaned towards the smaller of the estimates provided in Table 2, a considerable expansion had taken place by the middle decades of the 19th century in the coal used by manufacturing industry. Due to the growing dependence on coal, one authority has seen the industrialisation of Britain as 'a laying of population and enterprise upon the areas which had coal underneath.'[12] Correspondingly, there was a marked decline in the proportion of output devoted to domestic consumption. Domestic demand accounted for at least one-half of total output in 1800 but for less than one-fifth in 1869.

Hence the evolving technology of the iron industry and its growing demand for mineral fuel were primarily responsible for the rapid expansion of coalmining output. The problems stemming from the scattered and migratory nature of the iron industry were largely resolved in the 18th century by two major innovations. The first involved the use of coal in the blast furnace. As noted in Chapter 1, the Darby process freed the iron industry from total dependence on wood, but only from the 1750's when the cost advantages of smelting with mineral fuel became decisive. Moreover, Darby's discovery produced iron suitable only for castings or for conversion into bar iron of relatively low quality. High-grade bar iron still depended on charcoal-smelted pig and also required charcoal when refined in the forge. Since fuel consumption in the forge was higher than in the furnace, the iron industry was only partly released from its reliance on charcoal. Nonetheless from mid-century, iron-founders began regularly to use coke to produce a wide range of cast iron products.

It should also be emphasised that long before the introduction of Watt's engine, the first steam engine had been successfully applied to the iron industry at Coalbrookdale. Until the 1740's, the standard method of providing the blast for the furnace had been by water-powered bellows. In 1743, Abraham Darby II erected a steam engine of the Newcomen type to pump the water required by the water-wheel to blow the furnace. Subsequently additional engines were built at Coalbrookdale, fitted with cast cylinders made of iron rather than brass, to provide sufficient heads of water for blowing purposes. Hence a further vital link between coal and iron had been created — that of steam. Smelting ore successfully with coal or coke depended on the use of powerful bellows. Coke required a stronger air-blast than charcoal since more air in the process of combustion was necessary. At the Carron iron works in Scotland, John Smeaton produced a superior blowing cylinder driven by a water-wheel in the 1760's[13] but the long-term answer to the problem of providing a strong and regular blast lay with the direct application of the steam engine. It was left to John Wilkinson, using a Watt engine in 1776, to employ steam directly for blowing an iron furnace.

The second major technical breakthrough of the 18th century was the use of coal in the refining process: that is, in the manufacture of wrought iron. The refining sector had stagnated before 1750 since Darby's coke-smelting process could only produce poor quality bar iron. Credit for fully emancipating the iron industry from this dependence on charcoal has usually been accorded to Henry Cort who patented his 'puddling and rolling' process in 1783-4. But the key innovation was probably the 'potting and stamping' process developed in the early 1760's by the Wood brothers.[14] By enabling both coal and coke-smelted pig to be used in the forges, it brought significant cost-savings over the charcoal process in the refining sector. Thus by 1788 almost half of Britain's bar iron output of 32,000 tons can be attributed to the potting process. Only by the mid-1790's did Cort's innovation begin to exercise a significant influence over the iron industry, once technical difficulties had been overcome. Thereafter it made rapid headway and had superseded all other methods of manufacturing wrought iron by 1815. The great virtue of Cort's innovation was that coal fuel was used throughout, thus freeing bar iron from its dependence on charcoal. Already in the 1780's steam engines were being used in the forges and rolling mills to drive trip and tilt hammers and to slit and roll iron. By the early 19th century Cort's innovation, using Wilkinson's steam-hammer, could process 15 tons of bar iron in the time previously taken to produce one ton by the standard hammering method. Yet it was not until the 1840's when large-size iron bars were required for the shafts of ocean-going steamships that James Nasmyth invented the actual steam hammer.

Since coal was now required at all stages, the new technology in iron involved not only vastly increased inputs of the mineral but also the integration and relocation of the iron industry on the coalfields. During the second half of the 18th century iron manufacture made its home at or near the coalfields of the Midlands, Yorkshire, Derbyshire and South Wales, combining furnace, forge and mill in a single establishment. Average output per furnace rose from 565 tons in 1788 to 1,130 tons in 1806 and to 2,430 tons in 1827.[15] The scale and efficiency of furnaces were further increased by Nielson's invention in the next year of the hot-blast. By heating the air used in the blast, a much smaller tonnage of coke was required in the production of pig. Moreover, the process allowed raw coal to be used in smelting in those regions where good coking coal was absent.[16] It was a decisive step along the way towards greater economy in the use of fuel (see section 3 below).

Cort's innovation also permitted the steady replacement of wood by iron in the construction of machinery. The corollary of re-equipping British industry during the first half of the 19th century was the development of a new industry, mechanical engineering, and the emergence of machine tools. Nor was that all. The new techniques in iron stimulated the rapid development of canals not only to distribute the final iron products but more particularly to carry coal, the vital raw material, to the expanding iron plant. Civil engineering blossomed, therefore, as a necessary adjunct to the developing coal and iron industries. The smooth flow of heavy industrial products such as coal about the domestic economy depended during the Industrial Revolution upon a network of canals and the improvements effected in road and bridge construction.

The ability of the coal industry to respond to the demands made upon it enabled the iron industry to become the most efficient in Europe by 1815. The rapid expansion of iron manufacture can largely be attributed to the advantages of using coal fuel and the increasing application of steam in place of water power at all stages of iron production. In the latter context some progress had been made by utilising the Newcomen engine but most of the credit for designing a powerful and efficient steam engine can be assigned to James Watt. Significantly, Watt's patent, taken out in 1769, described the new engine as 'a method of lessening the consumption of steam, and consequently of fuel, in fire engines.'[17] His major difficulty probably lay less with the principles of design than with achieving completely accurate construction of engine-parts. It was this that led to his vital association with John Wilkinson whose cylinder boring-lathe achieved the precision of bore required to prevent the leakage of steam. Wilkinson was associated with the Boulton-Watt enterprise from its creation in 1775 until 1795. In that time he supplied virtually all the cylinders and many of the other engine-parts required by the new firm. In turn, Wilkinson made full use of the Watt engine in his own productive processes. As already noted, he was the first to apply steam power directly to blow the blast at the furnace in 1776; the first to use steam to work the forge-hammer in 1782; and again the first to employ steam in the rolling mill in 1784. In every sense, Wilkinson was therefore the pioneer who confirmed the relationship between steam power (and hence coal), iron-making and engineering. Where he led, other iron-masters were soon to follow.

Before the 1780's Watt's engine had virtually been confined to pumping water, finding ready employment in Cornwall where it drained tin and copper mines. Some engines were used in iron-works in

Shropshire and Staffordshire and others were erected for pumping at water-works. But in 1781, Watt patented rotary motion which allowed the steam engine to be applied directly to all types of industrial enterprise. The firm of Boulton and Watt became the centre of development, supplying engines both to the mining and manufacturing sectors of the economy and later diverisfying into transport, particularly in the form of steam navigation.

The ties between coal, iron and engineering were further consolidated during the early decades of the 19th century. The gradual innovation of the high-pressure steam engine meant that the economy became increasingly dependent upon a steady expansion in the supply of coal. Richard Trevithick had patented his high-pressure engine in 1802 but the amalgamation of high-pressure steam, with its subsequent condensation was mainly the work of Arthur Woolf using a compound (that is, two-cylinder) engine.[18] Opposed by Watt and others on the grounds that it was much more liable to explode than the traditional engine, the new technology was only gradually adapted to industrial use. It made its most significant contribution in the transport sector where it paved the way for the more rapid development of the steam railway locomotive. Here the increased power afforded by a compact, relatively small-sized engine proved ideal for the purpose of steam traction. In manufacturing, the great bulk of steam engines before 1850 remained of traditional design, built as low-pressure condensing steam engines.[19] Even so, the new technology made some impact in that there was a growing tendency for several of the standard designs to be converted to high pressure by strengthening the steam case and boilers and modifying the valves. The power of engines could also be greatly increased by 'compounding', as developed by McNaught in 1845.

3   FACTORS INHIBITING THE EXPANSION OF DEMAND FOR COAL

By the early decades of the 19th century, the rapid advances in industrial technology enabled a group of industries, firmly inter-related, to develop on a scale sufficient to transform the structure of the British economy. The coal and iron industries had become heavily inter-dependent, the latter using coal both as a material in smelting and as a source of power in the form of steam. Coal in turn increasingly employed iron in much of the technology applied to the processes of extraction and distribution. The metal was used for pumping and winding engines, tubbing, and above all rails, both above and below ground. Moreover important linkages had been established between these two sectors and steam engineering, the heavy castings trade and such infant industries as mechanical and civil engineering. Further progress in growth sectors like textiles depended upon the wider use of iron machinery, constructed with the help of coal and driven by steam engines stoked with coal.

However, it is important to place the influence of these technical improvements and developing linkages between heavy industries in proper perspective. For the most part, a considerable lag existed between the invention of a new technique or process and its wide-spread acceptance. Inventive activity is usually a gradual process, a cumulation of minor improvements, modifications and economies. Even when major inventions, which appear to represent sharp and dramatic departures from the past, can be distinguished 'there are usually pervasive technological as well as economic forces at work which tend to slow down and flatten out the impact of such inventions in terms of their contribution to raising resource productivity.'[20] The diffusion of steam power is a notable example. At the start of the 19th century, steam power was still in its infancy with little or no power-driven machinery installed in the great majority of manufac-tures. By that date, the firm of Boulton and Watt had turned out almost 500 engines with a total horse-power of only 7,500, an average of 15 h.p. per engine. Subsequently the use of steam power increased rapidly in cotton, coalmining and the primary processes of iron production; was prominent in water-pumping, engineering, brewing and several grinding and milling operations; but remained of relatively minor importance in all other manufacturing trades. By mid-century, total industrial steam power cannot have been much in excess of 300,000 nominal horse-power.[21] Allowance must be made for the fact that converting old engines to high-pressure raised nominal measurements so that indicated, or actual, horse-power may have been rather higher than this figure suggests. Yet it seems clear that, in terms of steam power and the volume of coal which it consumed, industry had by no means been 'revolutionised' by 1850.

Apart from lags in the development process, a further factor affecting the consumption of coal was the effort made to economise in the use of fuel in a number of manufacturing trades. This can best be illustrated with reference to one of the major coal-consuming industries, the production of iron. A rapid expansion in the output of pig iron from the late 18th century was accompanied by significant economies in fuel consumption. In Table 3 below, output and con-sumption estimates for the years up to and including 1840 are tentative and have been provided only to indicate the rough mag-nitudes involved. From 1855 the figures are more comprehensive and can be used with greater confidence.

On the basis of the figures presented in Table 3, the amount of coal consumed per ton of pig iron can be calculated from 1788. In that year, an average of 7 tons of coal was required to produce one ton of pig. The ratio fell steadily to 5 tons of coal per ton of pig in 1800-02,

Table 3

Volume of Coal and Coke Consumed in the Production of Pig and Bar Iron, Selected Years, 1788-1869

Year	Output of Pig Iron Smelted with Mineral Fuel	Volume of Coal and Coke Consumed in Make of Pig	Volume of Coal and Coke Consumed to Convert Pig into Iron Bar etc.	Total Volume of Coal Consumed in Make of Iron	Coal Consumed in Make of Iron as % of Total Coal Raised
	(000 tons)	(000 tons)	(000 tons)	(000 tons)	%
1788	53.8[1]	376.0	—	376.0	N.A.
1800-1802[2]	170.0	850.0	—	850.0	9
1840	1,396.4	4,877.0	3,550.0	8,427.0	25
1855	3,218.2	9,654.5	9,803.4	19,457.8	30
1860	3,826.8	11,480.3	11,672.0	23,152.3	29
1869	5,445.8	16,337.4	15,859.3	32,207.7	30

SOURCES:
Royal Commission on Coal, 1871, Committee E; figures for 1840 based on David Mushet, *On the First Production and Use of Cast Iron* (1840); *Report from the Select Committee on Coal,* 313, 1873.
NOTES:
1. A further 14.5 thousand tons of pig were produced in 1788, smelted by the charcoal process.
2. Annual average.

3.5 tons in 1840 and to about 3 tons during the third-quarter of the century. Further, between 1840 and 1869 some 3 to 3.5 tons of coal were needed to convert pig into bar iron. These ratios, averaged for the country as a whole, are confirmed by the experience of individual firms operating in different parts of the country. Economies in fuel-use, although significant in England and Wales, were even more pronounced in Scotland.[22] It was here that the rate of 'take-up' of Nielson's hot-blast was most rapid, with all furnaces using the technique by 1836. In regions of England and Wales, the rate of innovation was slower with only about one-quarter of the furnaces in Staffordshire and one-sixth in South Wales using the hot-blast by 1839. The speed with which the new process was adopted in Scotland and the large fuel savings which resulted can be directly attributed to the low carbon content of the coal in the region. Hitherto, the lower the carbon content the greater the volume of coal required for coking in order to yield a given tonnage of pure carbon. The major achievement of the hot-blast was to allow iron-masters to use raw coal in the furnace and dispense completely with coking. This meant a significant saving in costs.

Table 3 shows that during the first half of the 19th century, the output of the iron industry rapidly increased. In the 20-30 years after 1838 it was dominated by railway demand, particularly the requirement for iron rails.[23] As iron production expanded so, too, did the industry's consumption of coal, from just under one million tons in 1800 to over 30 million tons by the 1860's. By the latter date, iron was absorbing close to one-third of all coal raised. Dramatic though these figures were, they would have been higher still had significant economies not been made in the use of fuel. In pig iron alone, had the rate of coal consumption been the same in 1855 as at the start of the century, an additional 6.5 million tons of coal would have been required to produce the make of pig in that year. In short, the pig iron sector would have required two-thirds as much coal again to achieve the same level of output.

Similar economies in coal-use were effected in most branches of manufacturing. Committee B of the 1871 Royal Commission on Coal noted that for some time past, attempts to reduce the amount of coal consumed in the productive processes had been a major pre-occupation of British manufacturing industry. Even in relatively 'new' trades such as steel entrepreneurs were conscious of the need to reduce fuel costs to a minimum in order to keep production costs low and enhance their competitive ability. By 1869, an estimated 250,000 tons of coal were consumed in the production of steel, although the amount required per ton of steel was being rapidly reduced through the more widespread application of the Bessemer process and the introduction of Siemens' regenerative gas furnace.[24] Moreover, Hawke has shown that considerable fuel savings were involved in the change from coke to coal burning on the railways.[25] Coke had previously been preferred because it was regarded as more efficient and cleaner but by the late 1850's engineers had solved the problem of burning coal without creating large amounts of smoke. As a result, the replacement of coke by coal on the railways was complete by about 1870. In addition, by the 1850's large fuel savings were being made through the practice of collecting the gases which escaped at high temperatures from the top of the blast furnace and using these under the boilers for the production of steam and other functions. Indeed, so great were the efforts to reduce the consumption of coal that the 1871 Royal Commission believed that 'in some branches of manufacture...the limits of a beneficial economy appear to have been nearly reached.'[26] Apparently the Commission had little faith in the future of technical progress in this country!

4   COAL AND IMPROVEMENTS IN TRANSPORT

The developments in steam transport after 1800 had a number of important influences on British coalmining. As consumers, neither railways nor steamships were to have a large direct impact on the coal industry. Table 2 shows that they represented a relatively small, but stable, outlet for the mineral. On the other hand, in the provision of transport services, they did profoundly influence the structure and efficiency of coalmining. This was particularly true of the railways which brought lower distribution costs, regular and guaranteed deliveries and the opportunity to break down local monopolies. One example of this was the breaking up of the Limitation of the Vend, discussed in Chapter 2, section 1 above. But even in the case of railways, these advantages were derived only in the longer term, during and after the second railway investment boom of the 1840's. In the short term, when the foundations of the network were being laid, their benefits were rather less obvious, especially as carriers of freight. Although it was the need for better facilities to carry coal and other minerals that had largely 'induced' the development of railways, their first major impact was on passenger traffic. In freight they met stubborn resistance, mainly in the form of price-cutting competition from canals, and only managed to dominate this sector of the transport industry during the 1850's.

Similarly, the introduction of steam shipping had little immediate impact on the distribution of coal. There was a considerable time-lag between William Symington's successful experiments at Carron in the late 1780's[27] and the launching of the first commercially viable steamboat, Henry Bell's *Comet,* on the Clyde in 1812. Thereafter, development was rapid but concerned more with passenger than freight traffic. Registered steam tonnage in the UK rose from 10,000 tons in 1823 to 250,000 tons in 1853 but only a small fraction of this increase consisted of ships exclusively confined to the carriage of freight.[28] The great bulk was due to an unprecedented growth in the use of the steamship for personal travel. This reluctance to employ the steamship for the transport of goods before 1850 was partly a consequence of the greater amount of capital that had been invested in cargo sailing ships before the age of steam. However, more important were the high capital costs of building and equipping a steam cargo boat relative to a sailing ship and the heavy operating costs of the former type of vessel. In the east coast coal trade, a new steam collier, capable of carrying 600 tons of coal, cost approximately the same to construct by 1850 as six new sailing colliers of 300 tons capacity each.[29] Moreover, the operating costs of steamers were prohibitive since a large proportion of cargo space had to be sacrificed to accommodate the engine, boilers and coal storage area. Coal for the use of bunkers was a particularly serious problem in long-distance overseas voyages and together with space allocated to mechanical equipment could take up over half the freight-earning capacity of the vessel.

   The problems of heavy capital and operating costs were overcome with the substitution of iron for wood in construction and the introduction of more efficient engines capable of generating the power required by much larger merchant ships. But neither the use of iron nor the high-pressure compound engine became widespread until the 1860's. Only then was freight-earning capacity sufficiently increased to ensure the success of the steam cargo vessel. Compared with 30 years earlier boiler pressures had been trebled or quadrupled by the early 1870's and coal consumption cut by one-half, from roughly 4-5 lbs per horsepower per hour to 2 lbs or less.[30] Hence until at least mid-century, the coastal trade in coal continued to depend largely on very small vessels built of wood and driven by sail. Only in passenger services had the steamship made much headway; it was largely these vessels that account for the coal absorbed by the category 'steam navigation' in Table 2.

   In the case of railways, even the major phase of construction of the late 1840's had a relatively minor effect on the production of coal. It is true that between 1830 and 1845, coal output at least doubled but it was never dominated by the direct demand of either railways or steamships. Of greater moment were the expansion of exports which multiplied five times, imports of coal into London which increased by almost 80% and the demand of the iron industry which more than doubled. Hence on the demand side, the principal effect of the new forms of transport on coalmining was an indirect one, through the manufacture of iron.[31] On the basis of estimated train-miles and the fuel required per train-mile, it would seem that the total consumption of coal by the railways in England and Wales remained below one million tons until 1850.[32] Subsequently, railway consumption moved as follows:—

	1854	1860	1869
Total Coal Consumption (m. tons)	1.6	2.4	1.7
As % of Coal Output in England and Wales	2.8	3.3	1.8

Thus even in the third quarter of the century the railways' direct demand for coal amounted only to a small proportion of the total produced in England and Wales. The above estimates also give an indication of the fall in fuel consumption which followed the substitution of coal for coke. This change to coal-burning on the railways was accomplished mainly in the 1860's and was responsible for a rapid cut-back in total tonnage required.

   It was in the provision of transport services that railways exerted their most profound influence on the coal industry. Yet the relative cheapness of inland navigation and the earlier adaptation of manufacture and distribution to water-borne traffic allowed the canals to compete successfully with the railways until the late 1840's. Canals had permitted a rapid expansion of the coal industry from the 1760's, enabling inland collieries for the first time to distribute the mineral efficiently to markets remote from the coalfields. In so doing, they brought the Midlands, Yorkshire and Lancashire into direct competition with Northumberland and Durham. Owners in the latter districts protested bitterly against 'unfair competition' since coal conveyed inland was not subject to duty and could therefore be sold at a cheaper rate in southern markets (see Chapter 2, section 3 above). In one of several petitions to the House of Commons, northern coalmasters pointed out in 1816 that the demand for seaborne coal had been seriously affected by inland supplies carried free of duty.[33] It was alleged that this not only blighted the northern coal trade but also had grave implications for shipping interests, the large number of seamen employed in the coastwise trade and government revenue derived from the trade. The coalmasters estimated that a total of over 4 million Newcastle chaldrons of inland coal had been carried, free of duty, by canals and colliery railways in 1815-16, much to the detriment of capital and labour employed in the north. The suggested remedy involved both limiting the quantity of inland coal brought to London and taxing it at the same rate as seaborne coal.

On the grounds of equity, there was some merit in the northern owners' case. Between 1800 and 1830, government duty on seaborne coal brought into London amounted to about one-fifth of average selling-price at the ship's side.[34] This was in addition to local dues, port charges and other levies imposed on coal carried coastwise. But it was difficult for northern owners to plead hardship and 'unfair' competiton whey they were, at the same time, restricting supplies to London through the Limitation of the Vend. For the same reason, their complaints against the early public railways evoked little response from the Government. Owners of established collieries in Northumberland and Durham argued that they paid landowners relatively high wayleave rent to secure a right of way for their coal. In some areas, this amounted to as much as £350 per mile.[35] In contrast, under the Acts establishing railway companies in the 1830's, power was given to railway promoters to buy the surface of the land over which the public railways were to run at fair valuation. It was alleged that this enabled the new railways to operate at greatly reduced charges compared with the older railways in the north. Hence owners on the Tyne and Wear petitioned against the Stockton to Darlington railway and later the South-West Durham, South Durham and other lines on the grounds that they exonerated coal proprietors of those lines from paying wayleave rent.[36] Coalowners using such railways had been given 'a very great advantage over the occupiers of private [colliery] railroads in consequence of the heavy rents and other charges upon the latter.'[37]

New collieries had been opened in the vicinity of the public railways to take advantage of the low costs of distribution; even the prospect of a new line sometimes led to the sinking of pits in hitherto untapped parts of the coalfield. Where previously the best situated mines in the north had been located near the coast or on the banks of a river, the advent of the railways reversed the position. The best mines were now those situated inland, close to a public railway. According to Matthias Dunn, the number of collieries in operation in the north increased slowly during the early decades of the 19th century from 41 in 1800 to 59 in 1830 and to 76 in 1836. Thereafter the railways encouraged rapid development with the result that by 1844, 126 mines were actively engaged in producing coal.[38] The sudden increase in competition, it was alleged, meant that older collieries using private railways could not be operated at a reasonable profit on capital employed. But again the complaints of established colliery concerns foundered on the rock of output limitation which was being vigorously enforced by owners in the north to maintain prices, and hence profits, in the London market.

Nor before the 1840's were there convincing reasons for believing that railways constituted a major threat to those owners dependent for their livelihood on the coastwise trade. In view of the effective competition of canals in the freight market, the railway companies concentrated initially on developing passenger traffic which was not only easier to expand but also promised quicker returns. This was reflected in the delivery of coal to the London market. As observed in Chapter 2, coal brought into London by rail in 1850 amounted to a mere 2% of that by sea. Not until 1867 did the volume of railborne coal arriving in the metropolis exceed that of seaborne coal, almost 30 years after the initial rail link between the land-sale districts and the capital had been constructed. Thereafter the railways rapidly consolidated their position with the result that for more than one hundred years after 1850 the movement of coal was the bread and butter of British railways. Indeed, the tonnage of coal carried always amounted to well over half the total volume of freight traffic.[39] The railways made readily available throughout the economy the fuel which was the life-blood of the staple industries and encouraged in coalmining itself a jump on to an altogether higher plane of production.

Recently, an attempt has been made to measure the 'savings' made by the railways on the inland distribution of coal about the domestic economy.[40] By using the concept of 'social savings', an indication can be provided for the first time of the extent to which the railways benefited the economy by reducing the costs of carrying coal. Social savings are measured as the difference between the actual cost of the transportation services of a given year provided by the railways and the hypothetical cost of those same services in the absence of railways. Given the assumptions that the economy is not able to adjust in the absence of railways and that the prices used accurately reflect resource use, this also measures the difference in national income with and without the railways. In 1865, 50 million tons of coal were carried by the railways for an average of 34 miles. This yields a total of 1,700 million ton-miles of coal output supplied by the railways at a cost of £4.33 million. The alternative means of carrying coal inland would have been the canals. The cost of 1,700 million ton-miles at 2s. 3d. per ton-mile by canal would have amounted to £16.3 million. Compared with canals, railways therefore reduced the freight cost on coal by an estimated 75%. The direct social saving on coal transport of £12 million represented 1.46% of UK national income. This is a measure of the extent to which rail transport, by reducing the costs of distributing coal, augmented national income. On minerals other than coal the social savings, estimated in similar manner, amounted in 1865 to £2 million, 0.25% of national income. Hence direct social savings on all mineral freights due to the existence of railways amounted in total to 1.7% of national income in 1865.

However, in addition to the direct saving of transport costs, railways reduced the distance which wagon haulage had to travel in order to bring the mineral to a main transport artery. The indirect saving which resulted from this reduction of supplementary travel amounted in 1865 to over £7 million, 0.9% of national income. Thus the total social saving of the railways on all minerals in 1865 may be summarised as follows:

	£ million	as % of National Income
On coal and coke	12	1.46
On minerals other than coal and coke	2	0.25
On reduction of wagon haulage costs	7.1	0.90
Total	21.1	2.61

Viewed in relation to national income as a whole, the savings effected by the railways in transporting coal appear relatively small. But in the context of the individual coal industry, railways had a decisive contribution to make. By reducing delivery costs, they permitted a vast extension in the use of coal, both in manufacturing industry and the home. As a result, the output of coal which had doubled between 1750 an 1800, and doubled again between 1800 and 1830, increased by a factor of four during the so-called 'railway age' of the 1830's to the 1870's.

5 A REVOLUTION IN TECHNOLOGY?

The improvements made in mining technology during the Industrial Revolution are generally regarded to have been more modest in scale and influence than those in certain of the consumer durable trades. But such comparisons tend to be misleading. In relation to what had gone before, the changes in coalmining technique during the early 19th century affected output and methods of working to such an extent that the term 'revolution' is perhaps no less justified than in other sectors[41] — a point to be discussed further below, pp. 79-82. The increasing use of steam power and iron, above and below ground, profoundly altered ways of winning and moving the coal. As employment rapidly expanded from about 50,000 in 1800 to over 20,000 in the 1850's, industrial management techniques developed to become a model for other industries to follow. A large number of new collieries were opened, particularly in inland coalfields which for the first time assumed a national prominence. Even in older-established coalfields, the new technology had a major impact in that it allowed deeper sinkings and the re-opening of previously abandoned workings.

Perhaps the most fundamental change was the more general acceptance of the longwall system of mining which steadily replaced bank working in Yorkshire and the Midland collieries. By mid-century, it was also commonly found in other large coalfields such as Lancashire, Scotland and South Wales. By permitting a greater extraction of the seams, longwall reduced the incidence of waste in mining previously caused by leaving large pillars of coal underground to support the surface. Under the pillar and stall system, in extreme cases between one-half and two-thirds of the seam might be left intact in the form of barriers[42] and to support buildings on the surface. Moreover, under the longwall system less small coal was produced. Again this resulted in less waste since, due to inadequate market development, small coal was either left unsold by the collieries or used extravagantly.[43] Hence by minimising waste, longwall allowed the productivity of face-workers to increase, a trend accentuated from the 1780's by the steady replacement of wooden tools below ground by implements made of iron. Without such a general conversion to longwall working, either more men or more capital-intensive methods would have been necessary to sustain the expansion of output.[44]

Ironically, the one major coalfield which refused to make use of the longwall system was Northumberland and Durham, so often the pioneer of new methods and techniques. Many owners in the north mistakenly believed that ventilation under conditions of longwall working was inadequate. Moreoever in certain northern mines, longwall had been tried and found wanting. G. B. Forster, mining engineer at Blyth, confirmed in his evidence before the Royal Commission on the Coal Industry in 1871 that under *most* conditions, longwall working was capable of yielding more coal per acre than the bord and pillar system which he practised. However, he maintained that conditions in many areas of the Northern Coalfield proved the exception. For instance, around Blyth attempts to employ longwall methods had failed due to the nature of the roof and the fact that the floor in most collieries was undulating and wet. As a result, water had constantly seeped into the faces.[45] While Northumberland and Durham continued to resist longwall working, it was adopted in most other districts. The greater efficiency of the system was partly responsible for allowing these districts successfully to challenge the supremacy of the Northern Coalfield in the middle decades of the 19th century.

At the heart of developments in mining technology was the continuing struggle to improve ventilation and general safety in the pits. In the latter context, the introduction of the safety lamp was a major step forward, providing both the necessary illumination below ground and the early warning miners needed of the presence of gas. But it was never intended to be a substitute for improvements in ventilation. Certainly the lamp indicated the presence of firedamp in the workings and enabled avoiding-action to be taken. However, in too many collieries, this was regarded as sufficient. The very existence of the safety lamp provided a reason, or more accurately an excuse, for the tardy development of more efficient ventilation. Ironically, therefore, the principal short-term effect of the lamp was not upon safety, but upon output. Its introduction did not result in fewer accidents or fatalities. Between 1835 and 1850, no fewer than 643 explosions occurred in British mines, an average of over 40 per year. Only in the more progressive collieries were improved forms of ventilation and greater use of the safety lamp seen as being complementary to each other.

In the North of England, Spedding's air-coursing system, introduced about 1760, had been quickly adopted. Although it directed air through the underground roads, the danger of passing this air, which had often travelled between 20 and 30 miles,[46] over the ventilating furnace located in many collieries at the foot of the upcast shaft was all too obvious. This danger was compounded by the practice which had developed in the early 19th century of dividing the larger shafts into between 2 to 4 compartments.[47] In this way, separate compartments were provided for winding, pumping and ventilation. But in fact, these partitions, or brattices, were extremely dangerous. Constructed of wood, they were easily wrecked or set on fire, thus blocking the only exit from the mine.[48] Hence by the early 19th century, several practices conspired to produce a highly vulnerable situation in coalmining. Air-coursing, the custom in most northern collieries of locating a ventilating furnace at the foot of the upcast shaft and the use of bratticed shafts combined to produce a frequency of explosions and mounting toll of life that demanded action.

It was against this background that in 1813 the Sunderland Society for the Prevention of Accidents in Mines was formed and invited Sir Humphry Davy to recommend better means of detecting firedamp and reducing the risk of explosions. At roughly the same time, a new form of mine ventilation was innovated which was to herald a new era in British coalmining. Aware of the serious risk caused by the ventilating furnace, John Buddle had developed his 'dumb furnace' at Wallsend in 1810. In essence, the system comprised the leading of further passages to the upcast shaft through one of which (the dumb drift) the foul air could pass without coming into contact with the furnace at all.[49] In addition, the practice of splitting the air into several ground columns was developed. By dividing the mine into a number of *independent* ventilating systems, and splitting the main air current, separate sections of the face could be provided with different currents of air. The same current of air no longer had to travel 20-30 miles underground, becoming progressively more gaseous, and hence more dangerous, as it advanced. Rather, by maintaining as many as 11-16 air-splits, the length of any one air-course now did not need to exceed 4-5 miles. Members of the South Shields Committee found in their visit to Buddle's Wallsend colliery in 1839 that the longest air-course was 4 miles.[50] Air-splitting was rapidly innovated in both Tyne and Wear districts, with the result that by the 1840's air-courses of longer than two miles were uncommon.

Although a major advance, this was by no means the final answer to the problem of securing adequate ventilation in mines. While the new forms of ventilation were in general use, along with surface pumps, in the fiery mines of the North of England by 1850, they were slow to be adopted in other coalfields. Shropshire, S. Staffordshire, Warwickshire, South Wales and Scotland continued to rely on traditional means of ventilation, with gas firing and firelamps in the upcast shaft still in common use. Indeed, in the Midlands and South Wales many collieries existed which used no artificial aids of any description to promote better ventilation.[51] This was one of the principal explanations of the difference in mortality rates between the North of England and other coalfields by the middle of the 19th century. In the former, the striking and rapid success achieved immediately before 1850 in the control of mine gases resulted in a relatively low death-rate from explosions. Per 1,000 persons employed, the annual average death-rate from explosions amounted to 0.9 in the Northern Coalfield in 1851-53, as opposed to 2.4 in Lancashire,

Cheshire and North Wales, 1.1 in South Wales, and 1.1 in the area comprising Yorkshire, Derbyshire, Nottinghamshire, Warwickshire and Leicestershire.[52] Yet it was precisely in the Northern Coalfield that deeper working and extreme 'gassiness' of mines were most prevalent. Hence, necessity compelled an active interest in mine safety and more rapid innovation of adequate ventilation techniques. By the 1850's, powerful furnaces were used throughout the Northern Coalfield to produce general currents of air; splitting the air-current was widely practised; and between 15,000 and 16,000 safety lamps were in daily use in Northumberland and Durham.

Rather than wilful neglect by colliery managers in districts such as Lancashire and Cheshire, South Wales and Yorkshire, the principal cause of inadequate ventilation was probably sheer ignorance of what could be achieved.[53] Given the very different nature of mining conditions in different districts, no one form of ventilation could be recommended in all cases.[54] Nonetheless, devising a ventilation system geared to the needs of a particular colliery was always possible. It was the tragedy of coalmining during the first half of the 19th century that in many districts such measures were not even contemplated.

The innovation of the safety lamp after 1815 was one of the outstanding achievements of an age not altogether unfamiliar with spectacular technological improvements. Yet the introduction and early application of the lamp were surrounded by controversy and not a little animosity. It seems likely that credit for the first insulated lamp belongs to Dr Clanny. He insulated the candle in the lamp with glass and successfully concentrated attention on the urgent need to produce a stronger and more efficient insulated lamp. Authorship of the first commercially successful lamp was disputed between Sir Humphry Davy and George Stephenson. The latter strongly argued his claim to originality in the press and in pamphlets.[55] He particularly resented the fact that at the second of two meetings called by northern owners to bestow some mark of appreciation on Sir Humphry Davy, the title of the charter drawn up for the occasion was changed from 'the invention of his safety lamp' to 'his invention of the safety lamp' — a very different interpretation! Nor was Stephenson without his supporters. At a meeting held on November 1st, 1817, in Newcastle, it was decided that he was due a public reward for the service which he had rendered to mankind by inventing the safety lamp. A subscription was immediately opened and at the meeting itself a sum of over £600 was raised.[56]

The truth was probably rather different. Both men, and indeed several others, had been working independently to produce safer means of underground illumination. But beyond reasonable doubt, the important initial breakthroughs in concept and design were made by Davy.[57] Certainly it was his lamp, produced in 1815, that caught the public imagination. Before the end of that year, he had produced the wire-gauze safety lamp which was markedly more efficient than all other models. Lamps with 'a metallic tissue permeable to light and air and impermeable to flame'[58] were eagerly welcomed by a coalmining industry which for too long had suffered from inadequate illumination below ground and the dangers inherent in naked flame. The inestimable value of the Davy lamp was readily acknowledged at a meeting of owners of Tyne and Wear held at the end of November, 1817. They were in no doubt about the legitimate inventor of the new technology, asserting that 'the latest lamps made by Mr Stephenson are evident imitations of the lamps of Sir H. Davy, and even with that advantage, are so imperfectly made as to be actually unsafe.'[59]

Although he kept aloof from the dispute with Stephenson, Sir Humphry Davy was also assailed from other directions. In the early 1820's, William Martin had produced 'an improved lamp' and was not backward in extolling its virtures. His particular enemies were Sir Humphry and John Buddle who apparently wanted nothing to do with his lamp. In a series of letters to John Watson, viewer, urging the latter to introduce the lamp for the better management of his collieries, Martin modestly declared, 'You may venture to lay any wager with any gentlemen that they [his safety lamps] cannot be exceld for neither light nor safety.'[60] Later, in urging that his lamp immediately be manufactured, he advised that henceforth all gentlemen and coalowners 'need not mind if Mr Buddle and Sir Humphry and his manslayers [Sir Humphry's lamps] were thrown head long into Mount Vesuvas for neither of the two has done any good to their King and country…' Finally, quoting correspondence he had held with the Duke of Northumberland Martin suggested that, 'It is high time Sir Humphry was hiding himself…As for Buddle, I said my Lord [to the Duke of Northumberland] that the Country did him no justice by not trying him for his life.'

The furore which surrounded the early life of the safety lamp was further exacerbated by the allegation that neither explosions nor deaths had diminished with its use. However, it was not that the lamp itself was inherently dangerous under normal working conditions. This emerged clearly from the evidence given before the Select Committees of both the Commons and Lords, published in 1830, and the House of Lords Select Committee on the Prevention of Accidents in 1849. Rather, a variety of factors contributed to the persistently high number of deaths: careless and inefficient use of the lamp; the greater depths of working which it made possible; the wider use of gunpowder underground; and the rapid increase in the size of the labour force at risk. To obtain a better light, miners frequently took the cover off their Davy lamps, so exposing the flame to the atmosphere. As John Buddle confirmed, 'Scarcely a month occurs without the punishment of some of them for the mismanagement of the Davy lamps; they have been fined, and the magistrates have sent them to the house of correction for a month, yet they will screw off the top of the Davy, and expose the naked flame.'[61]

However, this does highlight a common criticism of the Davy lamp; namely, that it gave insufficient light for face-working. One witness before the House of Lords Select Committee in 1849 argued that the Clanny lamp provided four times as much light as that of the Davy. This may have been an exaggeration, but there was an element of truth in it. There was also some substance to the criticism that the Davy lamp was insecure in very strong currents of explosive air. It was alleged that where strong air-currents containing firedamp existed, the flame of the Davy, encircled only by wire gauze, might pass through the gauze to make contact with the firedamp outside. In this way, the Davy might actually cause explosions in strong currents of air.[62] Although this fear was well founded in currents of high velocity, these were rarely achieved before 1850. It was most unusual for velocities in the main air-ways to exceed 5 feet per second and in such conditions the Davy lamp was relatively safe. Much more a cause for concern was simply ignorance of the correct use of the lamp and a belief in its infallibility. From the outset it had never, of course, been intended as a panacea for all the dangers of underground working. Particularly, as observed earlier, it had never been regarded by its inventors as a substitute for fresh air. In too many collieries excessive reliance had been placed on the lamp as an alternative to effective ventilation. This was the basic misunderstanding. The one was a complement, not an alternative, to the other.[63]

It is true that increasing use both of the Davy lamp and the steam engine made possible mining in areas, and at depths, where no mining had been possible before. But the allegation that the principal short-term effect of the Davy lay, therefore, in increasing the risks, and hence mortality rate, of miners in the North-East cannot be substantiated. Such an argument totally neglects the rapid growth of employment after the introduction of the safety lamp. Despite an increase in the absolute number of deaths, relating these to the changing size of the labour force reveals a significant decline in the rate of mortality.[64] On the other hand, the Davy lamp did have an effect in an area, that of production, which had not been envisaged by its inventor. The experience of John Buddle is again revealing. The safety lamp, he claimed, had 'introduced quite a new era in coalmining, as many collieries are now in existence, and old collieries have been re-opened, producing the best coals, which must have lain dormant

75

but for the invention of the safety lamp.' In evidence, he cited the
fact that by 1830, 'almost all the collieries below the bridge on the
Tyne would have been at this time extinct but for the safety lamp; in
fact, the safety lamp has made a renovation of those mines.'[65]

Although it was in the Northern Coalfield, where mining was
conducted at greatest depths, that the Davy lamp made its largest
impact, similar evidence of the benefits it conferred can be derived
from most coalfields. In Scotland, for instance, the lamp was quickly
adopted and again enabled development to take place, particularly in
the west, where none had been possible before. Robert Bald, who
wrote one of the standard texts on the Scottish industry,[66] tested the
lamp for himself, descending into a fiery mine in Ayrshire. Mining
had previously been confined to shallow depths due to the dangers of
inflammable air. But the Davy afforded 'abundant light' and would
allow much deeper workings to be opened. Bald concluded that, 'I
would have no hesitation to descend into any mine however inflammable with Sir Humphry Davy's safety lamp and I know my life
would lie in safety as to an explosion.'[67] Hence, besides adding to the
security of life, the effect of the safety lamp was to make possible an
increase in output. Along with the steam engine, it was responsible
after 1815 for the opening up of new seams, the re-opening of old,
abandoned workings and the removal of pillars from areas which were
too dangerous to approach with naked lights. By creating these new
supply-points, the safety lamp and steam engine had much the same
effect on coalmining output as the railways some 20 years later. The
'revolutionary' increase in the supply of coal between 1800 and 1850,
initially made possible by the inventive genius of Watt and Davy,
was sustained in its later stages by the work of men such as Trevithick
and Stephenson.

Steady improvements were also taking place in other mining
operations largely associated with the steam engine. Advances in
both winding and underground haulage are generally associated with
the name of John Curr, viewer of the Duke of Norfolk. The new
methods which he pioneered during the late 18th century ultimately
did much to alleviate the back-breaking work of underground labour
but, being well in advance of their time, were not generally innovated
until 30-40 years later. His most important contribution was to
improve underground haulage and to link this directly with raising
coal up the shaft. His methods were mainly confined at first to shallow
pits about Leeds, Barnsley and Sheffield. Here, baskets had formerly
been used to carry coal from the face to the bottom of the pit.
Commonly these had been carried or dragged along, although in
Newcastle four-wheeled vehicles had been used to carry wicker corves
to the pit-bottom from the 1760's. Curr combined corf with wagon,
enabling the coal to be pulled along in wheeled carts by means of

either children or horses. Without unloading, the carts could be attached directly to the winding rope and raised from the pit. To facilitate this type of underground haulage, Curr fixed cast-iron plates on to the wooden rails, this giving way in the 1790's to rails made entirely of cast-iron. The first steam engine was installed underground for haulage purposes in 1804. Details are vague but this was again probably the work of Curr, although by that time he had been dismissed from the Duke of Norfolk's service.

As his reputation spread, Curr's wheeled corves were more generally accepted, although as noted below, the major advance in the technology of winding came in the 1830's with Hall's 'cage and tubs' system. In terms of haulage, more important was the gradual transition to steam, particularly after George Stephenson had shown in the early 19th century how successfully steam haulage could operate in practice. By the 1820's, underground steam haulage was being used in the Lancashire and Cheshire coalfield and high-pressure engines had been installed underground for the same purpose in Scotland. It was found that steam power was efficient where the inclination of the seams was steep, allowing self-acting planes to be used to propel the wagons on the return journey. On level roads, where power for haulage was necessary in both directions, the horse was still cheap and more popular.[68] As a result, it was not until the 1840's and 1850's that steam haulage became universal, with the introduction of both the Main and Tail Rope System and the Endless Rope System. Engines were located either on the surface or below ground, although already by that time experiments were being conducted with compressed air engines due to the large number of accidents associated with the use of steam.

The inter-relatedness of improvements can readily be seen in that the wrought iron rail, first introduced in 1815, was also widely innovated only by mid-century. At the same time, the advantages of both the wire rope and the steam engine for winding were being fully exploited by the coal industry. The flat wire rope was widely employed for the first time during the 1840's due to the greater security and qualities of endurance which it provided. However, before the decade was out, it was already being replaced by the cheaper and more efficient round wire rope. By the mid-19th century steam was universally used as the source of power for the winding engine, having steadily replaced the water-gin. In consequence, in the larger northern collieries winding capacity more than doubled between 1835 and 1850, from 300 tons to between 600 and 800 tons per day. Even so, it is important not to exaggerate the extent of progress. Although the winding engine was in general use, its power prior to 1840 had not in most instances exceeded 50 h.p. It was only after that date that increasingly large-capacity engines of 150 h.p. or more were installed, particularly in the Northern Coalfield. Nor did more powerful winding engines necessarily increase the volume of coal wound: rather the same tonnage could be wound from greater depths. The system of winding was also greatly improved by the innovation in 1834 of T. Y. Hall's iron cage and guide system to raise tubs up the shaft. Wheeled iron tubs were filled at the face, drawn on rails by horses or steam power to the pit-bottom and loaded on to the cage two at a time. The cage was raised up the shaft, being held steady by guide rails, to the surface where the tubs could be unloaded again on to iron rails. The system was rapidly introduced in the North of England since it was estimated that on average it enabled twice as much coal to be raised during a given time-period than the older system of lifting corves or baskets up the shaft. In addition, it allowed men and boys to be raised or lowered in much greater safety than had previously been possible.[69]

Steam had an equally important role to play in boring, sinking and pumping. By mid-19th century, all boring machines utilised steam power while in the sinking of heavily watered shafts, the most common practice was to employ sets of bucket pumps, powered either by a Watt engine or by a compound engine. The entire history of pumping reveals that the pumping engine has gradually moved from the top of the pit to the bottom. The standard engine used for much of the 19th century was the Cornish pumping engine, a development of the Newcomen-Watt models. Its advantages were to lie eventually in its comparatively small consumption of coal and low maintenance costs, but it was initially capable of generating only low steam pressures. As a result, it had to be located at the surface since the very size of engine required to deal with even limited quantities of water militated against underground installation. Moreover, there existed the constant danger of sudden inrushes of water into the workings. Pumps located underground could be overwhelmed and destroyed. Only as steam pressure increased, enabling the pumps to cope more easily with flooding, was it possible to install them in insets in the side of the pit. Even then, several such insets and several lifts of water were necessary since the total h.p. of the engines driving the pumps was not sufficient to force large quantities of water out of the pit direct.[70]

Finally an important, if rather neglected, area of coal technology was the spin-off derived from carbonisation. Along with coke, important products like tar and gases resulted from the carbonisation of coal. Not all of these were effectively used during the Industrial Revolution or even during the 19th century as a whole. Numerous attempts were made during the second half of the 18th century to secure by-products from coal, with considerable success initially attending Lord Dundonald's efforts to produce tar and pitch.[71] However, the emphasis was largely on the production of coke and, after 1800, on gas manufacture. In the former, the bee-hive oven was universally used, coke manufacturers showing a total disregard for such valuable by-products as gas and tar. Experiments with by-product ovens had proved a failure since they produced coke of a type and structure not suitable for metallurgical purposes. More spectacular success was achieved after 1800 in the manufacture of gas. It was commonly associated with the name of William Murdoch, whose early experiments at the Soho works of Boulton and Watt ultimately led to the creation of a flourishing gas-making industry. By the early 19th century, Murdoch had sufficiently refined his process of producing coal gas so that it was capable of being used as an out-door illuminant. In 1810, the first company, the London and Westminster Chartered Gas Light and Coke Co., had been authorised by Parliament to extend the public lighting system along Pall Mall in London.[72]

Again, neither the inventor nor his discovery were without their critics: numerous efforts were made to claim responsibility for discovering the valuable properties of coal gas. Although he had 'modestly forborn to lay his claim before the public' and was 'in danger of losing the credit for this major advance', Murdoch's admirers ensured in fact, through the press and in pamphlets, that his work received due acknowledgement.[73] Despite objections to the use of coal gas,[74] within a decade of the first company being formed, numerous towns throughout the country were busily manufacturing gas for lighting streets and houses. Company and municipal undertakings enjoyed a monopoly in the provision of street lighting before the emergence of electricity in the last quarter of the 19th century. By 1830, there were already over 200 gas undertakings in Britain, obtaining rights to supply by means of Private Act of Parliament.[75] Around the middle of the century, experiments were successfully conducted in the application of gas for heating purposes. Use of gas in this area rapidly developed after the invention of the Bunsen burner in 1855. By the same date, the vast majority of towns in Britain possessed gas companies. Rather than household consumption, the bulk of demand emanated from street-lighting requirements, factories, shops, railway stations and institutions of various types.[76]

Whether technical improvements effected within the coal industry amounted to a 'technological revolution' is rather a sterile debate. Many of the changes were innovated only towards the middle of the 19th century and many districts remained notably backward in their efforts to work the coal. By the 1850's, there was a significant gulf between 'best practice' techniques, to be found mainly in the Northern Coalfield, and those used in other parts of the country. But at least in the former, most of the 'ground-rules' had been laid for the solution of the major problems confronting the industry. Improved forms of ventilation, illumination, haulage and winding had all been introduced. The rest of the century was to be spent largely in further refining these improvements, in ensuring that the men complied with codes laid down for their safety, and in the strenuous efforts of other coalfields to catch up with the relatively advanced technology known and used in the north.

An indication of the extent of change is provided by the amount of investment undertaken in the industry. In this area, the evidence for the economy as a whole is fragmentary and for the most part unreliable. Although figures exist for certain firms at certain times, it is notoriously difficult to draw general conclusions from the experience of particular concerns. Coalmining is no different in this respect. However, the recent evidence gathered by Feinstein[77] at least provides an indication of the orders of magnitude involved. Table 4 below shows the estimated magnitude of domestic reproducible capital, distinguishing between fixed and circulating capital in coalmining during the period 1760-1860. For comparative purposes, similar evidence is provided for other sectors of the economy.

The figures shown in Table 4 should be treated with caution. Those provided for the stock of fixed capital are based on the replacement cost of fixed assets at 1851-60 prices. In coalmining, the figures would include such assets as shafts and equipment. Circulating capital consists of inventories and work in progress in industry, trade and agriculture. It can be seen that total reproducible capital increased by more than four times between 1760 and 1860, the annual average rate of growth being 1.4% (compound). But while the importance of capital in Agriculture and Residential Dwellings, Public Buildings and Works rapidly declined as a proportion of the total over the period, that of industrial and commercial capital rose very steeply from 11% in 1760 to 33% in 1860. This was largely due to the expansion of the stock in *fixed* assets which rose from a mere 5% at the start of the period to a dominant 25% by the end, larger than any other category in Table 4. Circulating capital in industry and commerce, originally more important than fixed, rose slowly with the result that over the century there was a sharp rise in the ratio of fixed to circulating capital. In 1760 the value of fixed capital was less than that of inventories. By 1800, the position had changed, the ratio between fixed and circulating capital standing at 1.5:1; in 1830 it was 2.5:1 and in 1860, 3.3:1.

The coal industry contributed to this rapid expansion in the stock of fixed capital. Growth was particularly marked between 1830 and 1860, confirming evidence previously presented in this chapter that there was a marked expansion in the coal industry towards the middle of the 19th century. Yet development was equally rapid in other industrial sectors so that coalmining did no more than maintain its

Table 4

Domestic Reproducible Capital in Great Britain by Sector and Type of Asset, 1760-1860 (£m at 1851-60 prices)

Industry and Commerce	1760	1800	1830	1860
Industrial and Commercial Buildings	25	75	204	460
Industrial Machinery and Equipment	9	26	61	160
Coal Mining[1]	1.5	2.5	7	28
Other Mining and Quarrying	0.5	1.5	1	7
Gas and Water	—	—	4	42
Total, Fixed Capital	36	105	277	697
Total, Circulating Capital[2]	40	70	110	210
Residential Dwellings, Public Buildings and Works	210	273	427	679
Agriculture, Fixed	210	270	340	440
Agriculture, Circulating[2]	140	190	220	240
Transport	38	81	139	504
Total, Fixed Capital[2]	490	730	1,180	2,320
Total, Circulating Capital[2]	180	260	330	450
Domestic Reproducible Capital	670	990	1,510	2,770

SOURCE:
Feinstein, op. cit., Tables 8, 12, 22 and 24.
NOTES:
1. Figures for coalmining calculated on the basis of the data provided by Feinstein, p. 42.
2. Figures rounded to nearest £10 million.

share of fixed capital stock between 1760 and 1860. In the former year, over 4% of the stock of fixed assets in British industry and commerce were to be found in the coal industry, this proportion falling back in the two intermediate years specified in Table 4, before regaining the same level a century later. As opposed to the stock of fixed assets, where only four observations are provided, a greater range of estimates can be given for gross domestic fixed capital formation. Annual average estimates for each decade from 1761/70 to 1851/60 show that in real terms, gross investment in mining and quarrying rose from £0.08 million in 1761/70, 6% of the total in industry and commerce, to £0.63 million in 1831/40, 5% of the total, to £1.71 million in 1851/60, 8% of the total.[78] More spectacular was the growth of investment in gas and water. Already in 1811/20, the gas industry accounted for an average of 3% of the total fixed capital formation in industry and commerce. By the 1850's, the proportion had risen to over 11%, a rate of investment considerably faster than that in coal.

Compared with other industrial and commercial sectors, the growth of investment and capital stock in coalmining was not particularly rapid or unusual over the hundred years from 1760. What can be said, however, is that the pace of change quickened in the latter part of this period, roughly from 1830 to 1860. These years witnessed a rapid expansion of output and significant changes in mining technique, a response to the increasing demand for coal particularly from the iron, general manufacturing and transport sectors. By 1860, the nature of coalmining and the environment within which it operated were very different from half a century earlier. Contemporaries at least were in little doubt that they had lived through a 'technical revolution' in the industry. Authorities such as Buddle and Dunn continually emphasised the rapidity of change since the start of the century. Perhaps it is as well to leave the last word on the subject to the latter who noted that, 'the march of improvement in the art of coalmining from this period has been extraordinary.'[79]

PART TWO

COAL IN THE MATURE ECONOMY, 1850-1914

4 Markets at Home and Abroad, 1850-1914

1 THE GROWTH OF THE DOMESTIC MARKET

According to Stanley Jevons in his *The Coal Question* (1865), 'Coal stands not beside, but entirely above all other commodities. It is the material source of the energy of the country—the universal aid—the factor in everything we do.' Britain was by that time an economic civilisation based on coal. The continued rapid expansion of coal output after 1850 enabled the country to consolidate the advances made in manufacturing during the Industrial Revolution and to become in the middle decades of the century 'the workshop of the world'. As noted below, a growing proportion of this increased coal output was sent overseas. But the developing needs of the home market also helped to sustain production at a high level. Despite economies in fuel use, the continued expansion of established industries like cotton, wool, iron and engineering ensured a steady growth in the demand for coal. This was reinforced by the requirements of the transport industries and, later in the period, by the emergence of certain new specialisms such as steel, gas and electricity. The increase in output and in consumption per head of population is shown in Table 1.

Output increased by more than four times between 1855 and 1913, a large part of this expansion being caused by the growth of shipments abroad. Over the same period, the volume of coal absorbed by the home market rose in absolute terms by a factor of three. Expressed per head of population, the demand for coal in Britain was roughly half as much again in 1913 as in 1855. Indeed, at just over 4 tons *per capita,* consumption in 1900 was higher than in any other country in the world. In the United States, consumption per head averaged 3.08 tons, in Belgium 2.89 tons and in the German Empire 1.72 tons.[1] However in the early years of the present century, demand grew more rapidly in the United States, with the result that from 1905 the level of *per capita* consumption regularly exceeded that of Britain. Nonetheless, the latter remained an important coal-using country, producing and consuming more per head of population than anywhere else in Europe. In fact, in terms of *output per head of population,* Britain still led the world before 1914. In 1910, for instance, she produced 6 tons per head, the United States 5 tons, Belgium 3.1 tons and Germany 2.3 tons.

Coal in the Mature Economy, 1850-1914

Table 1

Output and Exports of Coal, Volume Retained for Home Consumption and Consumption per Head of Population in the UK, Selected Years, 1855-1914

	Total Output	Coal Shipments Abroad[1]	Coal Remaining for Domestic Consumption	Domestic Consumption Per Head of Population
	(m. tons)	(m. tons)	(m. tons)	(tons)
1855	64.5	5.0	59.5	2.70
60	80.0	9.4	70.6	3.05
70	110.4	14.3	96.1	3.70
80	147.0	23.9	123.1	3.55
90	181.6	38.7	142.9	3.81
1900	225.2	58.4	166.8	4.05
10	264.4	84.5	179.9	4.01
13	287.4	98.3	189.1	4.11

SOURCES:
Royal Commission on Coal, 1871; House of Commons, Report of the Select Committee on Coal, 313, 1873; Mines and Quarries, General Report with Statistics for 1913 by the Chief Inspector of Mines, Part III, Cd. 7741, 1914.
NOTE:
1. Includes coal, coke, manufactured fuel and coal shipped for use of steamers engaged in foreign trade.

At the same time, major changes occurred after 1850 in the distribution of British coal output. The share devoted to the iron industry, one of the principal consumers up to the 1870's, rapidly declined in later years. By 1913, the industry was absorbing little more than one-tenth of total coal output. The proportion required for household and domestic purposes also declined steadily, but the greatest change was registered in the volume of coal devoted to exports. Of total coal raised, the proportion sent overseas rose from less than one-tenth in 1869 to about one-third in 1913. The principal trends are illustrated in Table 2.

In large measure, the continued rapid expansion of British coal output after 1869 was a response to the growing demand for the mineral abroad. Between 1873 and 1913, the volume of coal raised in Britain increased by almost 159 million tons to reach 287 million by the latter year. Of this expansion, 82 million tons, or more than 50% can be attributed to the increase in coal, coke and manufactured fuel (measured in terms of coal equivalent) shipped to foreign countries. Indeed, the rise in overseas shipments dominates the figures presented in Table 2. Nonetheless, certain trends within the domestic economy can be distinguished. In absolute terms, the demand of colliery companies, railways, gas and electricity increased rapidly with the result that they maintained, or expanded, their respective shares of a growing output. On the other hand, as noted earlier the iron industry declined in relative importance as a customer for coal. Here, economies in the use of fuel were allied to virtual stagnation in productive capacity during the late 19th and early 20th centuries. In terms of capital formation, existing capacity was at best maintained during the closing decades of the 19th century, but more probably there was some tendency to reduce investments.[2] Even in steel, which assumed a world-wide significance from the 1870's, the expansion in capacity during the latter part of the century was slow in relation both to previous experience and to development abroad.[3] In consequence, the blast furnaces in iron and steel absorbed a steadily declining share of the total quantity of coal retained for domestic use after 1869.

Significantly there was also a fall in the proportion of coal consumed by 'general manufacturing', due in part to greater efficiency in the use of fuel. In an age of mounting foreign competition, there was pressure on British producers to seek out and implement ways of reducing one of their major cost-items, that of fuel. They made some progress, but the extent of their achievement should not be exaggerated. In fuel conservation, Britain generally lagged well behind best Continental practice, particularly that of Germany. Coal was still used wastefully with many firms in manufacturing not even having an approximate notion of their heat losses. Similarly in

Table 2
Distribution of Coal Raised in the UK, Selected Years, 1869-1913
(Figures expressed as % of total)

	1869	1887	1913
Iron and Steel Industry	30	16.5	11
General Manufacturing	26	26	22.5
Mines	7	7	7
Steam Navigation	5	12.5	6
Gas and Electricity	6	6	8
Domestic	17	17	13
Exports	9	15	32.5

SOURCES:
Royal Commission on Coal, 1871, Committee E; Deane and Cole, op. cit., pp. 218-19.

shipping, where fuel was an important element in total costs, it was alleged that the marine steam engine used coal 'with a prodigality to contemplate which is humiliating.'[4] In absolute terms there was, of course, a large increase in the amount of steam power used in industry after 1850. Industrial steam power rose from an estimated 300,000 nominal h.p. in that year to 977,000 in 1870.[5] Of the latter total, well over half was concentrated in textiles, primarily in the spinning and weaving sectors, while a further one-third was absorbed by metal manufacture, engineering and shipbuilding. The rate of expansion was even more pronounced in subsequent years, with the amount used in manufacturing rising by at least ten times between 1870 and 1914. The *First Census of Production* in 1907 showed that the volume of steam power employed in British industry had increased to 9.7 million h.p. and also that electrical power had become steadily more important.[6] By that year, the textile category was no longer the largest user of mechanical power within manufacturing. It had been overtaken by the category iron and steel, engineering and shipbuilding. Its consumption of steam was also less than that of mines and quarries and public utility services.

Coal had become a vital producers' good from at least the 1840's and as such was subject to the violent fluctuations in price commonly associated with this type of product. But the mineral was particularly vulnerable for several reasons. First, a developing branch of the coal industry was devoted to the foreign market and was exposed to sudden fluctuations in demand due to changed economic circumstances abroad. Second, a slowing down, or fall, in the output of any power-using industry at home could have serious repercussions on coal-mining. Finally, as noted above, technical innovations after 1850 frequently involved greater economy in the use of coal. As a result instability on the demand-side, allied to inelastic supply and the industry's long-standing problem of diminishing returns, produced wide fluctuations in the value of coal output. Throughout the period up to 1913, London remained by far the most important domestic market for the industry. In that year, it absorbed more than 9 million tons, or 60%, of the 15.2 million tons of coal and coke received coastwise at the various ports of England and Wales. Table 3 compares average prices in the London market over specified periods with those prevailing at the pit-head in England.

The price data in Table 3 confirm the continued existence of a large 'spread' between pit-head prices and those prevailing in the London market. Between the 1870's and 1913, the latter were between two and three times as high as those obtaining at the pit's mouth. However, averaging the data over five-yearly intervals tends to obscure the wide price fluctuations which occurred in London on a year-to-year basis. Indeed, the relatively high prices prevailing in

Table 3

Annual Average Price of Coal per Ton in the London Market and at the Pit's Mouth in England, Selected Periods, 1873/77-1909/13

	Average Price in London		Average Price at the Pit's Mouth	
	s.	d.	s.	d
1873-77	22	7	—	
1883-87	15	5	5	2
1893-97	15	11	6	3
1900-04	18	3	8	3
1909-13	18	5	8	5

SOURCE:
Calculated from *Mines and Quarries, General Report by the Chief Inspector of Mines for 1913.*

London from 1871 had been the subject of a Commons' Select Committee enquiry.[7] It concluded that prices had been forced upwards by the boom in demand for pig iron and its conversion into various forms of rolled iron. The pressure of a greater demand for coal had been accentuated by a growing weakness on the supply-side of the industry. Output per man-shift had fallen, largely due to the success of miners in several districts in reducing the length of shift worked. Prices reached a peak in the early 1870's as demand far outstripped supply but after 1873 conditions rapidly changed. Excess capacity in the iron industry, particularly in the production of railway equipment, brought coal prices tumbling down. By 1880, the price of coal in London was less than half its 1873 level and even with some modest recovery in the following years, average prices between 1883-87 were still one-third below those of 1873-77. A recovery in the early 1890's was not sustained and coal prices during the 1873-1913 period reached an all-time low in 1896.[8] Subsequently, prices fluctuated widely until the first world war, although the underlying trend was decidedly upwards.

Annual changes in prices were so pronounced both in the London market and at the pit-head that large variations occurred in the *value* of aggregate output. It would be interesting to know which districts benefited and which suffered most from such variations, but a regional break-down of figures, according to value, costs and profits per ton, is not possible for the decades before 1914. However, the profitability of the industry at national level is shown in Table 4.

Table 4

Tonnage Raised, Value at the Pit-Head, and Costs and Profits per ton,
United Kingdom, 1889/93-1913

Average of	Tonnage Raised	Value at Pit-Head per ton		Costs Per Ton Raised						Profits and Royalties			
				Wages		Other Costs		Total		Per Ton		Total	
	(m. tons)	s.	d.	s.	d.	s.	d.	s.	d.	s.	d.	(£m)	
1889-93	178.0	7	4.18	4	7.16	1	5.24	6	0.40	1	3.78	11.7	
1894-98	195.5	6	2.16	—		—		5	3.48		10.68	8.7	
1899-1903	224.3	8	8.76	5	5.52	1	6.70	7	0.22	1	8.54	19.2	
1904-08	249.8	7	10.94	—		—		6	6.42	1	4.52	17.2	
1909-12	265.1	8	4.56	—		—		7	1.30	1	3.26	16.8	
1913	287.4	10	1.52	6	4.01	1	10.13	8	2.14	1	11.38	28.0	

SOURCES:
PRO, Power, 16/45; Gibson, op. cit., p. 179.
NOTE:
— = not available.

Table 4 shows that although output increased steadily, wide variations occurred in aggregate profitability due to fluctuations in the level of profits per ton. Within a quarter of a century, the total value of output rose from 3% of National Income in 1885 to over 5% in 1890, increased further to almost 7% in 1900 and then fell back again to about 4% in 1905? On balance these were good years for the coal industry but, even so, violent fluctuations in price made survival difficult for smaller pits and those in which the best seams had already been worked out. Increasingly, too, countries abroad were stepping up their own production of coal so that competition became fierce in world markets. The ability of the British industry to meet this competition is considered in the next section.

2   THE GROWTH OF THE OVERSEAS MARKET

The chief success of the British coal industry after 1850 lay in the exploitation of overseas markets. While total output increased four-fold between 1855 and 1913, the tonnage of coal shipped abroad rose almost 20 times during the same period. In 1855, the volume of coal exports, including bunkers, amounted to less than one-tenth of Britain's coal output and to about 3% of the value of total exports. By 1913, exports and bunker coal accounted for one-third of total British output and for more than 10% of the value of Britain's export trade.[10] The way had been cleared for this large expansion in overseas shipments by the removal of all duties on coal exports in 1850 and by the firm belief that, in the operation of both the domestic and foreign coal trade, there should be 'an inflexible resolution of non-interference on the part of the State.'[11] Although this created an environment conducive to the rapid growth of overseas sales, the principal causal factor at work was industrialisation abroad. The broadening of the industrial base of several European countries after 1850 created a steadily rising demand for coal, despite the forebodings of the 1871 Royal Commission on Coal Supplies that a significant increase in future coal exports was most unlikely. The Commission considered that keen competition in the coal trade would develop between Europe, America, Asia and even Australia. Moreover, new areas of supply would be opened up which hitherto had provided only a promise of valuable coal deposits. In consequence, countries abroad were likely to be much less dependent in future on British coalfields.

There appeared to be reasonable ground for the case advanced by the Royal Commission since the world's output of coal did increase sharply during the late Victorian era. Although British production rose from an average of 165 million tons in 1885-89 to 270 million tons in 1909-13, her share of world output fell from 41 to 25%.[12] Over the same period, rapid advances in technique and the opening

91

of new sources of supply allowed the United States to increase production from 115 million tons (29% of world output) to 458 million tons (43% of world output). Germany, too, had expanded output considerably from 60 to 163 million tons, enabling her to maintain her share of world output (15%) throughout the period. In addition several countries, including Russia and Japan, were emerging as important producers for the first time. This category also included the principal British possessions. Taken as a group, their output rose from an average of 7.5 million tons in the 1880's to 44.5 million tons in the years before the first world war.[13]

The Royal Commission was correct, therefore, to emphasise the growth of output in established coal-producing areas overseas and the opening up of relatively new sources of supply. Both involved increased competition for the British industry and in the long term, a decline in demand for British coal. But the Commission was quite wrong in its assessment of the timing of this increased competition. Although world supply increased by almost three times between the 1880's and 1913,[14] world demand increased faster still. The principal defect in the Commission's reasoning lay in its failure to appreciate how rapidly industrial development would take place overseas. The pace of development in general manufacturing, particularly of iron and steel, the spread of improved transport facilities, and the creation of gas and electricity undertakings ensured a steadily widening market for coal. The mineral enjoyed a monopoly position since the age of water power was passed while that of the petrol engine had still fully to develop. British coalmining took full advantage of these favourable trends in the international economy. A strong exporting sector developed as overseas markets, particularly in Europe, grew in size and prosperity. Details of the principal markets for British coal during the period of rapid expansion from the 1880's are provided in Table 5.

In absolute terms, British coal exports rapidly increased between 1886/90-1906/10 to each of the major markets specified in Table 5. Tonnage exported to Italy and France more than doubled, increased by over three times to Sweden, over four times to Germany and five times to Belgium. With the exception of the Russian Empire the consumption of British coal also formed a growing proportion of the domestic output of each country, notably of France where it amounted to 17% in 1886/90 and to 27% in 1906/10. In total, the countries listed in Table 5 accounted for almost one-half of total British coal exports at the start of the period and for almost three-fifths by the end. On the other hand, the *share* of British coal exports to several of these principal markets showed little tendency to increase. As Table 5 makes clear, this does not apply to Belgium or the German Empire, both of which absorbed a significantly higher proportion of

Table 5

(i) *Quantity of UK Coal Consumed* (ii) *Quantity of UK Coal as a Proportion of Domestic Output and* (iii) *Quantity of UK Coal Consumed as a Proportion of total UK Coal Exports, in Principal Foreign Markets. 1886/90-1906/10*

Period	Russian Empire (i) (000 tons)	(ii) %	(iii) %	Sweden (i) (000 tons)	(ii) %	(iii) %	Italy (i) (000 tons)	(ii) %	(iii) %	German Empire (i) (000 tons)	(ii) %	(iii) %	France (i) (000 tons)	(ii) %	(iii) %	Belgium (i) (000 tons)	(ii) %	(iii) %
1886-1890	1447	28	5.7	1298	*	5.1	3307	*	13.0	2375	4	9.3	3600	17	14.1	336	3	1.3
1891-1895	1574	21	5.3	1708	*	5.7	3789	*	12.7	3757	6	12.5	4173	17	13.9	381	3	1.3
1896-1900	2184	18	5.8	2524	*	6.7	4218	*	11.2	4927	6	13.1	5395	18	14.3	621	4	1.6
1901-1905	2372	14	5.3	3069	*	6.9	5228	*	11.7	5759	6	12.9	6197	20	13.8	649	4	1.5
1906-1910	2672	11	4.4	4218	*	6.9	7943	*	12.9	9854	9	16.1	9025	27	14.7	1687	10	2.7

SOURCES:
Calculated from *Statistical Tables Relating to Production, Consumption etc. of Coal in Each Year from 1886 to 1910*, 284, 1911; *General Report by the Chief Inspector of Mines for 1913*; Gibson, op. cit., p. 158.
NOTE:
*The domestic output of both Sweden and Italy was extremely small.

British coal shipments. But the share taken by Russia actually declined and that of the larger consumers, Italy and France, was only maintained. Hence the rapid expansion of Britain's coal exports from the 1880's was due only in part to the development of traditionally important markets. It can also be attributed to the increased demand of a host of new and smaller consumers. The Scandinavian countries, Egypt, Argentina, Brazil and even Japan absorbed growing quantities of British coal before the first world war.

By 1910, Britain was still by far the largest coal-exporting nation in the world. In that year she exported 63 million tons of coal and coke abroad, more than twice as much as the 28 million tons exported by Germany and well over four times the 14 million tons shipped by the USA. Exports on this scale made a substantial contribution to the country's favourable balance of payments in the pre-war era. Coal, unlike textiles, did not depend on an imported raw material and the income it earned from abroad was almost all pure gain.[15] Moreover, the mineral dominated British shipping. By reason of its weight, it afforded a vital outward freight from this country. At the end of the 19th century, more than four-fifths of the weight of British exports consisted of coal. Without it, the great bulk of shipping entering UK ports with food and raw materials would have been compelled to leave in ballast.[16]

The dominant position which Britain's coal exports held in the world economy was, to some extent, fortuitous. Her geographical position gave the ports of England and Wales easy access to markets in Europe and South America. This advantage was reinforced by the rapid decline in freight charges due to improvements in the efficiency of shipping. Jevons has shown that between 1863/65 and 1913 outward freight rates per ton from Cardiff to principal foreign ports like Bombay, Genoa, Buenos Aires and Port Said fell by anything between one-half and three-quarters.[17] Such falls conferred a great advantage on the British coal-exporting districts. Major competitors like Germany and the USA relied heavily on railway haulage to reach their foreign customers. Since the cost of carrying freight overland was still relatively high, producers in both countries were unable to compete effectively in most European and Mediterranean markets. Even in distant markets, where quality per bulk was a crucial factor, high-quality Welsh steam coal could compete on favourable terms.[18] For instance, it could be carried more cheaply by sea over the long haul from Cardiff to Buenos Aires than by rail and sea from the nearer inland coalfields of the United States.

But the competitive advantage enjoyed by British producers abroad was by no means solely due to geographical accident and declining freight charges. Of major importance was the fact that the price of coal at the pit-head was generaly much lower in Britain than in most other European countries. Germany alone could match British prices: in other countries, the level of efficiency was not sufficient to enable them to compete effectively. These differences in pit-head prices can be attributed to several factors. They reflect variations in the quality of coal mined, the accessibility of seams, the extent of royalties payable, the costs of labour and methods of operation. In several of these areas, Britain did not enjoy the type of advantage that would explain her greater competitive efficiency. On the contrary, in terms of quality and accessibility of coal this country was certainly in no better a position than Germany, France or Austria. Royalty payments were also greater than in other European countries,[19] although they never amounted to sufficiently high a proportion of selling price to be a serious weakness. Their influence was swamped in total price by other variables such as wage costs and the difficulties of mining. Nor was Britain advantageously placed with regard to labour costs. Comparative statistics on wages and earnings in different coal-producing countries are scarce and not generally reliable. Particular difficulties are introduced by differences in the nature of mining operations and in the length of shifts worked. Hence the estimates provided in Table 6 below should be used with caution. They give some indication of the scale of payments in coalmining in the principal European countries in 1889 and 1913, both years of rapidly rising prices.

Table 6

Annual Average Wages in Coalmining (1889) and Average Earnings Per Shift (1913), Selected Countries

Country	1889 Annual Average Wages	1913 Average Earnings per Shift
	£ s. d.	s. d.
France	47 18 4	4 1.20
Belgium	38 16 8	4 3.38
Germany:		
Saar	46 13 0	
Westphalia	47 1 0	5 5.79[1]
UK	60 6 0[2]	6 5.75[3]

SOURCES:
Royal Commission on Mining Royalties, 1893; Royal Commission on the Coal Industry, 1925, Cmnd. 2600, Vol. III (1926). (Henceforth referred to as *The Samuel Commission, 1925).*
NOTES: 1. Relates to the Ruhr Coalfield.
2. Relates to collieries in England only. 3. Relates to 1914.

95

Table 6 indicates that the relatively low level of pit-head prices in Britain was not the result of a low-wage coalmining industry. Indeed, by the first world war miners were among the highest-paid workers in the country and labour was being rapidly attracted into the industry (see Chapter 6, section 6). As noted above, international comparisons are difficult, but the data in Table 6 suggest that the average money wage of the British miner was relatively high. For instance, in 1889 the average wage in Britain was far in excess of that paid in Continental countries. The next highest was in France where the miner earned on average only 80% of the British level. The more detailed statistics available for 1913 provide much the same picture. Although the length of working shift was shorter in Britain than elsewhere, earnings per shift were almost half as high again as in France or Belgium, and one-fifth higher than in the Ruhr. Hence comparatively low pit-head prices in Britain were achieved in spite of, rather than because of, the price of labour. The fact was that wage costs accounted for a higher proportion of total costs in Britain than in other countries. Between the 1870's and 1910, as discussed fully in Chapter 6, wages in British coalmining amounted on average to between two-thirds and three-quarters of total costs. In contrast, in 1890, the proportion of average selling-price per ton taken in wages was 54% in Belgium, 50% in France and 33% in Westphalia.[20]

The success of the British coal export trade before 1914 can largely be attributed to a much higher level of labour productivity in the coalmining industry than was the case elsewhere. Although being rapidly overtaken in this respect in the years before the first world war, for most of the period between 1870 and 1914 output per man remained markedly higher in Britain than on the Continent. The position is shown in Table 7.

Output per man provides only a crude indication of the differences in coalmining efficiency between countries since it often conceals wide variations in the accessibility and nature of the seams, the organisation of mining, and methods of working. However, relative movements over time in output per man-year offer some guide to changing relationships in productive efficiency between competing nations. In both absolute and relative terms, the bituminous mining area of the USA was far in advance of any country in Europe, a reflection both of comparatively easy mining conditions and a more rapid adoption of mechanised equipment. Of these factors the first had the greater influence. American seams were generally thicker, closer to the surface, freer from faults, flatter and drier than those in Britain. According to one observer, the quantity and quality of resources rather than differences in capital inputs wholly explain the differential between American and British productivity.[21] Capital per man was about the same in both countries, being used as a substitute

96

Table 7

Output per Man-Year of Miners Employed Above and Below Ground,
1874/78-1909/13 (annual average, tons)

Period	UK	USA (Bituminous)	Germany	France	Belgium	Austria/ Hungary
1874/78	270	341[1]	209	154[2]	135	N.A.
1894/98	287	511	262	208	174	176
1909/13	257	698	256	195	159	190[3]
% Increase (+) or Decrease (−) 1874/8-1909/13	−5	+105	+22	+27	+18	+8[4]

SOURCE:
Samuel Commission, 1925; Gibson, op. cit., p. 227.
NOTES:
1. Figure for 1874/8 represents only one-fifth of the industry.
2. Relates to 1876-78 only.
3. Relates to 1908-12.
4. Increase measured over the period 1894/98-1908/12.

for poor and expensive coal land in Britain and for expensive labour in the United States.

With regard to the countries in Europe, Britain maintained a distinct competitive advantage until the closing years of the period. Greater output per man allowed her to produce coal relatively cheaply and thus dominate foreign markets. In part, Britain's greater efficiency in the early part of the period was due to sound mining practice, particularly a rapid expansion in the application of steam power and much improved haulage and winding techniques, as discussed in Chapter 5 below. Increasingly, however, the retention of a relatively high level of productivity came to depend on the exploitation of the best and most easily accessible seams. As these became exhausted,[22] Britain's apparent reluctance to mechanise the processes of production led to a steady erosion of her competitive advantage. She was the only country of those specified in Table 7 to lose ground in output per man-year over the whole period. In effect, the inexorable law of diminishing returns was taking its toll, more so in Britain than in the USA, Germany and France where exploitation of the coalfields had come later. Inevitably, the earlier development of British coal resources now entailed deeper working, the extraction of thinner seams and a longer travelling distance from the face to the shaft. The whole process of mining became steadily more difficult and was attended by greater costs. In these circumstances productivity was bound to fall if inputs of units of capital and labour remained unchanged. In the British case, the influence of more difficult mining conditions was not offset to any great extent by a greater application of capital in the form of mechanical equipment. The factor-mix employed in the coalfields was inappropriate and could not prevent a rapid deterioration in output per man.

While the warning signals had been hoisted for future years, for the greater part of the 1870-1914 period British coalmining enjoyed a comfortable superiority over its European rivals in terms of output per man. The resultant success in international markets meant that by 1912 exports accounted for one-third of total output in Britain as opposed to one-quarter in Germany and a mere 6% in both the United States and France. But the continued dominance of British coal in world trade concealed an important change which had taken place in the relative positions of the coal-exporting districts within the country. The export supremacy of the Northern Coalfield steadily declined during the second half of the 19th century. By the 1880's South Wales dominated Britain's foreign trade in coal, largely due to steamship demand. The steam coal of South Wales was held to possess several advantages over that of other districts, notably a higher evaporative power, an ability to ignite easily and the fact that it occupied less space per ton.[23] Therefore shipments from Cardiff, Barry and other ports in South Wales to such locations as Port Said, Aden, Genoa and Buenos Aires were largely used for bunkering steam vessels.

In 1850, a mere 13% of total British shipments had been sent through Bristol Channel ports, as opposed to a massive 64% through ports on the North-East coast. By 1880, both areas were exporting 39% of Britain's coal shipments, but thereafter the supremacy of South Wales was quickly established. During the period from 1900 to 1913, roughly 40% of total coal exports was shipped each year through the ports of the Bristol Channel while the contribution of the North-East fell to about one-third. By the first world war, the relative importance of the different coal-exporting districts in Britain may be judged from the statistics of distribution provided by the Secretary for Mines: —

From—	*Million Tons*	*% of total coal exports*
Bristol Channel Ports	29.9	40
North-East Ports	23.0	31
Scottish Ports	10.4	14
Humber Ports	8.9	12
Other Ports	1.2	3
	73.4	100

5 The Factors of Production
(i) Capital and Enterprise

During the second half of the 19th century, further important developments took place in mining technique and practice in an attempt to increase output and, at the same time, establish the principles of safe working. If the coal industry could hardly have survived in the 19th century without the steam engine, without improved systems of ventilation and underground haulage development after 1850 would have been seriously retarded. By the 1880's the main lines of advance had been laid down; subsequent expansion depended largely on making refinements to existing practice. There were exceptions, notably the mechanisation of activities at the face and the application of electricity below ground. But even here the rate of innovation was markedly slower in Britain than in the USA and Germany and the widespread application of these new techniques had to await the period following the first world war. Indeed the failure to innovate more rapidly before 1914 has frequently been regarded as the first indication of incipient weakness in British coalmining. The burden of increasing costs as deeper and thinner seams were worked could be shrugged off by the coalmaster as long as demand for his product was high and rising, as indeed it was for most of the period after 1850. But the corollary was a failure to keep abreast of modern techniques and a steady loss of ground to best mining practice abroad. The penalty for this relative decline in technical standards was not to be incurred in the generation before the 1914-18 war but rather in the ensuing period, when the British coal industry was confronted with new and unfavourable market conditions.

However, it will be argued in this chapter that there were important mitigating circumstances. A lack of enterprise and foresight was more apparent than real since in several British coalfields physical conditions did not readily permit the use of mechanical equipment. In many collieries, it was not until further improvements in the design and efficiency of machines had been accomplished that their innovation became not only practicable but vital to survival. Nor is it easy to find fault with an industry in which production and prosperity increased so rapidly before 1914. Output doubled between the 1850's and 1880, and had almost doubled again by 1913. Profits fluctuated widely but measured from peak to peak moved, in money terms, from an average of £11.7 million per annum in 1889/93 to £19.2 million in 1899/1903 and to £25 million in 1912/13. By the first world war, too, wages in coalmining were considerably higher than in most other industries, employment was rapidly increasing and unemployment was negligible. It is important, therefore, to put such problems as the industry experienced in perspective. From 1850 coalmining had experienced almost continuous expansion, developing better methods of getting and distributing the mineral and, at the same time, achieving a welcome improvement in its safety-record.

1 DEVELOPMENTS IN MINING TECHNOLOGY ALONG 'ESTABLISHED' LINES

While large improvements had been effected by mid-century in methods of ventilation, the high incidence of explosions underground was still a cause of grave concern. During the period 1850 to 1914, there was a growing awareness that the best safeguards were, first, more efficient ventilation to remove accumulations of firedamp and, second, to reduce as far as possible the amount of coal dust in the workings which served to carry along and extend the effects of an explosion. The stricture that 'no question is of greater importance in coalmining than that of the ventilation of the mine,'[1] was readily accepted. The emphasis after 1850 was increasingly placed on mechanical ventilators, this despite initial opposition from several quarters. In a Report to the Secretary of State in 1850, J. Kenyon Blackwell endorsed the furnace and steam-jet as the most effective forms of underground ventilation since the unreliability and inefficiency of mechanical ventilators 'seemed to preclude their use . . . in other than exceptional cases.'[2] It was recognised that, given the wide variety of mining conditions, no one form of ventilation would be appropriate in all cases, but both the House of Lords' Select Committee in 1849 and that of the House of Commons in 1852 favoured the application of the steam-jet. Further confusion was added when, after a more extensive survey, the House of Commons' Select Committee on Accidents in Coalmines in 1854 concluded that the furnace was both the most effective and the most economical means of ventilation, particularly where coal lay at considerable depths below the surface. It was alleged that mechanical methods, such as the machine invented by Struvé, were useful only in shallow pits and level collieries.[3]

Yet by the 1880's mechanical ventilators were being used throughout the industry, passing volumes of air amounting to between 100,000 and 250,000 cubic feet per minute. A variety of types were in operation, ranging from those open at the circumference like the Waddle and Rammell fans, quick-running fans, the Struvé cylinder apparatus and the drum type of ventilator. The most commonly employed made use of centrifugal force. Initially, mechanically induced air-flows supplemented existing forms of ventilation. For deep shafts, ventilating furnaces installed below ground remained in fairly general use until the closing decades of the 19th century, circulating air at rates between 200,000 and 400,000 cubic feet per minute.[4] This contrasted with the position on the Continent where mechanical methods had been applied, particularly in Belgium, well before 1850. Their success had led to the virtual disappearance of the underground furnace. From the 1860's the position began to change. Mechanical forms of ventilation were innovated in Britain at a much faster rate than abroad. At the same time a major step forward was taken in this country with the passing of the 1862 Coal Mines Regulation Act. To maintain safety standards, the principle was established that each mine with more than 20 workers must possess two shafts or outlets at each seam.[5] The practice was also adopted in the more progressive collieries of reducing the length of the air-courses while significantly increasing their number. By the 1880's, air-courses of between two and five miles were standard practice as opposed to the 20 to 30 miles previously travelled by the current. These improvements allowed British pits to introduce much larger volumes of air, with greater safety, than was the case in any Continental mine.[6]

Collieries still existed without adequate artificial aids and with too much ventilation left to the agency of diffusion alone. But in general a relatively high standard had been achieved in Britain by 1900. The mechanically driven fan had become the principal form of generating flows of air, steadily replacing the underground furnace. Where they supplied the main ventilation for the underground workings, these fans were placed on the surface with only auxiliary fans being used underground. This arrangement, and the use of mechanisation to induce air-flows, was endorsed by the Royal Commission on Mines established in 1906. After conducting a large amount of experimental work in different collieries,[7] the Commission laid down what it regarded as adequate standards of ventilation. Hitherto wide variations had existed in the proportion of firedamp classified as 'acceptable' by firemen and deputies in different collieries and coalfields. Anything exceeding 1% of firedamp in the air could readily be detected by an ordinary safety lamp, although a fully formed 'cap' in the flame was not visible until over 2% of firedamp was present.[8] While agreeing that a standard of ventilation common to all pits was difficult to establish the Commission concluded that air-flows should exist underground sufficient to prevent a fully-formed 'cap' appearing on the lowered flame of an ordinary safety lamp. It also recommended that on no account should men be allowed to work in places where more than 2½% of gas in the general body of air existed. Where mines were still worked with naked lights, this proportion was reduced to 1¼%? These recommendations were incorporated in the 1911 Mines Act which revised the General Rules under which collieries operated.

Even with relatively efficient ventilation to remove accumulations of firedamp, violent explosions running throughout the underground workings could still occur. The main culprit, although for long escaping retribution due to a succession of 'not proven' verdicts, was coal dust. Fierce controversy raged in the second half of the century over the danger of dust lying thickly on roads and nearby working-places, until extensive testing by the Royal Commissions reporting in 1886 and 1894 put the matter beyond all doubt.[10] Suspicions about the dangerous properties of coal dust had existed for a long time. Right at the start of the century, John Buddle, reporting on an explosion at Wallsend Colliery had noted that, 'the workings were very dry and dusty, and the survivors, who were the most distant from the point of explosion were burnt by the shower of red-hot sparks of the ignited dust, which were driven along by the force of the explosion.'[11] This view of the dangers of dust was confirmed by the report made to the Home Office in 1845 by Professor Faraday and Sir Charles Lyell following the explosion at Haswell Colliery in Durham in the previous year. Ninety-five lives had been lost by the ignition of firedamp but as Faraday and Lyell pointed out the resulting explosion had been greatly intensified by the prevalence of coal dust.[12]

Not everyone accepted this interpretation but there was more general agreement about one of the major causes of the ignition of firedamp—the use of gunpowder for blasting purposes. Up to the 1880's gunpowder was still commonly used for shot-firing to bring down coal and stone from the face. Once blown out, the shot frequently yielded a flame, particularly where the shot-hole had been over-charged or where insufficient tamping had occurred. This flame and the distance of its projection, or blown-out shot, could readily ignite coal dust in nearby workings. Although it was impracticable to prohibit shot-firing in mines, the 1886 Royal Commission strongly recommended that powder surrogates be found for gunpowder and other forms of blasting powder. Significantly, after discussing several possibilities, it advocated the further testing of electric shot-firing in the interests of safety. Its recommendations, along with those of the 1894 Royal Commission, were implemented in the first Explosives in Coal Mines Order of 1896. This introduced the principle of 'permitted' explosives in coal mines and contributed to a considerable reduction in the number of deaths resulting from explosions of firedamp or coal dust. Deaths due to this cause fell from 0.300 per 1,000 persons employed in 1896 to 0.057 per 1,000 in 1907.[13]

Just as it was impractical to prohibit the use of shot-firing so it was obviously impractical to try to remove all coal dust from mines. Yet thorough testing by the 1886 Commission demonstrated beyond reasonable doubt that dust when raised by the shot could be ignited so readily and could carry the flame so rapidly that explosive effects were generated similar to those caused by firedamp. Again both the 1886 and 1894 Commissions were in agreement that sides and floors should be kept sufficiently wet to prevent dust from becoming suspended in the air by the action of the rush of gas emanating from a blown-out shot. Despite these findings, it was clear that many coalfields considered the remedies to be either impractical or valueless. By the start of the present century, general watering was not systematically carried out in any coalfield other than that of South Wales. There was some justification for this apparent neglect. In many collieries the suggested remedies aggravated, rather than alleviated, the danger of accidents. To be effective, dampening the dust involved heavy watering not only of the floor but also of the roof and sides. In a large number of mines, watering on this scale was impossible due to the condition of the strata. After heavy applications of water the floor tended to heave and falls, or cave-ins, of roof and sides increased. Moreover, under wet conditions proper maintenance was often impractical with the result that haulage accidents, caused by greasy rails, became frequent. Colliery-owners in the Midlands, Yorkshire and Scotland were particularly sceptical alleging that effective watering might, or might not, reduce the incidence of explosions but greatly increased the risk of other types of accident.[14] Equally, watering the workings and roads was inimical to health since it meant that workers belowground operated in permanently damp and chilling conditions.

In view of these reservations, the 1906 Royal Commission was led to consider an alternative solution. By directing attention to the possibility of choking an explosion by sanding the workings and roads, the Commission paved the way for a real breakthrough in underground safety before 1914. It tentatively suggested salt or calcium chloride as possible 'sanding' agents or, even more effective, mixing the coal dust with shale or other forms of inert dust. The latter had previously been tried in several collieries with some success but it was the Commission's endorsement that led to further experimental work and the current practice of heavily sanding the face workings and roads.

Intimately bound up with the question of explosions, firedamp and coal dust, was the form of lighting employed underground. The Second Report of the Royal Commission on Mines, published in 1909, showed that of the 819 deaths caused between 1896 and 1907 by explosions of firedamp or coal dust, one-half could be attributed to underground lighting and one-third to shot-firing. In the former case, the chief reason was the persistent use of naked flame, especially in Scotland,[15] but deaths due to the ordinary safety lamp were still sufficiently high to be a cause for concern. They occurred despite important advances made after 1850 in the technology of the lamp. As before 1850, most accidents were due to inadequately maintained, or carelessly used, lamps. However, there was one significant difference between the pre- and post-1850 situations. In the former, the wire-gauze Davy, Clanny and Stephenson lamps had proved relatively efficient. Ventilation currents had been moderate, rarely exceeding a velocity of five feet per second in the main air-ways. But by the 1880's, current-velocities of between 20 and 25 feet per second were frequent in the air-ways, and 10-15 feet per second were common on the faces of longwall working. These velocities were too high for the unmodified safety lamp to withstand since they made the flame pass through the gauze.

The implications for mine-safety were serious since the lamp was widely used in most of the principal English coalfields. By mid-century, there were between 15,000 and 16,000 safety lamps in use in Northumberland and Durham alone and it could be confidently asserted that, apart from improper maintenance or careless use, there had been since its invention, 'no authentic case of any accident having happened from a safety lamp during the whole of that period. On the contrary, our explosions in the North of England have arisen from the contact of an inflammable atmosphere with naked lights.'[16] But times had changed. Improvements in ventilation had created a dangerous gap between the velocities of current being achieved underground and those with which the safety lamp had been designed to contend. It was estimated that the ordinary Davy became unsafe when a current-velocity approaching 400 feet per minute was attained, the ordinary Clanny at 600 feet per minute and the Stephenson at over 800 feet per minute.[17] At these velocities, the ignition of firedamp and air on one side of the gauze was communicated to the mixture on the other side of the gauze. In consequence, when the current became sufficiently charged with firedamp, these lamps ceased in any way to be 'safety' lamps. Bitter experience accounted for the growing popularity of a lamp of Belgian design, the Mueseler lamp, first produced in 1840. But in its standard form, it was not the final answer since the lower portion of the case which surrounded the flame consisted of glass. If this was cracked due to careless use or contact with cold water, the lamp was potentially dangerous.

The impetus given to the design of safety lamps capable of withstanding relatively strong currents in the main air-ways led to the marketing of a wide variety of models in the years after 1850. Most were modifications of those invented by the pioneers. The lamps of Hann and Gray were improved forms of the Stephenson model; the

Mueseler and Marsaut versions were bonneted lamps derived from the Clanny; and one of the most reliable, the Evan Thomas No. 7 lamp, was also a derivative of the Clanny lamp. By the 1880's these and several others were capable of providing both the degree of safety and amount of light necessary for underground working. But, initially the most successful innovation was a modified form of the Davy lamp. By casing the Davy, either in cans or in cases with glass windows, the air current was prevented from affecting the flame of the lamp. This type of lamp was found to be reliable in air-flows with a velocity of up to 2,000 feet per minute. Although higher velocities at that time were rare, they could occur when a shot blew out its tamping or a main current of air passed through a highly restricted passage. Since in these circumstances the modified Davy was much less secure, development work continued in an effort to produce a safer lamp. For instance, after an intensive series of experiments the 1886 Royal Commission endorsed both the Evan Thomas No. 7 which proved capable of withstanding an explosive atmosphere moving with a velocity of 3,200 feet per minute, and the lamp which later became known as the Ashworth-Hepplewhite-Gray.[18]

But of the many different types of flame safety lamp produced after 1850 the improved forms of Mueseler and Marsaut were to have the greatest long-term impact on the industry. By 1923, for instance, there were over 900,000 safety lamps in use in British coalmining. Of these, 403,000 were of the Marsaut type and 176,000 of the Mueseler type amounting together to almost two-thirds of the total.[19] However, the days of the flame-safety lamp were already numbered. By the late 19th century the possibilities of a totally new development were being explored, the use of electric lighting below ground. Among the first to use electricity underground was Earnock Colliery, Hamilton, in 1881. An installation at the pit-bottom and at a junction of three roads, 150 yards distant from the shaft, provided adequate roadway lighting. Here, as at the Risca Collieries and Harris' Navigation Colliery near Pontypridd where electric lighting was successfully employed in 1882-86, the major difficulty proved to be the development of an efficient portable electric lamp. Electric lighting was successful, but only within a limited area of the pit bottom. The miner, on the other hand, required a light both for travelling inbye and for illuminating his working place.

Hence while fixed electric lighting became steadily more common from the 1880's and was even tried in several collieries at the coalface, portable electric lamps remained an intractable problem until just before the first world war. Only by 1910 is there evidence that their use below ground was becoming increasingly common. Although they had to be carried by hand and were heavy and cumbersome, the number of such lamps rapidly multiplied. In 1911, it has been estimated that some 4,300 were in use: by 1913, the number had already jumped to 37,800.[20] Since in the latter year, 740,000 flame safety lamps were also being used electric lamps amounted to a mere 5% of the total. But by 1920 they numbered 246,000, 28% of the total, and finally became the predominant form of safety lamp used in British coalmining in 1930.[21]

One of the most important advances in mining technology in the second half of the century occurred in the methods of conveying the coal from the workings of the mine to the bottom of the shaft. Between 1850 and 1880 the practice of moving moderate amounts of coal by manual or horse power generally gave way to the traction of large amounts of mineral by means of ways fitted with ropes actuated by engines. The Main and Tail Rope system involved a single track along which the wagons were hauled by a stationary engine. The 'main' rope hauled the loaded wagons out of the shaft while conversely the 'tail' rope pulled the emptied wagons inbye. Alternatively the Endless Rope system required a double track, with the tubs attached to the rope at regular intervals. On one track the empty tubs travelled inbye, on the other the loaded tubs were pulled outbye. Mechanical power was used to move the endless rope continuously along the haulage roads. Both these methods significantly increased the amount of coal that could be shifted from the working faces.[22] By the 1880's the tubs were moving at speeds of between 8 and 10 m.p.h., a factor which, in itself, created a potentially dangerous situation underground (see Chapter 6, section 5). But more important was the danger inherent in the employment of steam to power the haulage systems. The use of steam boilers undergound with their necessary flues was the antithesis of what would now be regarded as safe mining practice. There was a constant risk of fire and explosions, with the result that steam engines steadily gave way to those powered by compressed air. The first such engine was used for power transmission at Govan Colliery near Glasgow in 1849.

Only from 1865 was compressed air used extensively instead of steam and its reign below ground was comparatively short. It was successfully applied not only to haulage but to longwall cutting machines and to pumping. Hitherto, the major difficulty encountered with the steam engine had been the transmission of power over long distances. Although steam boilers were housed underground, the further the workings from the shaft the greater the difficulty, danger and expense of transmitting the necessary amount of power. This problem was considerably eased with the introduction of the compressed air engine but was not finally solved until the widespread innovation of electricity during the present century. Long before that, of course, the use of electricity to transmit power had started to encroach on the monopoly previously enjoyed by steam and compressed air. It was first introduced for purposes of power transmission in the Forest of Dean in 1882 and became increasingly popular for such underground operations as haulage, pumping and lighting. Until the end of the century a direct current (DC) dynamo was employed for transmission, alternating current (AC) coming into general use only after 1900. Despite some initial opposition, the advantages of electricity were soon apparent: it was more convenient to apply, easier to maintain and more economical than compressed air.[23] Many owners found that while compressed air ceased to be efficient as a source of power at low pressures, the use of high pressures was frequently not practical in the underground workings. Moreover, there was often serious loss due to leakages, sometimes amounting to as much as 50%, in those collieries where the air-mains were relatively long.[24]

In both winding and pumping solid, if rather unspectacular, advance was made until the introduction of electricity once again accelerated the rate of change. However, electricity was to affect these two areas of mining activity in markedly different ways. In the years after 1850, improvements and better maintenance of winding engines resulted in a sharp fall in deaths caused by shaft accidents. In 1851/60 there had been one death per 1,160 persons employed but by 1881/84 the ratio had fallen to one death per 4,720 persons employed. This was largely due to the improvements made to the design of guided shaft-cages. Originally, guides had been constructed of wood or iron, but increasingly collieries began to make use of more durable and reliable wire ropes. By the 1880's some 420,000 men were being raised and lowered in the shafts each day in comparative safety, 'a major triumph of engineering' in the post-1850 period.[25] In the same decade the cross-compound horizontal winding engine was introduced, increasing both steam pressures and the speed of winding. But this was merely the forerunner of things to come. By the start of the present century limited use was being made of electric winders but these made such heavy demands on the electric transmission mains that attention turned to developing the potential of the exhaust steam turbine (see below, p. 109). The exhaust steam from high-pressure steam winding engines was transmitted to an exhaust steam turbine which generated electrical power for the rest of the machinery used at the colliery. In short, in the 50-60 years after 1850, the steam engine and use of wire ropes had transformed colliery winding practice. In the late 17th century it had been good practice to raise 5 tons of coal per hour from a depth of 100 feet, with an average shaft speed of 5 feet per second. By 1900, engines were dealing with about 360 tons of coal per hour, lifting from a depth of 2,400 feet at average shaft speeds of between 21 and 48 feet per second.[26]

Similarly in pumping, direct-acting underground steam pumps began gradually to replace the enduring Cornish engine after 1850.

Again, the rate of change quickened only in the 1880's and during the same decade the first collieries harnessed electric power to their pumping operations. Where these led others soon followed, with the result that by the turn of the century a revolution had taken place in pumping design and arrangement. The central feature of this transformation was the introduction from abroad of the centrifugal pump. It readily lent itself to electric drive, was immensely strong in relation to its size and above all was relatively cheap to operate. Its rapid innovation meant that in this field at least, electricity won an early and relatively painless victory over other sources of power. By 1914 compact pumping machinery was housed at the pit-bottom in the new 'pump room' off the pit-bottom sidings. Water could be pumped by means of electricity in one lift from the floor of the pit rather than the several lifts formerly required by the steam pumping engine.

2   NEW DEPARTURES IN MINING TECHNOLOGY

The foregoing discussion has shown that the introduction of electricity in the last quarter of the 19th century resulted in radical changes in mining technique. Already by 1910 electricity had been applied in virtually every mining operation requiring mechanical power. But within this short life-span a significant change had occurred in the method of transmitting electric power. Most of the early electric plants had been of the DC type mainly because it was regarded as more suitable for motors which had to be continually stopped and started. However, experience of using the DC system showed, first, that it involved relatively high costs of transmission and, second, that it was impossible to ensure spark-less working of the motors, thus obviously heightening the risk of accidents due to ignitions of firedamp or dust. For both these reasons the AC system was preferable, all the more so since a three-phase current had been developed which enabled varying voltages to be obtained by means of transformers. Hence different types of equipment in the mine could be supplied with voltages specially selected to meet their particular needs. By adopting the high-pressure AC system and transformers, collieries could secure high, or extra-high, pressures for transmission; high, or medium, pressures for large motors; and low pressures for small motors (including those of coal-cutting machines) and lighting.

By adjusting the strength of the current to the particular apparatus in use the AC system offered the prospect of greater reliability and safety and markedly lower transmission costs. As a result most of the larger collieries had converted to the three-phase AC system before the first world war. Nor was it only the underground distribution of electricity which changed. More stringent regulations were introduced after 1900 to control its use below ground. All metallic coverings of equipment had to be properly earthed as a precaution against electric shock, switchgear had to be completely enclosed in metal cases and motor-rooms had to be adequately fire-proofed. These rules ensured that in the years between the Reports of the first and second Departmental Committees on the Use of Electricity in Mines (1905 to 1910), the number of deaths caused by the new source of power never reached in any one year a figure higher than 1.54% of the total number of deaths in mines.[27] Even this low proportion could have been avoided since it was almost entirely due to a lack of knowledge or badly constructed and maintained equipment.

When electricity was first introduced for underground working in the 1880's the slow-speed horizontal direct-acting engine, which had replaced the Cornish type as the standard prime-mover, was adapted to drive the dynamo by means of belts and ropes. But once Parson's steam turbine had been invented, it was rapidly introduced into the mining industry. The first DC turbo-generators were installed at Ackton Hall Colliery in 1895. At this same colliery, the first AC turbo-generator in the world was put into operation in 1901. About the same time the possibilities of using the large quantities of exhaust steam from colliery winding engines in a steam turbine were realised. Thus in 1905 an exhaust steam turbine was installed, the forerunner of the colliery exhaust steam turbo-generating plant widely used in Britain during the present century. It was also discovered that another form of waste heat could be profitably employed to generate electricity. Surplus coke oven gas was used in gas engines before 1914 to drive electric generators. This gas, formerly wasted, became increasingly important in the provision of electric power during the course of the 20th century. By the first world war, a high proportion of collieries possessed their own small generating plants, using inferior slack or waste heat in the form of exhaust steam and coke oven gas. These small plants did not show high thermal efficiency but could generate current at relatively low cost per unit due to low overhead charges and the low value of the fuel used.[28]

Although electricity was used to great effect before 1914 in such diverse activities as lighting, pumping, haulage and winding, its most spectacular application was to the portable motors of coal-cutters and drills. As with so many other crucial breakthroughs in mining technique, the application of power to coal-cutting made possible operations previously regarded as impossible. The innovation of the mechanical cutter meant that very thin seams could now be exploited which had formerly been ruled out because they were uneconomic or physically incapable of being worked. A giant stride was taken before the first world war with the introduction of the electric coal-cutter but it was merely the final step in a long series of experiments that had started half-a-century earlier. The successful application of power to operations such as pumping, haulage and ventilation proved the stimulus to design more efficient methods of hewing the coal. In the 1850's patents were taken out for the three mechanical cutters that were later to dominate the industry. But taking out patents was a far cry from successful commercial development. The chain-cutting machine, patented in 1856, made little impact on British mining throughout the 19th century but was rapidly innovated in the United States. The more uniform mining conditions in that country, with thicker seams and softer coal, allowed the chain-cutter to be successfully applied. Subsequent American efforts to invade the British market with an improved version of the machine failed before 1914 and only succeeded in the inter-war years once it had been harnessed to another British invention, the compressed air turbine.[29]

Initially the greatest impact on the British industry was made by the disc machine, a crude form of which was patented in 1852. A year later, compressed air was applied as the source of power to a cutting machine but the major advance was made in 1863 when Thomas Harrison of Durham produced his turbine, powered by water, steam or compressed air, to drive the disc-cutter. With the arrival of the turbine, all efforts to emulate mechanically a pick-man came to an end. The power-driven disc symbolised the evolution from reciprocating to rotary motion and altered the principles of mining the coal. Rotary, or 'continuously moving cutters', ensured a large increase in cutting capacity. Where previously the swinging pick had fractured the coal by impact, the cutter of the rotary machine operated by sustained pressure which forced it to penetrate to a depth depending on the feed of the machine. In its circular path it removed the coal by tearing it from the face.

William Baird & Co of Coatbridge innovated the first chain machine to cut coal in 1864, the Gartsherrie coal-cutter, driven by compressed air. With steel-making still in its infancy, the poor quality of metals available to machine-makers meant that the chains were not strong enough to withstand the abrasion and, after a few years, production of the Gartsherrie was discontinued. Hence, largely due to the inferiority of available metals, British coalmining neglected the chain-cutter in favour of the disc machine, driven by compressed air. By the 1880's the disc and, to a lesser extent, the bar machines dominated the British industry. But experience soon proved that where the floor was undulating the disc had great difficulty in following irregularities of contour. At best, it could be used only where longwall mining was practised and was too inflexible to cope with all the widely different seam conditions of the British coalfields. Attention was increasingly directed towards the bar cutter which had lain dormant for some 30 years since the initial patent had been taken out. In 1887, electric power was successfully harnessed to the cutter: the Bower-Blackburn electrically driven bar cutter appeared to transform mining practice. It had a 10 h.p. engine, could be used in both longwall and pillar and stall systems and was soon found to be capable of hewing coal in seams no thicker than two feet which had previously been regarded as uncommercial.

By the closing years of the 19th century, coalmining had entered the modern era of mechanical cutting at the face. However development was slow and few collieries accepted machine mining unless force of circumstance compelled them to do so. Several coalfields remained notably backward in this respect, particularly Lancashire, the Midlands and North Wales. On a national scale, therefore, the development of mechanised face operations was relatively slight. Even in Scotland where the use of mechanical face-cutters had progressed furthest, only 3% of output was machine-cut in 1900. In England the proportion was lower so that, at best, only about 2% of Britain's total output of 225 million tons was mechanically cut.[30] At first sight, the rate of take-up of the new technology appears lamentably slow when compared to that of the United States. In that country, one-fifth of the 240 million tons produced was mechanically cut in 1900. But such a comparison is misleading. In large areas of the United States physical conditions, in the form of level floors and freedom from faults, were conducive to machine mining. A more detailed discussion of the reasons behind the apparently slow innovation of machine mining in Britain is given below, sections 3 and 4. It is more important to note that mechanical cutting made more rapid progress in Britain before the first world war than anywhere else in Europe. Moreover, cutting by electric machines made relatively rapid progress in Britain. Of the 483 mechanical cutters in use by 1903, 149, or almost one-third, used electricity as their source of power.[31]

If some districts were slow to appreciate the advantages of mechanical cutting, there appeared to be an even greater reluctance to make use of mechanical conveyors at the face. By 1900, the pattern of underground transport had changed little since the introduction of the Main and Tail and Endless Rope systems in mid-century. With more coal being cut, increasingly heavy costs were being incurred in forming and maintaining gate-roads for the transport of the coal from the face and in shovelling the coal along the face to the gate-ends where it could be loaded into trams. The Blackett face conveyor, of the scraper type, was introduced in 1902 in an effort to solve this problem. It was designed to transport the coal along the longwall face and from the face to the main haulage roads. Before the first world war, the jigger, or shaker, conveyor had also been put on the market and, in total, some 350 face conveyors were at work in British coalfields.[32] Again, this total compared unfavourably with best practice abroad. In part, this can be attributed to the belief in Britain that the mechanical conveyor was only suitable for thin seams where space restrictions hampered the free movement of the miner. Moreover, the many failures and disappointments associated with the earliest conveyors militated against their rapid innovation. Only in the inter-war period was it appreciated that the larger the quantity of coal to be dealt with per lineal yard of face, the stronger the case for mechanical conveying. Conveyors were particularly appropriate for thick seams, permitting an increase in output per man and significant cost-reductions due to the fewer haulage roads required and correspondingly, less timbering, rail-laying and maintenance of gate-roads.

3   MECHANISATION AND DIMINISHING RETURNS

It should be recognised at the outset that the colliery which undertook the type of face mechanisation outlined in the previous section did not, by definition, become 'efficient', nor was it guaranteed a relatively high level of profits. Analysis of the industry's progress tends to concentrate on mechanical cutting and conveying, not only because these were the main technical advances, but also because data on other aspects of colliery development are almost entirely absent. Little is known, for example, about machine use in other areas of coalmining activity or about the conduct of operations within the colliery, factors which would clearly have an effect on overall efficiency. Hence the application of capital-intensive methods should be regarded as only one of the aspects of colliery efficiency and even here, particular geological conditions could render such development largely inappropriate. Before 1914, force of circumstance played a major role in determining the rate of technological advance in the different coalfields. As already noted, it was wrongly believed that face conveyors were suitable only where thin seams prevailed. With more justification, it was also accepted that thin seams made it not only desirable but in many cases essential that mechanical cutters be employed. Mainly for these reasons the Scottish district led the way before the first world war in the application of the new technology.

In terms of the number of mechanical cutters and conveyors employed at the face and proportion of output cut by machine, Scotland was far ahead of any other coal-producing district in the UK. Moreover, Scotland was the heaviest user of electricity *below ground.* Table 1 shows that in absolute terms the Scottish district ranked third behind S. Wales and Northern in the consumption of electricity. But in the latter two districts there was a more even distribution of the electricity consumed above and below ground. In South Wales, for instance, the horsepower employed on the surface

112

Table 1

Number of Mechanical Cutters and Conveyors in Use, Proportion of Output Cut by Machines and Total Horse-Power Used in Districts Specified, 1913

District[1]	No. of Coal-Cutting Machines, Driven by:		% of Output Mechanically Cut	Total h.p. Used	No. of Conveyors at Coalface
	Electricity	Comp. Air			
			(%)	(000)	
Scotland	700	176	21.7	119.6	125
Northern	134	531	3.8	144.3	58
Yorkshire & N. Midland	331	342	10.2	107.2	86
Lancs, N. Wales and Ireland	36	354	7.7	30.8	22
South Wales	36	79	1.1	181.8	61
Midland & Southern	70	105	4.5	44.4	2
Total U.K.	1,307	1,587	8.5	628.1	354

SOURCES:
Reports of HM Inspectors of Mines for 1913, Cd. 7439 and 7439 I-VI, 1914; *General Report for 1913 by the Chief Inspector of Mines,* Part II, Labour Cd. 7721, 1914; *Annual Reports of the Secretary for Mines.*
NOTE:
1. The districts specified represent Inspector of Mines' divisions. For a definition of these divisions, see *General Report for 1913,* op. cit.

at 90.5 thousand was almost equivalent to the 91.2 thousand used underground. On the other hand, in Scotland a mere 26.3 thousand h.p. was employed on the surface compared to 93.4 thousand h.p. below ground. The greater technical efficiency of the Scottish district can be regarded as an attempt to offset diminishing returns. These are inevitable in an extractive industry since as the best seams are worked out, deeper and thinner seams have to be exploited. With the coal faces retreating further from the pit-bottom, costs of production rise and greater inputs of labour and capital are required to work the coal. When shallow seams are being worked, most of the effort is expended directly at the coal face but deeper and more distant seams involve more oncost (i.e. non-productive) labour being taken on for timbering, road maintenance, shifting the coal underground and activities on the surface such as banking. Inevitably the overall productivity of labour will fall. Of all districts, Scotland suffered this tendency to diminishing returns most severely before 1914. The richest and most easily accessible deposits in the Lanarkshire Coalfield had been worked out, deeper and thinner seams were being exploited and inrushes of water were a persistent problem. To a large extent, therefore, the increasingly difficult physical conditions encountered below ground and rapidly diminishing returns compelled mechanisation in the Scottish district. The alternatives were clear: mechanise the processes of production in an attempt to offset higher costs and keep prices competitive or eventually be forced out of business.

These considerations were largely responsible for the relatively heavy use of electricity below ground in Scotland. Mechanical cutters were suitable for working thin seams, particularly cutters fed by electric power. Where seams were of a thickness of two feet or less, the hewer cutting by hand unavoidably cut the mineral into very small particles not suitable as saleable coal. On the other hand, the machine could cut underneath the sill and save the whole two feet of the seam. For such tasks only the electric cutter could be used due to the relatively high horsepower it could generate relative to its size and weight. Robert Smillie, President of the Scottish Miners' Federation, made it clear to the *Departmental Committee on Electricity in Mines* of 1911 that electric coal-cutting had been developed to a greater extent in the West of Scotland than anywhere else in the country due to its preponderance of thin seams. Many of these would have lain idle but for the innovation of such machinery.[33]

Where force of circumstances was less compelling there was less enthusiasm for underground mechanisation. In part this reflected the conservatism of owners. Given a rising, and relatively price-inelastic, demand after 1850, profits were generally high: as a result, many owners were content to leave well alone. It was not fully established before 1914 that the mechanical coal-cutter reduced costs of production in the thick seams as well as thin and owners needed to be convinced before risking a heavy capital outlay on equipment and the inevitable reorganisation of underground operations.[34] But a reluctance to take risks was not the only reason for the delay in mechanising face activities. Before condemning owners for their lack of enterprise, certain mitigating factors should be taken into account. Foremost among these was the type of physical conditions encountered in the different coalfields of the country. At one extreme, geological conditions were, for instance, highly unfavourable in the long-established Lancashire Coalfield. At first sight, with deeper and thinner seams being worked, the coalfield would seem to have been in a situation similar to that of Scotland and therefore ripe for extensive mechanisation. But the presence of steeply inclined seams and a high incidence of faulting meant that much of the new technology, at the level of refinement then obtaining, was impossible to apply. At the other end of the spectrum, in South Wales the major retardative factor was simply the ease with which the mineral could be won by hand, although to this must be added the fact that the coal would hardly stand to be cut. Cutting machines, when applied to the face, tended to be buried by frequent falls. The relatively rapid innovation of face-conveyors before 1914 dispels the notion that owners in the district were lethargic or ignorant of the new methods. Hence rather than indicating inefficiency, the lack of mechanical face-cutters in South Wales simply reflected the adverse nature of conditions below ground. The requirements of the district were totally different to those existing elsewhere.[35] The other coalfields in Britain were variously placed between these two extreme positions. In sum, the lack of uniformity in mining conditions meant first, that unlike the position in the USA, it was difficult to devise machines adaptable to the needs of all and second, that in view of the existing state of technology the use of machines in some areas was precluded altogether.

In addition, technical difficulties acted as a brake on mechanisation, especially those related to the supply and servicing of machinery, and the provision of power. Breakdowns were frequent and the repair and maintenance of equipment were costly and rarely wholly successful. As noted earlier, for certain tasks neither the appropriate materials nor engineering skills were available. The early chain machines had to be abandoned due to lack of suitable metals and the compressed air turbine was taken up in America owing to the relatively backward state of the machine tool industry in Britain before 1914 (see section 2 above). The problem of distributing power underground also prevented more rapid acceptance of face mechanisation. Compressed air remained the most important source of power up to the start of the present century, although in seams of two feet or less it was of little value. It was impossible to use compressed air machines of the size necessary to generate 20 h.p. on a face two feet thick.[36] Leakages and the high cost of carrying pipes for the air added to the reluctance of coalowners to commit themselves wholeheartedly to machine mining. Even the introduction of electricity did not resolve problems of transmission and an exhaustive code of rules was quickly adopted, restricting the use of the new source of power in fiery mines or where there was major risk of explosion.

There was therefore some justification for the relatively slow introduction of the new face technology before 1914. It seemed clear, especially in thin seams, that mechanical cutters could reduce labour costs at the face but whether this gain was sufficient to offset the capital charges incurred in the innovation of such equipment remained an open question. On the other hand, several districts persevered with traditional methods for too long. But this was a cost that the following generation had to bear.

4 STRUCTURE, EMPLOYMENT AND EFFICIENCY

The early applications of electricity below ground and mechanical face-cutting in the 1880's roughly coincided with the industry's high-water-mark in output per man. From that time, the relatively slow acceptance of the new methods proved quite insufficient to combat diminishing returns to effort. Although output per man fluctuated widely over the next 30 years, the underlying trend was markedly downwards. From a peak of 319 tons above and below ground in 1879/83, output per man-year fell by 20% to reach 254 tons in 1909/13.

It is probable that between the 1850's and early 1880's, labour productivity had risen steadily in coalmining due to the wider application of the steam engine and the influence of improved ventilation and the underground haulage systems (see section 1 above). Particularly in the conveyance of coal below ground, a significant reduction had been achieved before the 1880's in the number of those engaged in haulage operations relative to the number employed directly at the face. Indeed, the widespread introduction of the stationary engine, replacing the horse in the main roadways, was probably the principal means of raising productivity below ground. The reversal of this trend from the 1880's can be attributed in part to a slowing down in the rate of innovation. But a full explanation of the fall in productivity requires several other factors to be taken into account.

The structure of coalmining by the late 19th century militated against the sustained growth of output per man. Unplanned and unco-ordinated development in the past now began to exact a heavy toll. The wide dispersal of the nation's coal resources had resulted in the creation of a large number of relatively small colliery companies catering in many cases for a purely local demand. Although technical economies of scale are probably not as important in extractive as in manufacturing industry, the high proportion of small independent units meant that commercial economies of scale were also relatively insignificant.[37] Inevitably, too, the finest and most easily accessible seams had been the first to be worked so that in several of the older coalfields a large number of collieries had long since passed their peak years of productive efficiency. As coal beds were depleted, the average product of labour was driven down. On the other hand, there was little incentive to close such collieries since in contemplating this course of action, the owner had to take a realistic view of the break-up value of his assets, the future trend in profits and the availability or otherwise of cost-reducing innovations. The scrap value of assets was low since few alternative uses could be found either for the machinery employed or obviously, for the pit itself. Going out of business meant, therefore, virtually writing-off existing capital investment. Moreover in view of past experience there was every reason to expect a continuation of the long-term rise in demand and an ability to make profits. Perhaps most important, the owner had access to a series of 'minor' innovations[38] which could be accommodated within the *existing* framework of the industry. These afforded the prospect of increasing the productivity of labour and reducing costs, so helping to offset diminishing returns.

This scenario accords well with the concept of 'defensive investment,'[39] a principle particularly relevant to the coalmining industry. Had the break-up value of his assets been high, profits rapidly falling and new techniques relevant to the industry not readily available, the owner would have scrapped his plant immediately. Provided that the scrap value of his assets had been higher than the aggregate value of gross profits in the foreseeable future, he would have preferred to go out of business rather than continue in operation. But none of these considerations applied to coalmining in the 30 to 40 years before the first world war. As noted in section 3, it was precisely in the smaller and older Scottish collieries that most advantage was taken of 'minor' innovations, in the form of mechanical cutters and conveyors. These went some way towards offsetting the tendency to diminishing returns and enabled such collieries to remain profitably in business.

On the other hand, the stubborn persistence of older collieries clearly delayed reorganisation in the industry and the concentration of labour and capital on newer and more productive seams, offering the possibility of higher rates of return. Even in 1925, the Samuel Commission showed that almost one-third of the miners in Britain were employed in collieries sunk before 1866 and that more than one-half were employed in collieries of pre-1876 vintage.[40] A greater emphasis on coalfields of more recent origin with more accessible seams, together with a willingness to make greater use of face mechanisation, would have cushioned the fall in labour productivity from the 1880's. It was not that the industry was under-capitalised; rather, its assets were too thinly and unevenly spread.[41]

The structure and attitude of the labour force also had a bearing on the efficiency of the coal industry. Allegations that there was a deliberate reduction in effort on the part of the work-force and that, in some districts and at particular times, the men opposed and deliberately obstructed the introduction of machinery can largely be discounted.[42] What can be substantiated is the tendency of prices, and hence wages, to move in the opposite direction to productivity.[43] In South Wales there is evidence that in the short term, hewers succeeded in levelling their earnings by adjustments in productivity. Since they were paid by the ton of coal hewn, they were able to determine their own rate of exertion and hence earnings. When wage-rates were low output per man tended to increase to maintain wage levels. Conversely with high wage-rates, far less effort was required to maintain earnings.[44] Miners were therefore capable of adjusting their rate of exertion in the short term in response to financial pressures. Whether in the long term they could have continuously sustained a higher intensity of effort, and therefore a higher labour productivity, is a more open question, although the evidence for South Wales points towards a positive answer.[45]

Again, although information on wages above and below ground is sketchy, data relating to collieries in County Durham show a strong positive relationship between rising wages on the one hand and rising absenteeism on the other during the late 19th and early 20th centuries.[46] As money wages rapidly increased so, too, did absenteeism from an average of 8% in the 1880's to 10% in the first decade of the present century. Since the Samuel Commission estimated that unavoidable absenteeism amounted to about 4½%, the increase in voluntary absenteeism which these figures represented had obvious implications for labour productivity, measured in terms of output per man-year.[47] In both Durham and South Wales, absenteeism tended in the short term to exacerbate the effects of high wages in bringing about a fall in labour productivity. In addition, time lost through workers' stoppages and disputes markedly increased from the 1890's and some districts experienced a decline in the hours of employment. In most coalfields the decline in working hours was of little consequence before the Eight-Hour Day Act, but in parts of Lancashire and at Barnsley in Yorkshire significant reductions were achieved between 1880 and 1890 (see also Chapter 6, section 6 below). This became a general reduction following the passing of the Eight-Hour Day Act in 1908. Thus, while allegations of a deliberate reduction in effort overstated the case, for a variety of reasons the miner by the first world war was working less strenuously than 30 to 40 years earlier. In this lies some part of the explanation for the deterioration in output per man over this period.

Equally important was the dilution of the work-force which occurred towards the end of the 19th century with a rapid increase in employment of less experienced men. Until mid-century, miners' wages had not been markedly higher than those obtaining in manufacturing industry. Thereafter, further market expansion and steeply climbing prices enabled wages in coalmining to rise relative to those of other occupations. Unskilled workers were sucked into mining from other industries such as agriculture and building. Between the 1880's and 1913 the labour force in coal doubled, with particularly rapid expansion occurring about the turn of the century as the demand for coal strongly revived in the general economic upswing after 1896. In the two years 1899 to 1901 alone, employment in the industry showed a net increase of 79,000 people, lifting the work-force to almost 807,000 by the latter date. Making allowance for normal labour turnover, this meant that by the end of 1901, about one in eight of the nation's miners had been employed in the industry for less than two years. With the industry working at virtually full capacity, increasing demand was met by taking on additional men. These were readily available since money wages were relatively high in coal and conditions of less than full employment existed in other sectors of the economy. But the very existence of this plentiful labour supply at a price which the industry could afford reduced the owners' incentive to substitute capital for labour. Unless there were compelling technical reasons, owners preferred to increase their work-force and move more men to the face rather than risk introducing expensive capital equipment, the returns to which were uncertain. However, the corollary was an inevitable dilution of the skilled labour force in the industry and adverse effects on labour productivity.

Finally, an important element in the decline of output per man overall must have been the decline in the proportion of productive underground workers (coal hewers) in relation to non-productive underground and surface workers. Other things being equal, a fall in the percentage of actual coal-getters and a corresponding rise in the proportion of oncost workers would adversely affect labour productivity. The problem before 1914 was not so much an increase in the proportion of surface workers. Indeed the composition of the labour force in terms of underground and surface workers remained remarkably stable between the 1870's and 1913, the latter commonly accounting for about one-fifth of the total. Where a significant change did occur was in the rapidly rising proportion of non-productive *underground* workers. It is not possible to obtain an annual series of statistics which distinguishes between hewers and underground oncost workers since government statistics made no such breakdown before

Table 2

Proportion of Hewers and Oncost Workers in UK Coalmining

	Hewers	Underground Oncost	Surface Oncost	Total
1889	49.6	32.5	17.9	100.0
1914	40.2	41.1	18.7	100.0

SOURCES:
Mines (Hours of Labour), Return Showing the Average Number of Hours and Days Daily and Weekly Worked by Men and Boys from Bank to Bank in and about Mines in the UK, 284, 1890; Gibson, op. cit., pp. 140-43.

1914. However, some indication of the extent of change between the years 1889 and 1914 is provided in Table 2.

During the period specified in Table 2 there was a considerable increase in the proportion of underground oncost workers. In part this reflected the growing tendency to diminishing returns in the industry as mines became deeper and the faces further from the pit-bottom. A growing number of men had to be taken on to act as putters, fillers and trammers, and for maintenance and safety work. As the share of such workers within the total labour force increased, that of productive underground workers fell.[48] This was bound to have an adverse influence on labour productivity, particularly since little attempt was made to offset diminishing returns with an adequate level of mechanisation.

6 The Factors of Production
(ii) Labour and the Social Issues

1 STATUS AND CONDITIONS OF HIRE

Within the working population, miners have traditionally been regarded as a 'race apart'. In large measure, this was inevitable since they were often physically separated from the rest of the working community. The location and commercial viability of the pit determined where, and how well, the miner and his family lived. Small enclaves developed in which habits and customs were handed down to each successive generation. Communities in mining districts such as Northumberland, Durham and Scotland often became inbred, suspicious of newcomers and intervention, and conservative in outlook. Until well into the 19th century, the rest of society treated miners and mining villages with disdain and not a little contempt. A stigma attached to the task of working underground, handling noxious material and, in the process, acquiring a dirt-ingrained and discoloured skin. In short, in most districts the working conditions and general life-style of the miner were far removed from the experience and activities of the rest of the population. To many, the base elements of society came together in the person of a miner with his crude and often anti-social behaviour and capacity for self-indulgence. But hard evidence of these characteristics is difficult to come by: for the 18th and early 19th centuries, contemporary observers and pamphleteers are the only sources of information. Since their examples generally relate to particular districts or communities at different time-periods, the reliability and relevance of their findings for the country as a whole are open to question.

With this caveat in mind, it is worth examining the principal criticisms made of the miner's way of life. Intemperance was regarded as one of his less endearing characteristics, children learning almost from infancy to attend the favourite alehouses and gambling houses of their father. With a relatively high money wage often supplemented by the earnings of his family, a miner could give rein to 'the indulgence of gross appetite so long as he possesses the power,' before sinking back again 'into filth and poverty until the opportunity returns of indulging himself in the same round of luxury.'¹ Nor was self-

121

indulgence confined to the men. The wives of pitmen were described as being in general, 'a very indolent set of women, either strangers to cleanliness, frugality or economy. It is no unusual thing to see a pitman, his wife and family, the first week after the receipt of his wages, indulging themselves in the finest food and extravagance three times a day and the next living on a little rye bread with oatmeal and water'.[2] This characteristically reckless spending, particularly on pay-days, market-days and Sundays was despised as, 'a devotion to mere animal indulgences.'[3]

A further common complaint before 1850 was that by pursuing his own pleasures in such single-minded fashion, the miner sacrificed the interests of his children. For the latter, an early introduction to the habits of intemperance hardly qualified as an appropriate form of upbringing: nor did frequent attendance at the brutal sports and pastimes of many mining communities. The first inspector of mines appointed under the 1842 Mines Act, H. S. Tremenheere, repeatedly condemned in his reports these aspects of mining village life and the despoiling effects which they had on the young. In 1850 he reported how the minister of a South Staffordshire mining community had told him that only 22 years earlier the baiting place of the village had witnessed, 'in one day, no less than 7 bulls, 3 bears, and a badger, besides dogs and cocks for fighting.'[4] Although the more bloodthirsty of these spectacles had died out by mid-century, dog-fighting still remained a frequent and popular pastime. In general, colliers were little concerned about the education of their children. The young learned their lessons not from any formal type of education but rather from the often bitter and unremitting experiences of their daily working lives. Such facilities for education as did exist before 1850 were largely dependent upon the benevolence of the coalowner. Hence, the provision of schools, books, materials and even schoolmasters differed widely in the separate mining districts.[5] By the 1850's it was reported that in nine cases out of ten there were schools at or near collieries in Northumberland and Durham. The Marquis of London-derry allegedly spent at that time between £400 and £500 per annum in educating colliery workers and children but, as his agent pointed out, this was 'the best organised system of schools that we have in the district.'[6] Even then, children left such schools at between 10 and 12 years of age, subsequently neglecting their education: 'they forgot how to write, and it is all to do over again.'[7]

Indeed before the 1870's lack of suitable education facilities and low standards of literacy, particularly in the under-15 age group, were common features of the coalmining communities. The 1860 Mines Inspection Act stipulated that children between 10 and 12 years old working in the mines must possess a certificate allowing them to miss education on the grounds that they could already read and write. Those without such a certificate were obliged to attend school for three hours per night, twice a week. However, the Act was difficult to enforce and was constantly evaded. This is not altogether surprising when it is recalled that even in the 1860's children under 14 years of age often worked for a longer shift than adult hewers. In the North of England for example, the young were employed as putters or trappers. They had to be ready to start underground by 4 a.m. and never left the pit before 4 or 5 p.m. Taking into account journeying time to and from work, 10- to 14-year olds in the Northern Coalfield worked on average a 14- to 15-hour day.[8] After such an arduous shift in the pits, they were in no condition to attend school in the evening for three hours. They were simply too fatigued and fell asleep over their books. Moreover, when back in the pits the children were often not fit for work and were a source of danger, through accidents, not only to themselves but to their work-mates.[9]

But if, as was alleged, a large part of the mining community was 'brutish' and 'ignorant', with children ill-educated and unwilling to learn,[10] the responsibility lay less with the miners themselves than with the industry for which they worked and an intolerant society. Until the start of the 19th century, the position of many miners in Scotland can be likened to that of slaves. The Scottish Parliament in 1641 had strengthened legislation passed in 1606 to control the movement of miners, making it necessary for them to possess a certificate before moving from their place of employment. The result could be to tie a man to one master for life. Those who escaped such bondage and remained at liberty for one year and one day became free men: but until then they could be hunted down and forcibly returned to their owners. The practice of accepting 'arles'—money payments or commodities—when initially engaged and at the start of each year's employment reinforced the system of servitude. This type of quasi-serfdom was hereditary, whole families being regarded as attached to an estate. Gifts from the employer at the baptism of children were accepted as part of a settlement under which the parents agreed to rear their child for colliery work. Hence a miner and his family could become 'the property of their landlords, appurtenances to their estates and transferable with them to any purchasers'.[11] Although serfdom had evolved in Scottish mining to guarantee an adequate supply of labour,[12] it proved unable in the long run to fulfil this aim. Nor was the system by any means universal in Scottish collieries. Increasingly during the 18th century, new entrants to mining stipulated that they should not become serfs as a result of their employment. Nonetheless the stigma of bondage remained: colliers and salters, to whom the system also applied, were regarded as having a lower status than any other class in Scotland.

Emancipation was secured only during the last quarter of the 18th century and can be attributed as much to economic as to humanitarian principles. The rapid expansion in demand for coal from the 1770's required an increase in the labour force which was difficult to achieve in view of existing employment conditions. Moreover, at a time of growing agitation over the question of slavery and the emancipation of negroes, the bondage of the Scottish miner seemed anomalous in a supposedly free society. The task of releasing him from his servile status was started with the Emancipation Act of 1775 and completed by the Act of 1799.[13]

Although serfdom was confined to Scotland, there had also been restrictions since the start of the 18th century on the free movement of miners in other parts of the country. Under the bond system most commonly practised in Northumberland and Durham, a collier committed his labour for a specified period to one employer. In exchange for a binding fee a worker tied himself for terms of varying length, the most customary being one year. Until the 1760's the fee for a bond of this duration was commonly between 6d. and 1/-, but after the Seven Years' War this sum escalated, due to high prices and labour scarcity, to between 3 and 4 guineas. During the rest of the 18th century, the binding fee varied according to the contours of the trade cycle, reaching a peak in the early 1800's at a time of acute labour shortage.[14] The system persisted during the early decades of the 19th century, being particulary welcomed by the men in periods of slack trade and a surplus labour market. On the one hand, it guaranteed to the employer a steady size of work-force; on the other, miners were afforded security of employment and a wage, albeit at a reduced rate, when coal prices were falling.

The success of the bonding system depended on all collieries in a district not only accepting the common fees to be paid to the men but also remaining faithful to the agreement reached. A typical binding agreement drawn up in the North of England for a one-year period is shown on p. 125.

While this type of binding lasted in the North until the 1840's, it was never a very rigorous or efficient means of determining the conditions of employment. The terms of the bond varied widely at different times and between different regions. In the North, a 12 months' bond was usual but the owners took the opportunity to reduce this according to circumstances. In 1809, for instance, the bond was reduced to 3 months and variations of between 3 and 12 months, or even longer, were also practised in other districts.[15] Security of employment was therefore often more apparent than real. Moreover, when the market was expanding, 'poaching' of workers and evasion of the conditions of the bond were widely practised. The system finally collapsed in the 1840's under the pressure of transport

The Factors of Production (ii) Labour and the Social Issues

At a General Meeting of the Gentlemen Coal Owners of the Rivers Tyne and Wear, Hartley and Blyth held in Newcastle, 24 September 1807

RESOLVED that the bindings of pitmen for the ensuing year be opened on 10th October and that the binding money shall be—

	Tyne			Wear		
	£	s.	d.	£	s.	d.
Hewer, being a Householder	1	1	0	2	2	0
Hewer, being a Single Man	1	11	6	2	12	6
Hewer, Driver		15	0	1	11	6
Driver		10	6	1	1	0
Tram Man	3	3	0	4	4	0

SOURCE:
Watson Collection, North of England Institute of Mining and Mechanical Engineers.

improvements which made it easier for labour to be mobile, and the men's growing awareness that freedom to work or move was more valuable than a tenuous guarantee of security of employment.

Periods of declining trade were characterised not only by the irregularity of employment but also by extensions of the truck system. Truck was widely practised in the Midlands, particularly in Staffordshire. Wages, instead of being paid in cash, were provided in the form of goods purporting to be of the same value or under conditions which forced the recipient to spend them in purchases from his employer. Such practices were exacerbated by the prevalence of the 'butty system'. Invariably, butties were working miners who had acquired sufficient capital to enable them to take over the working of a pit by contract. As contractors, they agreed with the colliery owner to deliver the coal on the bank, or at a wharf, at an agreed price per ton. Under such agreements the butty paid the wages of most of those employed in the pit, had the right to engage or dismiss workers and provided working capital like timber, tools, explosives, stores, horses and fodder. Fixed capital remained the responsibility of the owner. With no permanent interest in the mine, the butty's sole object was to win the coal at cheapest cost. This generally meant a total disregard for safety since economy came before safety, in the form of efficient timbering and ventilation in the mine, adequate provisions and the proper conduct of repair and maintenance work. More immediately, men and boys in the pit tended to suffer severely at the hands of the butty. Cases of ill-treatment and over-work were common, the men often being forced to undertake over-time without pay on penalty of dismissal. In Derbyshire, butty gangs of children were compelled to stay in the pit for 36 hours while working double shifts.

Worst of all was the fact that butties were commonly owners of alehouses or general stores in which the men received their wage. Under the terms of their employment, or various other pretexts, the miners were forced to spend all, or a large proportion, of their earnings in such premises. In some cases, where it was customary for the main wage-earner to try to forget his troubles by a rapid or excessive intake of alcohol, the system could work to the advantage of a household. At least it ensured that the family had something rather than nothing to eat. But more frequently, the system was used simply to exploit the miner and his family. Prices tended to be higher in the butty's shop, and the purchasing power of wages was considerably less than if freedom of spending had been allowed. Often the article wanted was not sold in the butty's shop with the result that other goods had to be purchased, then re-sold usually at a loss to acquire the money necessary to buy the article originally desired.

The blatant cruelty and exploitation of the butty system aroused the hostility not only of the men but also of the majority of owners, one of whom professed that he 'would go a hundred miles to see a butty hung'.[16] Yet both truck and the contracting system endured despite repeated attempts to eliminate them. Truck Acts were passed in 1817 and again in 1831,[17] forbidding the payment of miners' wages in kind, but both lacked adequate powers of enforcement. In the early 1840's the Midland Commission, reporting on the grievances of miners in Worcester, Warwick, Shropshire and Staffordshire, strongly recommended the suppression of truck, the abolition or strict supervision of butties and rigid enforcement of the law against wage payments in 'butty' public houses. Its report, together with that produced at roughly the same time by the Children's Employment Commission, presented a crushing indictment of the butty system. Virtually all mining acts after 1842 prohibited the practice of truck, yet both it and the butty system survived. This can be attributed directly to an unwillingness to condemn the system of contracting *per se* and a failure on the part of the authorities to enforce their own legislation. By the end of the 19th century, the butty system, although in decline, was still common in the Black Country, particularly in Staffordshire.

2 CONDITIONS OF WORK AND PROTECTIVE LEGISLATION BEFORE 1860

Iniquitous though they were, truck and the system of contracting constituted only part of a much larger national problem, the general conditions under which men, women and children worked in the mines. By directing legislation in the early 19th century at the practice of truck, Parliament was in fact only scratching the surface of the injustices and inefficiencies prevalent in the operation of the industry. In large measure, this reflected not so much wilful neglect as ignorance of the real nature of working conditions in the collieries. The Sunderland Society, formed in 1813, brought the issue of underground safety to public attention, but thought that it had achieved its aims once Davy had produced his safety lamp. The select committees of the Lords and Commons, reporting in 1830, queried the efficacy of the lamp but were concerned rather with the economics of the coal trade than with the question of safety. Nonetheless, the evidence which they gathered on the use of the lamp and frequency of explosions prompted the appointment in 1835 of a further *House of Commons Select Committee on the Nature of Fatal Accidents in the Mines.* Apart from vindicating the principle of the safety lamp, the Committee's findings were non-committal. The issue of government inspection of mines was not even discussed and it was thought that physical mining conditions varied too widely to permit the drawing-up of safety rules of general applicability.

It was, therefore, left to individuals such as Tremenheere and Lord Ashley and unofficial *ad hoc* groups to convince Parliament that legislation was necessary to protect the welfare of those working in the mines.[18] One such group, the South Shields Committee, set up at the end of the 1830's, had a pervasive effect on attitudes to technical and safety issues. It urged compulsory registration of the plans of mines, the creation of a system of government inspection and the prevention by law of employment below ground of women and children.[19] In 1840, mounting pressure to extend to children working in mines the same degree of protection as the Factory Acts conferred on their counterparts in manufacturing, resulted in the appointment of the Children's Employment Commission. The findings of this Royal Commission were to have a salutary effect on public opinion since, for the first time, the nature of working conditions below ground and the flagrant abuses perpetrated in several districts were fully exposed.

It is difficult to ascertain how well-founded or general the evils portrayed by the Commission were. The first Report dealing with mines, published in 1842, was based on surveys and evidence collected by sub-commissioners.[20] Much of this evidence took the form of allegedly verbatim accounts provided by children and young persons working in different mining districts. But if so, the vocabulary and turn of phrase of some of the witnesses, recipients of little or no formal education, was surprisingly advanced. Clearly, the sub-commissioners, if not actually putting words into the mouths of those they interviewed, must nonetheless have edited and rendered intelligible the accounts which they received. A pertinent question is, therefore, how far did such 'interpretation' go? Furthermore, in the context of the 1834 Poor Law Report, criticisms have been made of the Assistant Commissioners who reported on the workings of the Poor Law in the provinces. It has been argued that they were very selective in their coverage and fed back to London the type of evidence which they knew would be favourably received.[21] It may be that similar charges could be made against the sub-commissioners gathering evidence on child employment in the mines. The conditions which they described may have been typical of certain collieries and coalfields rather than of the industry as a whole.[22] Finally, the Commission collected a large amount of evidence on accidents in the different coalfields but failed to relate this to the number of men at risk. In attempting to show that mortality was high, the absolute number of estimated deaths from accidents was presented from incomplete information. Meaningful conclusions cannot, therefore, be drawn from the mortality figures in the Report.[23]

While the reliability of the evidence may be a matter of debate, the significance of the 1842 Report for the future of coalmining can never be diminished. It was a landmark in the development of the industry due to the effect which it had both on the public and on the future conduct of operations below ground.[24] According to the information collected by the sub-commissioners, in most districts children began work underground at the age of 5 or 6 and worked on average a 12-hour shift. In several, the hours of work were even longer. Table 1 below summarises for the most important coal-producing districts details of the employment below ground of women and children.

In total, the Commission found that about 6,000 women and girls were employed above and below ground in all types of mining, 2,350 of them in coal mines. Table 1 shows that by 1840 the employment of women and girls below ground was confined to Wales, Lancashire and Cheshire, Yorkshire and Scotland, although female employment had only recently been abolished in several other districts. In Yorkshire and Scotland, the work required of females was of a particularly brutal nature. They were commonly used to draw coal along in the passages. Where these were narrow, sometimes not more than 18 inches high, boys and girls would crawl on hands and knees, drawing the wagon by means of girdle and chain. The former was tied round the waist and attached to a wagon-chain which passed between the legs as the child crawled along, enabling him or her to 'draw' the coal. In East Scotland, where female employment was most common, woman and girls were used as bearers.[25] This involved removing the coal hewn at the face, carrying it on their backs in unrailed roads, in loads varying between three-quarters to two hundredweights, to the main roads of the mine. Such journeys often covered between 100

Table 1
*Employment of Children and Females Below Ground in Districts
Specified, 1840*

District	Earliest Age (Average) at which Children commenced work below Ground[1]	Employment of Women and Girls below Ground	Average Hours Worked per day by Children[2]
South Staffordshire	7		12
North Staffordshire	13[3]		12
Shropshire	6		12
Warwickshire	6		12
Leicestershire	7		12
Derbyshire	5-6		14
West Riding of Yorkshire (Southern part)	5	X	10-11
Lancashire and Cheshire	5-6	X	12
Cumberland	7		12[4]
South Durham	5		12[4]
North Durham and Northumberland	5		12[4]
East Scotland	5	X	14
West Scotland	8		11-13
North Wales	7		12
South Wales	4	X	12
Forest of Dean	7-8		8-10

SOURCE: *Children's Employment Commission, 1842.*
NOTES:
1. In many districts instances were provided of children starting work in mines at a younger age than that specified here. The figures in the Table were the most common of the 'earliest ages' cited. Large discrepancies exist in the statements of different classes of witnesses. Owners, butties, agents, and managers tended to give higher 'starting' ages than the children themselves, doctors, schoolmasters, magistrates and adults working in the mines. The ages specified in the Table represent, therefore, a balance of the views expressed to sub-commissioners.
2. Large discrepancies exist between the statements of owners and managers on the one hand and children, miners and independent witnesses on the other over hours worked.
3. Employment of children in the potteries prevented them being taken into the mines until a relatively late age.
4. Applies to well-regulated mines: frequently longer hours were worked in others.

to 200 yards, the women monotonously performing this back-breaking task for 12 to 14 hours each day. In more shallow mines, females were commonly used to carry the coal directly from the workings up steep ladders to the surface.

For the first time, the brutal conditions under which these women worked were exposed by the Commission. Witness succeeded witness in testifying before the sub-commissioners to the degradation and misery of those working below ground. Little wonder, therefore, that the Report in 1842 considered it 'revolting to humanity to reflect upon the barbarous and cruel slavery which this degrading labour constitutes.'[26] In other districts girls were used for hurrying or pushing the loaded corves outbye and filling and riddling the coal. The working lives of these girls were little better than those of their counterparts in Scotland. Typical of the conditions which they experienced were those described by Margaret Gomley, aged 9, who worked at the Waterhouse, Lindley pit near Huddersfield. Since it so accurately reflects so much of the evidence given to the sub-commissioners her statement is given in full:

> I have been at work in the pit thrusting corves above a year; come in in the morning sometimes at seven o'clock, sometimes at half-past seven, and I go sometimes home at six o'clock, sometimes at seven when I do overwork. I get my breakfast of porridge before I come, and bring a piece of muffin, which I eat on coming to pit; I get my dinner at 12 o'clock, which is a dry muffin, and sometimes butter on, but have no time allowed to stop to eat it, I eat it while I am thrusting the load; I get no tea, but get some supper when I get home and then go to bed when I have washed me; and am very tired . . . They flog us down in the pit . . . Thomas Copeland flogs me more than once in a day, which makes me cry. There are two other girls working with me, and there was four, but one left because she had the bellyache. I am poorly myself sometimes with bellyache, and sometimes a headache.[27]

The Commission expressed concern not only for the physical but also for the moral welfare of women and girls working below ground. Often females worked naked to the waist in close proximity to the men. In Scotland, girls commonly worked with their fathers but were also frequently 'rented out' to work with individual miners as hurriers or drawers. The moral dangers of this practice require no elaboration. The very young age at which children were taken down the mine can, in some districts, be attributed to the policy of restricting the day's work. Under this system, each individual was limited to the production of a fixed amount of coal per day. But in Scotland and South Wales, a parent, by taking a child into the mine, was entitled to earn more than if he worked alone. Hence instances were given to the sub-commissioners of children aged 3 and 4 being taken below ground, even though they were unable to perform any type of work whatever. It was in South Wales that the presence underground of children of very young age, virtually infants, was most common. Typical was the account given by William Richards, aged 7½, who worked at the Buttery Hatch Colliery in South Wales: 'I have been down about three years. When I first went down I couldn't keep my eyes open—I don't fall asleep now; I smokes my pipe'.[28]

Although conditions underground and long hours of work were bad enough it was principally the type of work which the children had to undertake that shocked the nation. They were used as pitchers, slack-boys and to drive the horses, but the most common job of the very young was to act as trapper. This menial task involved simply opening and shutting a door in the underground road when horses and men required to pass through. No strenuous effort was needed with the result that trappers were usually the youngest in the mine. Yet their job carried immense responsibility since it was vital for the ventilation of the pit that doors be kept closed to prevent the air-current from the downcast shaft escaping. By the nature of the work, too, the trapper had to descend the mine with the first and ascend with the last of the workers. Hence, the youngest children in the colliery were forced to work the longest hours. The monotony of the job, sitting in the dark for hours on end, simply opening and shutting the air-door when required, almost defies imagination. Indeed, had it not been for the passing of the horses and wagons, the work would have been 'equal to solitary confinement of the worst order'.[29] In the winter months, lads working the doors had the chance of seeing daylight only at the weekends. John Saville, aged seven, working at the Soap pit, Sheffield, told the sub-commissioners, 'I stand and open and shut the door; I'm generally in the dark, and sit me down against the door; I stop 12 hours in the pit; I never see daylight now except on Sundays; I fell asleep one day and a corve ran over my leg . . .'[30] Life was particularly hard for young apprentices who worked for butties. Many were paupers and were treated virtually as slaves, being subjected to indignities and various forms of cruelty until they were able to fend for themselves.

The 1842 Mines Act[31] which attempted to correct the worst of these abuses was important not because it brought immediate relief to exploited members of the work-force but because of its long-term implications. The central feature of the Act was that it embodied the principle of State intervention. Since the impetus for reform would not come from the industry itself, conditions governing safety, employment and the right of inspection had to be imposed by the State. In view of the evidence gathered by the Children's Employment Commission, the Act was in fact a moderate measure. It prohibited the employment below ground of women and girls, and boys were forbidden to descend the pit if less than ten years of age. Proprietors of mines and butties were not permitted to pay wages in public houses; the person in charge of a winding engine should not be less than 15 years of age; and finally, the need for government inspection was accepted. Although more might have been expected, particularly a higher age-limit for boys descending the mine, important points of principle had been conceded. But in the years which followed both the letter and spirit of the law were broken on an extensive scale. Many women in Scotland resented the fact that they were prevented from working underground, especially as little alternative employment usually existed. Hence in several mines, they continued to go down dressed and disguised as men.[32] More than ten years after the Act had been passed women were still to be found working below ground in Scotland and South Wales; boys under ten were still descending mines in South Wales, Staffordshire and Yorkshire; and wages continued to be paid in public houses or adjoining buildings. Moreover, the Mines Inspector appointed under the Act was far from satisfied with the powers conferred upon him, considering that they were too limited even to justify the title 'inspector of mines'.[33]

Despite these shortcomings, the reports produced by the inspector,[34] together with investigations into underground accidents by men like Faraday, Lyell and Playfair, exerted growing pressure on the Government to accept a larger measure of responsibility for the operation of the mines. Greater safety below ground became the over-riding issue and the Mines Acts of 1850 and 1855,[35] both designed as five-year measures, reflected the determination to minimise as far as possible the risk of accidents. The former consolidated the right of the State to intervene in the interests of safety by making provision for an increased number of mines inspectors (see section 4) and by stipulating that the plans of mines had to be produced on demand if required by these inspectors. Although only four posts (raised to six in 1852) were created additional to that provided for under the 1842 Act, the first reports of these 'safety' inspectors further increased the demand for stronger precautionary measures. They provided the first authoritative statistics of accidents in mines, showing these to be considerably higher than previously envisaged. The 1855 Act resulted, therefore, from the findings of a House of Commons' Select Committee,[36] established the year before, to investigate the circumstances of these accidents. The Act made a fundamental contribution by establishing a safety standard to be maintained by observing seven 'General Rules' applicable to all coal mines in the country. In addition, each *individual* colliery had to enforce its own code of 'Special Rules', devised in collaboration with the Home Office, and appropriate to its particular physical characteristics.

The legislation of the 1850's provided convincing testimony that the era of *laissez-faire* in coalmining was at an end. There was a much better understanding of the difficulties encountered by the individual miner and real efforts had been made since the start of the century to minimise the hazards of his work. Important principles had been established and there now existed rules which specified how each mine should be operated. Indeed, to the impartial observer, the conduct of the industry in the 1850's must have seemed light years away from that prevailing around 1800. Yet the miner was still regarded with some distaste by the rest of the community. Even in 1855, Tremenheere allegedly found great difficulty in finding men in any mining district 'raised in any degree above gross ignorance and capable of the lowest employment of trusts'.[37] Despite a growing concern for his welfare by the State, the occupational status of the miner had shown little, if any, improvement.

3 PATERNALISM AND CONCESSIONS

It would be quite wrong to suppose that for all those engaged in coalmining, adults as well as children, work was an unending round of drudgery, despondency and pain. The conditions which the individual miner experienced depended very much on the benevolence or otherwise of the mine-owner. Until the early decades of the 19th century, many of the important employers were landowners of substance or members of the aristocracy[38] and practised a form of benign paternalism. In both the 18th and 19th centuries, there is ample evidence of the care taken by many landowners of their colliery workers. In Scotland, a clear majority of lairds accepted that employing labour also implied shouldering responsibility for the weak and aged: that, indeed, this 'was part of the warp and woof of the social fabric'.[39] Much the same was true of other mining areas, particularly the Northern Coalfield and Yorkshire. Such paternalism shielded the worker from direct exposure to market forces. John Buddle indicated before the Select Committee of the House of Lords in 1830 that the humanity of many owners went unrecognised and unheeded. Accidents were inevitable in coalmining and owners in his experience did their best to take care of, and compensate, those injured or left as dependents due to the death of the main bread-winner. Jobs were always found for the injured, and widows were invariably granted a house and fuel for as long as they lived. Children were also provided with employment at 'advanced wages' in consideration of the loss of their father and/or brothers. Whether greater efforts might not have been made to prevent such accidents from occurring in the first place is a matter which might be pondered. At all events, Buddle was convinced that 'the coal owners, though their charity does not appear publicly, yet to a very great extent in the way of giving extra wages, or certain work to cripples, finding houses for widows, and so

133

on, they do charity to a much greater extent than they are even themselves aware of.'[40] In the North of England, one of the principal forms which this 'charity' took was the payment of 'smart money'. This practice, prevalent throughout Northumberland and Durham, consisted of a daily payment and free medical care to those adults and children injured or rendered idle due to colliery accidents.[41] It also served as an effective form of discipline since owners could always manipulate or withhold these and other types of charity payment.

In the early 19th century, 'smart money' varied between two and four pence per day in the North. By the 1850's, adults were paid ten and children five pence per day and this rate persisted throughout the 19th century. The practice in other districts varied widely. Paternalistic employers like the Lords Middleton in Nottinghamshire and Fitzwilliam in Yorkshire paid 'smart money', although their collieries were probably exceptional in this respect. In South Staffordshire the system was more widespread with employers contributing 6/- per week in 1843 and a further 6/- coming from the men's fund. Funds to which the men contributed became increasingly common by mid-19th century. In the North, a contributory scheme had been suggested as early as 1810 and came into operation a few years later. Its main purpose was to provide an increased allowance for disability over and above the usual 'smart money'.[42] In virtually all districts employers organised pit clubs to encourage insurance against injury or death. Both they and their employees contributed but the inadequacy of this type of insurance fund caused owners to abandon their interest and leave the provision of relief to other agencies (see section 5 below). Instead, owners in certain districts preferred to rely on the distribution of more direct and substantial benefits. In the Northern Coalfield it was customary for employers to provide the majority of married men with a house and fuel. For instance, at the beginning of the 19th century married men on the Tyne received 8 to 10 cartloads of coal per year and a cottage towards which they paid a contribution of 3d. per week.[43] Coal allowances became standard in virtually all districts, some owners, as those on the Tyne, initially making a token charge for this concession. But in the Northern Coalfield during the 19th century the practice rapidly developed of making available both fuel and miners' cottages free of charge. Towards the end of the century the coal allowance was valued at between 1/- to 1/6d. per week and the provision of cottages for married men at 2/-d. per week.[44]

As noted earlier, efforts were also made by paternalistic owners in certain districts to provide facilities for the education of miners' children. In general, the educational standards of children in the mining communities remained deplorably low, receiving no systematic thought or investigation before the 1840's.

Tremenheere, in his capacity as mines inspector, was one of the first to expose the lamentably poor facilities provided for the education both of adults and children employed in mining. Little was achieved until the Mines Act of 1860 at last stipulated that boys aged between 10 and 12 could only be employed underground if they possessed a certificate of ability to read and write. But even after that date the majority of owners believed that 'to be a skilled collier, a boy must begin not later than 12 years of age'.[45] Hence, while the more enlightened employers might try to raise the standards of literacy, their efforts were swamped by the general lack of facilities, inability and unwillingness of a large part of the mining community to learn, and the reluctance of most owners to allow time for children over ten years of age to attend school.

By the middle of the 19th century, landed coalowners were steadily declining in number and influence. Many had put the working of their minerals into the hands of professional coal- and iron-masters.[46] Others made way for new groups of self-made coalowners and later for joint stock companies which could more readily provide the capital required to mine at increasing depths. With the decline of paternalism the miners lost a safeguard which in several areas had been important in alleviating the harsh conditions under which they worked. But by that time, they had other forms of defence. The State was more fully conversant with the abuses perpetrated in the industry and a start had been made through legislative action to secure better and safer mining conditions. Moreover, through their own union organisations, the men could exert a growing influence after 1850 on standards of safety both above and below ground.

4 GOVERNMENT INSPECTION AND MINING LAW FROM 1860

'The Committee believes it may affirm that every witness, without exception, expressed an opinion more or less favourable to the establishment of Government inspection.' The unanimity of those giving evidence before the House of Lords' Select Committee on Accidents in 1849 paved the way for increased government supervision of the coal mines. Following the Committee's report, the calibre of inspectors appointed under the Mines Acts of 1850 and 1855 was very different from that of the original inspector, H. S. Tremenheere. Essentially, the new inspectors had to be practical engineers with at least seven years' service as colliery managers: they had also to be sufficiently trained, and educated, to pass an examination in mining science. Rigorous standards were therefore required of potential inspectors largely because of the steady expansion in the number of General and Special Rules governing colliery operation after 1850. The duties and responsibilities of inspectors increased more or less in line with the number of regulations. Moreover the specification of these duties was re-designed and re-stated in successive Mines Acts, with the result that the power of government inspectors was constantly a topical issue, pervading all others in coalmining.

Initially inspectors could enter a mine only by invitation or once a fatal accident had occurred. This arrangement was favoured by inspectors themselves since to make random or surprise visits to mines would greatly increase the work-load and require a considerable increase in their numbers. Even more important, a greater frequency of visits and the right to go underground would mean that their role was virtually equivalent to that of viewer. There would be, it was alleged, an undesirable shifting of responsibility for the safety and proper conduct of mines from colliery owners and managers to the State, in the form of government officials. The manager's job was to manage and his should be the responsibility for maintaining safety standards and proper maintenance of the pit. He should not be able to rely on the opinions of government inspectors and use these as evidence in mitigation if things went wrong. Acceptance of this view meant that first and foremost the inspector was an adviser. He could be called, usually after an accident had happened, to record, report and offer advice. More than that, he had an educational function in that the annual reports from 1851 not only listed casualties but also communicated information and offered suggestions for accident-prevention to colliery managers. Not surprisingly, perhaps, this rather limited role was favoured by the great majority of owners who wanted as little interference as possible in the running of their collieries.[47]

Valuable though they were, the services provided by the inspectors were regarded, particularly by the work-force, as peripheral to the proper task of mines inspection. By confining themselves to visiting mines once accidents had occurred or when dangers were reported to them, inspectors were, in a sense, 'locking the stable door after the horse had bolted'. More spontaneous and searching visits were necessary to further the objective of accident-prevention. As it was, inspectors tended to emphasise rather their 'recording' role: to outline the causes of accidents once they had happened and list the casualties. Those in the best position to observe the deficiencies of mines inspection were, of course, the miners themselves. Their criticisms were succinctly put before the Select Committee of the House of Commons established in 1865 to consider the operation of the Acts for the regulation and inspection of mines. As one miner from Staffordshire pointed out,

'If he [the inspector] came down and examined the workings, and did his duty, I think he would see that the place was properly ventilated, and would see if any place was short of props; so that *he should see the pits before the accidents happened, and prevent their happening.*[48]

The miners also rightly complained of the infrequency of the inspectors' visits. The same witness testified that he had worked in the pits for 21 years and never seen an inspector in his life[49] and Joseph Dickinson, inspector of the district which included Staffordshire, conceded that, 'it is fully possible . . . that a pit should exist without being inspected for several years'[50] Nonetheless, he managed to persuade the Committee of the greater disadvantages attached to more frequent and random visits. In one area at least the miners enjoyed some success. The 1860 Coal Mines Regulation and Inspection Act[51] not only increased the number of General Rules from 8 to 15 but also accepted that the miners should be able to appoint their own 'justice man', or checkweighman, to weigh the coal at the pithead. Payment by measure had caused ill-feeling and strikes, particularly since the size of coal trucks to be filled was far from uniform. Although measuring the coal was not forbidden under the 1860 Act, the Government had gone some way towards removing an injustice. In fact, the men had achieved more than simply the right to weigh the coal. By creating checkweighmen, the Act was at the same time providing the men with leaders, thereby strengthening developing union organisation. For many subsequent mining leaders, the post of checkweighman was the initial step which led to high office.[52]

The most fundamental legislation in the second half of the 19th century was the 1872 Coal Mines Regulation Act[53] It removed several of the anomalies which had caused difficulties and dissent in the industry. Payment for the quantity of coal produced was henceforth to be based on weight rather than measure, except in special circumstances. The Mines Inspectorate was strengthened by an agreement to allow periodic workmen's inspections and by the appointment, shortly after the Act was passed, of a number of sub-inspectors. The number of General Rules was increased to 31, including the stipulation that each mine manager must in future hold a certificate of competency. Above all, the Act reflected the increased strength and activity of miners' unions. A Miners' Petition had been submitted to the House of Commons in 1865 and considered by the Select Committee which reported two years later[54] The 1872 Act took account of several of the points raised in the Petition, notably those dealing with checkweighing, the competency of mine management and the need to strengthen safety legislation.[55] In essence, it codified and stabilised mining law for the next fifteen years. After 1872, legislation was of a different character, concerning itself rather with technical detail and the revision of safety standards which had been drawn up in previous years.

The Coal Mines Regulation Acts of 1887 and 1896[56] simply reinforced the legislation which had gone before. The former established that the minimum age of boys working underground must be twelve years, later raised in 1900 to thirteen; introduced eight new General Rules; and extended the provisions governing checkweighing and the certification of colliery managers. The latter took account of the 1891 Royal Commission's findings on the effects of coal dust in the workings and empowered the Secretary of State to impose stringent safeguards against the possibility of underground explosions. The weight and increasing complexity of this mining legislation, which had grown *pari passu* with the development of the coal industry, had obvious implications for mines inspection. The number of inspectors had risen from 4 in 1850 to 38 in 1906 but the Royal Commission on Mines established in that year considered that the latter total was still too small.[57] By the turn of the century spontaneous visiting was common and accounted for the bulk of the inspectors' work. Inspection was undertaken 'by sample', a particular section of the mine being examined and accepted as representative of the whole. Although there were evident dangers in this policy, these were minimised by making such visits without giving prior warning to the management and undertaking at least one inspection underground per mine each year. In practice, visits were usually more frequent as the following statistics provided by the Commission show:

No. of Mines	No. of Underground Inspections	Average per Mine	No. of Other Inspections	Total No. of Inspections	Average per Mine
3,245	5,624	1.73	2,531	8,155	2.51

While the number of visits was regarded as adequate, the Commission was concerned lest, in future, the increasing volume of clerical work which the inspectors had to undertake might reduce the amount of time they could spend 'in the field'. It therefore argued for a rationalisation of inspection divisions and an increase in the staff of the inspectorate.

The Coal Mines Regulation Act of 1908 (Eight-Hour Day Act) and Mines Act of 1911[58] represented the culmination of a process of

State involvement within the industry that had started some 60 years earlier. By 1911, the number of inspectors had risen to 83, the increase since 1850 reflecting the extent to which State intervention in matters such as safety and health had developed. The 127 sections included within the 1911 Act, revising and reinforcing earlier legislation, may also be regarded as indicative of the State's involvement. These sections brought the State into virtually every aspect of colliery operation and ensured that there were few surviving areas of inefficiency and danger.

5 ACCIDENTS AND MORTALITY RATES

The 1906 Royal Commission on Mines was in no doubt that the relatively rapid fall in the death rate per 1,000 persons employed underground during the second half of the 19th century could largely be attributed to government inspection and the general improvement in mining conditions. Before mid-century, details and statistics of accidents, fatal or otherwise, are far from comprehensive. Information collected from contemporary sources and newspaper accounts generally relate only to major disasters, invariably caused by explosions. But it is likely that the number of deaths resulting from minor accidents, involving small groups or individuals was almost as great, in total, as that from major explosions.[59] These lesser accidents received little publicity and the toll of lives which they took remains uncertain. It is probable that the greatest success in reducing mortality rates occurred in the North-East from the 1840's. By reducing the dangers of mine gas a substantial fall in the death-rate from explosions was achieved in the district. (See Chapter 3, section 5 above). As a result, by about 1850, the mortality rate per 1,000 employed per annum in Northumberland, Durham and Cumberland, at 3.5, was significantly below the national average of between 4.5 and 5.0. How many of the other coalfields achieved substantial improvements between 1800 and 1850 is not clear. Certainly by the latter date, the rate of mortality was still extremely high in the Black Country (between 6.0 and 7.0) largely due to the frequency of serious roof-falls, and relatively high in South Wales (between 4.3 and 6.8).

The first reliable statistics of deaths from accidents were provided by the inspectors' reports in the early 1850's. Table 2 shows the fall in mortality rates above and below ground in Britain from that period.

The rapid decline in death rate shown in Table 2 convinced the authorities that greater supervision of the collieries, together with safety legislation, were having the desired effect. The Table shows that the greatest part of the overall decline resulted from the fall in mortality rates underground. However, it is not possible on the basis of aggregate statistics to distinguish precisely those areas below ground

Table 2

*Death Rate from Accidents per 1,000 Persons Employed in the Coal Mines
During Periods Specified, 1851/55-1903/12*

Annual Average	Underground	Above Ground	All Accidents
1851-55	5.15	1.01	4.30
1861-65	3.79	1.11	3.24
1873-82	2.57	.92	2.24
1883-92	2.01	.96	1.81
1893-1902	1.52	.83	1.39
1903-12	1.46	.78	1.33

SOURCES:

Second Report of the Royal Commission on Mines, Cd. 4820, 1909; *Mines and Quarries, General Report with Statistics for 1913 by the Chief Inspector of Mines,* Part 1, Divisional Statistics, Cd. 7452, 1914.

where the largest improvements were effected. By disaggregating further, it is clear that success was mainly due to the continued reduction in fatalities resulting from explosions of firedamp and coal dust. This was made possible by improvements in ventilation, safety lamps and shot-firing which helped to prevent explosions occurring in the first place. But to these must be added a much better understanding of how to limit the effects of an explosion once it had started. Of utmost importance was a recognition of the dangers inherent in coal dust lying thickly in the workings. Watering the roadways was of some assistance in preventing the dust from carrying the explosion along but the principal breakthrough came with the introduction of stone dusting, described in Chapter 5, section 1 above.

On the other hand, deaths due to falls of roof and sides remained extremely high, reflecting a lack of systematic timbering in mines. In the decade 1903-12, the total number of deaths caused by underground accidents amounted to 11,296. Of this total, more than 50% was caused by falls of roof and sides, 30% by miscellaneous accidents, 12% by explosions of firedamp or coal dust, and over 7% by shaft accidents. By the first world war, falls of ground were clearly the miners' worst enemy. At the same time, miscellaneous accidents remained a persistent cause of deaths below ground. These resulted largely from the methods employed to convey coal from the face to the bottom of the shaft. Shifting large amounts of mineral by means of ways fitted with ropes and chains actuated by steam or compressed air, and later by electric power, was a constant source of danger. With the trams running at speeds of about 10 m.p.h., accidents were inevitable due to badly laid rails, weak couplings or because the roads were not wide enough for men to stand clear should anything happen to the trams. While it is true, therefore, that the death-rate in the mines had been notably reduced between the 1850's and 1914, there was still little room for complacency. In absolute terms, deaths from accidents had risen from an annual average of over 1,000 in the 1870's to over 1,100 in the decade preceding the 1914-18 war. Moreover, the number of fatal accidents in the pits still compared unfavourably with that in other occupations. The position is summarised in Table 3.

Table 3

Annual Death Rates from Accidents per 1,000 Living at Each Age-Period Coalmining and All Other Occupations, 1849-53 — 1910-12

Annual Average	Category	Age Group				
		15-25	25-35	35-45	45-55	55-65
1849-53	All Occupied Males	0.9	1.0	1.2	1.4	1.6
	Coalminers	5.7	5.3	6.2	6.9	5.9
1910-12	Occupied and Retired Males	0.4	0.5	0.6	0.8	1.1
	Occupied and Retired Coalminers	1.3	1.2	1.6	1.9	2.3

SOURCE:
J. S. Haldane, 'Health and Safety in British Coal Mines', in Mining Association of Great Britain, *Historical Review of Coal Mining.*

The dangers of coalmining as an occupation can be seen from Table 3. In mid-century, the accident death rate was between four and five times as high as that of other occupations. Over the 60 years covered by the Table, the decline in mortality rates was much more marked in coalmining than in other jobs. Yet the fact still remained that by the first world war, in every age-group, the accident death rate of colliery workers was more than double that of other males. Coalmining was still a high-risk occupation despite the technical improvements accomplished since the 1850's and the increase in government concern and supervision of the industry. Moreover, accident statistics take no account of other hazards associated with mining. A high incidence of lung disease, chest complaints and physical deformities were a natural corollary of working beneath the ground. Nor were miners and their families adequately covered in the second half of the 19th century against the distress caused by industrial accidents. They could call on a growing number of sources for relief, including assistance offered by the Poor Law, the courts,[60] the charitable public, benevolent employers and their own accident insurance funds. Despite such a wide range of agencies offering compensation, relief was far from adequate. It has been shown that the very multiplicity of sources supplying aid tended to produce inconsistency and inefficiency and that even the mining unions themselves failed to maintain payment of the 'friendly benefits' they had undertaken to provide.[61]

Some perspective on safety in the British industry can be obtained by comparing mortality rates in the principal coal-producing countries of the world. Data are provided in Table 4 on the incidence of fatality above and below ground in the generation before the first world war.

Table 4

Death-Rate From Accidents per 1,000 Employed Above and Below Ground in Leading Coal-Producing Countries, 1896-1912

Annual Average	UK	USA	Germany	France	Belgium
1896-1900	1.32	2.85	2.38[1]	1.23	1.11
1901-05	1.29	3.24	2.02	1.09	1.01[2]
1906-10	1.39	3.68	2.23	2.29[3]	0.99
1911-12	1.17	3.41	2.26	1.29	1.07

SOURCE:
Gibson, op. cit.
NOTES:
1. Relates to 1897-1900.
2. Relates to 1902-1905.
3. Distorted by unusually high death rate in 1906.

The fatality rate was lowest in Belgium where, as Tremenheere had reported in the 1840's, government supervision of the collieries had been established at an early stage and careful inspections had become normal practice long before they were accepted in Britain.[62] The British figures were roughly similar to those of France and compared favourably with those of Germany and the USA. Although high relative to other occupations, the over-riding impression is that considerable improvement had taken place in Britain's accident mortality rates. The higher number of accidents and fatalities shown by the early inspectors' reports in the 1850's had shocked the nation. It had given impetus to more thorough colliery inspection and an increase in the number of regulations governing underground operations. In consequence the greatest advances had been precisely in those parts of the industry most affected by good inspection. Between the 1870's and 1913, deaths from explosions and shaft accidents had been substantially reduced. On the other hand, deaths had increased in those areas where responsibility lay largely with the men themselves. These included accidents occasioned by falling roof and sides and careless use of machinery and equipment.

6   WAGES AND EMPLOYMENT

Definitive statements about the size and movements of miners' wages are not possible for the 18th century and most of the 19th, due to the scattered nature of the available evidence. For the most part, the information which does exist relates only to limited periods and particular districts or colliery undertakings. The task of deriving suitable wage data is made more difficult since in areas like the Midlands, miners were paid collectively in the 18th century while in other coalfields, payment was made per score of corves or per yard of level driven underground. Not only did the definition of corf-size vary widely from one district to the next but the rate paid per yard depended on the geological conditions prevailing. A comparison of wage rates between different collieries therefore reveals very little about the *real* reward for effort. Moreover, in the 19th century further difficulties are encountered in the shape of payments in kind and the custom of allowing free, or low-price coal, to those engaged in the industry. On the basis of contemporary estimates and the account-books of collieries in different parts of the country, there are plausible grounds for believing that despite wide fluctuations over time the real wages of miners rose considerably during the course of the 18th century. Around 1700 Nef has estimated that the average weekly wage of the collier in England varied between 4/- and 6/-,[63] but since mining was everywhere a seasonal occupation only between 20 and 30 weeks per year were worked. Annual earnings, therefore, amounted to between £5 and £7 which, with bounties and other bonuses, would have risen to £6-£8. In Scotland hewers earned on average between 7/- and 8/- per week, or £8 to £10 per year. Bonuses and other extras were rather higher in this district so that actual earnings must have been some £10 to £12. However, the wage paid to a hewer in Scotland was also regarded as remuneration for the bearers, commonly his wife or children, who worked with him. In fact, therefore, the hewer's wage covered an average of three people involved in mining the coal.

From a daily rate in the early 18th century of some 12 to 14 pence per day in the North of England and 14d. per day in Scotland, the average rose by mid-century to between 16 and 18d. per day, with rates of 24d. not unusual[64] Since the cost of living was falling over the period, the miner experienced an increase in his real wage. This is indicated in Table 5 below. The figures must be used with great caution in view of the inadequacy of the wage data, the neglect of differences over time in the length of the working-day and the narrow range of goods upon which the cost of living index is based. Moreover, the statistics relate only to skilled men in the East Midlands where rates were probably rather higher than in the rest of England. In 1805, for instance, overmen in the northern collieries of Pensher and North Rainton were, according to John Buddle, earning respectively 12/- and 14/- per week. Rolley drivers were receiving at most 2/- per day.[65] The magnitudes expressed in Table 5 cannot, therefore, be taken as representative of the industry as a whole and should be regarded as simply indicating the long-term trend.

Table 5

Average Day-Wage of Skilled Colliers in the East Midlands

	Day-Rate		Cost of Living Index	Real Wage Index
	s.	d.	(1451-75=100)	(1914=100)
C.1550	0	6	200	29
C. 1650	1	0	700	17
C. 1750	1	6	600	29
1790	2	6	871	34
1805	4	0	1521	31
1830	3	6	1146	36
1842	3	0	1161	30
1856	4	6	1264	42
1888	5	4	950	65
1914	9	10	1147	100

SOURCE:
A. R. Griffin, *The British Coalmining Industry* (1977), p. 80.

Despite the significant rise in money wages during the late 18th century as a result of war-time labour-scarcity and a substantial increase in the demand for coal for iron-smelting, the cost of living increased even more rapidly. As a result, real wages fell over the early years of the 19th century and tended to stagnate until about 1850. Rapid wage increases in times of good trading would be offset by equally rapid falls in the ensuing downswing of the cycle. Not until the 1850's did miners' real wages rise on to an altogether higher plane.

Necessarily movements in money and real wages before 1850 have to be painted with a fairly broad brush. But the trends noted above are supported by the findings of several contemporary observers. These show that by the end of the 18th century, the collier was better paid than most other types of worker. He was, for instance, better rewarded for his labour in England than either the agricultural worker or the skilled craftsman in textiles and the pottery trades.[66] In Scotland, Adam Smith confirmed that the miners' wage rate was significantly higher than the general rate of free day-labourers,[67] although as noted earlier his wage usually included payment for dependents working with him. But any comparative advantage enjoyed by the colliery worker disappeared during the first half of the 19th century. Although the evidence is fragmentary, it would seem that a slightly higher average money wage in the coal industry was generally offset by the irregularity of mining employment. This conclusion is supported by the fact that the industry failed to attract new recruits in significant numbers before the 1850's despite the notoriously low wages paid in such trades as framework knitting in the East Midlands and handloom weaving in Yorkshire.

Only in the second half of the 19th century with the rapid increase in demand for coal did the miners recover much of the ground lost. Money wages in most districts rapidly expanded from the 1850's, enabling those working in coal to improve their position relative to other employments. The upward drift was by no means smooth and continuous since wages fluctuated widely with the cycle.[68] For instance during the acute coal scarcity of 1871-3, miners' wages rose in most coalfields by more than 50%. It was alleged that this brought many 'novel luxuries within the reach of that laborious class, and even a Committee of the House of Commons had condescended to inquire whether the colliers do really indulge in champagne'.[69] Whether they indulged or not, the miners had little time to become addicted since the whole of the increase in wages was lost in the ensuing slump of 1875 to 1879. Cyclical influences apart, wage fluctuations were inevitable in most districts due to the adoption of sliding scales which involved tying wage rates to the ascertained selling-price of coal (see section 7 below). Several districts did not share in the increased prosperity of the industry until after the 1880's. This was particularly true of the Black Country where a high incidence of short-time working persisted. In 1878-9, the worst years of the Great Depression, miners' real income in this area fell to almost one-quarter of its 1850 level and remained depressed until 1887.[70] Thereafter, in common with the rest of the country, there was a major expansion of money and real wages.

In Britain as a whole, it is estimated that between 1888-1914, hewers employed on piece-work experienced an increase in money wages of 86%, firemen 70%, putters 78%, and underground labourers 88%. Since there was a relatively modest rise in the cost of living between these years, the real gains were not far below these nominal increases.[71] At the same time, output per man in the industry was steadily deteriorating from its high point of 1883. With face mechanisation still in its infancy and regarded with some suspicion by owners, the rapid expansion of demand for coal from the 1880's could only be met by increased inputs of labour. As a result, the industry claimed a growing proportion of the nation's labour force before the first world war. Between 1881 and 1911, coalmining employment doubled at a time when the total occupied male population expanded by less than 50%. The long-term employment position of the industry is shown in Table 6.

Table 6
Employment in Mining and Quarrying, 1851-1911

	Employment (000)	As Prop. of Total Occupied Population (%)
1851	394	4
1881	612	5
1911	1,210	7

SOURCE:
Census Reports, 1851-1911.

The large addition to the labour force after 1881 can be attributed to a more rapid expansion of wages in coalmining than elsewhere in the economy. By the start of the present century, miners' wages once again compared most favourably with those of competing occupations. This was due not only to the influence of market forces but also to institutional pressures in the shape of growing union bargaining strength and the activities of the small group of mining M.P.s at work in Parliament. Workers from other trades were drawn to the industry, mainly to occupy general labouring jobs above and below ground. Employment growth on this scale meant first, an increase in the aggregate wage-bill of the industry and second, an increase in labour's share of total costs per ton produced. As coalmining responded to the rise in demand, capacity began to be stretched. *Ceteris paribus,* labour under these conditions inevitably accounted for a larger proportion of costs per ton. At, or near, full-capacity working, overhead costs tended to fall and the ratio of labour to other costs rose per unit of output.[72] This change in relative costs did not affect all districts in the same way. Some employed much heavier amounts of capital equipment than others. Pressure was, therefore, greatest on those with relatively heavy average overhead costs such as Scotland, Yorkshire and North Midlands to maintain production at as full a level as possible.

Despite deficiencies in cost of production data, it would appear that labour costs amounted to a consistently high proportion of total costs between 1850 and 1914 and that this proportion probably increased during the latter part of the period. As a proportion of the total, labour costs averaged 66.3% between 1875 and 1879, rose to 73.3% in 1899-1903 and remained at, or near, that level until the first world war.[73] In part this increase was due to alterations in working time. There was some overall reduction in hours worked in the period before the first world war but this was not of a substantial nature and in many districts was insufficient seriously to affect production before the Eight-Hour Day Act of 1908.[74] More important in explaining the change in relative costs was the movement towards full-capacity working before 1914. The greater the utilisation of capacity, the higher the proportion of labour to other costs per unit of production. Thus, as noted in Chapter 4, the explanation of comparatively low pit-head prices in Britain was not that labour accounted for a relatively low share of total costs per ton produced. On the contrary, British labour costs loomed higher in total costs than was the case on the Continent. Rather, the greater competitiveness of the industry in Britain was based initially on the rapid growth of output per man. Ironically, the very fact that labour was so readily available, at a price which the industry could afford to pay, reduced the incentive to mechanise and contributed directly to the steady erosion of Britain's comparative advance in productivity from the 1880's.

7 MINING TRADE UNIONISM

As one of the leading industries in the economy, coalmining played a crucial part in shaping the nature of the labour movement in this country. Particularly in the second half of the 19th century, the industry had a decisive influence on the climate of industrial relations. There now exists a wealth of material on the activities and development of organised labour in the coal industry. Most of the geographical and chronological gaps in knowledge have been filled by the publication of regional histories covering the principal coalfields of the country.[75] This section concentrates only on the mainstream of development, emphasising the principal issues which, at national level, demanded the attention of miners and their leaders. In this sense, the organisation of labour in coalmining only 'came of age' in the 1840's since before then disputes and stoppages had been essentially of a local and regional character. Throughout the 18th century, a striking feature of the industry was the impermanency of any form of labour organisation. This was largely due to the overwhelming dominance of employers, the uncertainty of employment for much of the period and the lack of mobility which effectively restricted the communication of new ideas. Rather than lasting 'combinations' of miners, there were only transient strikes aimed at remedying specific grievances. To resolve a particular dispute, men might combine to exert pressure on owners but only on a temporary, *ad hoc,* basis and rarely was there detailed organisation, or planning, behind such action.[76] Frequently in the 18th century, miners' riots were directed against high food prices and stemmed from hunger and physical deprivation rather than issues specific to the coal industry. But 'collective bargaining by riot' was also a traditional and successful method of directly influencing particular employers.[77] Occasionally involving the wrecking of pit-head machinery and the burning of pits, it was an important weapon of trade unionism before the Industrial Revolution. It was not that the men were necessarily hostile to machinery *per se:* rather, through its destruction they could bring pressure to bear on recalcitrant 'bosses'.

Although involving no new principles of policy, the passing of the Combination Acts in 1799 and 1800[78] did reflect the Government's concern for public order at a time of revolution abroad. Yet they were unable to prevent, indeed may have stimulated, the growing sense of solidarity among wage-earners. Nor could they prevent strikes, the miners of Northumberland and Durham conducting their first general strike in 1810 against the owners' proposals to make more severe the conditions of the yearly bond. The strike was crushed, a factor which strengthened the miners' preference for friendly societies, concerned with sickness, old-age and funeral benefits, rather than trade clubs, or unions, with their more openly industrial aims. The latter were more susceptible to prosecution until the repeal of the Combination Acts in 1824. Following repeal, it was reported that, 'combinations have become the mania of almost every class of workmen',[79] but the miners remained largely devoid of permanent organisation during the early decades of the 19th century. They took little part in the agitation during the years of political discontent which followed the Napoleonic Wars or in the Chartist Movement. In general they were concerned with political activity and the aims of Chartism only in times of slump when unemployment was relatively high. Once their jobs had been restored they reverted to the more mundane objectives of trade unionism.[80] Widely scattered mining communities and variations in natural mining conditions acted as deterrents to collective action on a more extensive scale.[81] Moreover, many miners were not strictly wage-labourers but sub-contractors, or partners, in 'butty' gangs. In consequence, the division in other industries between employer and employee was much more blurred in coalmining.

In 1830, the miners dabbled with John Docherty's attempt to form a general union of all workers, the National Association for the Protection of Labour. About 150 unions affiliated, including a delegate conference of miners from Yorkshire, Staffordshire, Lanca-

shire, Cheshire and North Wales. The collapse of this 'grand design'
coincided roughly with the breaking of the miners' strike organised
in the North by 'Tommy' Hepburn.[82] These failures saw miners return
to more cautious, localised attempts to improve conditions. But a
turning point was reached in the 1840's, not as a result of Chartism
but rather of sustained rapid growth in the industry. A number of
county unions had been formed in Durham, Northumberland,
Lancashire, Yorkshire and Staffordshire. These were the prelude to
the creation in 1842 of the Miners' Association of Great Britain and
Northern Ireland, the first attempt to form a national union of miners.
It consisted of a federation of county unions, designed to promote
more concerted action. At the first national conference held in 1843,
200 delegates representing 50,000 members attended. Power quickly
passed into the hands of men from the Northern Coalfield and, under
the leadership of Martin Jude of Newcastle, organisers were appointed
to visit coalfields throughout the country in an effort to win more
support. At the same time, W. P. R. Roberts, the 'miners' attorney-
general', was retained in virtually all trade union cases to fight for
the men's rights in court. This served as a useful platform to solicit
public sympathy and to demonstrate that the courts were scarcely
impartial when dealing with labour issues. The collapse of the
Association not only discredited the ideal of a national union but
showed that the working-class movement as a whole lacked the degree
of solidarity essential for success on a national scale.

In 1844, the Association became involved with the disastrous and
bitter four months' strike of miners in Northumberland and Durham.
From the outset the owners determined to break the strike, called as
a result of wage reductions and stringent bond conditions. Lord
Londonderry, in his capacity both as coalowner and as Lord Lieutenant
of Durham County used all means at his disposal to ensure the men's
defeat, including evicting strikers from their homes and exerting
pressure on traders to refuse food supplies to those engaged in the
conflict. In the event, the downswing of the cycle and the importation
into the North-East of large numbers of non-union men, mainly
from Ireland and Wales, forced the miners to return to work on the
owners' terms. They had to accept the old wage rates, many were
dismissed and evicted from tied cottages and the Mining Association
came to an end. After struggling to survive for a few years, it disintegrated in the general slump of the coal trade in 1847-48.[83]

Positive benefits were achieved in that contract by yearly bond
disappeared in the Northumberland coalfield,[84] being replaced by a
monthly notice, and hours of work were reduced in the East Midlands.
But this was a high price to pay for the collapse of a national union
and the virtual disappearance in the 1840's of county unions. Mining
unionism did not cease to exist but adopted a much less ambitious

form by concentrating essentially on local issues and strengthening itself at lodge level. In the long term, this return to 'grass-roots' was to prove valuable. Colliery lodges became relatively powerful, producing leaders trained in union affairs who were later to assume control of the miners' movement.[85] But it was not until 1858 that a fresh start was made towards the ideal of national organisation. In that year, an effective county union reappeared, the South Yorkshire Miners' Association, and Alexander Macdonald, the controversial mining leader from Scotland called for a national conference, the precursor of the National Association of Coal, Lime and Ironstone Miners of Great Britain (the National Miners' Union). Macdonald believed in legislative regulation of the conditions of labour and that policies of moderation and arbitration could secure for the miners greater benefits than militant opposition to employers, frequent use of the strike-weapon and aggravation of the class war.

Under his auspices, the National Miners' Union (NMU), established in 1863, pressed for Acts of Parliament to secure the true weighing of coal, improved educational facilities, safety regulations and trained management. He could point to the fact that he had already made a significant contribution, along with the South Yorkshire Miners' Association, in having the checkweigher clause inserted into the 1860 Coal Mines Regulation Act (see also section 4 above).[86] However, his policy of moderation did not command universal support. Miners' battles in the 1860's were as fierce as the Northumberland strike of 1844.[87] The use of the lock-out, which had formerly proved a successful weapon for employers, dramatically increased. Indeed, the South Yorkshire owners used it so frequently that one Yorkshire miner complained in 1866 that he had been 'locked-out about 24 months in six years'.[88] With few concessions apparently being achieved, miners in Scotland, South Wales and Lancashire favoured a bolder, more militant policy which offered prospects of quicker gains. These sentiments resulted in the formation of a rival organisation, the Amalgamated Association of Miners, in 1869. Clearly, neither the 'Junta' nor 'New Model' concept of union development were able to gain a predominance in the coal industry. The split almost equally divided the miners' movement since both the NMU and the new Association claimed to represent about 100,000 men.

Macdonald has traditionally been regarded as one of the main driving forces behind mining unionism. In 1871, he was appointed chairman of the new Parliamentary Committee appointed by the Trade Union Congress. A year later, he succeeded in having further reforms in the conduct of mining inserted in the Coal Mines Regulation Act and in 1874, along with Thomas Burt, he entered Parliament. Despite such accomplishments, the extent to which he advanced the miners' cause is questionable. The NMU has been acused of being too concerned with safety in mining and not enough with labour and wage issues. It is also possible that Macdonald's importance has been exaggerated,[89] but at all events it was the NMU with its emphasis on the Parliamentary lobby which proved better able to withstand the vicissitudes of trade depression. The life-span of the rival Amalgamated Association was cut short by the slump of the 1870's.[90] It was swept away in the downward spiral of prices and wages, the last remnants being absorbed by the NMU in 1875. Nor was the latter organisation left in much better a position. Faced with a succession of 'arbitrated' wage-cuts, membership steadily drained away in virtually every coalfield. For instance in South Wales, trade unionism almost ceased to exist for the next 20 years. In a practical form, the NMU continued to survive only in its principal strongholds of the North-East and to a lesser extent in Yorkshire.

The problems confronting mining unionism were not solely due to the fierce cyclical downswings of the Great Depression period. Market forces in the last quarter of the 19th century were certainly inimical to a strong and healthy trade union movement but the difficulties were exacerbated by the existing institutional arrangements for settling disputes. The conciliation movement which developed after 1860 involved the adoption of arbitration, sliding-scales and conciliation boards. The first of these was associated with a Nottingham hosiery manufacturer, A. J. Mundella, who had achieved some local successes with arbitration boards in the Midlands in the 1860's. His efforts to extend the method of arbitration to other trades had an important influence on union leaders and employers in the 1870's. In the early years of the decade, both the NMU and Amalgamated Association successfully demanded that the principles of conciliation and arbitration be adopted in coalmining as a means of settling disputes. In practice this meant that the latter was generally used since compromise was difficult in the context of the 1870's. Few arbitrators, when settling cases submitted in the coal industry, were influenced by such issues as the subsistence level of miners or the level of profits being made in the industry. Indeed, profits were regarded as none of the workman's concern. Rather, the criterion most frequently adopted was a somewhat indeterminate notion of 'the state of trade'. Employers maintained that short-run changes in trading conditions largely governed the industry's capacity to pay wages: further, that in order to determine the state of trade, selling-price was the most reliable and useful indicator.

These arguments found a measure of support among union leaders of the North-East in the several arbitration cases settled before 1875-6.[91] But this emphasis on selling-price was to prove disastrous for the work-force. Since the chief characteristic of the Great Depression was the long-term fall in prices arbitrators, using prices as the principal indication of the state of trade, had little option but to hand down wage-reductions. Between 1873 and 1896, the awards made in the industry show a close correspondence to the trend of average industrial prices and short-run changes in the level of economic activity. Of the 21 wage arbitration awards in coalmining between these years, 19 involved wage-reductions and two no change. In the subsequent 1897 to 1914 period, there were 12 reductions, four no change and two cases of wage-advances.[92] Not surprisingly, most union leaders rapidly lost confidence in arbitration as a means of wage-fixing.

Yet in certain coalfields, notably Durham, union leaders were convinced that the practice of tying wages to selling-prices was the most equitable form of wage determination. Selling-price sliding-scales had been accepted as a means of regulating wage rates in South Staffordshire in 1874, South Wales in the following year and Durham in 1877. However, not until 1879 were they commonly adopted in other coalfields, and then only because unionism was weak and full-scale conflicts had to be avoided.[93] More than any other issue, the operation of these sliding-scales was responsible for the cleavage which developed within mining unionism. While leaders of the Northumberland and Durham miners were readily converted to the principle of a sliding-scale, miners in other districts insisted that wages should be regarded as a first charge on the industry. The gulf between the two sides was widened further by the continued objections of Northern leaders to the Eight-Hour Day principle.[94] Although not opposed in principle to a general reduction in the length of the working-day,[95] they alleged that legal regulation would create particular difficulties in the Northern Coalfield. For some time, hewers, fillers, and other skilled workers in the North had worked fewer than eight hours bank to bank, while hauliers and boys (transit hands) had worked on average a 10- to 11-hour shift. Most mines in Durham operated a system of two separate shifts of hewers per day, served by one shift of transit hands. At 'night-shift' pits, three shifts of hewers were worked with two of transit hands. To introduce a single-shift system by legislative action would reduce the hours of transit hands but increase those of hewers.[96] If double shifts of men and boys, of a uniform eight hours each, were introduced there might be an insufficient number of boys to work with the hewers.[97] Thus delays would be caused in moving coal from the workings, face-work would be disorganised and the earning-capacity of hewers adversely affected.

The NMU, based largely on Northumberland and Durham, found itself, therefore, increasingly out of touch with the rest of the labour movement in the coal industry. In contrast, the employers were united in their support of the sliding-scale principle. As noted in section 6, labour costs formed such a high proportion of total costs that they welcomed the opportunity given them by the sliding-scale to make frequent wage adjustments without risk of a dispute. During the Great Depression of 1873 to 1896, the mechanism provided employers with precisely the wage flexibility they wanted in their efforts to keep costs down and improve their competitive position. However, in 1881 miners in Yorkshire terminated their sliding-scale agreement[98] and were quickly followed by their counterparts in Lancashire, the Midlands and Scotland. These districts maintained that rather than tie wages to the ascertained selling-price of coal, a fairer return would be obtained if miners practised a common policy of output-regulation. Moreover, more militant industrial action was required than the NMU appeared capable of providing, particularly in the pursuit of minimum wage and eight-hour day legislation.

Accordingly with the support of most districts, the Miners' Federation of Great Britain (MFGB) was formed in 1888, based largely on outright opposition to the sliding-scale principle. Miners in Northumberland and Durham, most of those in South Wales and members of the Mid- and West-Lothian Miners' Association remained outside the new federation. The NMU survived but its conservative policies seemed increasingly out of place in an age of more militant, 'new' unionism which developed in 1889-90. Despite the rapid expansion of this so-called 'new unionism', the old unions retained in numerical terms by far the greatest strength.[99] Yet, the NMU, as one of the 'older' unions, failed to reflect the aspirations and new militancy of labour in coalmining. It was seriously weakened in 1899 when miners in South Wales joined the Miners' Federation[100] and finally disintegrated in 1908 with the transfer of the Northumberland and Durham County Associations to the Federation.[101] Although not in the mainstream of the 'new' unionism developing in the 1880's, the MFGB was a more militant organisation than most of its predecessors in the coal industry and in this sense was linked to the new wave of aggressive general unions.[102] It did not interfere with the financial independence or internal administration of its constituent bodies but did effectively centralise their industrial and Parliamentary policies.

Its creation coincided with a period of rapid growth in coalmining. As employment steadily expanded, so too did membership of the Federation, from a mere 38,000 in 1888 to approximately 360,000 by the turn of the century and to almost 900,000 by 1920. In 1893, the Labour Department of the Board of Trade was created specifically to collect and publish labour statistics.[103] Figures from that year show that union membership remained significantly higher in mining and quarrying than in any other individual industry before 1914. Moreover, the industry accounted for a high proportion of the total working-days lost through disputes in UK industry. Between 1893 and 1900, an average of 60% of the total number of working days lost in industry can be attributed to coal mining, this falling to 53% between 1901 and 1913.[104] These relatively high figures give the impression of an industry almost continuously at war. In fact, they can largely be explained by three major stoppages: the 1898 strike by miners in South Wales when owners refused to concede the principle of a minimum wage[105] and the lengthy national stoppages of 1893 and 1912.

In the latter two cases, the MFGB played a full part. The 1893 strike was called when the employers insisted on considerable wage-reductions in view of rapidly falling selling-prices. It lasted for four months but the men eventually accepted the findings of a conciliation board set up after mediation in the dispute by the foreign secretary, Lord Rosebery. In the light of this experience, district conciliation boards were established and remained in operation during the period up to the first world war.[106] It transpired that an important principle had been established in practice, though not yet officially: that there was a minimum below which there was to be no fall. The MFGB followed this up by successfully carrying the Eight-Hour Bill into law in 1908 and effecting major improvements in the 1911 Coal Mines Regulation Act. Finally, the nationwide strike of miners in 1912, involving almost one million men, lasted for over a month before the principle of a national minimum wage was officially recognised.[107] Joint Boards of employers and men were established in each coalfield under the Minimum Wage Act to determine district minima for underground workers which could vary considerably from one region to the next.[108] Although the minimum was considerably less than the men had hoped for, their ability to establish the principle encouraged them to work towards more ambitious objectives. The Triple Alliance, initiated in 1913-14 with railwaymen and transport workers, was potentially the strongest union association in Europe.

Along with the development of internal organisation went efforts to promote common interests and the solidarity of miners on a wider scale. The identity of interest between the British miner and his Continental counterpart presented an opportunity for international cooperation to seek common goals. The first international congress of miners was held in Paris in 1889 and the second in Jolimont in Belgium in the following year. Delegates at the latter unanimously agreed that one day's work in the mines, inclusive of descent and ascent, should not exceed eight hours in every twenty-four.[109] Significantly, a further resolution that the only effective means of achieving this limit in each country was through the intervention of the legislature was carried by all delegates except those of the British contingent representing Northumberland and Durham. At this and subsequent congresses, the issue of an international strike in support of the eight-hour day was considered but final agreement could never be achieved. The promise of international support was easier to make than to fulfil. The MFGB contented itself with sending financial support to Belgian miners on strike in 1891 to extend the suffrage. However, at the same time, a large increase occurred in English coal imports into Belgium, a factor which helped break the strike.[110] Although international conferences continued to meet each year until 1914, these confined themselves to a discussion of common industrial problems and general welfare schemes.

Miners' participation in domestic politics also changed character in the period before the first world war.[111] The first trade unionists to enter Parliament, Macdonald and Burt, won their seats with Liberal support in 1874 and sat as Liberals. They started what was to become a long Lib.-Lab. tradition among miners, adopting an essentially moderate outlook. Both they and their successors believed that progress could best be achieved through the parliamentary lobby and legislative reform. Even the new Independent Labour Party, founded by Keir Hardie in 1893, did not seriously weaken this politically conservative type of Lib.-Labbism. The development of the new party reflected the growth of Socialism within sections of the working class and the important role that Socialists had played in forming the 'new' unions.[112] But the Lib-Lab. tradition tenaciously survived in the coal industry, concentrating firmly on trade union issues such as the reform of mining law and improvements in safety regulations.

In the long term, a number of factors were responsible for changing the political complexion of the MFGB. In the late 1890's, Keir Hardie sought to weld the various working-class forces together into an alliance of labour interests. The Labour Representation Committee (LRC) was formed in 1900 but initially was regarded with some suspicion by trade unionists. However, a turning point in labour history was reached with the Taff Vale case in 1901. More than any other factor, the House of Lords' decision that a union was legally responsible for the damages caused by a strike of its members solidified the ranks of trade unionism. It was also responsible for the unions giving much warmer support to the LRC than had at one time appeared likely. Following the success of the LRC in the 1906 General Election, when 29 of its candidates were elected along with 13 Lib.-Lab. mining MPs, it changed its name to become simply the 'Labour Party'. In large measure, the party had resulted from the determination of trade union leaders to reverse the Taff Vale decision.[113] Two years later, the MFGB formally affiliated to the new party, thus bringing to an end the long-standing Lib.-Lab. tradition within the industry.

Assessing the achievement of mining trade unionism in terms of wages, hours and conditions of work is difficult for most of the 19th century because of the paucity of reliable information. The earlier sections in this chapter have shown that there was a considerable improvement in working conditions. Further, most districts experienced some reduction in the length of working day before 1870. But these advances can often be attributed to pressure initially exerted by individuals and private organisations such as the Sunderland Society and South Shields Committee.[114] Whether the mining unions made a significant contribution is open to question. After 1870, more tangible evidence of the condition of industrial labour and the number of trade unionists is available. Even so, it is not possible to provide a definitive answer to the perennial questions—did market forces lead to a rapid expansion of money wages and hence to trade union growth? Conversely, was it the growth and increased strength of unions during the upswing of the cycle which enabled them to exact higher wages?

In an attempt to minimise the importance of unionism, employers, not surprisingly, took the view that market forces were the main determinants of money wages. However in coalmining, there is evidence that both mechanisms were at work after 1870. It has been shown that the boom of 1870-73 brought higher wages only to those miners organised to press for them in South and West Yorkshire and Derbyshire.[115] Again, Ben Pickard in his presidential address to the fifth annual conference of the MFGB in 1893 could legitimately argue that whereas districts within the Federation had been able to withstand wage reductions, Durham, Northumberland, South Wales and Scotland (all outside the MFGB) had suffered considerably due to union weaknesses.[116] Yet, on balance, the weight of evidence in coalmining probably favours the reverse sequence: namely, that market forces determined the level of wages and thus the size and power of the unions.[117] Wage increases brought members into the union during the boom of the early 1870's in South Wales and West Yorkshire and mining unions generally appear to have benefited during the upswings of 1889-92 and 1898-1900. On the other hand, wage-cuts between 1874 and 1880 brought losses in union membership to South Wales and West Yorkshire, and to South Wales again between 1902 and 1906.

In sum, wage determination in the industry seemed to be largely a function of the market, despite the fact that mining unions were among the most militant and effective in the trade union movement. Perhaps G. D. H. Cole came closest to the truth when he concluded of the 1870-1900 period, 'unions cannot raise wages unless the economic conditions are in their favour; but even more favourable economic conditions may not bring better wages where unionism is lethargic or non-existent.'[118]

PART THREE
A CHANGE IN FORTUNES:
PROBLEMS OF CONTRACTION, 1914-1939

7 New Problems:
Markets and Technology from 1914

1 THE COAL INDUSTRY AT WAR

The first world war had an immediate and unfavourable impact on the coal industry. Government restrictions, labour shortages, and problems of distribution resulted in a substantial fall in output. By 1918 production was 60 million tons below the peak level of 1913, due almost entirely to the collapse of exports and bunker shipments. At the same time there was some deterioration in the level of employment, although more important than the quantity was the quality of the labour force lost to the mines. The loss of skilled men to the war-effort and the subsequent dilution of the work-force in coal with raw and untrained recruits had inevitable repercussions on labour productivity. Despite a small increase in the proportion of output mechanically cut from 8% in 1913 to over 12% in 1918, output per man-shift declined steadily from 21.5 cwts in 1913 to 17.23 cwts in 1918 and to 14.36 cwts in 1920. On the other hand, the scarcity of coal was responsible for a spectacular rise in pit-head prices from an average of 8/9d. per ton in 1909-13 to 20/6d. in 1918 and to no less than 34/7d. in 1920. But even this was surpassed by the escalation of coal export prices which, in common with domestic prices, more than doubled between 1913 and 1918, but then increased by a further 150% between 1918 and 1920.[1]

During the first year of war, an estimated quarter of a million miners enlisted.[2] The loss of manpower became so serious that in mid-1916 the Government prohibited the recruitment of miners to the armed services. But the decline in the quantity and quality of the work-force had essentially a short-term influence. This was also true of what, at the time, amounted to chronic problems of internal and external distribution. The use of merchant shipping to further the war effort, the loss of almost 40% of Britain's shipping tonnage and the congestion and deterioration of the railways at home all contributed to the difficulty of supplying waiting markets with coal. In 1916, the Coal Mining Organisation Committee noted that the problem was particularly serious in districts such as Scotland where frequently collieries were unable to get their coal away.[3] A partial solution was provided in the following year by the Board of Trade acting under Defence of the Realm Regulations. A national plan was devised to reorganise the railway transport of coal, a primary object of which was to cut down movements of coal by rail. Each region was to be as self-sufficient in coal as possible and where surpluses were produced, these were to be distributed only to adjacent or convenient areas. Although belated, the scheme operated with some success.[4] But it failed in one important respect, namely forcing compliance from private individuals owning wagons.

Of greater long-term importance for the coal industry were the effects of government intervention. The growing inability of the British mines to meet the needs of domestic industry and at the same time satisfy the demand both of allied and neutral countries overseas rendered some form of regulation necessary. When it came, government control had an immediate and crippling effect on the coal-exporting districts, although in truth restricted export facilities simply masked the fact that many countries no longer needed British fuel. As early as 1915, the State embarked on a policy of controlling the final destination of coal output. The initial measures taken, more rigid custom's regulations, the licensing of coal sent abroad to neutrals and subsequently the licensing of all coal and coke shipped overseas other than to British possessions, affected only the export sector. However, these restrictions were merely the first step along the way towards more complete control of the division of output between home and foreign consumers. With the passing of the Price of Coal (Limitation) Act, the Government achieved strict price regulation by class of coal at home, but in so doing upset the balance of the industry. By limiting the prices of domestically consumed coal to a maximum of 4/- per ton over the prices prevailing in the corresponding period of 1914, those collieries catering for the export trade were placed in an advantageous position.[5] Although some increases were allowed in domestic prices during the war years, strict control was maintained while export prices were left to find their own level in a sellers' market. On the other hand, exports were limited by the preference afforded to the domestic market and, from 1916, to the allied countries, France and Italy.[6]

After a series of disputes in the South Wales coalfield,[7] the Board of Trade, acting under the Defence of the Realm Act, assumed control of all mines in the district in late 1916. In March 1917, the State took control of output and distribution of all mines in the UK, with a Coal Controller being established to head a new department of the Board of Trade.[8] The policy of regulating the price of coal at the pit-head and to allies was continued, along with the licensing of exports to neutrals. The most important innovation of the Control Agreement was the imposition of a standard profit on each undertaking. The earnings of a colliery were limited to the standard of profits made in any one of the three years preceding the outbreak of war. In cases where this level of profits was not attained, collieries were compensated up to the standard on condition that output was maintained at the rate prevailing during the pre-war standard period. Of the profits earned over the standard level, 80% went to the Treasury, 15% to the Controller to enable him to compensate undertakings where profits were deficient and the remaining 5% was retained by the collieries. This 'pooling' arrangement was an attempt to achieve a degree of equity. It was recognised that control had brought great prosperity to some owners, particularly those in the export districts, while others suffered since they were forced to supply the inland market at a strictly controlled price.

Certainly not all exporting districts benefited to the same extent. For instance, exports from the Scottish collieries experienced almost complete collapse from 10.4 million tons in 1913 to 2.4 million tons in 1918 and to a mere 1.3 million tons in 1920. Tonnage sold overseas by the east coast pits, traditionally the most important sources of export coal, dwindled from 8.3 million tons in 1913 to a trickle of 0.9 million tons in 1917. Several factors were responsible, particularly the fact that Europe had always been the principal market for Scottish coal, absorbing 80% of the district's total exports in 1913. Of this, 28% had been consumed in Germany herself, and a further 30% in the Scandinavian countries which, as neutrals, were afforded lowest priority during the war.[9] Shipments to such neutral countries were limited by the Government, initially through customs control and later by the licensing system. In addition Scotland's export effort was dealt a severe blow by the compulsory closure of ports on the upper Forth. Outlets such as Grangemouth, Bo'ness, Granton and Burntisland were required for Admiralty use, with the result that coal shipments from the Forth alone fell from over 5 million tons in 1913 to less than 1 million in 1918.

Although there were exceptions, the scales were generally tipped in favour of collieries catering for export demand during the period of 'control'. This became all the more apparent with the extension of 'control' in modified form after 1918.[10] While certain restrictions on the domestic trade in coal were lifted in mid-1919, price schedules were issued in the same year with respect to coal exported to former allies and to neutrals. Indirectly, these maintained the former policy of distinguishing between eventual destinations of exported coal. Instead of fixed prices, the schedules laid down the minimum prices to be charged for different grades of coal. The minimum price of each grade exported to neutrals was approximately double that charged to allied countries. Such a policy contributed not only to the wild inflation of export prices but also forced neutrals to search for alternative sources of supply. There can be no doubt that the effects of government control were felt most unevenly over the different coal-producing districts. Experience varied widely, particularly between the land-sale and exporting collieries. Even within the latter group, collieries dependent on the demand of former neutral countries could experience hardship. For instance, in 1920, a year of unprecedented coal hunger and of immense prosperity for the majority of exporters,[11] Scotland alone of the principal exporting districts incurred a deficit.

Despite continuous pressure for the abolition of control,[12] the large surpluses accumulating to the Exchequer ensured that restrictions remained in force until 1921. A summary of the profits made in the industry is provided in Table 1.

The escalation of profits during the period of quasi-control from 1915 and full control from 1917 is shown in Table 1. At the same time, average earnings per shift of all classes of adult workers rose from an estimated 7.08 shillings in June 1914 to 16.21 shillings by the end of 1919. This increase of almost 130% can be attributed to district advances made during the period (58.4%), war wage increases in 1917 and 1918 (42.4%) and the Sankey pay award of 1919 (28.2%).[13] Moreover in March 1920, the miners obtained a further 20% increase in wages and a few months later prepared a claim for a further advance, based on the ability of the industry to pay and the rising cost of living. The sudden change in the economic fortunes of the industry from late 1920 led to a rejection of this claim and a national coal strike in October of that year. In fact, the pattern of rapidly rising profits and wages in coalmining belied the true condition of the industry. Agitation after the war over the nationalisation issue made owners reluctant to sink further capital into the industry, a factor which helps to explain the lag in face-mechanisation during the post-war years,[14] discussed further in section 5 below. Indeed development by private enterprise was amost wholly suspended. At the same time, the machinery which artificially distributed the coal 'was perpetually on the verge of disaster',[15] with some collieries enjoying large profits on exports while others were confined exclusively to the home market.

Under both the Coal Mines Control Agreement (Confirmation) Act of 1918 and the Coal Mines (Emergency) Act of 1919 provision was made for the pooling of profits made in excess of certain standards. Both also included a guarantee that the pool would be supplemented by the Exchequer in the event of it being insufficient to provide a specified standard of profit. In the event the Exchequer was called upon to fulfil its pledge. The sudden deterioration in demand for coal due to the general depression in trade both at home and abroad in late 1920 proved the catalyst necessary to return the industry rather hastily to private hands. Under the terms of both statutes, the State's liability steadily increased, reaching £32 million by end-March,

Table 1
Coal Mining Profits, 1909/13-1920.[1] *(£ million)*

Financial Year (1)	Estimated Profits of Coal Industry (2)	Deduct Coking etc. Profits (3)	Add Profits of Mines Subsidiary to other Industries (4)	Net Coal-Mining Profits (5)
		Adjustments to Arrive at Net Profits		
Prewar:				
Av. 1909/10-13/14	12.1	Counterbalanced by Col (4)	Counterbalanced by Col (3)	12.1
Pre-Control				
1914/15	12.4	2.0	2.5	12.9
1915/16	21.5	3.3	4.0	22.2
1916/17[2]	28.6	4.8	5.9	29.7
Average	20.8	3.3	4.1	21.6
Control:				
1917/18	15.5+3[3]	4.8	4.2	17.9
1918/19	15.6+4[3]	Adjusted in col. (2)		19.6
Average	19.05	2.4	2.1	18.75
1919/20	20.3	Adjusted in col. (2)		20.3

SOURCE:
PRO, Power 26/14
NOTES:
1. Includes loan interest but after deduction of royalties and all taxes including Excess Profits Duty, Coal Mines Excess Payments, Mineral Rights Duty where borne by colliery proprietor, and Income Tax.
2. Includes for South Wales four months, and for the rest of the country one month, during which the industry was under control.
3. For these years, profits were increased by payments of £3 million and £4 million respectively under the guarantee contained in the Coal Mines Control Agreement.

1922.[16] In consequence, the Coal Mines (Decontrol) Act was brought forward to take effect from end-March, 1921. It was estimated that to continue financial control, assuming continued depression in the coal trade and no reduction in miners' wages, would have cost the State a subsidy of £5 million per month.[17] The owners inherited, therefore, an industry desperately in need of large capital inputs; in which industrial relations were at a low and bitter ebb; and whose product was on the threshold of secular decline. This decline, resulting from rapidly developing foreign competition, economies in fuel use and the emergence of cleaner and more efficient substitutes, was to remain the fundamental problem until the closing years of the interwar period.

2 THE INTERWAR RECORD

The bitter experiences of the coal industry during the interwar years stand in marked contrast to the optimism and achievements of the previous generation. Progress and prosperity before 1914, gave way after the first world war to depression and decline. Output ceased to grow for the first time since the Industrial Revolution; overseas shipments, the basis of late Victorian prosperity, collapsed after the war with distressing effects on the several exporting coalfields; and, in consequence, employment which had grown so rapidly before the war, declined almost continuously after the 1926 General Strike. The capacity of the industry was substantially reduced, with the number of mines in operation falling by more than one-third between 1913 and '37. But even this was insufficient to equate supply to steadily declining demand until the very end of the period, when the pressures of rearmament provided a flagging industry with much needed relief. Hence after the brief post-war boom, surplus capacity became the hallmark of the coal industry; inevitably it was accompanied by a persistently heavy rate of unemployment and the alienation of the work-force during the 1920's.

The contrast between pre- and post-first world war experience was all the sharper because in 1913 the industry seemed set on a course which assured it of a prosperous future. Since the 1880's, coalmining had enjoyed a period of relative stability, set against a trend of steadily rising output. Britain was still the largest coal-exporting nation in the world and in 1913 production had hit an unprecedented high. Along with the United States, she dominated the world's coalmining industry. Together these two countries accounted for almost two-thirds of total output in 1909-13, Britain alone contributing almost one-quarter of the world's supply.[18] Of course, there were problems but these were essentially of a minor nature. Continued efforts to economise in the use of coal had achieved some degree of success and substitutes for the mineral were steadily being developed.[19] Gas, oil and hydro-electricity were all at a relatively early stage of application but had already served notice that in certain sectors the future of coal as a source of fuel and power was limited. There was a tendency towards rapidly rising production costs, particularly in those districts like Scotland, Durham and Lancashire where the best and most favourably situated seams were approaching exhaustion. As noted in Chapter 5, mechanisation had not been introduced on a sufficient scale to prevent rapidly diminishing returns and a decline in output per man. Perhaps most serious was the growth of foreign competition. New areas of supply were being opened up which in later years would have a damaging effect on Britain's sovereignty of overseas markets.

Although a cause for concern, these difficulties weighed little in the scales when set against the 'extraordinary success and activity of the period.'[20] Coal prices were high and rising at home and abroad, handsome profits were being made and the industry could with some justification be regarded as the corner-stone of British prosperity. It was not the war alone which shattered dreams of continued expansion and transformed the industry into the ailing giant of the 'twenties and 'thirties. Certainly the war jolted coalmining out of any sense of complacency but its main effect was to lay bare and exacerbate existing problems.

In comparison with the stability of the pre-war era, the coal industry between the wars was characterised by extreme fluctuations in output. Significantly these were superimposed on a declining secular trend. The performance of the industry is summarised in Table 2.

The data in Table 2 reveal that the fall in coal output between the wars was largely due to the collapse of export demand. Production fluctuated widely but over the period 1909/13-38 as a whole there was a fall of more than 40 million tons. Nine-tenths of this decline can be attributed to the loss of overseas shipments since domestic demand was relatively well maintained. Consumption of coal per head of population in Great Britain had been 89 cwts in 1913, fell to 66 cwts at the trough of the world depression in 1933 but then recovered to 79 cwts in 1937.[21] In view of the fall in output, the capacity of the industry was significantly reduced. Both employment and the number of productive units fell by about one-third during the period specified in Table 2. Even so, the capacity to produce remained far in excess of demand for most of the period.

Of course, these difficulties were not confined to Britain alone. Similar problems of demand deficiency, surplus capacity and unemployment existed throughout the major coal-producing regions of Europe. Yet it was in Britain that they assumed their most extreme form. In terms of output, European coalmining had recovered from the war by 1927 and ten years later production was 25% higher than

Table 2

*UK Coal Mines, Output, Exports, Domestic Consumption and Employment,
Selected Years, 1909/13-1938*

Year	No. of mines in operation	Output (m. tons)	Exports[1] (m. tons)	Domestic Consumption (m. tons)	Employment Above and Below Ground (000)
1909/13	3179	269.6	85.1	184.5	1,069.5
1920	2851	229.5	38.8	190.7	1,248.2
1925	2721	243.2	67.2	176.0	1,102.4
1929	2419	257.9	76.7	181.2	956.7
1932	2158	208.7	53.1	155.6	819.3
1935	2075	222.3	51.2	171.1	769.5
1938	2125	227.0	46.4	180.6	790.9

SOURCES:
Annual Reports of the Secretary for Mines; Mitchell and Deane, op. cit., pp. 115-19.
NOTE:
1. Includes exports of coal, coke and manufactured fuel and bunker coal.

the 1909-13 level.[22] On the other hand, output in Britain never regained its pre-war peak and by 1937 was still more than 10% below that of 1909-13. Hence, viewed against the background of a slowly developing European industry, the performance of British coalmining was the more disappointing. In terms of world production, Britain's share fell from 25% in the years before the first world war to about 20% by 1927. This level was only maintained in the 1930's at a time when the rest of Europe accounted for a growing share of world output.

In part, instability and decline in Britain stemmed from a series of random shocks, generated both by the intransigence of those engaged in the industry and by forces in the world economy outwith the control of either owners or men. With the end of the post-war boom in demand for coal and with prices already falling, the Government de-controlled the mines in 1921. The depression in output was aggravated in that year by the strike of coalminers, allowing the German collieries to benefit from Britain's temporary absence from world markets. Similarly, the General Strike of 1926 allowed the Polish mines to invade the Scandinavian market in the late 1920's and capture a larger share of demand than would otherwise have been the case. On the other hand, the British industry benefited from the strike in the American coalfields in 1922 and the occupation of the Ruhr in 1923. In the latter year, exports of British coal reached a peak for the interwar period, thereafter falling steadily, apart from a brief revival in 1929, until the end of the 1930's. The world depression of 1929-32 had serious repercussions for all coal-producing nations: yet, in contrast to the rest of Europe, Britain failed in the ensuing recovery of the 1930's to regain her 1929 level of output.[23]

For the most part, these were short-term influences but the basic problem of the interwar period was essentially a long-term one. Economies in coal use, the development of substitutes and the opening up of new areas of production created a growing imbalance between demand and supply. The major difficulty was not so much *actual* over-production since the mining of coal remained relatively sensitive to fluctuations in world demand. Rather, there was a persistent problem of *potential* over-capacity in that the industry was capable of supplying a much larger output than the market could absorb at prices which at least covered production costs. It is estimated that in the century before 1914, world demand for coal increased by about 4% per annum. In the interwar period, demand grew at an average rate of only 0.3% per annum.[24] As the largest coal-exporter in the world, Britain was bound to be adversely affected by these trends.

Here was the problem of the British coal industry. Since the mines could never be worked to capacity, the burden of fixed charges in the form of plant and equipment became increasingly heavy. Already by 1929 the margin of surplus capacity as a proportion of actual output amounted to between one-quarter and one-third in Britain, one-quarter in Germany and approximately one-half in Poland.[25] To streamline the capacity of the British industry in line with prevailing demand would have required a much clearer understanding of the issues than was demonstrated by most contemporary analysts and the application of much stronger measures than were in fact implemented (see Chapter 9, section 1 below). In the event, paying lip-service to rationalisation and setting up the necessary machinery to devise plans and schemes, while in practice achieving very little, was possibly the right policy. The Government in the early 1930's was well aware of the heavy social cost that successful rationalisation measures would inevitably incur. A serious displacement of labour would have resulted, with the likelihood of whole mining areas being left derelict. At a time when unemployment was already abnormally high, the cost was too great. Hence in the 1930's, as in the previous decade, hopes of a solution to the problems of coalmining rested largely with the demand- rather than supply-side of the industry.

3   THE DEFICIENCY OF DEMAND: EXPORTS

Approximately nine-tenths of the coal mined in the world during the interwar period was destined for domestic consumption within the separate national economies, with only one-tenth entering international trade. Yet for several countries, including Britain, foreign trade in coal assumed a much greater importance. Between 1913 and 1937, Britain's exports of coal varied between one-fifth and one-third of her coal output and accounted, along with foreign bunkers, for an average of 10% of the value of total British exports. In consequence, the violent fluctuations which characterised British coal shipments and their secular decline from a peak in 1923 had a significant impact not only on coalmining itself but on the overall trading position of the nation. In part the factors which reacted unfavourably on the British coal trade were common to all countries in competition for world markets. But Britain's coal exports suffered more than proportionately, falling from 55% of world exports in 1913 to 37% in 1937-8.

Initially responsible for the sharp downturn in exports was the war and its immediate aftermath. With the British industry under Government 'control' for about five years, exports were limited to conserve the quantities essential for domestic requirements. Customers abroad were obliged to follow one or more of the following courses: they could develop more fully their own coal resources; economise as much as possible in the use of coal; or seek other forms of fuel and power. The most striking example of a country choosing the first of these options was Holland. Output rose from a mere 1.9 million tons in 1913 to 10.9 million tons in 1928. There was also particularly rapid development in Russia and the Succession States. In fact, the Russian Empire was the most important single market lost to Britain, imports of British coal falling from 6 million tons in 1913 to a mere 0.5 million tons in 1928.[26] At the same time, by encouraging domestic production after the war countries such as India, Spain and Japan considerably increased the world's coalmining capacity. The result was to decentralise the output of coal. There was a shift in emphasis away from older-established centres like Britain, the United States and France to 'newer' producers such as the Soviet Union, Japan and India. Established customers also forced on domestic development to the detriment of British output. By 1928 the post-war territory of France was producing 7.5 million tons more and that of Germany over 10 million tons more than in 1913. Over the same period, British shipments fell by between 3 and 4 million tons to each country.[27]

The enlargement of the area of supply was accompanied by rapid progress abroad in the conservation of heat, the extraction of maximum energy from coal burned, and the development of substitutes. During the 1920's, Germany achieved an economy of 10% in the use of coal in industry through the greater efficiency of boilers and furnaces. In the USA, major advances were made in fuel efficiency by both manufacturing industry and the railways. Between 1909 and 1929 average fuel consumption per unit of output in these sectors had fallen by about one-third.[28] Whereas in 1913 over 84% of the total energy employed had been derived from bituminous and anthracite coal, the proportion had fallen by the later 1920's to 64%. A similar displacement of coal was taking place throughout the world economy. Measured in terms of coal equivalent, all forms of energy supply increased by over 400 million tons between 1913 and 1929. Of this increase, coal accounted for just over 100 million tons. By far the most important competitor was oil which contributed more than 200 million tons to the world's increased energy supply over the same period.[29] The influence of oil was most seriously felt in shipping and, to a lesser extent, in railways. Between 1913 and 1937, world tonnage of coal-fired merchant shipping fell from 44 million, 97% of the total, to 32 million, 49% of the total. Correspondingly, the tonnage of oil-fired (steam-raising) vessels increased from one to 20 million, a jump from 3 to 30% of the world's total. Even more spectacular was the expansion of oil-burning diesel vessels, the tonnage of which increased from 0.2 million, less than 1% of the total, to 14 million, 21% of the total. This actually understates the move to oil-using vessels since the figures take no account of the almost complete displacement of coal by oil in the naval shipping of the world. The shift to oil, together with the depression of world trade and economies in burning, resulted in a serious fall in British bunker coal from 21 million tons in 1913 to 12 million tons in 1937.

All coal-producers were affected by the alteration of the coal map of Europe following the Treaty of Versailles and the increase in competition which resulted. After adjusting to these changes it became clear that the most serious losses had been suffered by Britain. Under the peace-terms, Germany lost more than one-quarter of her coal resources, including the cession of Alsace-Lorraine to France and the loss of the Saar. The effect was to stimulate rationalisation in the Ruhr and enable the district greatly to increase its output of coal and lignite.[30] In addition, Germany was obliged to deliver reparation coal to France, Belgium, Italy and Luxembourg, a factor which distorted normal trade flows within Europe. In aggregate, it is unlikely that reparation deliveries directly affected the volume of the British coal trade. Rather, they entailed a reorganisation and re-routing of trade.[31] The most striking result of the alterations in national boundaries within Europe was the emergence of Poland as an important coal-exporting nation. Having acquired the mines in East Upper Silesia from Germany, Poland found the natural market for her coal in Germany herself. However in 1925 the latter placed an embargo on coal coming from East Upper Silesia. As a result, Poland was forced to seek outlets elsewhere, a quest greatly assisted by the 1926 General Strike in Britain. Her invasion of the Scandinavian market was achieved largely at the expense of British coal[32] and by the 1930's Polish coal was also firmly entrenched in French and Italian markets.

Besides forces at work in the international economy, Britain's coal exports were adversely affected by domestic economic policy, received little in the way of preferential treatment and were unable to compete effectively in overseas markets due to technical deficiencies within British coalmining itself. Controversy still exists about the effect which the over-valuation of the pound sterling had on Britain's exports. Whatever the general implications of the 'return to Gold' in 1925, the least that can be said is that such a policy cannot have benefited the export trade in coal. Nor was the position materially altered when Britain left the Gold Standard in 1931 and allowed sterling to depreciate in value. Her chief rivals, Germany and Poland, negated any advantage that might have been obtained by quoting in depreciated sterling when in competition with British coal. Germany, in particular, resorted to drastic price-cutting to meet the potential threat to her coal export trade. By 1932 the average price of her exported coal had fallen to two-thirds of its 1929 level.[33] Moreover, long-term contracts entered into before Britain left the Gold Standard had still to be honoured and prevented any immediate improvement in her export position. A further obstacle lay in the restrictions imposed by a wide range of protectionist policies adopted abroad. Throughout the international economy market forces were subordinated to interventionism in the shape of tariffs, quotas and preferential clauses. Again, Britain was hardest hit, not only because she was the world's leading coal-exporter but because efforts were made to discriminate particularly against her coal.

Indeed, British owners could justifiably claim that compared to other countries, little was done to smooth the path of Britain's exporting districts. Tariffs abroad protected domestic coal production while at the same time exports were subsidised to provide them with a competitive edge in world markets. Discrimination between home and export sales was reinforced by preferential rates charged by railways abroad on the carriage of coal. For instance, Poland's ability to compete depended not only on relatively low wages but on abnormally low railway freight rates charged on export coal and price discrimination between inland and overseas sales.[34] Little of a comparable nature was done to assist the British exporting districts until the 1930's. Railway charges on the carriage of coal increased rapidly after the first world war. Already by 1925 the rate charged per ton of coal was on average 80% higher than in 1913, a rate of increase which compared unfavourably with the 40% recorded in Germany.[35]

170

Despite the operation of the Railway Freight Rebate Scheme from the end of 1928, British producers were correct in their assertion that the level of assistance in this country did not match that provided abroad. In this respect Britain failed to exploit what should have been an important natural advantage. With the exception of a small part of the Midland Coalfield, all British coal-producing districts were within easy reach of the sea, the average length of haul for export coal being a mere 25 miles. The corresponding distances in Belgium were 50 miles, in the Ruhr between 100 and 150 miles and in Polish Upper Silesia between 300 and 400 miles.[36]

Of greater long-term significance in accounting for the decline in Britain's export performance were supply-side weaknesses in the domestic industry. The relatively low rate of growth of productivity and high costs of British coalmining contributed directly to the loss of competitiveness in foreign markets. A full discussion of the relationship between mechanisation, labour productivity and costs of production is provided in section 5. However, it is useful to note here that labour costs bore more heavily on British coalmining than was generally the case abroad. Comparability between countries in this respect is extremely difficult and conclusions must necessarily be tentative. Nevertheless it may be accepted that while labour costs in all countries constituted a relatively high proportion of the total costs involved in mining the coal, Britain carried one of the heaviest burdens in this regard. Expressed as a proportion of average pit-head prices, wage-costs per ton in Britain varied between 60 and 70% over the period 1927-36. In Belgium and the Netherlands, they were generally about one-half of pit-head prices and in Germany and Poland, the proportion was even lower, varying between 40 and 50% in the 1930's.[37]

Reductions in labour costs may be accomplished by one or both of two principal methods: an increase in output per man-shift and a decrease in wage rates. In contrast to the marked progress in productivity achieved in all other European countries between 1927 and 1936, the increase in output per man-shift in Britain remained disappointingly low.[38] At the same time, although details of changes in wage rates are not available, movements in average money earnings per man-shift are highly illuminating. Average earnings per man-shift (per employed worker) remained practically constant in Britain between 1929 and 1935, before rising sharply in 1936-7. On the other hand, there was a considerable fall in average *earnings* per man-shift in Germany, Poland, Belgium and the Netherlands, precisely the areas where *output* per man-shift had risen most strongly.[39] These trends accentuated the competitive weakness of the British coal industry. Wide divergences in movements of productivity were inevitably reflected in major changes in wage costs per ton in the principal European countries.

Table 3

Movements in Wage Costs per Ton of Coal, Selected Countries, 1929-36
(1929=100)

	Belgium[1]	Germany (Prussia)	Netherlands	Poland	UK[1]
1929	100	100	100	100	100
1932	74	65	78	90	99
1934	59	64	69	67	94
1936	54[2]	63	62	60	100

SOURCE:
ILO, op. cit., p. 216; PEP, op. cit., p. 155.
NOTES:
1. Excluding allowances in cash and kind.
2. Relates to 1935.

To the extent that wage costs were an important determinant of competitiveness, Table 3 shows that Britain's major rivals enjoyed a growing advantage during the 1930's. Indeed, throughout the inter-war period, the simple truth for British coalmining was that wage costs were too high to allow the industry to function at a profit. The operation of minimum wage provisions forced up the share of net proceeds accruing to labour to a level higher than the industry could possibly afford. In most districts, therefore, the owner found himself squeezed by low selling prices on the one hand and relatively high wage costs on the other.[40]

Due partly to greater cost efficiency and partly to the preferential treatment accorded to coalmining abroad, Britain's rivals in foreign trade substantially improved their competitive position in the 1930's. In terms of national currencies, average prices per ton of exported coal in the UK moved from 100 in 1929 to 102 in 1935 and to 129 in 1938. Between the same years, Germany's export prices moved from 100 to 48 to 62 and those in Poland from 100 to 53 to 67.[41] Hence UK export prices remained relatively high during the 1930's and rose sharply in the latter part of the decade due to the pressure of rearmament demand. In contrast, both German and Polish prices in 1935 were approximately half their pre-depression level and by the end of the 'thirties were still more than 30% down on 1929. Nor did Britain find adequate compensation in the series of bilateral trading agreements negotiated during the decade. Concessions were granted to British coal under agreements negotiated with the Scandinavian and Baltic countries, Argentina, Ireland, France, Spain and several other countries.[42] But these were not sufficient to offset the markets lost due to declining competitive ability, and the discrimination and protectionism practised in other areas. Between 1929 and 1937, the tonnage of British coal sold overseas fell by one-third while over the same period that of Germany increased by more than two-fifths.[43]

4 THE DEFICIENCY OF DEMAND: THE DOMESTIC MARKET

The rapid decline of British coal exports during the interwar years was accompanied by stagnation and a tendency towards decline in the home market. For the first time since the Industrial Revolution a check was placed on the long-term growth of domestic consumption. This can be attributed to depression in the major coal-consuming industries at home and, in common with the rest of the international economy, the effects of economy and substitution. The staple trades had always been the largest customers of British coalmining, particularly iron and steel, textiles and the transport industries. Ironically, the collieries themselves were also heavy consumers of coal, in the form of engine fuel. Depression in these sectors and the extent to which they successfully reduced production costs by economising in the use of fuel inevitably had an adverse effect on coal output. According to the *Fourth Census of Production* for 1930 some 36.3 million tons of coal were consumed in that year for the purpose of providing power in British industry. A quarter of a century earlier, the *Royal Commission on Coal Supplies* (1905) had estimated that about 52 million tons of coal were used to provide power. The latter may have over-estimated the coal required at the earlier date but it is clear that significant economies in the use of coal had been achieved, especially since over these 25 years the engine-capacity installed at industrial undertakings had doubled and industrial production had risen by over 40%.

The distribution of coal between domestic users is shown in Table 4.

For those trades which can be separately distinguished, Table 4 confirms that the greatest reduction in coal consumption occurred in the heavy industrial sector. It was this group of industries that was most severely affected by the world slump of 1929-32. Table 4 shows that by 1932, the volume of coal absorbed by blast furnaces was less than one-third of its 1913 level while over the same period tonnage used in Other Iron and Steel Works had fallen by 50% and in collieries by 33%. Of the total decline in domestic coal consumption by the end of the world depression, these three categories accounted for no less than three-quarters. Together they would have had a most

173

Table 4
*(i) Volume of Coal Consumed in Great Britain (million tons) and (ii) Volume
Expressed as Proportion of Total Available for Domestic Consumption*

Consumer	1913 (i)	(ii)	1929 (i)	(ii)	1932 (i)	(ii)	1937 (i)	(ii)
Gas Works	16.7	9	16.8	10	16.4	11	18.2	10
Electricity Generating Stations[1]	4.9	3	9.8	6	9.8	7	14.8	8
Railway Companies	13.2	7	13.4	7	11.7	8	13.1	7
Vessels Engaged in Coastwise Trade (Bunkers)	1.9	1	1.4	1	1.2	1	1.2	1
Iron Works (Used in Blast Furnaces)	21.2	12	14.5	8	6.5	4	14.8	8
Other Iron Works and Steel Works	10.2	5	8.9	5	5.2	3	8.9	5
Collieries (Engine Fuel)	18.0	10	13.7	8	12.0	8	12.2	7
General Manufacturers and All other purposes (including domestic use)[2]	97.7	53	95.0	55	86.7	58	98.8	54
Total	183.8	100	173.5	100	149.5	100	182.0	100

SOURCE:
Annual Reports of the Secretary for Mines.
NOTES:
1. Belonging to authorised undertakings and railways and tramway authorities.
2. This residual is subject to changes in stocks held by producers and consumers about which information is not available. During the 1920's the consumption of coal used for domestic heating, lighting etc. was estimated at 40 million tons per annum but in the 1930's no information was provided by the Mines Department. During the war years, estimates of consumption in domestic premises were based for the first time on statistical returns. These showed that 61.9 million tons of coal were consumed in 1938 for domestic purposes. Ministry of Fuel and Power, *Domestic Fuel Policy: Report by the Fuel and Power Advisory Council, Cmd. 6762, 1946.*

damaging effect on the coal industry's output between 1913 and 1937, had it not been for compensatory movements elsewhere in the economy. The increase in the output of coal required by electricity generating stations and to a lesser extent by gas works almost wholly offset the dwindling tonnage used by iron and steel and the collieries themselves.

While the stagnation of the staple trades accounted for some part of their smaller consumption of coal, improvements in fuel efficiency were also important. The latter were particularly marked in the iron and steel industry where a saving of one-fifth was achieved between 1913 and 1936 in the volume of coal required for each ton of pig iron smelted. Indeed, had the 1936 volume of pig iron output been smelted according to the techniques practised in 1913, an extra 3.1 million tons of coal would have been needed for the blast furnaces.[44] Further, although the tonnage of steel output rose by more than 40% between 1920 and 1937, no corresponding increase in the use of pig iron (and hence of coal) occurred in the steel furnaces. This was due to the steady rise in the use of scrap, rather than pig, in the steelworks. By the end of the interwar period, scrap amounted to almost 60% of the total output of steel ingots.[45] Similar economies in coal use were effected in trades of more recent origin such as the electricity supply industry and gas works. In the former, the coal and coke consumed per million Kw. hours fell from 1.49 tons to about 0.67 tons between 1920/21 and 1934/5. In gas undertakings the yield of gas per ton of coal carbonised increased by more than 10% between 1925 and 1934.[46]

The desire to economise in the use of coal was given impetus by the trend of pit-head prices. In the 1930's, it was justifiably argued that in relation to overseas experience, domestically produced coal was becoming more expensive in Britain. At a time when domestic coal was getting steadily more cheap for industry abroad, the price of British coal was well maintained. For instance, taking 1930=100, pit-head prices had risen in Britain to 112 by 1937. In Belgium, they had fallen to 91 and in Germany (excluding the Saar) to 74.[47] These relative price movements increased the cost-burden that had to be carried by Britain's exporting industries. Not surprisingly, every effort was made to reduce fuel costs and particularly those of coal.

A further problem, of greater long-term significance, was also beginning to affect the domestic demand for coal—the emergence of substitutes. This was an issue complicated by the fact that different degrees of substitution existed, both between coal and other forms of fuel and power, and between different grades of coal itself. Coal is not a homogeneous product and the degree to which it can be replaced by other grades or other fuels depends on the type and quality of fuel, and the intended economic use. The demand for certain grades, like anthracite and high-quality steam coal, was relatively inelastic while for others, large changes in the elasticity of demand, both seasonal and long-term, could occur. It was these latter types that were susceptible to substitution by oil, gas and electricity. Nonetheless, as shown in Table 5, coal remained by far the most important source of energy consumption in Britain before the second world war.

Table 5

Fuel Consumption by Principal Categories, 1935 (million therms)

Consumer	Coal	Coke	Fuel, Gas & Diesel Oil	Purchased Electricity	Gas
Traction (railways and Tramways	4,000	—	—	70	
Iron and Steel	2,900	3,100	60	40	
Clay and Building Materials	2,700	70	50	30	
Textiles	2,400	40	10	30	
Chemicals	1,400	120	70	10	300
Food, Drink and Tobacco	1,100	180	40	20	
Paper	900	30	10	10	
Engineering and Shipbuilding	500	250	60	40	
Other Industries, Government Departments etc.	1,500	400	74	100	
Small Firms and Commercial Works, Domestic Consumers	15,700	1,700	—	180	1,000
Total	33,100	5,890	—	530	1,300

SOURCE:
PEP, *The British Fuel and Power Industries* (1947), p. 329.

The figures provided in Table 5 are estimated on the basis of 1935 *Census of Production* statistics. Time series data showing the importance of the different fuels used by various categories of consumer are not available for the interwar years. The table shows that in 1935 coal was still by far the most important fuel used in Britain. In terms of the thermal value of fuels consumed, it dominated in all categories except iron and steel where coke was marginally more important. However, the data in Table 5 cannot answer the important question of how quickly substitute fuels had emerged during the interwar years. Was the challenge to coal from other fuels growing consistently and to what extent was the mineral being replaced?

Lack of information prevents a definitive answer to these questions but some insight is afforded by the estimates in Table 6 below. It should be emphasised that the data are tentative and provide only a rough indication of trends in fuel usage in Britain.

Table 6
Energy Consumption in Britain by Source, 1913-34
(figures expressed as % of total calories)

	1913	1930	1934
Total Energy (billion calories)	1,299	1,307	1,210
Energy Source	%	%	%
Coal, Metallurgical Coke and Briquettes	89	83	78
Gas from Coal	2	2	3
Gas Coke	5	5	6
Electric Power from Coal	3	5	7
Motor Spirit, Fuel Oils etc.	1	5	6
	100	100	100

SOURCE:
Buxton, 'The Coal Industry.'

Table 6 shows that total energy consumption in Britain stagnated between 1913 and 1934, the product of a generally depressed industrial environment and the rapid advances made in fuel economy. However, by disaggregating to the level of individual energy sources, it can be seen that the virtually stationary total conceals significant movements in the consumption of different fuels. The contribution of coal, metallurgical coke and briquettes fell from nine-tenths of the total in 1913 to just over three-quarters by 1934. Over the same period, fuel oils etc. and electric power increased their share of total energy consumption from 3 to 13%. Although the substitution of coal had not proceeded very far during the interwar period, a warning-note had been sounded that in future years the coal industry might expect serious competition from alternative sources of energy.

5   MECHANISATION, LABOUR PRODUCTIVITY AND COMPETITIVENESS[48]

As already noted, the decline in competitive efficiency of British coalmining between the wars can partly be attributed to weaknesses on the supply-side of the industry: specifically, to the relationship between mechanisation, labour productivity and costs of production in the different coalfields of the country. It is difficult to compare efficiency in coalmining between districts and between countries since so many factors impinge on the criteria adopted for measurement. However, an examination of costs of production and profitability provides a useful starting place. To the extent that the latter is dependent on market conditions over which the industry may have little control, production costs are likely to be of greater value. By far the largest component of total costs was the price of labour and here British coalmining operated at a disadvantage. As observed in section 3, wage costs amounted to a much higher proportion of average price per ton at the pit-head in Britain than was the case abroad. Moreover, movements in wage costs per ton in the European coal industry in the 1930's led to a further decline in the competitive position of the British industry (see Table 3). But relatively high labour costs in Britain were themselves largely a function of the natural difficulties of mining, the extent of mechanisation, and the rationalisation of mine lay-out and the sequence of mining activities. This section concentrates on the relationship between mechanisation, physical mining conditions, labour productivity and costs. The organisation of the industry is considered in Chapter 9.

A major cause of the imbalance between supply and demand during the interwar period was the higher output obtained per unit of capital and labour as a result of mechanisation. Hand-hewing was steadily replaced in the United States and Britain by coal-cutting machines, and in Germany, France and Belgium by pneumatic picks. Similarly, hand-loading increasingly gave way to loading and conveying by machine and underground haulage systems were extensively mechanised. Electric power replaced steam in most underground operations as well as in hoisting coal up the shaft. In addition, considerable progress was made on the surface in the preparation of raw coal for the market, with the installation of plants, operated electrically, for washing, breaking and sizing. With rapid innovation taking place, virtually all countries were able to achieve large improvements in output per man-shift. Britain proved to be the exception, securing a relatively small increase in labour productivity between 1914 and 1937. This was largely due to the physical difficulties encountered in mining the coal and to a lag in the mechanisation of the pits during the 1920's. Table 7 compares trends in mechanisation and output per man-shift in several of the leading coal-producing nations of Europe. Some indication is also provided of the natural mining conditions prevailing in each country.

Table 7 shows that the proportion of output mechanically cut was relatively low in all countries before the first world war. It was during the 1920's that Britain signally failed to keep pace with Continental mining practice, so that by 1929, less than 30% of output was cut by

178

Table 7

Percentage of Coal Output Mechanically Cut, Output per Man-Shift (O.M.S.) and Natural Mining Conditions in Selected Countries, 1913-35

	Great Britain				Germany (Ruhr)				Belgium				France (Pas-de-Calais)			
	Output Mech-anically cut (%)	O.M.S. Statute Tons	O.M.S. 1913 =100	Physical Mining Conditions	Output Mech-anically cut (%)	O.M.S Statute Tons	O.M.S 1913 =100	Physical Mining Conditions	Output Mech-anically cut (%)	O.M.S. Statute Tons	O.M.S. 1913 =100	Physical Mining Conditions	Output Mech-anically cut (%)	O.M.S. Statute Tons	O.M.S. 1913 =100	Physical Mining Conditions
1913	9[1]	1.016[1]	100[1]	High Pro-portion of thin seams worked,	2	0.930	100	Seams worked on average thinner	10	0.530	100	Thin seams worked at considerable depth below surface.	—[3]	0.690	100	Seams worked on average thinner
1925	20	0.901	89	lying at considerable depth below surface.	66[2]	1.096[2]	118[2]	than most economical sections.	63	0.465	88		44	0.569	83	than most economical sections.
1927	23	1.031	102	Moderate number of faults: seams fairly flat.	80	1.114	120	Heavily faulted and seams steeply inclined.	81	0.505	95	Heavily faulted and seams steeply inclined.	65	0.596	86	Heavily faulted and seams steeply inclined.
1929	28	1.085	107		91	1.251	135		89	0.567	107		72	0.683	99	
1932	38	1.100	108	Gas prevalent and heavy pumping demand for drainage.	96	1.599	172	Gas prevalent and pumping demand for drainage fairly heavy.	95	0.599	113	Gas prevalent and pumping demand for drainage fairly heavy.	85	0.771	112	Gas prevalent and pumping demand for drainage fairly heavy.
1934	47	1.147	113		97	1.651	178		97	0.723	137		—[3]	0.844	122	
1936	55	1.177	116		97	1.683	181		99	0.781	148		88[4]	0.858[4]	124[4]	

179

SOURCES:
Calculated from data provided by *Royal Commission on Coal, 1925, Minutes of Evidence* (1926); League of Nations, *Memorandum on Coal*, I, pp. 39-40; ILO, op. cit., I, pp. 106-10; PEP, op. cit., pp. 153-4; *Reid Report*, 1945.
NOTES: 1. Figures for mid-1914. 2. Figures for 1926. 3. Not available. 4. Figures for 1935.

machines in this country as opposed to approximately 90% in both the Ruhr and Belgium and over 70% in France. During the 1930's, efforts were made to make up lost ground: even so, by the closing years of the decade, British coalmining with something less than three-fifths of output mechanically cut compared unfavourably with the virtually complete mechanisation achieved in Germany and Belgium. Whilst the rate of growth of output per man-shift was not solely a function of greater mechanisation,[49] there can be little doubt that the rapid innovation of machine-cutting techniques was the most important single determinant of the increases recorded in Table 7.[50] Given the greater degree of mechanisation abroad, output per man-shift increased much more rapidly between the wars than in Britain. As Table 7 shows, productivity in the British mines increased by a modest 16% between 1913-36; the corresponding increases in the Ruhr and Belgium were some 80 and 50% respectively, whilst even in France, a growth of 24% was recorded.

The fact that, in absolute terms, output per man-shift remained higher in Britain than in either Belgium or France can largely be explained in terms of the natural difficulties encountered in mining the coal. Although mining conditions were far from ideal in Britain and were, for instance, markedly inferior to those of the bituminous mining areas of the USA, they were, nonetheless, still superior to those in France and Belgium. Table 7 indicates that both these countries had to contend with thin, steeply inclined seams, worked (in the case of Belgium) at some considerable depth below the surface, heavily faulted terrain and the ever-present dangers of flooding and inflammable gas in the pits. Indeed, in the context of the world coalmining industry, it has been estimated that the natural difficulties experienced in mining were at their *most* severe in Belgium; were relatively difficult in France, Czechoslovakia and Britain; were relatively easier in Germany, good in Poland (East Upper Silesia) and were clearly best of all in the bituminous mining regions of the USA.[51] This 'degree of difficulty' thesis accords very well with the output per man-shift statistics of the countries specified in Table 7. Together with mechanisation, physical mining conditions played a large part in determining the differences which existed between countries in labour productivity.

Apart from coal-cutting, one factor which deserves particular emphasis within the general term 'mechanisation' is the variation which persisted between countries in underground haulage techniques. It was here that British mines fell far short of 'best practice'. So much so, indeed, that inadequate underground haulage may be regarded not only as the most important deficiency in British coalmining between the wars but also as the major reason, perhaps, for the relatively slow growth of labour productivity in the industry. As one authority noted, 'no single operation associated with coal production in Britain offers more scope for improved efficiency than that of underground transport.'[52] In a sense, this was the more ironic since it was precisely in this area that British pits should have enjoyed a comparative advantage. As indicated in Table 7, the seams in Britain were relatively flat, as opposed to those more steeply inclined on the Continent. This should have permitted a more rapid and economical system of underground transport in this country. It was, however, precisely because the difficulties were less acute that British coalowners failed to innovate the efficient haulage techniques developed and fully exploited abroad. Given flatter seams, British owners preferred simply to follow the seams and draw coal through roads in the seam, first by hand and ponies, and later by rope haulage and to a lesser extent conveyors.[53] The undulating and frequently circuitous nature of these roadways, extending far from the shafts, placed British mines at a serious disadvantage when locomotive haulage techniques were innovated in the Ruhr, Holland and Belgium.

Adherence to traditional methods of haulage meant that by the end of the interwar period, a haulage worker handled on average 5 tons of coal per shift in Great Britain, between 20 and 25 tons in Holland, and 50 tons in the United States.[54] This was one of the main explanations of the relatively slow growth of output per man-shift in this country. In 1939, Britain's output per man-shift *underground* was 30 cwts: it could have been almost 10 cwts higher had the same tonnage per haulage worker been handled as in Holland. Hence a meaningful analysis of variations in labour productivity between countries must take account of a number of issues. On the technical side, developments in mechanically cutting the coal must be considered in the light of the significant differences which existed in underground haulage and loading techniques. These, in turn, must be taken in conjunction with the physical difficulties encountered in mining the coal in the separate coal-producing areas.

However, the foregoing analysis tends to overstate the degree of technical backwardness in British coalmining between the wars. Reliance on aggregate figures of mechanisation and labour productivity can be misleading. They conceal important differences between regions in the application of technology and the level of efficiency. By the end of the interwar years, less than 60% of British coal was mechanically cut, a proportion well below that of the main coal-producing nations in the rest of Europe. But this figure was depressed by mining practice in one or two coalfields of the country. In the great bulk of districts, the proportion of output cut by machines compared not unfavourably with that of other countries. Table 8 provides a comprehensive view of the physical conditions and performance of the major coalmining districts within Britain.

Table 8

Costs and Profitability Per Ton, Aggregate Horse-Power, Mechanisation and Labour Productivity in British Coalmining, Selected Districts, 1924-37

		Wage Costs s. d.	Total Costs s. d.	Gross Proceeds s. d.	Profit(+) or Loss(−) s. d.	Aggregate Horsepower of Electric Motors in Use (000)	% of Output Mechan. Cut %	% of Output Mechan. C'veyed %	Output Per Manshift cwts	Physical Mining Conditions
Durham	1924	12 9¼	18 9¼	19 11	+1 1¾	240.3	14	—[1]	17.16	Large proportion of mines worked out, or nearing exhaustion. Extensive mining, therefore, of undersea coals at considerable depths, with constant danger of flooding. Difficult mining conditions.
	1927	9 0¼	14 5¼	13 9	− 8¼	255.9	18	—	21.68	
	1929	7 9½	12 6½	12 9¾	+ 3¼	262.2	22	7	21.65	
	1932	7 9¾	12 10½	12 6	− 4½	273.7	33	11	22.09	
	1937	8 10¼	13 11¾	14 6	+ 6¼	328.7	40	22	21.75	
North-umberland	1924	12 6	18 2¼	18 7½	+ 5¼	75.3	25	—	17.30	District highly mechanised: mining conditions fair.
	1927	8 7¼	13 6¾	12 10¾	− 8	92.4	42	—	21.66	
	1929	7 0¼	11 2¼	11 8	+ 5¾	100.1	55	14	22.54	
	1932	7 1½	11 7¾	11 2¾	− 5	114.9	75	28	22.76	
	1937	8 1¼	13 2¾	14 3½	+1 0¾	144.4	91	49	23.28	
Yorkshire	1924	—	—	—	—	186.5	16	—	—	South Yorks. a relatively recent and modern coalfield, characterised by the uniformity and thickness of its seams. West Yorks., an older field, possesses shallow seams. Mining conditions relatively good.
	1927	10 8¼	15 2	15 2¾	+ 0¾	223.7	17	—	21.93	
	1929	9 2½	13 1½	13 8¾	+ 7¼	231.9	18	9	23.49	
	1932	9 0½	13 3½	13 9¼	+ 5¾	254.7	26	16	24.42	
	1937	9 8½	14 1¼	15 5¼	+1 4	306.3	51	51	26.34	

South Wales[2]	1924	14	3	20	11	21	4	+	5	376.3	5	—	16.07	Coal near surface and cannot be easily mined with machines. Hand mining often appropriate.
	1927	11	2	16	11½	15	10	−1	1½	421.6	7	—	19.52	
	1929	9	11¾	14	11½	15	1	+	1½	426.0	9	16	20.46	
	1932	10	0	15	8	15	8½	+	0½	436.6	12	20	19.36	
	1937	10	9½	16	8½	17	1½	+	5	462.2	24	40	20.59	
Lancs., Cheshire & N. Staffs.	1924	14	7¾	20	6	21	1¼	+	7¼	108.0	17	—	14.45	Heavily faulted: many of richer seams worked out. Less productive seams being mined, often at considerable depth. High levels of efficiency in N. Staffs. Difficult mining conditions in Lancs.
	1927	13	1½	18	10¾	18	4½	—	6¼	118.4	20	—	16.46	
	1929	11	7	16	11¼	16	10	—	1¼	124.0	29	19	17.62	
	1932	11	2½	16	7½	16	9¼	+	1¾	125.9	45	39	18.46	
	1937	11	3	16	10¼	18	3¾	+1	5½	148.1	71	73	20.77	
Scotland	1924	12	10¾	18	2¼	19	0¼	+	10	274.2	47	—	18.82	Heavily faulted: thin seams worked at considerable depth. Strata often steep and varied. Water prevalent. Difficult mining conditions.
	1927	9	4	14	1	13	3	—	10	285.3	56	—	22.74	
	1929	8	5¼	12	7¾	12	11	+	3¼	300.8	63	29	23.74	
	1932	7	10¾	11	11	11	6½	—	4½	296.7	69	42	24.41	
	1937	9	4½	13	11½	15	9¼	+1	9¾	359.4	79	57	23.96	
Gt. Britain	1924	13	3	18	8¾	19	10¾	+1	2	1,481.9	19	—	17.59	
	1927	10	7½	15	8¼	15	2½	—	5¾	1,684.1	23	—	20.61	
	1929	9	2	13	7½	14	0	+	4½	1,753.7	28	14	21.69	See Table 7
	1932	9	0¾	13	9	13	11	+	2	1,855.3	38	25	21.99	
	1937	9	9¾	14	8½	15	11¼	+1	2¾	2,162.0	57	51	23.35	

SOURCES:

Annual Reports of the Secretary for Mines: Jones, Cartwright & Guenault, op. cit., pp. 57-8 *passim;* Neuman, op. cit., pp. 43-6 *passim;* PEP, op. cit., pp. 43-61; Scottish Home Department; *Scottish Coalfields: Report of the Scottish Coalfields Committee,* 1944; *Samuel Commission 1925,* pp. 46-9; The Fuel Economist, *Britain's Fuel Problems* (1927).

NOTES:

1. — = not available.
2. Particulars for this district relate to the twelve months Feb.-Jan. inclusive.

Table 8 shows that not much more than half of Britain's output of coal was mechanically cut and conveyed by the end of the interwar period. As noted above underground conveying remained an intractable problem and was probably the greatest technical weakness of British coalmining. But the table also illustrates that in several districts, notably Northumberland, Scotland and Lancashire and Cheshire, cutting by machinery was relatively far advanced. The proportion cut was also extremely high in several of the small coalfields not included in Table 8. For instance, three-quarters or more of the output of Derbyshire, Nottinghamshire, Leicestershire and North Wales was mechanically cut in 1937. Hence retardation in the use of coal-cutting machinery in only a few coalfields of the country served to deflate the overall level of mechanisation achieved. Two districts, South Wales and Durham, were particularly backward in this respect but in both special factors militated against the extensive use of machinery[55] (see Chapter 5, section 3 above).

A blanket condemnation of British owners for their lack of enterprise is therefore not appropriate. Their record of innovation compared reasonably well with that overseas in both mechanical cutting and the employment of electricity above and below ground. Aggregate horse-power of electric motors in use increased by 46% in Britain between 1924-37 and in several districts expansion was very much greater. Moreover, in assessing the rate of technical innovation in British coalmining, the depressed profit margins of the industry and complete absence of any form of government control over the exploitation of the seams must be borne in mind. The former meant that British owners lacked the reserves of capital necessary for technical re-equipment on a scale commensurate with that achieved in several European countries. The opportunity to mechanise more fully had existed during the period of heady prosperity before the first world war but already by the late 1920's it was too late without the heavy assistance or 'control' of the State. Without government intervention the collieries could not operate as efficiently as those in Germany, where 75% of production during the interwar period came from the Ruhr. Here was a relatively homogeneous area in which natural conditions were similar for all pits and the orderly extraction of the seams by mechanical means was supervised by the State.[56]

Table 8 also permits mechanisation and output per man-shift to be examined in conjunction with the natural difficulties involved in mining in each district. These were the principal determinants of total production costs. It has been demonstrated[57] by means of simple regression analysis that a strong positive relationship existed between the development of mechanisation and increasing productivity in the great bulk of the coal-producing districts of Britain. Indeed, an increasing degree of mechanisation between the wars 'explained' a significant proportion of the increase in labour productivity.[58] The data provided in Table 8 support this conclusion. As mechanisation developed so too did labour productivity and hence, the greater was the effect on the major cost item in coalmining, wages. In general, the greater the advance of mechanisation, the greater the rise in output per man-shift, although natural mining conditions could influence this relationship—as in the case of the Yorkshire coalfield, for example, where a comparatively modest increase in mechanisation was accompanied by a major rise in output per man-shift due to the relative ease of mining the coal. Hence, coalmining mechanisation and labour productivity directly and significantly affected *total costs of production* but were not, in themselves, the sole determinants of *profitability.*

This can be readily demonstrated by referring to Table 8. Both Scotland and Northumberland achieved a relatively advanced degree of mechanisation between 1924 and 1937. Indeed, during the 1920's, the Scottish district was in the forefront of those applying the new technology, having a percentage of output mechanically cut and conveyed that was never less than *twice* as high as in Britain as a whole.[59] In both districts, an advanced degree of electrification below ground existed by the end of the interwar period. In view of extensive mechanisation, output per man-shift in Scotland and Northumberland was relatively high as both fought to keep their prices competitive and offset the disadvantage of possessing relatively small shares of the valuable, high-quality grades of coal. The great bulk of output in the two districts consisted of ordinary types of coal which commanded relatively low prices.

Because of their achievements in expanding mechanisation and labour productivity, total production costs remained comparatively low in Scotland and Northumberland. Indeed, in this respect, both districts were consistently below the average level of costs obtaining in British coalmining as a whole (See Table 8). Yet, while costs were relatively low, so too were gross proceeds—a function largely of the demand for, and hence selling-price of, the grades of coal produced. *Greater efficiency did not, therefore, necessarily mean greater profitability.* In the last resort, market conditions determined profitability. Table 8 indicates that the level of profits per ton in each district was generally well below the national average. That demand conditions were largely responsible for this relative lack of prosperity in the two districts is confirmed by the details provided in Table 9 of prices and qualities of coal produced.

Table 9, which illustrates the average net selling-price per ton in the main districts over selected years, makes clear that it was precisely in Scotland and Northumberland that prices obtained for coal were at their lowest. In absolute terms, the price of coal per ton raised in

185

Table 9

Average Net Selling Value Per Ton of Coal Raised in Districts Specified 1924-37, and Grades of Coal Produced
In Each District (Current Prices: 1924=100)

District	1924	1927	1929	1932	1937	Grades of Coal Produced[1]
	s. d.	s. d.	s. d.	s. d.	s. d.	
Durham	19 5.79	13 6.85	12 7.18	12 2.46	14 2.54	Coal possesses excellent coking qualities. Gas and coking coal produced in quantity.
Index	100	70	65	63	73	
Northumberland	18 0.34	12 7.35	11 7.54	11 4.29	14 0.26	Gas, house and particularly steam coal produced. Virtually no coking coal.
Index	100	70	65	63	78	
Yorkshire, South	18 1.13	14 2.48	13 0.51	12 9.10	14 4.56	Wide variety of coal produced, including excellent quality coking coal.
Index	100	79	72	71	80	
Yorkshire, West	18 8.46	15 6.82	14 0.00	13 11.60	15 5.26	
Index	100	83	75	75	83	
South Wales (Anthracite)	27 4.78	20 10.20	19 10.02	20 7.84	20 9.25	Large deposits of anthracite present, plus wide variety of other grades including high-quality steam, household and gas coal.
Index	100	76	72	75	76	
Other	19 9.48	15 0.43	13 11.35	13 10.59	15 4.58	
	100	76	71	70	79	

Lancs, Cheshire & N. Staffs.	19	10.65	17	5.49	15	11.71	16	2.00	17	5.74
Index		100		88		80		81		88
Scotland	17	5.19	12	3.47	12	0.39	10	9.17	14	9.59
Index		100		71		69		62		85
Great Britain	18	10.11	14	7.34	13	5.21	13	3.11	15	2.36
Index		100		78		71		70		81

Lancs, Cheshire & N. Staffs.: Common grades of coal predominate, including gas, steam, household and manufacturing coal. Limited production of coking coal.

Scotland: Common grades of coal predominate, especially gas, household and manufacturing coal. Limited output of anthracite.

SOURCES:
Annual Reports of the Secretary for Mines; Neuman, op. cit., pp. 508-23; The Fuel Economist, *Britain's Fuel Problems*; Rowe, *Wages in the Coal Industry*, pp. 16-34.

NOTE:
1. After 1945, an effort was made to systematise the classification of coal. Different grades were ranked according to their calorific value, which in turn depended largely on carbon content. On this basis, the ranking of coal, in order of value, was as follows: anthracite, low volatile steam (semi-anthracite), coking, gas, household, and manufacturing coal. See A. Beacham, 'The Coal Industry', in D. Burn (ed.), *The Structure of British Industry* (1958), I, NIESR, pp. 108-10.

each district generally remained well below that of any of the other districts specified in Table 9. Indeed, by the end of the 1929-32 world depression, it can be seen that the average price per ton of Scottish coal amounted to only 80% of that in Great Britain as a whole and to a mere 52% of the top selling-price available for anthracite coal in South Wales. Moreover, between 1924-32, the rapidity of the price fall in Scotland and Northumberland, as measured by the index of prices for each district, was matched only by the Durham district. The effect of these low selling-prices was more than sufficient to offset the comparative efficiency, as measured by the levels of mechanisation and labour productivity, prevailing in both Scotland and Northumberland. The reverse was also true. High selling-prices, as in Yorkshire and particularly in South Wales, could compensate for a relatively low level of mechanisation. Machine mining was therefore important in that it helped to reduce money wages, the major cost-factor in coalmining, but its effect on labour productivity and on profitability could be more than outweighed by adverse mining conditions in particular districts, the low selling-prices of the coal produced, or by a combination of both. One further factor could materially influence the relationship between these variables—the organisation and layout of mines in the different coalfields of the country. This forms the subject of the chapter which follows.

8 Industrial Relations, Employment and Wages, 1919-1939

1   THE PROBLEM OF INDUSTRIAL RELATIONS

The most acute and bitter struggles in the field of industrial relations during the interwar period occurred in the coal industry. Indeed, it may be said that the miners were in large measure responsible for shaping the nature of employer/employee relationships after 1918. This stemmed from the basic importance of coalmining, both as a major employer of labour and through its provision of fuel to other sectors of the economy. However, the nature and outcome of the industrial conflict between miners, owners and Government are sufficiently well known to require no elaborate repetition here. A massive literature has been published in recent years on the climate of industrial relations between the wars and particularly the causes and consequences of the General Strike.[1] Rather the purpose of this section is to emphasise only certain aspects of the struggle between capital and labour: those necessary to the analysis of employment, wages and profitability which is undertaken in the following sections.

From the outset the Triple Alliance, formed in 1914, held no revolutionary connotations for the miners. It was simply a means of ensuring co-operation against common opponents. Strikes 'in sympathy' by partners in the Alliance were generally regarded as a last resort, a method of applying more effective pressure when action in an individual industry had failed, or appeared to be failing. It is true that between 1918 and 1926 the policy of the MFGB was strongly influenced by syndicalists whose first objective was to bring the industry under public ownership. If such a formal take-over of the mines was not possible, they were determined at least to secure a legally enforceable system of pooling of revenues throughout the industry in order to permit the creation of a national wages fund.[2] Syndicalism retained its appeal down to 1925 but it is clear that the General Strike owed more to the experience acquired and the practical effects of the militancy which existed between 1910 and 1914.[3] The Triple Alliance was revived after the war in response to the miners' claims for higher wages and shorter hours. Although the industry still operated under Government 'control', there had been no significant reorganisation or regrouping. Moreover, while wage rates had been substantially increased from 1914, miners not only felt they were falling behind in the race to keep up with the rising cost of living but also wished to assert their claim for national wage agreements.

Above all else loomed the issue of nationalisation of the mines. The matter had been first raised by miners in the late 1880's in the belief that, under State ownership, a larger share of the proceeds of the industry would accrue to labour and greater attention would be paid to safety and the proper maintenance of equipment. It was argued that nationalisation would be in the best interests not only of the miner but of the country as a whole. It would promote more economical working of the mines and reduce the existing 'great waste of our mineral supplies'.[4] From the beginning, mines nationalisation had been complicated by the question of ownership of the minerals. State acquisition of mineral rights was persistently demanded by most sections of the mining labour force as a necessary first step towards nationalisation of the entire industry. Most also believed that the State had no obligation to compensate proprietors for the loss of mineral ownership, a view typified by Keir Hardie who argued that 'no one has created minerals; they do not belong to any person in particular, but to the people as a whole.'[5] However, over this and indeed the whole question of mines nationalisation, there was a lack of unanimity among miners' leaders. Several of the men's representatives argued against any form of nationalisation before the Royal Commission on Mining Royalties in 1893. This was particularly the view of those from the Northern Coalfield who argued that royalty payments acted as a 'leveller' between well-endowed and less favoured collieries. High royalties were paid by pits which enjoyed good natural conditions and special advantages. If royalties were abolished these pits would experience the greatest reduction in costs, enabling them to drive their less fortunate counterparts out of production. Ralph Young, secretary of the Northumberland Miners' Association, put it plainly when he declared that since royalties in his district 'were less than the average royalty paid throughout the United Kingdom and especially by our competitors, it would not be an advantage to us as Northumbrians to go in for abolition.'[6]

Lack of agreement within the labour movement persisted down to the first world war and was partly responsible for the failure of Nationalisation Bills in 1893, 1907 and 1913. Over time, the miners modified their commitment to nationalisation from simply demanding public ownership to a form of reorganisation that would permit them to play a substantive part in the management of the industry.[7] As Robert Smillie, president of the MFGB pointed out, 'the capitalist is not the only person who invests in the mines. He invests his money.

The miner invests his labour, his time and his life. Yet he has no say in the conduct of the industry in which he lives'.[8] To the embarrassment of the Government this view was endorsed by the Majority Report of the 1919 Royal Commission (the Sankey Commission) which urged that miners be given an effective voice in the industry's development.[9] The Commission, set up by Lloyd George in an attempt to side-step the several issues being pressed by the miners, was unable to produce a unanimous report. This was hardly surprising since it comprised an equal number of masters and men. The subsequent division of opinion along predictable lines allowed Lloyd George to escape the commitment previously given that the recommendations of the Sankey Commission would be implemented.

Although the miners' side on the Commission and Sankey himself voted in favour of nationalisation, making 7 out of a possible 13 votes, the concept of radical reorganisation was unacceptable to the Government. Instead, Government 'control' of the mines was pro-longed and the Seven-Hour Day conceded by Act of Parliament. At a critical time, outright confrontation with the miners was therefore avoided, but at the cost of further embittering relations within the industry. Neither side was happy with the type of 'compromise' reached in 1919, a factor which in part explains the inflexibility and en-trenched positions taken up a few years later.

Of greater importance in shaping the events of 1926 was the defeat of 'Black Friday' in 1921. With the end of the post-war boom, the threat of strike-action in 1920 had secured for the miners a temporary increase in wage rates, pending a permanent settlement to be made by end-March 1921. When no agreement had been reached,[10] the miners appealed to the Triple Alliance for support in their efforts to resist wage reductions and the type of profit-sharing by district which was envisaged with the return of the mines to private enterprise. After both railwaymen and transport workers had withdrawn their promise of assistance in the debacle of 'Black Friday', the miners were left to strike on their own. Defeat was inevitable and after a stoppage of 94 days they returned to work under the new Wages Agreement of 1921 (details of which are given below in section 3). It implemented a profit-sharing scheme for wage regulation and a minimum level beneath which wages could not fall. At the same time, a sum not exceeding £10 million was voted to the industry to make the fall in wages in the three months from July more gradual in those districts where immediate and substantial reductions were regarded as necessary.

In the event, although the subvention of miners' wages cost the Exchequer only £7 million, the residue was not devoted to the assistance of coalmining. Both the Prime Minister and Baldwin, President of the Board of Trade, made it clear to Frank Hodges,

Secretary of the MFGB, that the coal industry would not receive preferential treatment. 'At a time such as the present', wrote Baldwin, 'it is impossible to single out the Coal Mining Industry, or any particular industry, for special assistance; the whole available resources of the State must be devoted to the financing of schemes for the relief of unemployment and for the restoration of trade generally.'[11]

The collapse of the Triple Alliance in 1921 was followed by the longest period of industrial peace that coalmining had known since 1910. Defeat in 1921 had left the MFGB in a weakened condition[12] and, anyway, it was able to negotiate peacefully a major wage increase (see section 3) due to modest economic recovery in 1923-4. But for neither masters nor men did peace signify satisfaction with the current position. With the deterioration in commercial activity in the first half of 1925, owners felt obliged not only to terminate the new Wages Agreement of 1924 but to seek an extension of hours of work. In the dispute which followed, first the General Council of the TUC and later the Government were drawn into the negotiations. The result was the rather unexpected, and temporary, triumph for the miners of 'Red Friday'. Under the terms of settlement in July 1925, it was agreed to grant a £10 million subsidy to coalmining for a period of nine months. During this time a Royal Commission would be established (the Samuel Commission) to produce a policy for the reorganisation and reconstruction of the industry. The findings of this Commission, when they were published in 1926, were to have a vital bearing not only on the immediate dispute within the industry but on attitudes and policies which shaped its long-term development.

The Samuel Commission presented a comprehensive and wide-ranging report, emphasising the major problems of loss of effective demand and the chronic surplus capacity which had subsequently been created. The industry required thorough reorganisation, involving amalgamation into larger units of production rather than state ownership. Royalties should be nationalised—in other words, public ownership of the coal but not of the mines—the distribution of coal improved, and reforms introduced to promote better working conditions and the general welfare of miners. But on the immediate issue of wages, the Commission recommended on the one hand that national wage agreements should continue and on the other that the Government subsidy should be terminated. Hence, in the short term, wage-reductions would be inevitable while measures were taken to reorganise the structure of production. Although the Commission accepted that mining wages were 'even now lower than we desire and hope to see them', it pointed out that 'the minimum wage since 1924 has been fixed so high relatively to the economic ability of the districts as

192

practically to obliterate and replace the economic wage; to a large extent it did so even between 1921 and 1924'.[13]

So much has been written about the subsequent negotiations and the dominant part played in them by the Samuel Report that it is unnecessary to dwell upon them here. The intransigence of both sides, the inability of the General Council and Baldwin's Government to come to terms and the failure of various initiatives rendered a general conflict inevitable. The General Strike at the beginning of May 1926 lasted for nine days, but the miners stayed out until the end of November in the longest, most costly and bitter stoppage in British industrial history. By the following month, the last of them were back at work, having to accept the most humiliating of terms. There was a return to district agreements, in most districts the eight-hour day was restored and in several, immediate wage reductions were imposed. In the following year, it seemed that the Government was intent on reaping the fruits of victory by passing the Trades Disputes Act which outlawed General Strikes and stipulated that in future union members would have to 'contract in' to pay the political levy to the Labour Party. The MFGB was effectively destroyed as a fighting force for almost a decade, suffering a severe loss of membership and funds.

There can be no doubting the severity of the treatment handed out to miners after the collapse of 1926. They were forced back to work on terms considerably worse than they could have obtained, with much less grief, during the pre-strike negotiations. However, on a wider stage, there is much less certainty about the long-term effects which the General Strike and its aftermath had on the trade union movement as a whole. There seems little case for regarding the events of 1926 as a watershed in the history of the labour movement: whatever its short-term consequences the General Strike had no lasting effect on general union membership. Nor does it appear to have had much impact on union behaviour in terms of strikes and working days lost.[14] Yet in other ways it left its mark on working-class sentiments. It weakened trade unionism in the sense that it led to a loss of trust in the General Council and in joint action by unions. Moreover, it deepened the gulf between official union leaders and the rank and file.[15] On a more positive note, it demonstrated just how powerful unions could be if, and when, they could be brought together in common cause. Many employers heeded the lesson that, in future, co-operation was likely to be more advantageous than confrontation. This attitude was reflected in wage negotiations after 1926. The district wage agreements which were drawn up, terminable at different dates, still incorporated relatively high minimum percentage additions. In all districts, except Northumberland and Durham, these minimum percentages varied between 20 and 30%

above the 'standard'.[16]

The bitter industrial relations of 1918 to 1926 had little effect on one vital area, the structure and organisation of the industry. As observed in Chapter 9 below, the Mining Industry Act of 1926 was a watered down version of the proposals advanced by the Samuel Commission to encourage amalgamation. The Railway and Canal Commission entrusted with the task of securing such amalgamation, was rendered impotent by the failure of the Act to provide it with compulsory powers. Nor were the miners any longer in a position to press for the reconstruction of the industry into larger groupings. It is doubtful, anyway, whether they would have supported reorganisation along these lines, even as a second-best to nationalisation.[17] After the General Strike militant policies were impracticable, particularly once the economy had entered the downswing of 1929-32. Hopes that the Government might regard coalmining as a 'special case' came to nothing, just as they had at the start of the 'twenties. At the first meeting of the Cabinet Committee on the Coal Industry, chaired by Ramsay Macdonald in 1929, it was emphasised at the outset that 'the Government saw no source from which wages could be paid other than the proceeds of the industry itself.'[18]

Already by that time the coal industry was being operated on lines far removed from those obtaining earlier in the decade. Collective marketing arrangements, drawn up in each of the major coalfields, were given statutory force by the 1930 Coal Mines Act. In contrast to the bitterness engendered after the war by the threat of nationalisation, the Act of 1930 brought the State fully into the conduct of the industry with relatively little fuss. At the same time, the length of the working day was shortened to 7½ hours despite opposition from the coalowners. The latter argued that a reduction of half an hour in the existing eight-hour districts would increase costs by an average of between 9d. and 1/6d. per ton according to the district. Many collieries, it was alleged, would be unable to continue at all on 7½ hours, especially those heavily committed to machine-mining.[19] However, the reduction was enforced with few noticeable consequences since, at the same time, the 1930 Act ensured that all collieries were given a share of the market. A few years later the miners secured a return to national wage settlements, again in face of the serious misgivings of employers.[20] In these respects, therefore, much of the ground lost by the defeat of 1926 had been made good before the second world war.

If industrial relations, militant or peaceful, failed to influence the structure of coalmining, they were little more successful in improving the unemployment position and safety record of the industry. Mining unemployment remained at a relatively high level due to the deficiency of demand and the gradual rationalisation of the industry during the

1930's (see section 2). Perhaps most disappointing was the failure to bring about a significant reduction in fatal and non-fatal accident rates. From 1922, statistics of man-shifts worked, collected by the Mines Department, can be used as the basis for calculating accident rates. They provide a more accurate assessment than accident rates based on employment since they take into consideration the time during which workers were exposed to risk and eliminate errors resulting from irregularities of employment. Table 1 below shows accident rates during the interwar period on the basis of man-shifts worked.

Table 1

Persons Killed and Injured by Accidents at Coal Mines, 1922-1936
(Average Annual Rates per 100,000 man-shifts worked)

| Period | Killed Under- ground & Surface | Killed and Injured[1] by Type of Accident | | | Surface All Causes | Under- ground & Surface All Causes |
| | | Underground | | | | |
		Falls of Ground	Haulage Accidents	All Other Causes		
1922-26	0.40	28.5	21.0	27.7	24.7	65.5
1927-31	0.43	31.6	22.5	29.8	22.2	69.7
1932-36	0.44	31.1	22.6	26.9	20.9	65.9

SOURCE:
Report of the Royal Commission on Safety in Coal Mines, Cmd. 5890, 1938.
NOTE:
1. Defined as being disabled for more than three days.

The death rate above and below ground actually increased between 1922/26 and 1932/36, despite better supervision by officials and improved maintenance of the roads underground. The Mines Department was established in 1920 under the Mining Industry Act of that year and accepted responsibility for health and safety previously shouldered by the Home Office. By the late 1930's, the average number of visits made by inspectors per mine per year was a little over ten, four times the frequency of inspection before the first world war. The increase in death rate between the wars is all the more surprising when it is remembered that the use of machinery was steadily increasing, performing exhausting and dangerous work instead of men. However the beneficial influence which these factors might have had was more than offset by several forces working in the opposite direction.

The machines themselves involved risk when in operation, requiring constant care and skilful handling. Moreover they emphasised the economic necessity of maintaining a steady cycle of operations, spread over three or more successive shifts in several districts. Intensive working meant less time available for face ripping and repair. There was also a substantial increase during the period in the number of shots fired per ton of coal brought down and in the use of electrical equipment, particularly at the face. Finally, the more rapid advance of the face brought with it not only new problems of roof control but also an increase in the rate of emission of firedamp and coal dust. In contrast, therefore, to the steady reduction before 1914, there was a long stagnation, and even some tendency to rise, of fatality rates during the interwar period. In most years, mining was still the most dangerous of the major industries. A man was nine times more likely to be killed in a mine than in a factory.[21] The safety-record in British coalmining was, in fact, inferior to that of certain principal European coal-producing countries. The mean rate of those killed and injured in Britain per 100,000 man-shifts worked above and below ground stood at 66.7 in 1930-34. This was considerably better than the rates of 99.3 in the anthracite coal mines of the United States and 136.4 in French coal mines. On the other hand, it compared less favourably with the 61.6 and 64.0 achieved in Poland and Germany (Prussia).[22]

2 MINING EMPLOYMENT

An examination of the distribution of gross national product in Britain vividly illustrates the change in fortune of coalmining during the present century. The contribution of mining and quarrying fell from 6.0% in 1907 to 5.4% in 1924 and to 3.1% in 1935.[23] Nowhere was the effect of this relative decline felt more keenly than in the labour market where conditions confronting miners rapidly deteriorated after the 1926 General Strike. Until that year, coalmining employment had been sustained at or near its pre-war level due to the effects of the post-war boom, the 1922 strike in the United States coalfields and the occupation of the Ruhr in the following year. After 1926, employment in the industry steadily declined, a trend accelerated by the 1929-32 world depression. The partial recovery in the late 1930's was not able to make good the ground lost since 1929, let alone that since the first world war. By 1937/8, employment in coalmining stood at just over three-quarters of a million, one-fifth below the 1929 level, and 30% below that of 1913. Moreover, the decline was greatest in the more productive groups, those working underground.

The extension of the Unemployment Insurance Scheme in 1920 afforded a clearer impression of the extent of unemployment in the industry. Although criticism has been made of the statistics published as a result of the Scheme,[24] the data at least give an indication of the general trend. At the same time, details published by the Ministry of Labour of the number of insured workers in coalmining can be used to check the employment totals provided on an annual basis by the Mines Department. Not surprisingly in view of the very different methods employed to collect and classify the statistics, there is some divergence between the two series. In Table 2 estimates of the labour force are provided by both sources, together with the percentage unemployed in coalmining and in UK industry as a whole.

Table 2

Size of Labour Force in UK Coalmining and Per cent of Insured Workers Unemployed in the Coal Industry and All UK Industries

Year	Number of Persons employed in and about Coal Mines (000)	Insured labour force in coalmining[1]		% of insured labour force in coalmining unemployed[1]	% of insured labour force unemployed in all industries
		(000)	as % of total insured labour force		
Aver.	(1)	(2)	(3)	(4)	(5)
1909/1913	1,069.5	—	—	—	—
1925	1,102.4	1,233.3	10.4	25.5	11.0
1929	956.7	1,074.7	8.9	19.0	10.3
1932	819.3	1,044.9	8.2	40.7	21.9
1934	788.2	981.5	7.6	36.5	16.6
1937	791.7	868.4	5.7	19.5	10.6

SOURCE:
Annual Reports of the Secretary for Mines; Ministry of Labour Gazette, published annually.
NOTES:
1. As at July of each year.
2. Taken at June of each year.

Table 2 shows that while Ministry of Labour estimates of the work-force in coalmining (Col. 2) consistently exceed those published by the Mines Department (Col. 1), the trends indicated by the two sources are very similar. Each shows that the size of the labour force fell steadily from the mid-1920's, with the result that the proportion of coalminers in the total insured work-force dwindled from over 10% in 1925 to 5.7% in 1937 (Col. 3). Table 2 also indicates that the proportion of workers unemployed in coalmining was roughly almost twice as high as that in UK industry as a whole. No fewer than two-fifths of the labour force in the coal industry were out of work at the trough of the world depression in 1932 and even by the end of the period, when the pressure of rearmament resulted in some increase in output, about one-fifth of the miners were still without a job. Unemployment on this scale was particularly serious for the coal industry because occupational rehabilitation was extremely difficult for coalminers. Moreover, the coalfields were generally located in the most severely depressed parts of the country, conditions which they, themselves, had helped to sustain. As a result, alternative work could not readily be found in the same vicinity and geographical mobility of labour was the most difficult to obtain. The operation, and marginal achievements, of the Industrial Transference Scheme bore adequate testimony to the problems of shifting men from areas of labour-surplus to regions offering greater employment opportunities.[25] The Scheme, initiated in 1928, was designed to assist geographical mobility, and particularly the movement of miners, to the expanding regions of the South and Midlands. In the event, it did little to even out the geographical incidence of general unemployment but did achieve a limited success in reducing unemployment in coalmining, the purpose for which it had been originally designed.

The serious decline in coalmining employment can be attributed to the combined influence of several factors: the business cycle, technical progress and structural changes. The relative importance of these varied at different periods, but it can safely be concluded that the cyclical influence was not the starting-point of the slump in mining employment. The run-down of the labour force in mining was a steady and consistent trend, the result of a secular decline in the demand for coal, notably from overseas countries. Even when general economic activity revived, as for instance in the 1930's, the decrease in employment in coalmining continued. This was quite contrary to the employment trend in British industry as a whole. General industrial employment did not sink as low as that of mining in 1932 and subsequently recovered rapidly in the 1930's. The cyclical factor would therefore appear to be of relatively small importance in British coalmining. Clearly other forces were at work. Of these, a minor role can also be assigned to technological change. As observed in Chapter 7 the rate of growth of labour productivity was relatively low after 1918, largely due to the hesitant introduction of mechanical methods of coal-cutting. In addition, the substitution of capital for labour in face operations could, in the short run, be offset by the increase in oncost workers required to service the new equipment.

Rather, employment in the coal industry was most seriously affected by the structural factor: that is, by changes in the demand for coal. Between the wars, structural unemployment in world coalmining was principally due to the transfer of demand for the mineral from some countries to others, the transfer of demand from coal to other sources of energy, and economies effected in coal use. The British industry suffered in full measure from each of these influences. Indeed the most striking example of structural unemployment caused by a shift of demand to other countries occurred in Britain. The resultant collapse of the export trade entailed cutting back on production and a decline in employment. As Table 2 indicates, there was not only an absolute fall in the number of miners but also a marked deterioration in the ratio of miners to the total number of industrial workers. Coalmining was, in effect, a 'special case', in which factors operated, particularly on the demand-side of the industry, to an extent not evident in other trades.

3 WAGES AND COSTS

The depressed market environment and low profitability of the coal mines inevitably had repercussions on wages. In turn, since they formed such a high proportion of total costs, movements in wage rates and earnings had a vital bearing on the general well-being and prosperity of the industry. It was alleged that, at one and the same time, the level of wages after the war represented a wholly inadequate remuneration of labour and a formidable drain on the owners' resources.[26] To understand how the cost of labour affected the industry, it is necessary to have some knowledge of the factors governing the determination of wages.[27] The National Wage Agreement of 1921 established a common system of wage determination for the whole industry, although it did allow for district variations in wage earnings. It specified for each district a flat rate per shift known as the 'basis rate', with piecework rates being negotiated locally. To the 'basis rate', which varied according to the type of work done in the district, was added a system of profit-sharing.[28] The standard wage[29] applicable in the district was deducted from gross proceeds, along with all other costs of production. From the surplus remaining, a standard profit equal to 17% of the standard district wage was deducted, thus leaving a residual which was then divided up between profits and wages in proportions which varied between districts.

Of crucial importance was the fact that the wage, so determined, was not to fall below a given minimum wage: that is, the 'basis rate' plus profit-sharing had to sum to a given minimum which in all districts consisted of standard wages plus 20% thereof. This minimum wage inevitably varied from one district to the next since it was founded on a 'basis rate' which itself varied between districts. In the event of net proceeds being insufficient to meet the minimum wage requirements the owners' share of net proceeds was encroached upon, or foregone altogether. This amount foregone by the owners was

199

either carried forward until profits recovered or written off after a specified period of time had elapsed. Finally in the case of low-paid day-wage workers, where the rates of wages determined in any district did not provide a subsistence wage, district boards, established to administer the new wages system assumed responsibility for 'making-up' the wage to a subsistence level. In practice, therefore, two minimum wages operated in the coal industry: the first automatically determined by a 20% addition to standard wages and the second by intervention when such an arrangement did not produce a subsistence wage. The intention of the wage-system was therefore to provide a minimum standard below which no wage-earner would fall while at the same time allowing district differences in profitability to be reflected in wages through profit-sharing.

Important modifications were made to this system of wage determination by the new Wages Agreement drawn up under a Labour Government in 1924. The Miners' Federation demanded that the deductions to be made on account of 'profits' in the district ascertainment of the 'wages fund' should be reduced from 17% of standard wages, and that the owner's proportion of the residual should also be reduced. More important, it was also proposed that the guaranteed minimum district percentage should be substantially increased from the prevailing 20% on standard wages. Under the terms of the new agreement in 1924, it was established that deductions on account of profits should be reduced from 17 to 15% of standard wages, and from 17 to 12% of the residual. Moreover, the minimum district percentage was increased from 20 to 33⅓% above standard wages, with adequate provision being made for the lower-paid men to bring any 'short-fall' in wages up to subsistence level. These provisions came into force at the beginning of May, 1924 and had an immediate impact on the industry. Their effect was to increase wage rates by about 11−12% in districts on the minimum percentage and by about 2-3% in other districts. At the same time, average proceeds during the last eight months of the year fell by 1s. 6d. per ton from their level during the first four months and 'other costs' rose by almost 2d. per ton. Hence for three-quarters of the year, not only were wage rates at a higher level but the fund available for their payment fell by approximately 1s. 8d. per ton.

Given a prosperous coal industry, this type of profit-sharing system might have worked well. In the event, the decline in demand for coal during the 1920's and hence the depressed level of proceeds meant that the minimum wage provisions had to be repeatedly invoked. With some justification the owners constantly brought to the forefront of the wages debate 'the ability of the industry to pay'.[30] The simple truth for the industry was that these provisions forced up the share of net proceeds accruing to labour to a level higher than the industry

200

could possibly afford. Indeed between 1921 and 1926 when the National Wages Agreement was in force, labour's share of net proceeds turned out in practice to be higher than that provided for under the Agreement of 1921 and higher than that intended under the Agreement of 1924. It was also higher than that envisaged once a return had been made to district agreements following the 1926 General Strike. This was because, even under district arrangements, the system of profit-sharing on the basis of ascertainments for each district and the enforced payment of minimum wages were retained.

In short, the misfortune of coalmining was that from the owners' point of view, the financial condition of the industry was critical and they were frequently compelled to make up wages to the agreed minimum at times when they could not afford it on economic grounds.[31] From the men's point of view, it was obviously not possible for them to accept less than a reasonable minimum standard of remuneration. Thus a gap existed between the economic level of wages on the one hand, and the social level on the other.[32] It was this gap which was directly responsible for the owners' termination of the 1924 Wages Agreement in July 1925, the Government's subvention of wages between 1925 and 1926 in an attempt to avert a national stoppage of the mines, and the General Strike which was called at the start of May, 1926.

The effect of this system of wage determination, operating under both national and district agreements, is examined by principal coalfields in Table 3 below.

Table 3 shows that in practice the proportion of net proceeds accruing to labour was at least 90% of the total and more frequently stood well above that figure. Indeed, since wage costs often exceeded available net proceeds, the owners' share had to be foregone altogether. Between 1925 and 1935, proceeds remained so depressed that only rarely were rates paid above the minimum. More specifically, in the years 1926-31 the existence of this floor beneath which wages could not fall was responsible for an expenditure of no less than £78 million in excess of the sum which the industry could afford on the evidence of the ascertainments.[33] The methods by which wages were determined therefore conferred on them a rigidity which, at certain periods, placed owners in an invidious position. In most districts they were squeezed throughout the interwar period by depressed selling prices and relatively low proceeds on the one side, and relatively high wage rates on the other. When, faced with a wage bill that he was often in no position to afford, the owner attempted to reduce wage costs by direct cuts in rates, his attempts were, not unnaturally, fiercely resisted by the workforce. In the years before 1926, when miners' disputes dominated industrial relations, the situation was exacerbated by the fact that National Agreements governed the structure of district

Table 3

(i) Average Earnings per Shift; (ii) Per annum[1]; (iii) Percentage of Wage Costs per Ton to Net Proceeds and (iv) Average Number of man-shifts Worked in Districts Specified, Selected Years, 1924-37

Year	Durham				Northumberland				Yorkshire				South Wales				Scotland				Gt. Britain			
	(i) s. d.	(ii) £	(iii) %	(iv)	(i) s. d.	(ii) £	(iii) %	(iv)	(i) s. d.	(ii) £	(iii) %	(iv)	(i) s. d.	(ii) £	(iii) %	(iv)	(i) s. d.	(ii) £	(iii) %	(iv)	(i) s. d.	(ii) £	(iii) %	(iv)
1924	10 2	129	92	254	9 10	125	97	254	N.A.				10 6	139	97	266	10 10	151	94	277	10 8	138	92	260
1927	9 2	116	108	252	8 8	109	108	252	10 10	125	100	230	10 1	124	111	246	9 8	136	110	283	10 1	123	105	244
1929	8 0	106	97	268	7 5	100	94	270	10 1	119	94	237	9 6	129	99	272	9 2	136	97	297	9 3	118	96	257
1932	8 1	99	105	244	7 8	99	106	260	10 2	107	95	210	8 11	113	100	253	8 10	128	105	291	9 2	109	98	239
1934	8 1	105	103	261	7 10	110	101	282	10 2	114	90	225	9 1	119	101	264	8 9	133	94	304	9 2	110	98	242
1937	9 1	125	94	275	9 0	126	88	280	11 11	150	88	252	10 5	143	96	275	10 4	158	84	306	10 8	144	89	270

SOURCE:
Annual Reports of the Secretary for Mines.
NOTES:
1. Excluding the value of allowances in kind.

wage rates. A reduction in wage rates in any one district was, therefore, almost impossible to achieve. On the other hand, any proposals for *general* wage reductions were met by national strikes in the industry as in 1921 and 1926.

Nor can it reasonably be argued that, by increasing productivity through greater mechanisation or rationalising the structure of the industry in order to eliminate small units of production, the owner would have been better able to accommodate his wage costs. In the former case, it has already been shown in Chapter 7 that relatively high productivity, as in Scotland and Northumberland, was no guarantee of a correspondingly high level of profitability. On the contrary, the financial results of several districts between the wars show unequivocally that a relatively high output per man-shift was little compensation for the inability to produce certain types of coal for which world demand was reasonably strong. In the latter instance, streamlining capacity by means of amalgamation into larger units was again not certain to promote a rapid increase in efficiency. As is shown in Chapter 9, smaller units could, and did, operate at least as efficiently as their larger counterparts during the interwar period.

Certain districts were, of course, more seriously affected than others by the depressed interwar environment. In Northumberland and Durham, for instance, selling-prices were relatively low with the result that minimum wage provisions dictated a level of profits well below the national average. Similarly in Scotland, a comparatively high output per man-shift could not offset low selling-prices together with a minimum wage only marginally below that of the UK as a whole. Again, the level of profits in the district generally remained well below the national average. Yet from the standpoint of the miner in Scotland not all was gloom and despondency. Table 3 illustrates that although earnings per *man-shift* in the district were generally less than the national average, *annual* earnings were extremely high. Throughout the 1930's, they remained consistently above those of other districts.[34] This apparent anomaly can be explained by referring to column (iv) of the district data shown in Table 3. In the 1930's for example, the highest number of man-shifts of any district was worked in Scotland. An average of 297 per annum was worked north of the border as opposed to only 252 in Great Britain as a whole. The miner in Scotland enjoyed higher annual earnings simply because he worked harder and completed, on average, a greater number of shifts.

PART FOUR

THE MODERN ERA:

RISK AND UNCERTAINTY UNDER NATIONALISATION

9 The State and Structural Change in Coalmining

1 STRUCTURE AND ORGANISATION BETWEEN THE WARS

Although the miners' call for nationalisation received short shrift after the first world war, the organisation and control of the industry continued to be central issues. In common with other staple industries, coal experienced a growing measure of Government intervention during the interwar period. Essentially, policy was drawn up according to the needs of the industry as a whole, with regional implications being largely ignored. Not until 1934 was some attempt made to differentiate between the various coal-producing districts, and then not on the basis of different regional requirements. Rather, a distinction was made between districts according to whether they catered for the inland or export market. However, it is possible to contrast State policy towards the industry in the 1920's with that of the subsequent decade. In the former, the State confined itself to exhorting owners to increase efficiency, believing that this could best be secured by amalgamation into larger units of production. There existed, it was alleged, a strong and positive correlation between size and efficiency. The larger the size of units, the greater the economies of scale: at the same time, amalgamation would facilitate the process of shearing off capacity surplus to requirements.[1] Yet, while favouring a policy of rationalisation, the State simultaneously provided the means whereby existing units of supply could remain operational without having to undertake reorganisation.

Financial assistance was offered to the industry in a variety of ways during the 1920's in an attempt to mitigate the effects of a depressed demand both on money wages and on the operation of the mines. The object was to provide a breathing-space during which collieries could be reorganised and wages reduced gradually. Thus, besides direct subsidy payments in 1921 and again in 1925-6, the industry benefited from several indirect forms of assistance. These included the exemption from duty of by-products produced from *British* Coal, the Rating and Valuation (Apportionment) Act, the Railway Freight Rebates Scheme and the Development Act.[2] Such measures were designed to ease the financial difficulties facing the collieries, but were incompatible with the aim of eliminating excess

207

capacity. The Samuel Commission in 1925, wrestling with the problems of demand-deficiency and surplus capacity, believed that the best prospect of creating a viable industry lay with rationalisation. This could be achieved through the amalgamation of hitherto competing units of production. Hence the Commission argued against the provision of subsidies to the industry on the ground that they constituted 'a dole to the inefficient to the disadvantage of the efficient'.[3] Accordingly the Government subsidy to coalmining was not renewed when it expired in 1926. Instead, the Samuel Commission's recommendations were used as a basis for the Mining Industry Act of 1926: rationalisation was accepted as offical policy for the first time.

Whereas it can be argued that before 1926 the State in its relations with coalmining had done no more than make bulges in the fence of orthodoxy, in that year it made an unmistakable hole in the fence and stepped outside. Already known in the roles of protector of the employees and consumers, the State now assumed the novel role of protector of employers against each other. While doing its utmost under the 1926 Act to encourage voluntary amalgamation, in the last resort Parliament gave power to the Court, upon application of coalowners, to coerce other owners into a planned organisation. Path-breaking though it may have been, the response to the Act was very disappointing. Compulsory powers were never used and of the voluntary amalgamations subsequently completed only a minority took advantage of the Act's provisions. Coalowners apparently preferred locally agreed amalgamations to any measure of reorganisation conducted under the auspices of the State. This was reflected in the late 1920's in a number of voluntary schemes, undertaken by the owners themselves, which had as their objective the stabilisation of the coal trade. Following the recommendations of a Departmental Committee on Co-operative Selling in 1926 (the Lewis Committee), the first voluntary marketing scheme commenced operations in Scotland in 1928. It was shortly followed by the South Wales scheme and a more important plan designed to cover the Midland Coalfield. The Central Collieries Commercial Association in the Midlands (the Five Counties Scheme)[4] regulated output and paid grants in aid of the export trade. Yet none of these marketing schemes achieved a lasting degree of success since under each the burdens and benefits experienced by different collieries were most unevenly distributed. Moreover, there was a lack of co-operation *between* existing district schemes with the result that fierce price-cutting and hostility developed. This could be resolved only by a nationally administered and fully co-ordinated plan for promoting the rationalisation and efficiency of the industry.

The Coal Mines Act of 1930 was an attempt to secure just such a national regulation of the trade. The Act carried to its logical conclusion the process started in 1926 of introducing a measure of state control over the industry. Henceforth the emphasis was on securing the reorganisation considered necessary to eliminate surplus capacity and thus increase productivity. Where before the State had relied mainly on encouraging voluntary amalgamation, more clearly defined compulsory powers were written into the 1930 Act. It was drafted in four parts, the first two of which had a vital bearing on the conduct of the industry during the 1930's. The remaining two sections, reducing hours of work from 8 to 7½ per day and making provision for a Coal Mines National Industrial Board to inquire into industrial disputes, had a considerably smaller impact on the industry. Under Part 1, machinery was created to regulate production, supply and sale of coal while Part 2 made provision for the creation of a Coal Mines Reorganisation Commission (CMRC) to secure, by compulsion if necessary, the rationalisation of the industry. Most of the conflict within coalmining during the 1930's stemmed from the contradictory policies which these two sections of the Act attempted to implement. At the very least the Act closed the book of *laissez-faire* with a bang. But whereas Part 1 tried to make the best of the existing structure, Part 2 sought to create a very different one.

Under Part 1 Britain was divided into 21 districts, each of which had its output and sales controlled by a district council composed of representatives elected by the coalowners of the district. Final power, however, rested with the Central Council which presided over the whole industry. The duties of this body were to allocate to the districts, on the basis of previous trading experience, the maximum output each could produce over specified periods; to co-ordinate the operations of the districts; and to impose penalties on any district that contravened its orders. On receipt of its allocation, the district council had to determine first, the proportion of each grade of coal that would be produced by the individual mines within the district and second, a minimum price for each grade of coal which the district supplied. Although drawn up with the best of intentions, there were numerous weaknesses in this plan for output and sales regulation. It made no distinction between districts according to the markets which they served, and failed therefore to recognise the greater difficulties facing those districts catering mainly, or in part, for the export market (see Chapter 7). Further, allocating output between all collieries in a district prevented the more mechanised and progressive enterprises, with heavy fixed charges, from capturing that share of the market which their greater efficiency might otherwise have warranted. While certain mines could operate fairly efficiently below full capacity others, in which there had been heavy capital investment, could not. Yet they were prevented from producing that level of output which would reduce overhead costs to a minimum. Finally, while *intra*-district competition was strictly controlled, there was no effective mechanism for the control of *inter*-district trade.

An effort had been made by drawing up a schedule of minimum prices to be charged by each district for different grades of coal. But these schedules could be easily evaded and there was no redress against districts which set unduly low prices. Scotland was the main culprit, switching sales between export and inland markets and fixing minimum prices in the latter at a level substantially below that at which business had been conducted in the past—the criterion adopted by other districts. These artificially low prices provoked bitter complaints from other districts and accusations of 'dumping'.[5] Minimum prices, it was argued, had 'shipwrecked on the stony truths that it is impossible to enforce any law unless it commands the goodwill of the bulk of those whose conduct it professes to regulate'.[6]

Only in 1934 were new restrictions introduced which limited total sales by each district in both export and domestic markets. Although criticised for not providing a permanent solution to district problems and for being simply 'a patch on a worn tyre', these measures did effectively prevent the *switching of supplies* between home and foreign consumers. On the other hand, *price co-ordination* remained an intractable problem before the second world war. Regulation was extended in 1936 with the object of restricting price competition within districts by means of organised selling-schemes.[7] Not only did these finally prevent inter-colliery competition but they went some way towards securing inter-district co-ordination of prices. However, the price of coal remained largely responsive to market conditions, rising with the trade recovery of the late 1930's. Thus price regulation was only important in preventing competitive price-cutting in the slump of 1937-8.

Undoubtedly the greatest weakness of Part 1 of the 1930 Act was that its objectives came into direct conflict with those envisaged in Part 2. While the former apparently guaranteed all collieries a share of the market, the latter was concerned to use compulsion if necessary to force individual units to amalgamate. This conflict had been recognised when the Act was drawn up but Part 1 had been regarded as merely a temporary expedient.[8] It was designed to bring relief to the collieries while machinery was created under Part 2 to effect a permanent cure to the industry's problems. In the event, the CMRC, set up under the chairmanship of Sir Ernest Gowers, found its freedom of action continually restricted by the inadequate compulsory powers placed at its disposal and the extensions of Part 1 of the Act. The Commission began its task of 'rationalising' coalmining confident that to preserve the *status quo*, as envisaged under Part 1, was simply to perpetuate the problems of the industry. Amalgamation was essential and Gowers regarded his role as being 'attached to the industry as a sort of therapeutic blister and I am going through that phase which is, I suppose, the experience of every blister—that its irritant effects upon the patient are immediately and abundantly apparent, while its ultimately remedial effects lie hidden in the womb of hope.'[9] Amalgamation schemes were rapidly drawn up for different districts but the Commission soon ran up against the entrenched opposition of owners.

This was based partly on the rejuvenating medicine given them by Part 1 of the Act and partly on the long tradition of individualism in the industry. As Gowers noted, even under competitive conditions, 'the unfit are most tiresome in their reluctance to die ... Even when one of them does die, it is as likely as not to rise Phoenix-like from the ashes of liquidation.'[10] Under the threat of imposed amalgamation, owners were all the more adamant about their right to survive. Moreover, the CMRC discovered through bitter experience in court that it did not possess sufficient powers to enforce schemes on reluctant owners. The truth was that successive Governments in the 1930's were not prepared actively to pursue a rationalisation policy. The choice was between spreading available employment over the maximum number of men (as envisaged under Part 1) or concentrating the work and giving the maximum employment to the minimum number of men (as envisaged under Part 2).[11] At a time when unemployment was already abnormally high, no Government was prepared to accept the heavy social costs which the latter option inevitably involved.

Baldwin, himself, was fully aware that alternative schemes of employment had not been worked out to cater for those likely to be displaced by amalgamation. If the CMRC was given its head there might be whole villages or areas to be dealt with.[12] This obstacle assumed forbidding proportions when a preliminary estimate by Sir Ernest Brown, Secretary for Mines, showed in 1934 that the labour force was likely to be reduced by a policy of concentration from 780,000 to 600,000. This was almost certainly an exaggeration since the Inter-Departmental Committee set up in the same year considered that displacement would be unlikely to exceed 100,000.[13] But this figure was still large enough to make the Government shy clear of compulsory amalgamation. Instead the virtues of voluntary measures were extolled. According to the Inter-Departmental Committee, voluntary amalgamation would lead to a more gradual reduction in employment. It would be easier to handle a gentle fall in numbers through the transfer of labour, restrictions on recruitment and possibly work-sharing schemes. Rather than compulsory amalgamation, the Government should, therefore, seek out means of facilitating a voluntary concentration of holdings. In line with this belief, the Committee was asked to prepare a scheme for the unification of mining royalties under national ownership. This would be 'helpful to the industry and financially sound' since it was recognised that the existing system of royalty ownership constituted a major impediment to planned reorganisation.

Not surprisingly then, not a single compulsory amalgamation was effected throughout the 1930's under the auspicies of the CMRC. Such closures and amalgamations as did occur were accomplished wholly by voluntary agreement. Between 1926 (when encouragement of concentration became official policy) and 1938, a mere 90 voluntary schemes were completed, reduced by subsequent amalgamation to 65, affecting in all some 307,000 employees.[14] These cold statistics meant that between 200-300 of the original thousand or so companies had combined to form 65 new units—and added up to the failure of the CMRC. Instead, it was assigned a new role by the end of the 1930's. Under the Coal Act of 1938, it was to be the acquiring authority of all mining royalties in Britain. A Central Valuation Board, set up under the Act, divided the country into ten valuation regions. The statutory purchase price of the royalties was fixed at a total of £66,450,000, each of the ten districts being allocated a share of this global sum. On July 1st, 1942 all coalmining royalties became the property of the Coal Commission although the valuation of royalties was not finally completed until 1945.

2 THE RATIONALE OF AMALGAMATION

The failure of the amalgamation movement between the wars has commonly been attributed to the intransigence and intense individualism of owners. Their independent outlook and faith in private enterprise made them reluctant to submerge their interests in a large unit, with consequent loss of identity and control. There was some substance to these allegations in that certain employers displayed an obduracy and perversity in their dealings with both labour and Government that aroused unnecessary animosity. Lord Birkenhead's oft-quoted remark, that 'it would be possible to say without exaggeration that the miners' leaders were the stupidest men in England if we had not had frequent occasion to meet the owners', contained an element of truth. In addition, in their opposition to the principle of amalgamation, several owners showed that they had not sufficiently grasped the need for a measure of technical reorganisation.[15] This, it was alleged, also delayed the move towards more efficient working which the large combine could have achieved. But these charges have been overstated. No satisfactory evidence was brought forward to show that the type of amalgamation being proposed would materially have improved the industry's situation, given the levels of technology and technical expertise then prevailing.

Official endorsement of amalgamation policy was based in the first instance on the findings of the Samuel Commission which reported in 1925. The Commission claimed to have established a positive relationship between large-scale enterprise and increased efficiency. The former could be secured by a vigorous policy of amalgamation which would help to eliminate surplus capacity and allow important economies to be made on both the technical and commercial sides of the industry. A qualitative assessment of the economies which might result was reinforced by quantitative evidence purporting to show that the larger the productive unit, the higher the level of efficiency as measured by output per man-shift and trading results. However, rather than these shaky statistical 'proofs', a more convincing account of the benefits of large-scale production was provided at the end of the second world war by the influential Reid Committee. This body emphasised that efficiency could be improved only by making sweeping changes in current technical practice. It recommended that major changes should be made in methods of working, underground face mechanisation and haulage, the use of power and lighting, and in surface equipment and layout.

Of these, the greatest scope for improved productivity lay in underground haulage which lagged far behind best Continental and American practice. Existing methods in Britain should be drastically revised with the introduction of locomotive haulage on the main roads. In turn this would require a major reorganisation in the size and layout of mines, since level roads would be necessary. Hitherto, the main haulage had generally followed the seams which were often steeply inclined. Thus the widespread use of the locomotive underground would entail the introduction of 'horizon' mining, whereby the main roads would be driven horizontally through the strata at different levels and intersect the sloping seams of coal. Clearly the initial outlay would be very large, these measures requiring larger-sized mines than were general in this country.

In face of such apparent unanimity of opinion in favour of merging conflicting interests into compact and unified commands of large-size, the owners' reluctance to amalgamate appeared perverse and contrary to the national interest. However, on closer inspection, good reasons existed for resisting the rationalisation proposals then being advanced. During the interwar period, meaningful amalgamation along the lines advocated by the Reid Committee was a non-starter. Simply, the necessary conditions had not been created to enable sweeping revisions in organisation and technique to be put into effect. A pre-requisite was the unification of mining royalties, a process set on foot only with the Coal Act of 1938 and not completed until the second world war. In Europe all mineral rights were the property of the State with the result that the working of the seams could be centrally controlled and provision made for working-concessions to cover large areas, thus reducing the number of separate undertakings to a minimum. In Britain, the position throughout the interwar years was very different. The Samuel Commission estimated in 1925 that each mine had on average to obtain leases from five different mineral owners before it could commence operations.

Moreover, the environment within which the industry operated was hardly conducive to vigorous amalgamation since the State appeared incapable of deciding between a policy of labour dispersal or concentration (see section 1). That is, whether it should guarantee a share of the market to all producers as implied by the subsidies of the 1920's and Part 1 of the 1930 Act or streamline capacity as implied by the Acts of 1926 and 1930 (Part 2). It may well have been true, as argued by Ernest Brown, that Part 1 acted 'as a buffer between the Government and economic and industrial strife in the coal industry,'[16] but the cost in terms of reorganisation was extremely high. The industry in the 1930's could hardly take seriously the policies of successive Governments, the avowed intention of which was to concentrate capacity while at the same time everything was being done to preserve the existing structure in an attempt to protect employment and wages. Given such confusion in policy, it is difficult to place the main responsibility for lack of a determined drive towards amalgamation at the owners' door. As noted above, the Government's hesitancy stemmed in part from the likely social consequences that would ensue from rationalisation. There was also a recognition that compulsory amalgamation might be inappropriate due to the wide variety of physical mining conditions in Britain. Unifying collieries and areas where natural conditions were easy and seams good with those where conditions and reserves were inferior might threaten the profitability of the former and hold back the more progressive mines.

In addition, there was the legacy of small and comparatively old mines and the unsystematic exploitation before 1914 to consider. Even if amalgamation meant eliminating the smaller units of production altogether, this would have contributed little to solving the problem of surplus capacity. The Samuel Commission showed that some 2,900 collieries operated in Britain in 1923, producing almost 253 million tons of saleable coal. Of these collieries 1,300, or 45% of

214

the total, contributed in aggregate a mere 5% of saleable output.[17] Closing these units down would, therefore, have had little effect on the industry's capacity to produce.

Important as the above considerations were, major obstacles to interwar amalgamation lay in two further inter-related issues. First, a meaningful programme of reorganisation involved wholesale changes in technique and layout as demanded by the Reid Committee in 1945, together with an extensive programme of new sinkings. As noted in Chapter 7, the time for reploughing profits back into the industry had been before and immediately after the first world war. The owners had indeed spent an estimated £53 million on improving the methods of production between 1918 and 1925[18] but this appeared trivial when measured against the investment programme considered necessary by the Reid Committee. The latter refrained from providing a firm estimate of the total cost of the best-practice techniques which it recommended but the final figure would inevitably have been well beyond the industry's own resources.[19] Nor could coalmining realistically have hoped to attract large amounts of new capital without first devising plans for radical reorganisation. The reforms advocated in both the 1920's and 1930's fell a long way short of the comprehensive technical reconstruction which was required.

Second, there was no satisfactory evidence, particularly of a statistical nature, to suggest that amalgamation undertaken with more limited objectives would give rise to significant economies of scale and improvements in efficiency. According to one observer.[20] The controversy over amalgamation should be confined solely to undertakings (ownerships comprising one or more mines) since this was the unit-size adopted by the Samuel Commission in its investigation into the desirability of the move to large-scale production. But this would be merely to scratch the surface of the debate current at that time. In fact, the Commission conducted its analysis both in terms of undertakings and disaggregated further to the level of the individual mine.[21] It anticipated, as did the Reid Committee in 1945, that commercial and technical economies of scale would be obtained by enlarging the size of the productive unit. Commercial economies were related to the size and strength of the undertaking: technical economies to the size-distributions of both undertakings and mines. In the latter case the more relevant unit is, in fact, mine-size since, as the Reid Committee made clear, increasing the size of individual mines and making appropriate changes in layout and technique offered the best prospects of securing technical economies of scale.

In the discussion which follows, the arguments in favour of amalgamation are considered first, in the context of undertakings and second, since technical economies depended largely on reorganising processes and layout underground, at the level of the individual colliery. In terms of the former the Samuel Commission argued that grouping undertakings into large units might give rise to both commercial and technical economies. Commercial economies were seen as the ability to create a stronger sales organisation, eliminate the middleman in selling, secure better distribution services and, where appropriate, promote a more efficient export drive. But to a large extent the industry was already in a position during the interwar period to take advantage of these improvements. In all mining districts a high degree of unified control over output already existed. For instance by 1930, over nine-tenths of district output was produced by a mere 16 undertakings in N. Staffordshire, 17 in Northumberland, 21 in Durham and 24 in South Wales. Even in Scotland with its traditionally small enterprises, three-quarters of the tonnage produced came from fewer than 20 undertakings.[22] Given this concentrated control of output in all districts, the scope for achieving further commercial economies through amalgamation was extremely limited. In large measure they were already being exploited since the concentration of output in relatively few hands allowed the co-ordination of collieries' sales efforts, the better promotion of exports and sufficient market strength to secure favourable terms for supplies and provision.

In the case of technical economies which included the central provision of power and pumping facilities and the rationalisation of staff and management, the statistical data used by the Samuel Commission are open to criticism. On the basis of evidence presented in terms of both undertakings and mines, the Commission claimed to have established a positive relationship between increased size and increasing efficiency. With regard to undertakings, the strength of the relationship depended largely on the higher productivity and lower costs of the large enterprises in South Yorks and Nottinghamshire. As the Commission itself pointed out (pp. 46-7), these operated in a large new coalfield with rich seams of good-quality coal, albeit situated well below the surface. Deep pits, involving heavy capital outlay, could only have been sunk on the basis of securing a correspondingly large output and the fact that the seams in the coalfield were three feet and upwards in thickness was directly correlated to the larger output per man-shift. The thickness of the seams, together with an 'immense outlay' on equipment, virtually guaranteed a high output per man-shift irrespective of the size of the undertaking. Professor Dron has shown that if the two districts of Yorkshire and Nottinghamshire are eliminated from the analysis and an average taken of all other districts examined by the Samuel Commission, the smaller undertakings in its survey actually had a rather lower cost per ton than the larger undertakings.[23] The same source also casts considerable doubt on the several technical economies which, the Commission alleged, might result from the amalgamation of undertakings.[24]

The most convincing argument in favour of economies of large-scale production relates to the size and structure of the individual mine. According to the Reid Committee and authorities such as Professor Beacham, meaningful technical economies could be secured only by increasing mine-size, reorganising underground roads and processes and rationalising existing surface layouts. The case advanced here is that nothing short of the wholesale reorganisation, replanning and enlargement of mines along the lines advocated by the Reid Committee would have produced significant results: certainly not the type of amalgamation envisaged in the interwar period. To some extent, such extensive restructuring was undertaken by the National Coal Board once the industry had passed into public ownership. But in the interwar period, the time was not ripe for such sweeping changes. The piecemeal measures envisaged by the Acts of 1926 and 1930 were no substitute for the massive technical reconstruction and large capital inputs which were necessary to secure important scale-economies. Since neither the capital nor the plans for radical reconstruction were available, owners were rightly suspicious of inadequately financed 'half-way house' measures.

Indeed, there was no empirical evidence to suggest that the larger-sized mines which might have resulted from the CMRC's efforts in the 1930's would have operated any more efficiently than their smaller counterparts. Districts in which the average size of mine was relatively small could operate at least as efficiently as those where the average size of productive unit was much larger. In Scotland for instance, with its traditionally small collieries, productivity was relatively high and costs per ton low. In Kent and Durham, the average size of mine was relatively large, yet output per man-shift remained comparatively low.[25] Rather than size *per se,* other factors were obviously more important in determining the overall level of efficiency. Not surprisingly, therefore, the type of amalgamation advocated in the 1930's was regarded by many owners as irrelevant to the real needs of the industry.

3 WAR AND THE DEVELOPMENT OF STATE CONTROL

A turning-point in the organisation and control of coalmining was reached with the publication of the Government's White Paper on coal in mid-1942.[26] Until that year, the Government had simply 'taken over' the machinery created by the 1930 Coal Mines Act to regulate output and prices, subsequently strengthened by the centralised control of sales in 1936. A Coal Production Council had been established in 1940 to promote increased output and to co-operate for this purpose with owners, men and appropriate Government departments. The industry was asked substantially to increase supplies in order to facilitate armament production; expand exports and thus earn vital foreign currency; and to provide the French with necessary fuel.[37] The Council immediately recognised that the major constraint would be lack of skilled manpower, especially since a large number of miners had already enlisted. It strongly urged, therefore, that the recruitment of pitmen for the forces be stopped and that they be returned where possible from other industries and the armed services. However, the Council was overtaken by events. The collapse of France and entry of Italy into the war dealt a severe blow to exports and with the temporary return of surplus capacity men were allowed once more to drift out of the industry.

This critical loss of manpower between 1940-41 was never subsequently made good and contributed to the continuous fall in output during the war years.[28] The measures taken during and after 1941 to prevent the drain of labour out of the industry were too little and too late. Between 1938 and 1941 the number of colliers fell by more than 10% and the exodus was only halted by the Essential Work (Coalmining Industry) Order of May 1941. Even this was incapable of supplying the 25,000 skilled hewers or extra labour force of 65,000 that the industry was estimated to need.[29] In the following months, compulsory registration was introduced of all those who had left coalmining since the start of 1935 in an effort to secure their return to the industry. In this way, over 50,000 men from other trades and the armed services were reabsorbed by October 1942 but their influence on the labour force was largely offset by natural wastage and an inability to prevent further leakages from the existing workforce. Successful recruitment clearly depended on the level of wages and conditions of work and although the number of wage-earners on colliery books climbed from the floor of 1941, recovery was marginal. Even the introduction of compulsory employment in the mines in 1943 was unable to restore the labour force to its prewar level. Selection for the mines from the able-bodied was made by means of a ballot. All those born in 1918 who were physically fit and would otherwise have been called up for military service were eligible for drafting into the coal industry. Yet in 1945 there were still 73,000, or about 10% fewer people in coalmining than the 782,000 employed in 1938.

The loss of skilled manpower and subsequent dilution of the labour force contributed to the decline in productivity during the war.

The State and Structural Change in Coalmining

Between 1938 and 1945, output per man-shift overall fell by 12%, from 1.14 to 1.00 tons. Other factors were also at work in bringing about this fall. By mid-1942, more than 40% of the men in the industry were over 40 years of age and 20% were over 50. Absenteeism substantially increased from 6.4% in 1938 to 16.3% in 1945 and the level of mechanisation was insufficient to compensate for the loss of skilled labour, let alone generate an increase in output per man. Above all, as hostilities dragged on, the work-force suffered from an increasing degree of war-weariness, tired of being continually exhorted to work to their utmost capacity. This was reflected in the tonnage of coal lost through disputes which had fallen from 0.9 million tons to 0.3 million tons between 1938 and 1941 but thereafter rose substantially to over 3 million tons in 1944.

Obviously it was not possible to explain the considerable increase in wages and earnings in coalmining during the war in terms of productivity increases. Wage rates rose more rapidly than in almost all other industries, reflecting in part the rise in the cost of living but, more important, the extent to which wages in coalmining had fallen behind those of other industries in the 1930's. The trading results of the industry during the war years are shown in Table 1.

Table 1

Weekly Earnings and Costs, Proceeds and Profits Per Ton in Coalmining, Selected Years, 1938-1945

Year	Average Weekly Cash Earnings			Wage Costs		Total Costs		Proceeds		Adjusted Credit Balance[1]	
	£	s.	d.	s.	d.	s.	d.	s.	d.	s.	d.
1938	2	15	9	10	6	16	1	17	5	1	4
1940	3	8	8	12	9	18	11	20	6	1	7
1943	5	0	0	20	3	28	2	29	1	1	6
1945	5	12	8	25	5	35	11	38	4	1	7

SOURCES:
PEP, *The British Fuel and Power Industries,* pp. 85 and 98; Court, op. cit., p. 344.
NOTE:
1. After transactions with Coal Charges Account taken into consideration.

Between 1938 and 1945 the output of saleable coal fell by almost 20% from 227 to 183 million tons. Between the same years, output per man-shift steadily deteriorated, yet wages paid per ton increased by nearly 150% and average weekly cash earnings more than doubled. Indeed, the increase in wage payments alone accounted for no less than three-quarters of the total increase in costs. In view of the fall in productivity, this escalation of wage payments could not have been accommodated by simply raising prices. Abnormal price-increases would have been necessary which would not only have seriously affected household consumers but would also have resulted in unacceptably high costs of production throughout manufacturing industry. Wage and price regulation, and the guarantee of a credit-balance in the industry, inevitably had to be the responsibility of Government. The State therefore assumed control in 1942, coalmining becoming a privately owned industry operating under Government direction.

The Coal White Paper in 1942 introduced the new policy, emphasising the need for more efficient regional organisation to secure maximum output from all mines. A wholly new form of organisation was imposed on the industry, headed by a Ministry of Fuel and Power responsible for planning and co-ordinating the output-drive of the regions. The new Minister, Gwilym Lloyd George, possessed full control in law over the operation of all coalmines and the allocation of coal raised. A Controller-General was also appointed to assist the Minister in grafting control of a large and complicated industry on to an ordinary Government department. Power was centralised in a National Coal Board, chaired by the Minister, which assumed responsibility for planning the allocation of regional and district targets, improving efficiency, supervising the provision of supplies and equipment and controlling aspects such as welfare, health and safety. To prevent too top-heavy a structure from emerging, elaborate regional machinery was created with the country being divided into eight coal-producing and four non-producing regions. A Regional Controller and three directors planned the output and distribution of coal in each of the eight regions,[30] assisted by a Regional Coal Board consisting of representatives of owners, men, management and technical staff. Finally, at grass-roots level, Pit-Production Committees were, as the name suggests, responsible in each colliery for output, technical aspects of production and the meeting of targets.

In the following year, national planning of the industry was further tightened with the creation of the National Conciliation Board, based on the successful National Joint Standing Committee which had been formed in 1935. The task of the new body was to supervise wages and conditions of employment in the industry. It consisted of a Joint National Negotiating Committee on which owners and men were equally represented and a National Reference Tribunal whose decision on issues submitted to it would be binding on both sides of industry.[31] This at last achieved one of labour's major objectives, comprehensive conciliation machinery on a national basis. It brought to a triumphant conclusion the process started in 1935 for securing national negotiations and ended any lingering hopes of owners for a return to local wage bargaining. At the same time as these measures were being taken on the supply side of the industry, further restrictions on demand had to be imposed. By 1942, exports of coal had fallen to 10% of their 1938 level and although attempts were made in 1942-3 to maintain supplies to valuable neutral customers, the Minister of Fuel and Power had to announce in early 1944 that exports to neutrals had temporarily ceased. Restrictions on exports remained in force for the remainder of the war and in the immediate postwar years, despite the desperate need for coal abroad and the loss which this represented in terms of foreign exchange.[32] A similar tightening of restrictions had to be imposed on the home market in an effort to allocate steadily falling supplies between competing demands. From the outset, the Government had made every effort to encourage the stocking of coal.[33] This was reinforced in early 1943 by the payment of compensation on a tonnage basis for the retention of existing ground stocks and a bonus payment for any increase in stocks secured during the summer-to-autumn stocking-period.

Nonetheless, the state of coal stocks was causing grave concern towards the end of the war. By early 1945, suggestions that a crisis was looming due to a grave shortage of supplies were dismissed by Gwilym Lloyd George as alarmist. Not everyone was as complacent. Lord Cherwell, formerly an 'optimist' about the coal position, complained to the Prime Minister in early 1945 that 'although he forecasts a fall in distributed stocks to the lowest level on record by the end of April, the Minister of Fuel and Power does not regard the position as serious.'[34] In the event, Cherwell was proved correct and in a matter of weeks, Lloyd George was forced to acknowledge the gravity of the situation. In his 'Coal Budget' for 1945-6, presented to the Lord President's Committee, he outlined a powerful programme designed to relieve pressure on existing supplies.[35]

Impetus was also given to the fuel economy campaign in 1943 and 1944, designed to reduce both industrial and household consumption. With regard to the former, qualified fuel technologists visited factories to advise on how best to save fuel and technical information was distributed widely throughout manufacturing industry. Increased industrial output and changes in the quality of coal supplied make it difficult to judge the success of these measures. It has been estimated that had changes not occurred in industrial output or quality of fuel used, a saving of 10% in coal consumption would have been achieved throughout industry. Economy in household consumption depended upon publicity and technical advice, reinforced by statutory regulations. The 'rationing' of coal was introduced under the Fuel and Lighting Order of September 1939 and further restrictions and adjustments were enforced in subsequent years. These determined the maximum quantities of coal available for disposal for periods

221

ranging between one and six months. However at best this was a loose type of rationing scheme since 'control' depended not on the volume of coal to be consumed by each individual or household but rather on a maximum number of deliveries which could be made. Beyond this number, consumers were not allowed to acquire additional fuel unless their stocks had fallen below a certain 'critical' level.

All these measures on the demand- and supply-sides of the industry depended on centralised planning and regulation. In effect, from 1942 the State acted 'in the national interest' by assuming full control of a scarce resource and determining how that resource should be allocated between competing uses. In exercising this responsibility it made use above all of the Coal Charges Account (CCA), set up in 1942 to handle the problems of prices and costs. The abiding principle was that in war-time, output was more important than finance: that supplies even from low-productivity, high-cost districts were vital to further the war effort. In view of the falling productivity at national level, the rapid increase in costs during the war bore more heavily on the weaker districts. Certain of these would have ceased production altogether had not the CCA taken responsibility for spreading costs over all producers in the country. In essence, the stronger undertakings and coalfields helped to subsidise their weaker counterparts. The system adopted was to average the rise in costs over the whole output of the industry, levy the funds needed to meet successive cost increases by means of a national average charge per ton, and recoup the industry for the levy by national average price increases. Provision was also made for those coalfields with specially high costs by the continuation of the Necessitous Undertakings Scheme.[36] An undertaking whose financial difficulties were such that they could not be met by district price increases was given grants to cover ascertained working losses, plus 3d. per ton on the output of the undertaking. This became a significant charge on the new Account, as did taking over the operation of the guaranteed wage first implemented under the 1941 Essential Work Order.

It was, in fact, the successive increases in wages and their growing weight in total costs that came to dominate the operation of the Account. These were related to a system of district price allowances and standard district credit balances. The procedure adopted was that used to implement the wage award made in June 1942 by Lord Greene's Board of Investigation. The increase of 2/6d. per shift to all adult workers could only be met by substantially increasing prices. Had undertakings been left to bear the entire cost through district prices rises, widely different increases per ton would have resulted throughout the country in view of the high-cost structure and low productivity of certain coalfields. In the event, the existing levy[37] was increased from 7d. to 3/7d. per ton and the Minister of Fuel and

Power paid from the CCA the entire cost of the wage-award to each colliery. The increase in costs was met by a national price increase of 3/- per ton. On the one hand, this would *not* have been sufficient to meet the needs of the high-cost undertakings but on the other, would have contributed a bonus to low-cost concerns, being higher than their real needs. Hence by pooling the proceeds of the price-increase those with greatest need could be recompensed without having to impose an exorbitantly high national price increase, weighted to meet the needs of undertakings with higher than average costs.[38]

To this was added a system of district price-allowances whereby changes in district costs, other than those due to wages, were henceforth met through the price allowance system. The proceeds of the high-cost districts were increased by allowances from the CCA. No individual district price increases were allowed; rather, any increase that was required was administered on a national basis. The proceeds were then pooled and the weaker districts 'put on allowance' by the Account. In this way, one district helped to finance another, a far cry from the fierce inter-district competition of the interwar years. In turn, price allowances were bound up with standard district credit balances. In mid-1942, the *national* average credit balance was set at 1/9d. per ton, with the provision that if profit became less than 1/6d. or more than 2/-, price adjustments would take place. *District* standard credit balances were then fixed, ranging from 6d. to 2/9d. per ton and averaged out to 1/9d. per ton for the industry as a whole.[39] Thereafter, the mechanism was relatively simple. District price allowances were designed to produce the agreed standard credit balances, plus the increase in district costs resulting from a 1/- per ton pit-head price-increase imposed in January 1943. The coal levy was at the same time increased from 3/7d. to 5/- per ton and paid back out of the CCA at a flat-rate per ton to those districts which failed to meet their agreed standard credit balances.

Falling output and rising costs meant that in practice a *national* average credit balance of 1/9d. per ton was never achieved. It amounted to 1/2d. per ton in 1942, 1/4d. in 1943 and 1/7d. in both 1944 and 1945. As a result, the balance was made up to the stipulated minimum of 1/6d. per ton by supplementary payments (district price allowances) of £3.5 million in 1942 and £1.25 million in the following year. The simple truth was that despite major increases, the coal levy was still insufficient to meet the charges made on the Account. The levy increased from 7d. per ton in June 1942 to 12/- in 1944, and finally to 15/- per ton in May, 1945. The latter increase brought it up to about 45% of the average costs of production for the country as a whole. Correspondingly, rapid price increases were also imposed. Between the outbreak of war in 1939 and end-1944, general *additions* to the price of coal totalled 15/11d. However, since in the early stages of the war district adjustments of price had taken place up to permitted levels, the average increase over all supplies amounted to 18/- per ton.[40] With the increase in levy during the following year, prices were accordingly adjusted once more, with a further increase of 3/6d. per ton being announced. This brought the overall increase in the wholesale price since the outbreak of war to almost 100%.

Large though it was, the increase in levy could not withstand the steadily mounting calls made on it. It was asked to finance four persistently heavy items of expenditure: guaranteed wage payments under the Essential Work Order; wage additions; assistance to necessitous undertakings; and district price allowances. In addition, various other items were charged to the Account as the war progressed.[41] Of the four main items, by far the most onerous were wage additions, particularly those occasioned by the Green award in 1942, the Porter award in January 1944 and the National Wage Agreement in April of the same year.[42] Since outgoings began to run far ahead of receipts the CCA, and the coal industry with it, incurred progressively greater debts with the Exchequer. By end-1944, total advances made to the Account by the Exchequer amounted to £32.5 million. When disaggregated, these showed that the excess of charges over levies had been

£6.25 million in 1942
£6.00 million in 1943
£13.50 million in 1944

Total deficiency £25.75 million, plus balance of £6.75 million in the forms of advances of working capital for the current operation of the Account.[43] It was intended that this deficiency should be repaid whenever improved trading conditions allowed.

Translated into a district effect, the operation of the CCA entailed the heavy subsidy of certain districts by others. Seven districts with lowest output per man-shift never contributed to the Account at all; of these, three—Durham, South Wales and Monmouthshire, and Lancashire and Cheshire—accounted for some 30% of total output in 1945.[44] On the other hand, five districts with the highest output per man-shift in the country, N. Derbyshire, Nottinghamshire, South Derbyshire, Leicestershire and Warwickshire consistently contributed. The first four of these, constituting the North Midland Region, accounted for about 20% of total output.[45] The policy of spreading the incidence of war-time costs was vital to the survival of the low output per man-shift districts. Indeed, had the strong not been used to subsidise the weak, Durham, South Wales and Lancashire could hardly have continued in production. Their costs by 1945 ranged from 40/2d. to 49/4d. per ton at a time when average costs in the industry as a whole amounted to 35/11d. and in the lowest-priced district (Leicestershire) to only 24/6d.

Although a legacy of debt was left for the post-war industry, on the whole war-time 'control' achieved its primary objective, securing the nation's supplies of fuel and power during a period of extreme pressure. The Government's policy was to leave routine control of the industry in private hands and, at the same time, keep as many pits as possible in production by spreading increased costs over all producers. To this extent, piecemeal and hesitant though it may have been, the policy worked well. The miners clearly achieved a great deal since they secured not only a substantial rise in real earnings,[46] but also a minimum wage and the right to negotiate at national level. On the other hand, the owners argued that such a large measure of Government intervention was not the way to increase production, pointing to the rapid expansion of wages unrelated to productivity gains and the increase in absenteeism.[47]

However, they were prepared to co-operate with the measures taken, particularly since every effort had been made to retain the money incentive to greater efficiency. Competition between collieries was maintained by guaranteeing the credit balance not of the individual *undertaking,* but of the *district* as a whole. Since district profits were guaranteed under the price allowance scheme, any increase in the costs of an individual colliery would reduce the district balance and therefore increase the price-allowance to *all* collieries in the district. But this increased price-allowance would obviously amount to only a small fraction of the increased costs of the *individual* colliery. Hence, there was still every incentive to colliery management to be as efficient as possible. For a brief spell after the war, the principles of competition and working the coal by private enterprise survived and owners entertained hopes of retaining control of the industry's development. These were dispelled by the Labour Party's landslide victory at the polls in July 1945. The new Government immediately made clear that one of its priorities was to bring the fuel and power industries under public ownership.

4 NATIONALISATION OF THE MINES

After the war, the coal industry was in a run-down condition with output and productivity falling, exports insignificant, the size and quality of the labour force at a low ebb and absenteeism extremely high. Above all, there was a large proportion of relatively old mines with reserves nearing exhaustion and the industry was heavily in debt to the Exchequer. These facts were not an indictment of the operational control of the Government during the war but the inevitable aftermath of years of 'coal at any price' and insufficient time for proper maintenance and replacement. Even by 1948, estimated net fixed capital per employee in coalmining, a labour-intensive industry, amounted to only £100, compared with £5,070 per employee in electricity and £1,080 in manufacturing industry as a whole.[48] Nor, with the end of hostilities, was coalmining afforded a 'breathing space' since British coal was in urgent demand both at home and abroad. All concerned with the future of the industry accepted that technical reorganisation along the lines suggested by the Reid Committee would be necessary to promote greater efficiency. Apart from larger-sized mines, both the Committee and the *Regional Surveys of the Coalfields,* submitted between 1944 and 1946 to the Ministry of Fuel and Power, recommended grouping undertakings into larger units.[49] In this way compact and unified commands would be created, responsible for finance, technical reorganisation and development.

Where serious divergence of view occurred was over how this necessary reorganisation should be brought about. The owners pinned their hopes mainly on the Foot Plan,[50] devised by the chairman of the Mining Association, which rejected nationalisation and upheld the principle of the autonomy of individual colliery undertakings. In essence, the Plan was a compromise based on self-government for the industry while at the same time accepting that it must be operated as a national service. Policy would be the responsibility of a Central Board, composed entirely of representatives of colliery managements, which would be supported by a number of District Boards. Despite the owners' natural enthusiasm, the Plan was eventually written off as a fine example of 'Bourbon self-Government-Government of the coal-owners, by the coal-owners, for the coal-owners.'[51] All controversy came to an end when the Nationalisation Bill, placed before Parliament in December 1945, was finally passed in May 1946. A period of frantic activity followed during which preparations were made for the transfer of the industry to public ownership. A National Coal Board (NCB) was to be created, ready to assume control on the vesting date, 1 January 1947.

The immediate problem was to determine precisely what constituted 'the coal industry'. Most of the assets owned by colliery companies were transferred to the Board.[52] These were classified in three groups:—

— essential productive assets, including the coalmines themselves, plant and machinery used for mining coal, unworked deposits etc. *These were transferred automatically on vesting date.*

— the property owned by colliery companies such as water-works, wharves, housing, farms, stores, etc. *These were transferrable either at the option of the Board or the owners, whether or not the other party acquiesced.*

— Brickworks and any remaining assets of colliery companies. *These were transferrable at the option either of the Board or owners, provided the other party acquiesced.* Where no agree-

226

ment could be reached an independent arbitrator was to decide the issue.

Even by the end of 1949, the NCB did not know the full extent of its inheritance. The listing of its assets was likened to the making of the Domesday Book, but at very least it had acquired 1,400 collieries,[53] 30 manufactured fuel plants, 225,000 acres of farmland, carbonisation and by-product plants, brickworks, hotels, shops, swimming baths, a cinema, holiday camp and mortuary. To manage these efficiently, a new organisational structure had to be created which would operate 'in the national interest' and ensure that revenues were sufficient to meet outgoings on an average of good and bad years. The Board itself comprised nine members (including a chairman and deputy chairman) who were responsible for framing general policy; each ordinary member also assumed charge of an executive department such as Production, Marketing and Finance. In line with the recommendations of the Reid Committee, collieries were grouped into planning units, or Areas, regarded as the chief instruments of technical development and reorganisation, and the main units of general management. It was envisaged that the 48 Areas created would become large commercial organisations, having an average capital of £8 million and an annual turnover of about £10 million.[54] This fulfilled the object of maintaining responsibility for policy at the centre, in the shape of the Board, but devolving managerial responsibility to the parts.

However, the NCB was very conscious of the danger of over-centralising the decision-taking processes and recognised the need for an intermediate authority in the coalfields. Eight divisions were therefore established, based broadly on the regional organisation employed by the Ministry of Fuel and Power during the war. Each was operated by a Divisional Board with a composition similar to that of the National Board and to which the latter devolved as much responsibility as possible. The Divisional Boards acted as the link between the National Board and the Area managements. The new structure of the industry is illustrated in Table 2.

The type of organisation outlined in Table 2 could not be achieved overnight. Essentially it depended on grouping collieries as quickly as possible into Areas, these being about the same size as the few larger undertakings in the industry under private ownership. Since few Area managements had developed sufficiently to take full responsibility by vesting date, arrangements were made during an 'interim period' for the headquarters of most colliery companies to carry on as before. Immediately, the new organisation was required to address itself both to short-term production problems and to the task of devising a long-term strategy for the development of the industry. In the former case, a new understanding with labour was urgently

Table 2

Divisions and Areas of the NCB with Approximate Annual Output, 1946-7

Division[1]	No. of Areas	No. of Collieries	Approx. Annual Output
			(m tons)
1. Scottish	5	187	21.9
2. Northern	10	213	34.0
3. North Eastern	8	117	37.4
4. North Western	5	75	12.6
5. East Midlands	8	102	32.6
6. West Midlands	4	60	16.1
7. South Western	8	222	21.8
8. South Eastern	*	4	1.3
	48	980[2]	177.7

SOURCE:

NCB, *Annual Report for 1946.*

NOTES:

1. The geographical areas included within each division can be found in NCB, *Annual Report for 1947,* Appendix 1, pp. 193-4.

2. Over 400 small mines, not managed by the Board, are excluded throughout.

*. No separate Area organisation.

needed. As Emanuel Shinwell, the Minister of Fuel and Power, had noted in 1946, 'relations between owners and men, generally speaking, are soured and embittered, and the efficiency of the industry relative to that of our Continental and other competitors is distinctly back-ward.'[55] The NCB took over, in modified form, existing conciliation machinery both at national and at district level. The Joint National Negotiation Committee and National Reference Tribunal were retained and district conciliation boards continued to exist, enlarged by means of amalgamation to conform more readily with the new divisional organisation of the Board. A new departure was the agreement reached between the Board and NUM[56] to provide conciliation machinery at colliery level. A Pit Conciliation Scheme, worked out in 1946, was ready to start on vesting day.

A wide variety of salary and wage systems existed at the end of the war with different companies paying different rates for the same job. The National Wages Agreement of 1944, in an effort to stabilise wages, had stipulated that no applications for wage increases could be made before end-June 1948. The effect had been to dam up all claims for changes in wage-rates at the collieries and to create frustration and impatience on the part of the men. The transfer of the industry to public ownership provided the opportunity for a fresh understanding to be reached between the NCB and NUM. The 1944 Agreement was to continue but the ban on wage claims at collieries was removed once pit conciliation machinery had been in force for 6 months (i.e. by the start of July 1947). Moreover, agreement was reached on payment for statutory holidays, a guaranteed weekly wage, and the introduction of a 5-day week. The last of these depended on the men's acceptance of 'increased tasks' to ensure that, despite a reduction in the length of the working week, output was not only maintained but increased.[57]

Introduced in May 1947, the Five Day Week Agreement stipulated that the normal working week for underground workers should consist of five consecutive shifts of 7½ hours plus one winding time and for surface workers, five consecutive shifts of 8½ hours. In the event, mineworkers proved unwilling to accept the increased duties that shortening the working week entailed and output steadily fell below the rate required to meet the target set for the year. As a result, an Extension of Hours Agreement was signed in October 1947 in response to the Government's appeal to the basic industries to work longer hours to increase output at a time of growing economic difficulty. Under the Agreement, hours of work belowground were temporarily increased from 7½ plus one winding time to eight plus one winding time. In most coalfields, this involved Saturday-working, although in Northumberland and parts of Durham it was decided to work the extra half-hour each day. In return, the NCB agreed to a raising of the minimum wage and increasing the wages of lower-paid workers as from November 1947.[58]

Further short-term difficulties were created by the fuel crisis arising from the exceptionally severe winter of 1946-7 and the fact that the Board had to operate under a system of Government 'control', distributing the coal as the Government directed. The fuel crisis threatened to close down power stations and gas works since stocks at the former had fallen by early February 1947 to little more than one week's supply. Coal allocations to firms were suspended, all but essential industries were asked to stop using electric power, exports were prohibited and about 2 million people were unemployed. The greatest difficulty was simply to keep coal-class traffic moving in view of snowed-up railway lines and blocked roads. Although the crisis totally disrupted the economy in the two months of February and March, ironically the actual output of coal in these two months was more than one million tons up on the corresponding months of 1946. More than anything else, the 'freeze-up' in early 1947 confirmed the need first, to make provision for an adequate distribution of stocks and second, to devise measures capable of securing an immediate increase in production. In the latter area, the industry was afforded preferential treatment within the Government's system of post-war controls.[59] It was agreed that mineworkers should not be called up for military service; the industry's requirements for materials and equipment were given priority; the capacity of Government training centres was expanded to allow for double-shift training; and local authorities were asked to give priority to the housing needs of miners.

Difficult though the solutions to these short-run problems were, the real test of the nationalised industry lay in the long-term planning and reconstruction of colliery output. The Board accepted that sweeping technical changes along the lines suggested by the Reid Report were necessary. These involved an active policy of colliery reorganisation and the preparation of long-term output targets. To assist in this work, the deficit incurred by the CCA during the war years was written off and under the terms of the Nationalisation Act the Minister of Fuel and Power could advance up to £150 million to the Board in the first five years for capital expenditure and working capital. Thereafter he was empowered to advance such amounts as Parliament might determine. The pressure for immediate increases in production delayed the formulation of long-term plans for the reconstruction of collieries. Until a national plan could be devised, the Board took over schemes for new sinkings and reconstructions prepared by the Ministry of Fuel and Power during the war. To these, it added new schemes of its own which were required whatever future decisions were taken on reorganisation. In total, schemes valued at £22.7 million had been approved by the end of 1947.

Although the way had been cleared for amalgamation and the concentration of control by the 1938 Coal Act which transferred mining royalties to the State, the reverse side of the coin was that the Board had to accept liability for the stock issued in compensation.[60] Moreover, compensation to owners for the main assets of collieries was fixed at £164.7 million. After taking subsidiary assets (coke-ovens, brickworks, interests under freehold leases etc.) into account, the total value of assets taken over by the Board was finally fixed in 1956 at £388 million, on which annuities averaging 3½% were payable for 50 years. All interest on the compensation stock and on capital advanced by the Treasury was regarded as a compulsory charge on the industry. This was a heavy burden to place on the industry, all the more so since the Board was not allowed complete freedom in its pricing policies. These were conditioned by the view of the Minister of Fuel and Power that the industry should provide a 'service' in the national interest. Since it was not allowed to charge the level of prices which would have covered capital expenditure, the industry was forced to borrow heavily to meet its requirements. As a result, it incurred a large deficit on capital account. This was to be particularly relevant in later years when it had to meet the competition of other fuels with an inflated structure of capital borrowing (see Chapter 10, section 4 below).

On the whole, the transfer of coalmining into public ownership was accomplished smoothly and without noticeably disrupting colliery output. This was a remarkable achievement in view of the speed with which the transfer had been effected and the complex administrative, financial and organisational structure which had to be developed. Full control by the State was the logical outcome of developments within the industry during the preceding fifty years. The tendency to diminishing returns and the relatively low level of output per man during the interwar years required colliery reorganisation and capital expenditure on a scale which private enterprise, given prevailing market trends, could not hope to provide. The regulation of output and sales under the 1930 Coal Mines Act and the failure of the CMRC were simply a prelude to a system of control 'imposed' from outside the industry. Once the State had taken charge in 1942, a full return to private ownership always seemed unlikely despite the owners' rapid acceptance of the Foot Plan and their attempts to put it into operation. War-time control had confirmed that the industry could, and should, be operated in 'the national interest'. Whether this should have extended in the first expansionary decade of the nationalised industry to subsidising the domestic consumption of coal or whether the consumer should have been asked to pay a more realistic market price is a more open question.

10 Fluctuating Fortunes: Coal in the Modern Age

The problems confronting the nationalised coal industry were of a different character from those encountered in former years. Since the industry was unable to satisfy European demand for coal before 1957, exports and the competitive struggle for overseas markets ceased to be one of the principal determinants of prosperity.[1] British coal-mining became more preoccupied with competition between different types of fuel rather than competition between different coal-producing countries. An increasingly desperate struggle developed, notably with oil, to retain as large a share as possible of the domestic market. For about ten years after 1947 the coal industry enjoyed market conditions akin to those experienced before the first world war. Acute coal shortages existed and with the mineral still in virtually a monopoly position as a source of fuel and power[2] a rapid expansion of capacity was necessary to lift supply to a level more closely in line with demand. Over-investment in the boom, and inefficient means of financing it, were to exact a heavy penalty in the ensuing slump. From the mid-1950's, Britain moved gradually from a two-fuel (coal and oil) to a four-fuel economy (with the addition of nuclear power and gas). The greater flexibility now possible in energy use and planning placed intolerable pressures on the coal industry.

Committed to an expansionary programme rendered obsolete by changed market conditions, the industry was saddled from 1957 with a large margin of surplus capacity. It was also weighed down by heavy interest payments on debt incurred to finance capital spending and in no position to withstand, unaided, growing competition from cleaner, more efficient and, for some uses, cheaper fuels. In face of these pressures, the industry was allowed to contract for over a decade with successive Governments doing what they could to slow the rate of run-down and reduce social costs through various forms of assistance. Not until the 1970's was this decline brought to a halt with the emergence of a 'new energy situation'. Significant changes in relative fuel prices presented the coal industry with an opportunity to make some degree of market recovery and to plan, for the first time for over 15 years, once again for expansion.

Three distinct periods can therefore be identified in the development of post-war coalmining. The first, from 1947 to 1957, was

233

characterised by prosperity and a rapid expansion of capacity; the second, from 1958 to about 1970, brought all the problems of a contracting industry—lack of profitability and a steep decline in output, employment and number of productive units. In the 1970's, coalmining stood on the threshold of a third period, poised to recover some of its former markets by taking advantage of the escalation of fuel oil prices. The conflicting fortunes of the industry during these periods form a convenient starting-place for a study of efficiency and profitability in the modern era.

1   THE RECORD UNDER NATIONALISATION

Apart from witnessing a steady expansion in the demand for coal, the first ten years after nationalisation are notable for the attempts made by the NCB to stamp a system of control over the output and organisation of the industry. When it took over, it became the largest employer in the western world and had an annual turnover of some £360 million. The immediate problem was to reconcile the need for substantial increases in output with hardly less urgent long-term policy objectives. Not only had the industry to be reorganised and re-equipped, but a rational prices and wages structure required to be drawn up. For instance, on vesting date about 8,000 different prices for coal existed throughout Britain. Inevitably, long-term planning tended to be over-shadowed by short-term considerations. With energy requirements rising by an estimated 4.5 million tons of coal equivalent per annum between 1947 and 1957, attention was concentrated on how best to meet immediate targets.

On the demand-side, coal was not finally de-rationed until 1957 and exports were restricted in favour of the home market. To supplement existing supplies imports of coal had to be allowed, these reaching a peak of 11.6 million tons in 1955 (5% of total domestic consumption). Moreover, large consumers were required to find alternative sources of energy. The Ridley Committee in 1952 urged that scarce fuel resources 'should not continue to be subject to waste on the present scale in rail transport.'[3] In consequence, railways embarked upon a programme designed to find other forms of traction, leading to the development of diesel power and ultimately to the electrification of main lines. Electricity, too, was authorised to convert power stations to oil-burning and in 1955 the first nuclear power programme was published with the long-term objective of reducing pressure on coal supplies.[4]

These changes indicated that coal was simply not capable of meeting the heavy demands made on it, despite a rapid expansion of capital investment in the industry. Weighted at 1947 prices, capital expenditure in the mines rose from an annual average of £24 million in 1949-50 to £60 million in 1958-9 and mechanisation, notably in the form of power-loading, made rapid progress.[5] Encouraging as these trends were, two difficulties persisted on the supply-side of the industry which prevented output from rising as quickly as it might have done. Due to the urgent need for coal, poor pits with a high-cost structure and low record of productivity were kept in production for the sake of output. At the same time, there was a national shortage of skilled labour despite a vigorous campaign of pit-recruitment and a doubling of money wages between 1947 and 1957. Employment fluctuated widely but by the latter date was no higher than it had been when the NCB took over. The combined effect of these factors—poor pits maintained in production, large wage increases and heavy capital costs—was a disappointing rate of growth of productivity. Output per man-shift overall rose from 21.9 cwts in 1947 to 24.9 cwts in 1957 (Table 1), an increase of 14% during a period in which capital expenditure, in real terms, had more than doubled.

Operating costs rose steeply from a total of 41/3d. per ton in 1947 to 81/6d. per ton in 1957, a problem exacerbated by the fact that with demand high and rising, the Board was unable due to a 'gentleman's agreement' with the Government to charge the going price for coal (see section 4).[6] Reserves were not, therefore, built up during this period of prosperity, a factor which was to be of great importance to coal since the industry had nothing to fall back on in the lean years to come. Had surpluses been accumulated these might have cushioned coalmining from the full impact of depressed demand conditions in the 1960's. As it was, in the first decade of operations the Board was just about able to break even, making a profit after interest payments had been taken into account in six out of the ten years.[7] Ominously on capital account, the industry was saddled with a heavy debt structure since it had borrowed to finance investment rather than secure the reserves it needed through appropriate pricing policies (see section 4).

Since it was estimated to take an average of ten years to complete a new sinking and over eight to carry through a big reconstruction scheme,[8] the NCB necessarily had to adopt a long-term policy for future output expansion. In its original *Plan for Coal,* published in 1950, a deep-mined production target of 240 million tons was set for 1961-5, subsequently reduced in the revised *Investing in Coal* (1956), to 230 million tons by 1965, with 10 million tons to come from open-cast mining.[9] This margin to be supplied by open-cast mines represented a departure from previous policy. Started during the second world war as a supplement to deep-mined output, open-cast working was, according to the original *Plan for Coal,* to be phased out by 1965. Under the revised formula, it was rescued due to its low cost of working, high output per man and the speed with which open-cast sites could be brought into production. More important in the 1956 revision was a recognition that previous targets for deep-mined output had been over-optimistic. Indeed, in the light of operating experience, the history of the Board's planning up to the 1960's was one of reduced targets and escalating capital expenditure. This does not imply a condemnation of the development strategy drawn up in the 1950's but reflects rather the increased difficulties of making forecasts in an essentially fluid energy situation. As the *Plan for Coal* pointed out any estimate of long-term demand could be little better than an informed guess. For instance, the Board could not have predicted the developments which occurred in the supply of energy during the 1960's. Along with a large increase in the use of fuel oil went rapid progress in natural gas and nuclear energy. While the 1956 Plan had still been expansionary in outlook the *Revised Plan for Coal,* published in 1959, took account of the radical changes in demand for coal. The output targets for 1965 were scaled down once again to between 190 and 205 million tons inland consumption and 10 million tons exported.

Together with these reduced estimates of future colliery production went a growing awareness of the difficulties involved in financing reconstruction. It was estimated in 1955 that about four million tons of coal, or about 2% of the then existing productive capacity, was lost each year due to exhaustion of reserves.[10] Major new schemes had to make good this loss simply to maintain existing potential. To ensure that output was not only maintained but increased, the £635 million (at mid-1949 prices) envisaged by the 1950 Plan as necessary for the period 1950 to 1965[11] was raised substantially by the 1956 Plan to £860 million for collieries and associated activities, plus £140 million for ancillaries for the period 1956 to 1965. Between 1950 and 1955, £287 million of the £520 million devoted to collieries had actually been spent. The new allocation to collieries, when added to that already spent, gave a total capital investment of £1,147 million. Thus to reach the target of 240 million tons in 1965, investment at over double the rate envisaged in 1950 was regarded as necessary. This can be attributed not only to modifications and additions to the original programme but also to serious under-costing in the original Plan and steadily rising prices since its publication. The further amendment of 1959 had to adopt a different approach, revising and rephasing the capital expenditure programme in the light of falling markets. Targets had now to be set 'in the expectation that demand will be within the potential capacity of the industry in 1965'.[12] It was accepted that coalmining would not develop as originally expected: rather than expansion, the emphasis was placed firmly on achieving greater productive efficiency. According to the revised formula, over 400 of the original collieries taken over would be closed by 1965 and 80% of total output would come from new and reconstructed mines.[13]

236

Although experiencing difficulty with its long-range output forecasts, in other areas the NCB had cause for satisfaction. Despite
criticisms that its administrative organisation was top-heavy and that
a bureaucratic structure made two-way communication difficult
between headquarters and those operating in the field, the Fleck
Committee found little evidence to support such allegations.[14] On
the contrary, the operating structure of headquarters, divisions, areas
and collieries was found to be relatively efficient. Within the framework of a generally favourable examination of the Board's activities,
the Fleck Committee had several recommendations of its own to
make. These included an expansion in membership of the Board,
tighter control over capital expenditure schemes, more rigid enforcement of the Board's policies and the adoption of budgetary control
and standard costs. Overall, the effect of the Committee's Report
was to vindicate the administrative structure under which the industry
operated. Equally gratifying was the sustained fall in the number of
fatal accidents after nationalisation. Between 1942 and 1955, the
size of the labour force remained virtually unchanged, yet in absolute
figures, the number of fatal and serious accidents fell by more than
one-third. The death rate, underground and surface, per 100,000
man-shifts worked fell from 0.43 in 1942 to 0.24 in 1955 and the
reportable injury rate from 1.38 to 1.06.[15] In the 1960's, the numbers
at risk declined in view of the considerable reduction in employment,
with the result that a fall in the actual number of fatalities and
serious accidents might have been expected. On the other hand, the
rapid expansion in mechanisation after 1955 greatly increased the
potential hazards of winning the coal. The fact that the death rate
continued to fall while the rate of serious injuries remained relatively
stable can be counted a considerable achievement. Per 100,000 man-
shifts, the rate of fatal accidents had fallen to 0.11 in 1975/6, while
the serious injury rate had moved to 1.01.

A turning-point for the coal industry was reached in 1957 when it
was confronted with altered market circumstances. Although the
fall in demand for coal in that year was thought to be the result of
temporary industrial recession, it soon became clear that coalmining
was on the verge of a long-term decline in markets. The fall in
demand is examined in greater detail in section 2 but it may be noted
here that the principal factor at work was coal's lack of competitiveness, in terms of price, relative to other fuels. The chief culprit was
oil which in several markets quickly eroded any technical or price
advantages previously held by coal. After 1957, not only the railways
and gas works but private industry swiftly converted coal-burning
equipment to oil. As a result, Britain's total petroleum consumption
rose from almost 21 million tons in 1957 to over 60 million tons in
1965 and to 84 million tons in 1974/75. By the 1970's, petroleum

had become Britain's major source of primary energy. The dominant role which coal had played in the economy since the Industrial Revolution was at an end.

The effect of changed market circumstances on the capacity and performance of the industry in shown in Table 1.

Table 1

NCB Output, Exports, Employment, Productivity and Number of Collieries in Operation, 1947-75

Year	Output Deep-Mined (000 tons)	Open-Cast	Exports (inc. bunkers) (000 tons)	Employ- ment at End-Year (000)	Output per Man-shift Overall (cwts)	Number of Producing Collieries
1947	184.4	10.2	5.3	705	21.9	958
1950	202.3	12.2	16.9	683	24.5	901
1955	207.8	11.4	13.9	695	24.7	850
1957	207.3	13.6	7.9	704	24.9	822
1960	183.7	7.6	5.5	583	28.0	698
1965	178.0	7.3	3.7	447	35.9	504
1970	133.3	7.8	3.2	283	44.1	293
1975	114.7	10.2	1.8	245	44.9	241

SOURCE:

NCB. *Annual Reports and Accounts;* Department of Energy, *Digest of Energy Statistics.*

The change in market conditions in 1957 forced the NCB to announce in the following years that for the first time since vesting day it had taken deliberate measures to restrict output. These included selective restrictions on recruitment, the ending of voluntary Saturday morning and over-time working, and the advancing of plans to close old and uneconomic pits. But these measures were both too little and too late. Despite scaling down the forecasts of future demand, output and employment, the estimates contained in the *Revised Plan for Coal* in 1959 were still too optimistic. Once started, the run-down of the industry gathered momentum with the result that during the second half of the 1960's, colliery closures were taking place at the rate of almost one per week. Increasingly the Government was obliged to intervene to slow down what would otherwise have been an unmanageable rate of contraction and to mitigate, as far as possible, the social consequences of decline. Coalmining therefore became a Government-assisted and heavily protected industry in the 1960's. Along with measures taken directly to increase the demand for coal, heavy financial support was forthcoming.

238

Between 1959 and 1969, imports of coal were prohibited and in 1961 an additional tax of 0.83 p. per gallon on heavy fuel oil was imposed which added at that time about 25-30% to the price of oil. By 1967, it was estimated that this tax was worth between four and five million tons of output to the coal industry.[16] Moreover, under the provisions of the Coal Industry Act in 1967 both the electricity supply industry and to a lesser extent the gas industry could be requested to burn more coal than strictly economic considerations would have warranted. Between 1967 and 1969, this 'extra-burn' amounted to six million tons per annum but fell to two million tons per annum in 1969-70 and to zero in 1970-71. By the latter date, dramatic changes had occurred in the price of imported oil and hence in the competitive positions of coal and oil. However, in 1973, the 'extra-burn' was re-established at about five million tons per annum.[17] The most important support given to coal was the strict control, amounting virtually to a ban, exercised on the conversion of coal-fired stations to oil or natural gas. Again, this was only eased in 1970-71, when coal markets began to improve. In 1970, it was estimated that this form of control was worth about 20 million tons of output to coalmining. At the same time, coal was afforded preference as a fuel for public buildings where price differences between it and alternative fuels did not exceed 5%. In aggregate the effect of these measures was to prop up the output of an ailing coal industry and to prevent what might otherwise have been an irreversible rate of contraction.

Along with these measures to hold up the demand for coal went a considerable measure of financial assistance. This included capital reconstruction with £415 million of capital debt, incurred in re-building the industry, being written off under the terms of the 1965 Coal Industry Act. In consequence, the NCB's accounts improved by about £30 million per annum due to the reduction of interest charges. Substantial relief payments were also made available by both the 1965 and 1967 Coal Industry Acts to mitigate the social costs which resulted from rapid contraction. Under the former, the Exchequer met one-half of the costs arising from redundancy payments and travel and transfer allowances, this subsequently being raised in 1967 to two-thirds. The Exchequer's contribution on these counts rose from £1.3 million in 1966/7 to almost £10.8 million in 1968/9. In addition, the 1967 Act stipulated that the State would meet the cost of supplementing the income of miners over 55 years of age who became redundant. These measures, due to expire in early 1971, were subsequently extended subject to certain amendments. For example, discretion could be exercised in setting the age-limit for the early retirement scheme and instead of meeting a rigid two-thirds of the social costs identified in the 1967 Act, grants were operated on a tapering basis over a number of years.[18]

Whether more could, or should, have been done is open to question. In view of the uncertainty of the energy position in the 1970's it would seem that the authorities were at least justified in providing the level of support which they did. Even then, between 1957 and 1970 the consumption of British coal fell by almost one-third, employment by one-half and the number of productive collieries by almost two-thirds (see Table 1). A faster rate of run-down would have reduced capacity to a point from which there could be virtually no way back. Collieries, once closed, cannot easily be reopened: to all intents and purposes a policy which involves closure for an extended period of time is irreversible. While there was, therefore, every reason to allow the industry to contract by shearing off uneconomic and virtually exhausted pits, there were equally strong grounds in the 1960's for intervention to prevent the remaining 'hard-core' of relatively efficient units from being overwhelmed by the tide of market forces. The vital question was, of course, at what level the industry should be stabilised.

In the event, far-reaching changes in the energy position of the country during the 1970's largely resolved the issue. From the start of the decade coal benefited from a factor 'external' to the industry altogether—the successive increases in the price of imported oil. These began in 1970-71 but the real disruption came a few years later when the actions of the Organisation of Petroleum Exporting Countries (OPEC) led to an escalation of world oil prices in 1973-4, at a time when Britain was entirely dependent on foreign sources.[19] The higher oil prices were raised the more competitive indigenous coal production became and the more assured its position within an admittedly uncertain global energy future.[20] The nature of the coal debate changed, discussion now concentrating on how best to stabilise production with a view to planning for expansion in the years ahead. The stabilisation process started with the Coal Industry Act of 1973 which again reduced the book value of NCB assets, wrote off accumulated deficits and provided a new structure of borrowing powers for the Board. In addition, grants were to be made available to meet the social consequences of colliery closure, the cost of the 'extra-burn' of coal at power stations and the cost of stocking aids and regional aid as allowed under European Coal and Steel Community regulations.[21] In aggregate, these measures conferred grants on the industry of up to £720 million for the following five-year period.

It was against this background of continuing State support that the NCB presented its new *Plan for Coal* in 1974. For the first time in 15 years provisions were made for an expansion of capacity. In what amounted to a massive rescue plan for the industry, an investment programme of £1,400 million (at January 1974 prices) was outlined for the period up to 1985. By that date, 42 million tons of new capacity were to be created, 22 million tons by expanding existing capacity and 20 million tons from new pits, including the giant 10 million tons per annum colliery planned for Selby in Yorkshire.[22] This investment would ensure that output was not only maintained but actually increased by 1985. Existing output in 1974 stood at about 120 million tons and, if nothing was done, exhaustions were likely to reduce capacity during the following decade to between 80 and 90 million tons. The proposed new capacity would therefore compensate for this exhaustion rate and permit some increase in output over the next ten years. In the enthusiasm for expanding indigenous energy supplies following the oil crisis, these targets were endorsed by a tripartite group consisting of Government representatives, NCB board members and officials of the mining unions.[23]

Yet, two years later, the tripartite group was forced to announce a massive increase in the cost of the Board's investment plans from £1,400 million to £3,200 million.[24] There was also to be a further £200 million allowed for projects which had slipped for a couple of years beyond the original time-limit of 1985. In particular, the completion of the Selby project was not now envisaged until 1987. This escalation in costs can be attributed to serious underestimation of equipment costs in the original Plan, the addition of several new projects and the fact that the NCB had been hit harder than most industries by inflation. Acceptance of these new investment totals was combined with official backing for the Board's expansionary plans after 1985. Although promises given in the 1970's to support an investment programme between 1985 and the year 2000 cost nothing, the tripartite review of policy indicates how far the debate on coal had been transformed within a comparatively short time-period. Pessimism and retrenchment had given way to optimism and the prospect of an expansionary future.

2   THE DEMAND FOR COAL

The most striking aspect of post-war coal demand was the extent to which the mineral switched from being directly consumed by final users to being an input for the fuel conversion industries. In 1955, one-half of the total supply of coal was destined for direct consumption, principally by industry, households and the railways. Twenty years later, this proportion had fallen to one-fifth (see Table 2), largely due to the slump in industrial and domestic demand and the virtual disappearance of railways as a consumer of coal. Indeed, over the period, Table 2 shows that the quantity of coal absorbed by each of the main direct consumers fell continuously, resulting in a fall of almost 80% in the volume *directly* marketed. Up to 1970, some part of this lost demand was switched to the full conversion industries but the great bulk was lost entirely, consumers switching to cleaner and more efficient fuels.

Table 2

Markets for British Coal, 1955-75 (m. tons: figures in brackets represent proportions of Total Consumption)

	1955	1960	1970	1975
Input to Secondary Fuel Producers:				
Power Stations	43.5	51.9	76.0	73.4
Gas Works	28.2	22.6	4.2	—
Coke-Ovens	27.4	28.8	24.9	18.8
Carbonisation and Patent				
Fuel Plants	2.2	2.3	4.1	4.0
	101.3 (44)	105.6 (52)	109.2 (69)	96.2 (79)
Directly Consumed by Final Users:				
Industrial	45.4	34.9	19.3	9.5
Collieries	8.7	5.0	1.9	1.2
Railways	12.3	8.9	0.1	0.1
Domestic	38.1	35.5	19.9	11.5
Miscellaneous	9.4	6.8	4.0	1.8
	113.9 (50)	91.1 (45)	45.2 (29)	24.1 (20)
Exports (plus Bunkers)	13.9 (6)	5.5 (3)	3.2 (2)	1.8 (1)
Total Consumption	229.1(100)	202.2(100)	157.6(100)	122.1(100)

SOURCE:
Digest of Energy Statistics.

In contrast to the direct demand for coal, input to secondary fuel producers rose steadily, reaching a peak in 1964/5 before slipping back during the 1970's. Had it not been for the tonnage consumed by the power stations, partly enforced, the decline of coal markets would have been disastrous. In 1955, the generation of electricity accounted for almost one-fifth of the total consumption of coal, rising to about one-half in 1970. Although this proportion actually increased to 60% in 1975, this reflected the continued rapid contraction of total coal consumption rather than an increase in the absolute tonnage sent to the power stations. Indeed during the 1970's, even the secondary market for coal deteriorated due mainly to the conversion to natural gas and the consequent loss of demand from the gas works. In large measure, the decline of both primary and secondary coal markets can be attributed first, to technological developments which enabled great improvements to be made in fuel-burning efficiency and second to the switch by consumers to other fuels.

Between 1955 and 1975, the increase in Britain's total consumption of primary energy did not keep pace with the rate of growth of real GDP.[25] As a result the energy ratio, defined as tons of coal equivalent per £1,000 GDP, fell from 8.6 to 6.8.[26] This reflected increased efficiency in energy use: there was a steady fall in the amount of energy required to generate a standard 'unit' of GDP.[27] Some part of this improvement in fuel-burning efficiency was due to better use being made of coal. Over the past twenty years there has been a marked improvement in the efficiency of household fires, steel has steadily used less coke per ton of pig iron due to improved blast furnace design and fuel oil injection processes, and industry in general has proved more ready to make use of waste-heat. Above all, there has been a rapid improvement in the efficiency of steam-raising plant in the electricity supply industry. Due to better plant design and advances in metallurgy which have permitted higher pressures and temperatures, the thermal efficiency of steam stations rose from 21.1% in 1948 to 28.4% in 1970. This meant burning about 17 million tons of coal equivalent less than if the 1948 level of thermal efficiency had prevailed throughout.[28]

More important, however, in accounting for the depressed coal market has been the switch by consumers to other forms of fuel. Initially encouraged by the Government in the period of coal shortage up to 1957, this transfer of allegiance, notably to oil, gathered momentum in the 1960's at a time when coal was plentifully available. The trend in favour of other fuels is brought out in Table 3.

Between 1947/50 and 1972/75 there was a spectacular decline in the coal industry's contribution to the total energy requirements of the nation. From an overwhelming nine-tenths of the total, coal had slipped to little more than one-third while over the same period the consumption of petroleum increased from 9 to 46%. By the latter date, too, natural gas had gained for itself an important share of the market although it is unlikely ever to occupy one of the larger roles in a future energy programme. Potentially the greatest source of competition to coal in the long term could be nuclear power, but the nuclear thrust by the mid-1970's had run into appalling difficulties.[29] The second nuclear programme was years behind schedule, the five AGRs in the programme had experienced serious construction problems and there was very little operating experience.[30] According to one estimate, the development costs of the AGR had reached £3,000 million by 1977, a cost over-run of more than £1,000

Table 3

Inland Energy Consumption: Primary Fuel Input Basis, UK
(m. tons of coal or coal equivalent: figures in brackets represent proportion
of total energy consumption)

	1947/50	1952/55	1962/65	1972/75
Coal	194.2 (90.5)	210.9 (87)	189.2 (66)	121.4 (36)
Petroleum	19.7 (9)	29.7 (12)	90.0 (32)	151.4 (46)
Natural Gas	—	—	0.5 (0.2)	47.6 (14)
Primary Electricity[1]	0.8 (0.5)	1.1 (1)	5.3 (1.8)	12.7 (4)
Total consumption	214.7(100)	241.7(100)	285.0(100)	333.1(100)

SOURCE:
Digest of Energy Statistics.
NOTE:
1. Nuclear and Hydro Electricity except generation at pumped storage stations.

million—higher than that of Concorde.[31] Ahead lay the prospect of considerable redesign to overcome maintenance difficulties if further AGRs were to be placed on order. Alternatively, there might be a switch to American-designed pressurised water reactors which are allegedly cheaper to build. The deciding issues in any future programme might well be safety and environmental factors. However, even if commissioned now, the next generation of nuclear power stations would take years to build and come into full operation. In the short and medium terms therefore, coal's major enemy, as in the past twenty years, will continue to be oil.

To some extent, the steady fall in demand for coal from 1957 reflected non-price factors in fuel choice. Other fuels were simply cleaner, especially for household use, and easier to control, handle and store. At the same time, the move away from coal was given added impetus by the Clean Air Act of 1957 and subsequent amendments. But of far greater significance was the growing inability of the mineral to compete effectively in terms of price with other sources of power. For instance, the price of coal to the power stations rose from 1.5 pence per therm in 1955 to 2.1 in 1966 and 2.9 in 1972. In contrast, the price of oil per therm fell from 2.0 to 1.7 between 1955 and 1966, before rising to 2.5 in 1972.[32] At the latter date, it still had a considerable advantage over coal. Only after the substantial price rises in imported fuel oil in 1974 was the balance tipped back in favour of coal, but successful future performance will depend on the retention of this price advantage in face of competition from indigenous North Sea oil.

Similarly private industry rapidly converted coal-burning equipment to oil in view of the latter's growing competitiveness during the 1960's. Undoubtedly the electricity supply industry would also have converted from coal-fired stations on a larger scale had not the Government prevented such a move as part of a comprehensive programme designed to protect the coal industry. Falling markets and dwindling coalmining capacity appeared to be permanent features until the escalation of fuel oil prices in the 1970's. The industry was suddenly presented with an opportunity to recover some of the ground lost since the 1950's. The chance can be seized only if coalmining possesses sufficient flexibility to respond rapidly enough to the changed market environment. The major problem has been that customers, particularly power stations, are unwilling to pay enough to make large new coal investments attractive. A considerable measure of Government intervention will be necessary, a factor already accepted in the review of the NCB's 1974 *Plan for Coal* conducted in 1976 by the tripartite group of ministers, management and unions (see section 1).

3 TECHNOLOGY, PRODUCTIVITY AND COSTS

In the competitive energy environment in which coal found itself after 1957, productivity increases became all-important in order to offset diminishing returns and hold back the natural tendency of costs to rise. The doubling of mine productivity in the 1960's, associated with the introduction of powered roof supports, coal shearers and conveyor belts, contrasted strongly with the disappointing achievement of previous years. Between the 1880's, when machines first appeared in any number at the coal face, and 1955, output per man-shift overall had not significantly increased. Even with nationalisation and the commitment to reconstruction, productivity rose by only 14% between 1947-8 and 1956-7, from 21.9 to 24.9 cwts. This can largely be attributed to the policy of production at all costs which entailed keeping low-productivity pits in operation. Such closures as did take place were due mainly to exhaustion of reserves rather than a conscious desire to concentrate capacity and promote greater efficiency.

The contraction of markets from 1957 evoked an altogether different response from the industry. Although rationalisation was inevitable, the programme of colliery closures was accompanied, under the chairmanship of Lord Robens, by a speeding-up of face-mechanisation.[33] By 1975, output per man-shift had risen to 45 cwts, an increase of 80% over the level of 1956-7. At first sight, this was an impressive achievement but it was still far below the optimistic forecast made by the NCB in 1969. In its submission to the Select Committee on Nationalised Industries the Board had predicted an increase from the 47 cwts per man-shift existing at that time to a spectacular 75 cwts in 1975-6, leading to a total demand estimate of 135 million tons by the latter date. In the event, output per man-shift was 30 cwts short of this target and demand about 10 million tons short. Moreover, there has since that time been a tendency for productivity to fall, a movement which must be reversed if coal is to remain competitive with oil.

The growth of output per man-shift between 1957 and 1975 was the outcome of several conflicting forces. The main impetus came from the NCB's determination after 1957 to close down less economic, low-productivity pits and to introduce in the remaining nucleus of comparatively efficient collieries an extensive programme of machine-mining. By closing the less profitable mines and deliberately concentrating output in fewer units, the NCB ensured that the average level of productivity would increase more rapidly than in the past. Capacity was streamlined to bring it into line, as far as possible, with the new market situation, the rate of closure speeding up in the second half of the 1960's. As shown in Table 1, the number of producing collieries fell by little more than 10% between 1947 and 1957 but had declined by a further two-thirds by 1970. Even the subsequent rise in oil prices could not prevent an additional 50 collieries from being taken out of production between 1970 and 1975. More important than the actual closure of pits was the rationalisation of working faces, resulting in less dispersal of effort and greater ease of organisation. The number of major longwall faces in operation fell from about 2,500 in 1963 to 1,260 in 1967 and to just over 750 in 1975.

However, within this declining total important changes had taken place in an attempt to increase productivity. The fall in number of faces was exclusively confined to longwall advancing, while every effort was made to increase production from longwall retreating. The development of retreat mining was largely due to the growing difficulties, in the shape of poor roof conditions and faulting, encountered in winning the coal. By driving the roadways first and working the seams from the end of the roadways to the start, an indication was provided of the lie of the seams and the incidence of faulting. This system permitted a much higher output per man-shift than advance mining but could not be used in many deep mines due to the pressure on roadways. Development has, therefore, been modest although, where it has proved possible, retreat mining has yielded impressive results. In 1967 there were 37 retreating faces in Britain each producing a daily output of 471 tons, as opposed to 1,223 advancing faces producing 443 tons per face. By 1975 93 retreating faces each produced 774 tons, a 64% increase in their daily output from the level of 1967. In contrast, the number of advancing faces had fallen to 661, producing 556 tons per day, an increase of only 25%.

A major obstacle in the way of further productivity gains from retreat working in the 1970's proved to be the speed with which underground roads could be driven. Attempts to increase the proportion of output won by retreat methods led to an increase in the yards of drivage per 1,000 tons of output. At the same time, however, the efficiency of this drivage declined. Despite an increase in the number of heading machines in use from about 250 in 1970 to almost 600 in 1975, the average daily advance remained the same. Between the same years the number of man-shifts per drivage shift increased by almost 20%. This, together with the increase in amount of drivage required to support operations, resulted in a rise in the man-shifts per 1,000 tons devoted to drivage from under 8 in 1970/71 to almost 12 in 1975.[34]

Important though they were, retreat methods of working and mechanical road head drivers were still at a comparatively early stage of their development. A more sustained contribution to productivity growth between 1957 and 1975 came from the innovation of power loaders and powered supports and the development of more efficient processes in coal-working. According to the NCB in their evidence to the Select Committee on Nationalised Industries in 1969 these, rather than pit-closures, had been primarily responsible for the increase in efficiency since 1957. Until that date, undercutting the longwall face by machine had been prevalent. Coal was brought down by explosives, hand-loaded on to a face conveyor, transferred to a roadway conveyor and taken either to the shaft-bottom or the surface. Roof supports of wood or metal were advanced by hand. From 1947 the power loader had been very slowly adopted, largely due to the run-down state of the industry. Since there were far more urgent requirements such as new sinkings and the reconstruction of existing collieries, a low priority was inevitably given to face mechanisation. In addition, combined cutting and loading by machine had been developed in America to suit the room and pillar system of working and substantial modifications had to be made before the new technology could be applied to British longwall faces.[35] Only in the mid-1950's, when a large part of the reconstruction programme had been completed, was attention increasingly diverted to work at the face, and especially to power-loading techniques. Whereas between 1947 and 1957 the proportion of British output power-loaded had only increased from over 2 to 23%, by the end of the next ten years the ratio had jumped to 86%. In the 1970's, the mechanisation process was virtually completed, with more than nine-tenths of output obtained in this way.

The increasing speed with which the face could be advanced meant that the manual advancing of roof supports delayed production. Hydraulically powered supports were therefore developed to complement power loaders. These held the roof by means of hydraulic pressure and were moved forward by the same force. Progress in this area was astonishingly swift. The first full face installation of powered supports was introduced in 1954 but they were hardly in use on a production basis until a few years later. Yet by the 1970's they were generally applied throughout the industry. Whereas in 1960 about 90 powered support faces produced 10% of NCB output, by the mid-1970's over 800 were in operation, contributing 91% of total output. Indeed, the NCB regarded powered supports and their adoption for general use as 'a technical revolution of major significance which has resulted in great improvements in productivity and safety'.[36] Moreover, successful research work continued with the development of more advanced systems of power support control. These offered a considerable saving in manpower in combined conveyor and support advancing, making possible much higher rates of advance and more accurate support setting. At the same time, growing use of the chainless power loader and the increase in weight and capacity of these advanced machines created a need for heavy-duty face conveyors. Trials and experimental work undertaken by the NCB offered the prospect of important productivity gains in this area.

In one important respect success has continued to elude the Board in its attempt to improve the efficiency of face-working. In 1963-4, a system of fully automated mining, remotely operated longwall face (ROLF), was used on experimental faces and put into production in the following year in Nottingham. Serious geological and technical difficulties led to the withdrawal of the system and it was only reintroduced in 1971. Since it used remotely controlled power loaders and supports, ROLF required no men at the face. But it was virtually impossible to keep the cutting machine on the face and to prevent it straying into the roof or roads. Quite apart from technical difficulties, there were also difficulties on the labour side. In view of its high capital cost—about £0.5 million compared with £150,000 for a standard power loader face—ROLF requires to be worked intensively. At Nottingham, seven-day working was initially introduced but labour problems led to a return to a five-day week. Because of the problems encountered, the system was discontinued, making it unlikely that fully automated face working will significantly affect productivity figures in the foreseeable future.

On the other hand, away from the face, considerable advances were made in underground operations. These took the form of remote-controlled conveyor systems, the development of man-riding by truck or conveyor to speed up the journey to and from the face, more efficient repair systems and improvements in winding.[37] On the surface, progress was also maintained with the introduction of automatic loading of wagons and a growing use of automatic monitoring and control systems. Efficiency was further improved by better organisation of both production and administration. The former area was particularly important since it was estimated in 1969 that after taking unavoidable delays into account, coalmining achieved only two-thirds of possible output. This was due to deficiencies in the organisation and planning of face advance and frequent delays caused by machine breakdown. In best-practice German collieries round-the-clock working on five over-lapping shifts is practised. In mechanised British collieries two-shift working is common, the coal face lying idle the rest of the time. Weekends and off-shift time are being used for maintenance in Britain but for cutting coal in Germany. This highlights a serious obstacle in the way of greater productivity in Britain, the high incidence of mechanical failure. Coal ripped from the face by the coal shearers frequently jams conveyors and crushers and faults develop in power and water cables (needed to keep down dust). Stopping and starting on the face can cause surges of coal on the conveyors so that the coal-raising apparatus cannot cope. A further important cause of delay is the disorganisation at each end of the coal face caused by the inability of road-tunnelling machinery to keep in step with face-advance.

While this in no way minimises the unfavourable effects on productivity of difficult geological conditions and the reluctance of unions and management to move towards multiple-shift working, it does suggest that technical problems, in the shape of unreliable machinery, have been central in checking the improvement of efficiency. The answer probably lies in the introduction of more thoroughly automated techniques and electronic monitoring throughout the pit which will make the entire colliery run smoothly as a unit. In terms of the administrative structure of the industry, substantial changes have already taken place. In the late 1960's rationalisation resulted in a fall of managerial and clerical personnel from 44.0 thousand in 1967 to 28.5 thousand in 1975. This was achieved mainly by trimming the former five-tier structure of Headquarters, Divisions, Areas, Groups and Collieries down to three, Headquarters, Areas and Collieries.

However, the impact of measures taken to improve the organisation of production and administration was less than it might otherwise have been due to the influence of certain factors working in the opposite direction. The steadily increasing average age of the workforce was accompanied by a significant rise in involuntary absenteeism, due to illness and other unavoidable causes, from an average of 6.55% in 1950-52 to 12.76% in 1973-75. This easily offset the decline in voluntary absenteeism from 5.56% to 4.07% over the same period.

The rising average age of labour reflected the difficulties of recruiting young and especially skilled men into coalmining. This in turn was caused by the apparent lack of career prospects up to 1970: the future of the industry to say the least appeared uncertain and the consequent difficulties in recruiting for craftsman-training inevitably had a detrimental effect on productivity. Nor during the 1960's were earnings in coalmining sufficient to encourage an inflow of skilled men. The reward to labour did not rise as rapidly as in British industry as a whole with the result that between 1955 and 1970 miners' weekly earnings fell from being the highest of all manual workers to 16th place (although still 4th in terms of hourly earnings). Dissatisfaction with the decline in relative living standards resulted in 1972 in the first official national stoppage of the mines since 1926. The strike, which followed a 10-week ban on overtime, lasted for 7 weeks and was only resolved by the setting up of a special Court of Inquiry under Lord Wilberforce.[38]

The Court of Inquiry confirmed that the miners had slipped steadily down the 'earnings league-table' and could properly be regarded as a 'special case'. In 1952, average weekly earnings in coalmining had been 28% above the average for all manufacturing industries. By 1970, earnings in coal were below the average and even the Wilberforce award placed them only about 5% above, in a period of rising wage inflation. Besides an increase in wage rates, the age at which adult rates could be paid was to be lowered at annual intervals down to 18 and 5 further days of holiday were granted per year. Heralded as a triumph for the miners, this award in fact only restored to them some of the ground previously lost. Inevitably, it neither solved the industry's recruitment problems nor for long satisfied the men in view of the constantly rising cost of living. The further national stoppage in January 1974 can be regarded as part and parcel of the same struggle, the miners on this occasion being unwilling to settle within the limits of the Government's counter-inflation policy, phase 3 of which had started in October 1973. With the gains secured under the Wilberforce award quickly being eroded, the miners were in a strong position to press their claim due to the steep rise in price of imported fuel oil.

In the bitter dispute which followed the Government, as in the former instance, declared a state of emergency and placed severe restrictions on heating and lighting. To preserve fuel supplies industry was required to work on only three days per week and coal stocks were rapidly run down. The entrenched positions taken up both by miners and the Conservative Government drove the latter finally to call a general election, a central issue of which was the alleged attempt by the NUM to use its industrial strength to defeat the policy of an elected Government. The minority Labour Government which came

250

to power took a broader view of the points at issue. It not only agreed that the average weekly earnings of male manual workers in the industry had fallen from a ratio of 105.6% of those in manufacturing in 1972 to 102.3% in 1973 but also accepted that a long-term view demanded the reversal of the previous policy of contracting the coal industry. In view of the pricing policies of OPEC, miners' earnings should be boosted to a level that would encourage an inflow of new recruits and permit the industry to plan for an expansionary future. 'Exceptional' payments were therefore made to the miners, raising the NCB's wage bill by £95 million per annum rather than the £44 million which had been offered. In 1975, for the first time since 1957, the Board was able to report that recruitment into the industry had exceeded wastage.

However, this highlights the major problem of the miners. It is generally accepted that they have a disagreeable and dangerous job to perform. If, nonetheless, the work has to be undertaken 'in the national interest', then those involved are entitled to a reward significantly higher than the average available for other types of manual labour. The sentiments expressed by J. R. Clynes in 1920 still hold good today that, 'however much we may mourn the demands which they make, we will not go down the pits to take their place'.[39] The crucial question is whether in future the job will continue to be 'in the national interest' or, more precisely, whether so many jobs in mining will continue to be necessary. The miners' leaders must continually walk a tightrope, pushing the return to labour to as high a level as possible in the interests of those they represent, without pushing so hard that they undermine the competitive position of the industry. There is a cut-off point, determined by the availability and pricing of other forms of fuel and power. If wage costs, which form such an integral part of total mining costs, pushed the industry into this 'no-go' area the future of coalmining would be jeopardised since there would be every incentive to develop more strongly alternative forms of fuel and power. The final irony is that for all their recent militancy the miners have lost much of the real advantage which they gained from the last two national stoppages. Other unions in different industries, using the miners as pace-setters, have followed their lead with similar, and in some cases, higher settlements.

The pay claims of 1972 and 1974 emphasised the delicate balance which must be maintained to ensure a just return to labour and, at the same time, preserve the competitiveness of the industry. The extremely good record of industrial relations in the 1960's gave way in the 1970's to bitterness and conflict and a massive deterioration in tonnage lost through disputes. In the former decade, output lost due to disputes averaged only 1.2 million tons per annum. In 1970-71, 3 million tons were lost, in 1972 over 26 million and in 1974,

21 million. Justified or not, the danger of these stoppages lay in the harm done to the NCB's financial position; the price increases which became necessary to minimise trading losses; and the erosion of consumer confidence, especially on the part of large customers like electricity. The Board's chairman, Derek Ezra, rightly warned at the end of 1973 that 'our customers will not accept our arguments about security of supply if we go on in this way'.[40] On the other hand, from the point of view of productivity it was desirable to bump up relative earnings to a level which would encourage an inflow of young and fresh talent into the industry.

The dampening effect which the age-structure of the labour force, rising absenteeism and the slow growth of earnings before 1970 had on productivity made the increase which was obtained all the more commendable. It was this increase which enabled labour costs per ton to be held at a relatively steady level between 1957 and 1970/71, a striking achievement in such a labour-intensive industry. Movements in costs and proceeds per ton are shown in Table 4.

Table 4

Operating Costs, Proceeds and Profits per ton, Selected Years, 1950-1974/5

	1950		1957		1970/1		1974/5	
Costs	£	%	£	%	£	%	£	%
Wages and related expenses	1.47	65	2.41	59	2.83	49	6.32	51
Materials, repairs and power	0.47	21	0.95	23	1.52	26	3.25	27
Other costs (incl. depreciation)	0.32	14	0.71	18	1.45	25	2.71	22
Total Costs	2.26	100	4.07	100	5.80	100	12.28	100
Proceeds	2.39	—	4.10	—	5.84	—	11.89	—
Profit (+) or loss (−) per ton before charging interest	+0.13	—	+0.03	—	+0.04	—	−0.39	—

SOURCE:

NCB, *Annual Reports and Accounts.*

The relative stability of labour costs ended with the pay-awards of 1972 and 1974. These had the effect of raising wage costs per ton by more than 120% between 1970/71 and 1974/75. But at the same time, the cost per ton of materials, repairs and power rose by 114% and other costs (including depreciation) by 87%. As a result, Table 4 shows that only a slight increase occurred in the share of total costs absorbed by wages. The labour side of the industry could rightly claim that the ratio of wage costs to total costs per ton in the mid-1970's was still far below that of the 1950's. This can be attributed to the very large input of capital, the rapid growth of productivity between 1957 and 1970 and the fact that wage rates in coalmining had advanced less quickly than in several branches of · manufacturing. Following the awards made to labour in 1972 and 1974, the problem in the 1970's will be to ensure that further large increases do not tilt the balance in such a way that coal is unable to compete effectively with other sources of energy. This becomes all the more vital when the recent tendency of productivity to fall is borne in mind.

4 PROFITS, PRICING AND THE COALFIELDS

The operating results of the industry reveal that between vesting day and 1970-71, a profit was made before taking interest payments into account in all but three years.[41] Up to and including 1957, the average annual profit amounted to £15 million on an annual turnover of some £600 million. To these profits must be added those made by NCB ancillary activities, such as coke-ovens and brickworks, of about £2.6 million per annum. However interest payments on debt and borrowing, averaging about £17 million per annum, virtually absorbed the whole of these profits, allowing the NCB to do little more than break even. Between 1958 and 1970-71, the financial position of the Board deteriorated rapidly. Operating profits continued to be made in most years, the average for the period reaching almost £17.5 million per annum on a yearly turnover of about £810 million. Profits from ancillary activities averaged £10.7 million, but swamping all these margins was a massive increase in interest payments. These had to be spread over a constantly dwindling output and converted operating profits into heavy deficits which averaged about £9.2 million per annum.

The increasingly heavy burden of interest which the industry had to pay can be attributed not only to a rise in interest rates over the period but also to the large amount of borrowing undertaken to finance extensions of plant and equipment and the higher level of stocks held after 1957. By 1964-5, it was clear that the coal industry was seriously over-capitalised. It had borrowed heavily to finance investment on the expectation of a demand and level of output that never in fact materialised. The Government therefore agreed in 1964 to write off about 40% of the NCB's capital debt, amounting to £415 million. This immediately reduced the burden of interest charges which fell from £42.7 million in 1964-5 to £25 million in the following year, but the respite was short-lived. By 1970-71, they had risen again to about £35 million due to increased borrowing from the Government to finance investments.

If financial performance was poor up to 1970-71, it was even more depressing during the first half of the 1970's. Where before the industry had generally made an operating profit it now consistently made a loss, despite grants received under the 1973 Coal Industry Act. With interest charges steadily rising on capital debt, coalmining again benefited in 1973 when the value of its assets was written down by the Government. This brought some relief but as in the previous decade the reduction in interest charges was short-lived. Heavy borrowing to finance capital expenditure was responsible for a formidable increase in the size of outstanding loans. These had been reduced from £630 million in 1972 to £472 million in the following year due to the writing down of assets. But by the year ending March 1976 they had spiralled upwards to £732 million. The industry was paying heavily, in the form of interest charges, for the methods which it had been obliged to use since vesting day to finance capital spending.

The parlous state of coal's finances in the 1970s reflected not only the current market situation but also the pricing policies which had been implemented in the past. There is no doubt that had the NCB been given a free hand in pricing during the period of rapidly expanding demand prior to 1957, much larger profits would have been made. The reserves, thus accumulated, could have been used to cushion the effects of a declining demand from that date. As it was, the Board was obliged to enter into a 'gentleman's agreement' with the Government in the pricing of its product. The latter was concerned to keep fuel prices down in the national interest: specifically, to reduce the impact which the price of coal might have on general inflation. Although this sacrifice, in terms of profits foregone, was large enough, the NCB's freedom of action was still further curtailed. Rather than employ price increases or other forms of self-financing, the Board was 'encouraged' to meet its capital requirements through Exchequer borrowing. Indebtedness to the Exchequer therefore rapidly increased during the expansionary 1950's in line with the NCB's programme of new sinkings and reconstruction schemes. The more it financed capital expenditure in this way, the heavier the interest burden the Board was forced to carry and the greater its dependence on Government for renewed borrowing facilities. In addition, the NCB was asked by the Government to finance the losses accumulated on imported coal, amounting to more than £70 million between 1951 and 1959.

The benefits of the 'gentleman's agreement' may appear a little one-sided in the period up to 1957 but in the years which followed the balance of advantage tipped decisively in coal's favour. Recognising its obligations in a period of falling demand, the State increasingly intervened to protect the industry. As noted in section 2 several forms of assistance were provided, including capital reconstruction, increases in the Board's borrowing limit and various 'protectionist' measures. These were designed not only to slow down the fall in demand for coal but also to cushion the social costs of contraction. Both the NCB and the national interest might have been better served before and after 1957 by more realistic and efficiently managed pricing policies. This is an issue which leads to much wider considerations about the proper role of the nationalised industries. Whether they should be left to operate as efficiently as possible within narrowly defined industrial limits or be used in a wider role as instruments of Government policy has been widely debated elsewhere and lies beyond the scope of the present enquiry.[42]

Since coal is not a homogeneous product and is produced under widely different cost-conditions throughout the country, a uniform price-structure is not possible. Competition in certain qualities is severe while in others it remains relatively slight. In addition, the NCB had to take account of the provisions of the 1946 Nationalisation Act. As noted earlier, revenues had to be sufficient to meet outgoings on an average of good and bad years and undue preference to particular consumers had to be avoided. From the outset, the Board apparently felt bound by the Act to charge prices which would roughly cover its costs. Prices were therefore based on average, rather than marginal, costs with appropriate adjustments being made to reflect the quality and costs of particular grades of coal. For household consumers, coal was classified into different grades according to quality. The country was divided into zones, each of which operated its own set of prices for the various grades. Initially, prices in each zone were determined by the average national cost of mining different qualities but in the early 1960's adjustments were introduced to reflect supply cost differences.

In the case of coal for industrial use, a nationally fixed cost per unit of heat content was applied before 1970 to each particular grade to give a basic price. To this different 'adjustments' were made, including a size and preparation adjustment, adjustments to reflect unfavourable characteristics of the coal (high sulphur or ash content) and a flat-rate 'coalfield adjustment'. The last of these tried to ensure that similar grades of coal from different districts sold in a given market at roughly the same price. Since it did not, however, reflect the thermal quality of the coal, the 'coalfield adjustment' was abolished in 1970 in favour of area point values. Under the new measures, an area cost per unit was introduced to replace the national cost per unit of heat content. The area basic price was then modified by a code of simplified 'adjustment' procedures also introduced in 1970. Despite the existence of this formal pricing system, the NCB retained an element of flexibility in order to negotiate favourable agreements with large customers.

Throughout, pricing strategy made no concessions to marginal cost pricing policies despite the injunction to do so in 1967. In that year the nationalised industries were exhorted to align prices to marginal costs in an attempt to secure a more efficient and co-ordinated system of pricing.[43] The long controversy over average cost or marginal cost pricing has been adequately documented elsewhere[44] but some general points may be made here. Economic theory suggests that by setting all prices equal to long-run marginal costs, the optimum allocation of resources will result since the prices consumers pay for an additional unit of output will exactly equal the value of resources used in producing that additional unit. In practice, problems are created by the need to consider marginal social cost rather than marginal private cost; the difficulty of calculating even an approximation to marginal cost;[45] and whether marginal cost pricing will lead to a better or worse allocation of resources if other sectors are pricing non-marginally. Although criticised for not moving towards marginal cost pricing, the NCB was in no sense defying Government policy. The rules set down for the nationalised industries in 1967 did not require that prices be *equated* with long-run marginal cost; rather that they should be *related* to long-run marginal cost and it was recognised that necessarily there would be deviations from this principle.

It is true that the NCB has, perhaps, deviated more than most. It has not attempted to relate prices to costs at the margin, despite the policy statement in *Review of Economic and Financial Objectives* and the recommendations of the National Board for Prices and Incomes.[46] On the other hand, there was no statutory requirement to move in this direction and any major departure from existing pricing policies entailed a high degree of risk. In the event of change it was not only the financial position of the coal industry at national level that had to be considered but the viability of individual coalfields and the regional implications of a further wave of closures. Between 1957 and 1976, the rate of run-down was most unevenly spread throughout the country. By the latter date, both Scotland and the North-East were operating less than one-fifth of the number of collieries which they had in production in 1957, the North-West (including Staffordshire) about one-fifth and the South-West about one-quarter. In contrast, closures were much less marked in the East Midlands (including Nottinghamshire and Derbyshire) and in Yorkshire. These latter Areas accounted for almost 60% of total output by the mid-1970's as opposed to 43% in 1957.

Differing rates of closure corresponded closely with regional productivity differences. Despite shutting down uneconomic, low-productivity pits, in 1976 outputs per man-shift in Scotland and the North-East, at 39.4 and 38.6 cwts respectively, were 50% below the 59.2 cwts obtained in North Derbyshire. They were almost as far behind the other high-productivity Areas, the South Midlands and North and South Nottinghamshire. In turn, these productivity differences inevitably found reflection in the profit/loss accounts of the various districts. As noted in Chapter 7, profits per ton in the separate coalfields are the product of several different influences, including geological factors, the structure of demand and an ability to produce scarce and high-quality grades. Over the past decade, average price per ton has generally remained high in South Yorkshire, South Wales and Kent but in each of these Areas so, too, have costs. On the other hand, in North Derbyshire and North and South Nottinghamshire, prices per ton remained generally below the national average. Yet a high output per man-shift in these Areas and correspondingly low costs of production usually allowed the Midland region as a whole to be the most profitable in the country. In contrast, Scotland and the North-East, with low output per man-shift, have consistently been among the least profitable regions.

Variations in regional costs will probably diminish in future years as more low-productivity pits are closed down. But differences will always remain due to geological circumstances, levels of absenteeism and organisation, extent of multi-shift working and managerial competence. The survival of several British coalfields will, therefore, largely depend on their level of operating efficiency as measured by output per man-shift and costs, and the competitive position of coal in relation to other forms of fuel and power. This is the criterion adopted by the European Coal and Steel Community (ECSC) which encompasses the relevant industries of the nine member countries. Formed in 1951, the ECSC executive was merged with the EEC and EURATOM Commissions in 1967. The single Commission which resulted was empowered to borrow and lend and to raise revenue by charging a levy on coal and steel production. In its *Guidelines for Coal 1975-85,* published in 1975, the ECSC recommended that in view of OPEC pricing policies dependence on the rest of the world for energy supplies should be reduced to a minimum.[47]

As a result, an important future role was envisaged for the European coal industry: capacity which had averaged over 250 million tons coal equivalent in the first half of the 1970's should be maintained at that figure. However, it should be concentrated in those fields where potential productivity made coal production competitive with alternative energy sources. Other things being equal, the bulk of British capacity would continue to be viable on this basis. Britain and Germany are by far the largest coal producers in the Community, accounting in aggregate for more than four-fifths of total output.[48] In a 'scarce energy' situation, all but the most unremunerative of their coal would be vital to the Community. Coalmining productivity in the member countries is outlined in Table 5.

Table 5

Average Output per Man-Shift Underground in Community Countries. 1964/5-1974/5 (tons)[1]

	1964/5	1970/71	1974/5
W. Germany	2.72	3.93	4.06
France	2.01	2.59	2.74
Belgium	1.79	2.59	2.47
UK:—	—	3.37	3.41
Scotland	—	2.87	2.83
Northern	—	2.68	2.70
Yorkshire	—	3.80	3.72
North-West	—	3.16	3.31
Midlands	—	4.57	4.33
South Wales	—	2.32	2.04
Kent	—	2.25	1.93
Total Community (nine members)	2.39[2]	3.42	3.51

SOURCE:
Calculated from Statistical Office of the European Communities, *Energy Statistics Yearbook.*
NOTES:
1. Converted on the basis 1 ton=1016.047 kilos.
2. Relates to the six founding members of the Community before the addition of the UK, Ireland and Denmark.

The relatively high level of output per man-shift underground in the Community as a whole reflects the importance of UK and German production. In both France and Belgium, productivity is well below that of the two leading countries, although in the former the relatively high output per man achieved in the Lorraine district is concealed by the poor performance of the other coalfields. Within the UK, the future of the Yorkshire and Midland Coalfields, which contribute

258

the bulk of output, seems assured. Underground productivity in these districts compares favourably with best-practice German coalfields, the Ruhr and Saar. On the other hand, productivity is low in Kent and South Wales (in both of which special considerations apply), and relatively weak in Scotland and the North-East. The output of the latter two districts is essential if Community production is to be maintained at 250 million tons coal equivalent per annum. Yet the dispersion of productivities and costs relative to revenues confirms the view that efficiency and profitability are significantly higher in the central coalfields of the country.

In marked contrast to experience in the 1960's when investment in primary coal-producing capacity within the Community fell almost to zero, the oil price increases of the early 1970's gave rise to a constantly expanding investment programme. The bulk of this increased capital spending was undertaken by Britain under the terms of the 1974 *Plan for Coal.* By the mid-1970's she accounted for 60% of the capital expenditure taking place in the coalfields of the Community. In terms both of actual and estimated future investment, the Yorkshire and Midlands Coalfields were singled out for special treatment. Concentrating on high-productivity and profitable coalfields is of course, in line with Community policy; it also suggests that, within the UK, output in future years might be wholly concentrated in the central coalfields.[49]

11 Epilogue

The growth of State protection for coal in the 1960's indicated how serious the pressure from competitive fuels had become. In the second part of the decade the move to a four-fuel economy was particularly rapid, with growing use being made of two new indigenous primary fuels, gas and nuclear power. Until the early 1960's nearly all gas in Britain was manufactured from coal but the industry then switched to new processes based on oil. The subsequent discovery of natural North Sea resources changed the circumstances of the gas industry. It ceased to be a secondary fuel industry and became instead a supplier of primary fuel for direct use. At roughly the same time, nuclear power stations were developing in competition to coal. Britain had pioneered the Magnox reactors in the 1950's and, although slipping behind in the nuclear technology race, launched a second generation of reactors (AGRs) in the mid-1960's. With the addition of these two sources of primary energy, there was a clear need for a co-ordinated and comprehensive fuel policy.

This had been recognised in the preparation of the National Plan in 1964, part of which was devoted to a thorough examination of the energy sector. Its conclusions were contained in the White Paper on *Fuel Policy* in 1965 but the pace of development was such that the review of policy was continued. A second White Paper appeared in 1967[1] which underlined some unpalatable truths for the coal industry. The emphasis was to be on swift progress towards cheaper energy. This involved not only moving as quickly as possible to a four-fuel economy but inevitably entailed a further run-down of coalmining. It was argued that a continued fall in demand for coal could not be avoided, even by holding back the development of nuclear power and natural gas. As observed in Chapter 10, every effort was made to minimise as far as possible the social and regional consequences of contraction under the provisions of the Coal Industry Acts of 1965 and 1967 but neither the Government nor the NCB doubted that such contraction was necessary.

Where fierce controversy did arise, particularly after publication of the 1967 White Paper, was over what constituted 'an acceptable rate of run-down' and the level of protection which it was desirable to extend to the industry.[2] The NCB argued that while in the short

261

term extended protection and a slower rate of run-down would involve higher costs, there was every prospect in the longer term that coal would become highly competitive again due to the uncertain availability and pricing policies of alternative fuels. In this sense, further investment in coal was a long-run 'insurance policy'. In addition, there were important externalities associated with coal production which were not reflected in its price. These included improving the balance of payments by reducing the need for imported oil, greater security of supply and the heavy social costs which would have to be borne if the contraction of the industry was allowed to continue. These arguments were countered by those critical of the amount of protection afforded to coal and those which questioned whether the industry was sufficiently flexible to allow rapid expansion in the future.[3] The policy of protecting coal involved a considerable cost which the rest of the economy had to bear. Apart from heavy financial support and increased short-term costs incurred by such users as power-stations through having to consume coal rather than cheaper forms of energy, protectionism inevitably implied a less than optimum allocation of resources. Resources of labour and capital were kept in coal rather than released for expanding industries with greater potential for rapid productivity growth.

In the dynamic energy situation of the 1970's, further support for coal was required, if for no other reason than to keep all existing energy options open. The level of assistance was largely determined by the introduction of several new factors into the 'energy equation'. First, the huge increases in the price of imported oil transformed the competitive positions of different types of fuel within Britain. Second, the new possibilities which were opened out for coal had to be evaluated against a background of North Sea oil discoveries and the likely extent of indigenous oil reserves. Finally, while it seemed safe to assume that Britain's short-term energy requirements could be comfortably accommodated, growing concern was expressed over the long-term position and the likelihood of critical energy shortages by the 1990's. Planning an energy programme for such a distant figure is to say the least hazardous but a more substantial role can be envisaged for nuclear power and possibly for several new energy forms (solar and tidal). However, in the short and medium terms, the deciding factor for coal will be its ability to compete with oil, particularly in the supply of fuel to the power stations.

The discovery of North Sea oil introduced a totally new element into the planning of future energy programmes. It is already clear that competition between different indigenous fuels creates problems just as complex as competition between indigenous and imported fuels. The North Sea fields currently under commercial development have 'proven' reserves of about 1,000 million tonnes and will permit an estimated annual production of between 100 and 150 million tonnes throughout the 1980's.[4] Britain should, therefore, be self-sufficient in energy, including oil, from the early 1980's until the mid-1990's and possibly beyond. Under the Petroleum and Submarine Pipelines Act, the British National Oil Corporation (BNOC) was set up, taking over the offshore interests and expertise built up by the NCB since 1968. In 1976, its first year of operation, BNOC acquired interests assuring it of a quarter-share of total North Sea oil output in the early 1980's and through further participation agreements and new licensing rounds, this will slowly rise to about one-half. Under the Act, the Government also assumed powers to control depletion rates which will be governed largely by expected future price levels and the availability of foreign supplies. In the final analysis, it is the relationship between this price level and that of coal which will dictate the future course taken by British coalmining.

This is because the major concern about the coal industry's own development plans, contained in the 1974 *Plan for Coal,* is not the immediate cost, greatly increased though that was by the 1976-77 revision. Rather it is how to sell the coal that is to be produced up to 1985. This is where the ruling world price for oil becomes critically important. It may well be the case that the *long-term* future of coalmining has seldom seemed more promising. Oil and gas reserves are relatively small and will run out long before those of coal, while nuclear energy is still burdened with technical difficulties and growing environmental objections. The prospects for coal are, therefore, bright if, as predicted, energy shortages begin to develop in the 1990's. But this is cold comfort for those whose livelihood depends on the survival of the coal industry *during the intervening period.* By the mid-1970's, coal was rather cheaper than oil for use in power stations but this fragile advantage could disappear due to a fall in oil prices or a disproportionate rise in coal prices. This is the danger of pressing mining wage-claims, not backed by productivity increases, beyond the limit which the industry can afford to pay.

Coal's principal customers, the CEGB, the basic industries and householders, have clearly indicated that they are not prepared to subsidise coalmining for its own sake. The problem of markets is exacerbated by the fact that before 1982, three giant oil-fired power stations will come on stream. Since they are likely to be highly efficient, the CEGB wishes to use them intensively at the expense of coal-fired capacity. There is, therefore, every prospect of a steady increase in coal stocks even without significant increases being made to coalmining capacity. To date, the Government has proved willing to help the coal industry over temporary falls in sales through stockpiling grants and direct subsidies. For instance, it has agreed to a £7 million subsidy for Scottish coal, since the new Inverkip oil-fired power station built by the South of Scotland Electricity Board would otherwise damage the prospects of the Scottish pits. But there is a limit both to the support that can be provided and to the surpluses that the power boards can be expected to mop up. It is imperative that the coal industry should increase its sales to other industrial consumers and for this to happen price-competitiveness with oil must be maintained.

Notes

CHAPTER 1

1. J. U. Nef, *The Rise of the British Coal Industry* (1932), I, p. 109.

2. As early as 1306, Parliament had successfully petitioned Edward I to prohibit the burning of coal in London due to the environmental pollution it created. *Report of the Commissioners Appointed to Inquire into the Several Matters Relating to Coal in the United Kingdom,* Vol. III, Report of Committee E, C.435-2, 1871 (Henceforth *Royal Commission on Coal, 1871, Committee E).*

3. R. Galloway, *Annals of Coal Mining and the Coal Trade* (1898, reprinted 1971), I, p. 122.

4. D. C. Coleman, *Industry in Tudor and Stuart England* (1975), Studies in Economic and Social History, pp. 46-7; see also the discussion between Coleman and E. Kerridge in *Econ. Hist. Rev.,* Second series, Vol. XXX (1977), pp. 340-5.

5. Nef, op. cit., II, pp. 74-8.

6. P. S. Bagwell, *The Transport Revolution from 1770* (1974), p. 61.

7. Parliament placed an embargo on all trade with the Tyne valley in 1642-44. As a result, the price of coal arriving in the Pool of London, which had been fixed at 17/- per Newcastle chaldron in summer and 19/- in winter, jumped to £4 per chaldron in 1643. For the effects of the War on the coal trade, see Galloway, op. cit., I, pp. 142-3.

8. Coleman, op. cit., p. 47.

9. Although the output of the Midland district in Table 1 exceeds that of Northumberland and Durham in 1781-90, the production of several different coalfields ranging from Yorkshire in the east to Lancashire in the west and Warwickshire in the south have been aggregated to produce the Midland total.

10. Several good texts are available which outline the nature and scale of industrial developments during this period. See, for example, L. A. Clarkson, *The Pre-Industrial Economy in England, 1500-1750* (1971); C. Wilson, *England's Apprenticeship* (1965); D. C. Coleman, *The Economy of England, 1450-1750* (1977); B. A. Holderness, *Pre-Industrial England: Economy and Society from 1500 to 1750* (1976).

11. Galloway, op. cit., I, pp. 149-50.

12. J. R. Harris, 'Skills, Coal and British Industry in the Eighteenth Century', *History,* Vol. 61, No. 202 (1976), p. 172.

13. D. Dudley, *Mettallum Martis: or Iron made with Pit Coale, Sea-Cole etc.* (1665, reprinted 1851).

14. For further details of Dudley and his battles with the charcoal iron-masters, see Galloway, op. cit., I, pp. 194-5; G. R. Morton & M. D. G. Wanklyn, 'Dud Dudley—A New Appraisal', *Journal of the West Midlands Regional Studies,* Vol. I (1967), pp. 48-65; G. Hammersley, 'The Charcoal Iron Industry and Its Fuel, 1540-1750', *Econ. Hist. Rev.,* Second series, Vol. XXVI, No. 4 (1973), p. 611.

15. Galloway, op. cit., I, pp. 195-6, 215, 223-4, 227-8 *passim;* Hammersley, loc. cit., p. 611.

16. C. K. Hyde, 'The Adoption of Coke-Smelting by the British Iron Industry, 1709-1790', *Explorations in Economic History,* Vol. 10, No. 4 (1973), pp. 399-400.

Notes

17. See for instance T. S. Ashton, *Iron and Steel in the Industrial Revolution* (1924), pp. 24-38; Nef, op. cit., I, p. 251, note 2.

18. Hammersley, loc. cit., pp. 610-12; Hyde, loc. cit., pp. 397-418.

19. Coke-smelted pig iron was profitably produced at Coalbrookdale largely because of the relatively high returns from a new by-product of the process, namely thin-walled castings. Hence, it was Darby's casting technology that initially made coke-smelting profitable. Hyde, loc. cit., pp. 406-7.

20. For further details of fixed rents and royalties, see *Final Report of the Royal Commission Appointed to Inquire into the Subject of Mining Royalties* (1893), c. 6980, Vol. XLI.

21. Many instances could be cited but one of the most notable was the colliery at Denton. By the first decade of the 17th century, the output of the colliery, leased by the Crown for a mere £10 per annum, was estimated to be worth some £1,200 per annum to its operators.

22. Maximum production of charcoal bar iron in Britain, around the mid-18th century, cannot have exceeded 27,000 tons per annum. To convert ore into finished bar iron required at most 2,100 cubic ft of solid wood per ton of bar; Hammersley, loc. cit. The remainder of the paragraph in the text is based largely on this source.

23. Ashton and Sykes, op. cit., p. 30.

24. These latter depths were exceptional and specific to the Northern Coalfield. Elsewhere, in the land-sale mining districts of the Midlands, Lancashire and Yorkshire, collieries were generally much smaller, often being operated by only a handful of workers.

25. J. C., *The Compleat Collier: Or, the Whole Art of Sinking, Getting and Working, Coal Mines etc. As is now Used in the Northern Parts, Especially about Sunderland and Newcastle* (1708), p. 22.

26. ibid.

27. The implication of Lord's study, *Capital and Steam Power* (1923), that the 321 engines produced by Boulton and Watt represented the entire increase in steam power in Britain in 1775-1800 has now been shown to be seriously in error. Although their patent did not expire until 1800, there was a high degree of 'pirating' of the Boulton and Watt engine. Even more important, the older type of Savery and Newcomen engines continued to be built and other engine-builders were also active in the years before 1800. It has been estimated, for instance, that at least 110 non-Watt engines were employed in Lancashire in 1775-1800, about two-thirds of the total supplied to that county over the period. Similarly in Derbyshire, only 6 of the 28 engines supplied between the construction of Watt's first engine and 1800 came from Soho, and in Cornwall barely half the engines in existence by the end of the century had been built by Boulton and Watt. See J. R. Harris, 'The Employment of Steam Power in the Eighteenth Century', *History*, Vol. LII, No. 175 (1967), pp. 145-6; A. E. Musson and E. Robinson, 'The Early Growth of Steam Power', *Economic History Review*, Second series, Vol. XI, No. 3 (1959), pp. 424-9.

28. E. O. Forster Brown, 'The History of Drainage', in Mining Association of Great Britain, *Historical Review of Coalmining* (1923).

29. P. Mathias, 'Who Unbound Prometheus? Science and Technical Change, 1600-1800', in A. E. Musson (ed.), *Science, Technology and Economic Growth in the Eighteenth Century* (1972), p. 87.

30. In the latter context, see especially A. E. Musson and E. Robinson, *Science and Technology in the Industrial Revolution* (1969); also A. E. Musson, 'The Diffusion of Technology in Great Britain during the Industrial Revolution', in Musson (ed.), *Science, Technology and Economic Growth,* op. cit., pp. 108-9.

31. Thomas Newcomen had apparently no personal contacts with the leading scientists of the age. See D. S. L. Cardwell, *Steampower in the Eighteenth Century* (1963), p. 18.

32. A. E. Musson and E. Robinson, loc. cit., pp. 420-4; 439.

33. See especially L. T. C. Rolt, *Thomas Newcomen: The Prehistory of the Steam Engine* (1963); D. S. L. Cardwell, op. cit.,; a most fruitful source of information is the *Transactions of the Newcomen Society:* see particularly R. A. Mott, 'The Newcomen Engine in the Eighteenth Century', Vol. XXXV (1962-3); A. Raistrick, 'The Steam

266

Notes

Engine on Tyneside 1715-1778, Vol. XVII (1936-7).

34. There is particular uncertainty as to when and where the first Newcomen engine was erected. Ashton and Sykes prefer the vague form of 'sometime before 1717', op. cit., p. 38; Harris, 'The Employment of Steam Power', p. 138, plumps for 1712 but admits the possibility of an earlier date; S. Pollard, *The Genesis of Modern Management: A Study of the Industrial Revolution in Gt. Britain* (1965), p. 85, also favours 1712 claiming, presumably on the basis of Galloway's evidence, that a Warwickshire colliery was the first to use a Newcomen engine in that year. This contradicts an earlier assertion (pp. 79 and 81) that the first engine had been installed at Whitehaven in Cumberland in 1715; Galloway, op. cit., I, pp. 239-45, gives reason to suppose that the engine at Griff in Warwickshire was erected about 1713, but that an earlier model had been built at a Staffordshire pit in 1712; Robert Edington, *A Treatise on the Abuses of the Coal Trade* (1817), points out that 'it is perhaps not generally known that the first steam-engines used in this country were erected at Elswick, Byker and Ouston, about the year 1914', p. 131; the author of *The Compleat Collier* (1708) was already aware that a 'fire' engine existed, p. 23. He was probably referring to Savery's engine, but may have heard rumours about Newcomen's model and its construction.

35. By the mid-18th century the Newcomen engine consumed at least 30-32 lb of coal per horse-power hour; Smeaton's improvements in the construction of the engine reduced fuel consumption to about 20 lb of coal per h.p. hour, and not until James Watt's improved engine of the late 1780's was the amount of coal consumed reduced to the level of some 10 lb per h.p. hour. In the 19th century, consumption was eventually to be reduced to approximately 3 lb per h.p. hour. See E. O. Forster Brown, loc. cit., p. 187.

36. For most of the 18th century, the soft small coals that were fed to the Newcomen engine were virtually unsaleable, so that coalmasters were relatively indifferent to the heavy fuel consumption of the new technology.

37. Harris, 'The Employment of Steam Power', pp. 138-9.

38. Matthias Dunn, *History of the Viewers,* unpublished manuscript (1845?), North of England Institute of Mining Engineers.

39. See, for instance, Rolt, op. cit., p. 84; Mott, loc. cit., p. 69.

40. *Grand Allies Minute Book, Partnership Minutes etc.,* op. cit., computations for 1738.

41. Harris, 'Skills, Coal and British Industry', p. 170 and note 10.

42. This system was itself attended by a high degree of risk. Often the air current had to travel some 30 miles between the downcast and upcast shafts. In a fiery mine, the dangers of passing such air over the ventilating furnace at the foot of the upcast shaft were all too obvious.

43. A further danger was, of course, the developing use of gunpowder in the mines for blasting. It was probably first used in this country by German miners in the 1630's, but the practice was not adopted by British miners until the 1680's when it was employed in the Cornish tin mines and Somerset lead mines. It is unlikely that gunpowder was used in coalmining until the early 18th century. See H. M. Crankshaw, 'History of Explosives used in Coalmining', in Mining Association of Great Britain, *Historical Review of Coalmining,* pp. 82-8; Galloway, op. cit., I, pp. 226-7.

44. *Report of the South Shields Committee Appointed to Investigate the Causes of Accidents in Coal Mines* (1843).

45. Dunn, op. cit., pp. 16-17.

46. Galloway, op. cit., I, pp. 151-3.

47. *The Compleat Collier,* p. 6.

48. In Scotland, progress in winding was notably retarded. Even by the early 19th century women and children were still commonly used as bearers to carry the coal to the surface. Since they could be used only in relatively small and shallow pits, these remained the rule until approximately the 1830's.

49. The whim gin was a refinement of the earlier cog and rung gin which consisted of a drum mounted over the mouth of the pit. Rope was coiled round the drum and descended

into the shaft, the apparatus being wound by horse power. This practice had impeded the work of the banksmen and was highly susceptible to being blown apart by pit explosions. Hence the whim was located some distance from the pit-head, being replaced there by a simple pulley over which the winding rope passed. For further details and an illustration of the whim gin, see Galloway, op. cit., I, p. 178.

50. According to Nef, op. cit., I, pp. 244-5, the first evidence of rails being used in England related to the years 1597-8 and the first comprehensive account of a wagon-way was provided by a contemporary in 1606, for the track laid between Broseley colliery and the river Severn. See also P. S. Bagwell, *The Transport Revolution from 1770* (1974), who claims that the first wooden rails were laid in Nottinghamshire in 1603-4 (p. 89).

51. Interesting accounts of the operation of these early haulage systems, both above and below ground, can be found in Galloway, op. cit., I, pp. 154-7 *passim,* G. Poole, 'The History and Development of Underground Haulage' in Mining Association of Great Britain, *Historical Review of Coalmining.*

52. For evidence on this point, see Galloway, op. cit., I, pp. 177-8.

53. The use of horses, by minimising the problem of distance between the face and pit-bottom, had the further effect of prolonging the life of single-shaft pits. Moreover, horses allowed the increased sinkage charges, incurred by mining at greater depths, to be accommodated more easily.

54. See, for instance, T. C. Smout, 'Scottish Landowners and Economic Growth, 1650-1850', *Scottish Journal of Political Economy,* Vol. IX (1964); T. J. Raybould, 'The Development and Organisation of Lord Dudley's Mineral Estates, 1774-1845', *Econ. Hist. Rev.,* Second series, Vol. XXI (1968); E. Richards, 'The Industrial Face of a Great Estate: Trentham and Lilleshall, 1780-1860, *Econ. Hist. Rev.,* Second series, Vol. XXVII (1974); J. T. Ward, 'West Riding Landowners and Mining in the 19th Century', *Yorkshire Bulletin of Economic and Social Research,* Vol. XV (1963); Nef, op. cit., II, pp. 31 ff.

55. See G. E. Mingay, *English Landed Society in the Eighteenth Century* (1963); J. T. Ward, *'Landowners and Mining,'* in J. T. Ward and R. G. Wilson (eds.), *Land and Industry: The Landed Estates and the Industrial Revolution* (1971), pp. 63-116; Nef. op. cit., II, pp. 3-78; D. Anderson, *The Orrell Coalfield, Lancashire 1740-1850* (1975), pp. 21-7 and 146-96.

56. Nef, op. cit., II, pp. 35-8.

57. See, especially S. Pollard, 'Fixed Capital in the Industrial Revolution in Britain', in F. Crouzet (ed.), *Capital Formation in the Industrial Revolution,* Debates in Economic History Series (1972), pp. 146-51; also Crouzet's 'Introduction' to the above volume, pp. 34-9.

58. Pollard, loc. cit., p. 151.

59. Nef, op. cit., I, p. 379.

60. These were the East India Co, Royal Africa Co, New River Co, White Paper Makers, and Bank of England (ibid.).

61. By the start of the 19th century, for instance, a pit of 993 ft. had been sunk in Cumberland. Ashton and Sykes, op. cit., p. 10.

62. A ten of coals was regarded by the Grand Allies as being equivalent to 19 Newcastle chaldrons.

63. P. Cromar, *Economic Power and Organisation: The Development of the Coal Industry on Tyneside 1700-1828,* unplublished Ph.D. thesis (Cambridge 1977), pp. 145, 151, 180.

64. *Buddle-Atkinson Collection, Vol. 23, Letter from John Buddle, Wallsend Colliery, to Mr George Silvertop, 27th August 1808.*

CHAPTER 2

1. Nef, op. cit., I, pp. 101-2; A. R. Griffin, *The British Coalmining Industry* (1977), pp. 127-8.

2. The Bishop of Durham had granted a 99-year lease in 1582 on all his coal lands in the manors of Whickham and Gateshead. The terms of the lease, which covered some of

Notes

the best and most conveniently situated deposits in the Tyne district, were highly favourable to the lessees.

3. For details, see P. M. Sweezy, *Monopoly and Competition in the English Coal Trade, 1550-1850* (1938), pp. 6-7.

4. For details, see D. J. Williams, *Capitalist Combination in the Coal Industry* (1924), pp. 19-20.

5. The term 'Hostman' meant one who owned parts in the colliery enterprises and undertook the marketing of his share of the output. At the start of the 17th century the term was used particularly to describe the large mine-owners who dominated both the municipal government of Newcastle and the Company of Hostmen. This began to change during the course of the century, especially after the Civil War. Owners became increasingly independent so that by the early 18th century Hostmen were regarded rather as fitters, or agents supervising the details of sale, shipment and the like.

6. For details see Sweezy, op. cit., pp. 16-21.

7. *Grand Allies Minute Book, Partnership Minutes, Memorandums etc.*

8. The rent paid by lessees for the right to work coal on an annual basis was referred to as a fixed or dead rent. This was a minimum: if output exceeded a certain level additional rent or royalty was payable *pro rata.*

9. *An Enquiry into the Reasons for the Advance of the Price of Coals within Seven Years Past* (1739).

10. ibid.

11. *A Brief for the Coal Owners Against the Petition of Certain Consumers of Coals in the City of London etc.* (1738).

12. Sweezy, op. cit., p. 143.

13. Ashton and Sykes, op. cit., p. 212; *An Enquiry into the Reasons for the Advance of the Price of Coals.* However, for a different view of the causes of these price fluctuations see Cromar, op. cit., pp. 90-106, 177.

14. Matthias Dunn, *An Historical, Geological and Descriptive View of the Coal Trade of the North of England* (1844), p. 43 (Henceforth, *View of the Coal Trade).* Even so, the partnership of the Grand Allies persisted for a long time. By 1800, the term was still being used to describe the owners of certain leases in the North.

15. Cromar, op. cit., pp. 119-22.

16. Sweezy, op. cit., p. 144; Cromar op. cit., pp. 122-3.

17. For details of the creation of the Vend, see the evidence of Francis Thompson who initiated the 1771 Agreement, *Commons Reports, Report of the Committee Appointed to Consider the State of the Coal Trade of this Kingdom* (1800), Vol. X, 1785-1801 (Henceforth, *House of Commons, Select Committee on the Coal Trade, 1800).* Thompson was described as ship-chandler and ironmonger but had formerly been head manager of Washington Colliery; Williams, op. cit., pp. 28-54.

18. *Royal Commission on Coal, 1871, Committee E.*

19. An indication of the timing of agreements is provided by Sweezy, op. cit., pp. 39-41.

20. *Report from the Select Committee of the House of Lords Appointed to take into Consideration the State of the Coal Trade in the United Kingdom, 1830* (Henceforth, *House of Lords, Select Committee on the Coal Trade, 1830).*

21. House of Commons, *Report of the Select Committee on the State of the Coal Trade,* 633, 1830 (Henceforth, *House of Commons, Select Committee on the Coal Trade, 1830);* Dunn, *View of the Coal Trade,* pp. 80-85.

22. Evidence of Nathaniel Clayton, town clerk of Newcastle in *House of Commons, Select Committee on the Coal Trade, 1800.*

23. Actual sales in 1835 amounted to 1.3 million chaldrons, just over three-quarters of that allotted. *Report from the Select Committee of the House of Commons on the State of the Coal Trade,* 522, 1836 (Henceforth, *House of Commons, Select Committee on the Coal Trade, 1836).*

269

24. ibid.

25. As early as 1800, Francis Thompson had pointed out that this was one of the main effects of output-regulation. See *House of Commons, Select Committee on the Coal Trade, 1800, Minutes of Evidence,* p. 542.

26. *House of Commons, Select Committee on the Coal Trade, 1830, Minutes of Evidence,* p. 322.

27. There was a long history of legislation designed to prevent combination and the restraint of trade in the coal industry. It had been uniformly unsuccessful.

28. Sweezy, op. cit., pp. 119-20.

29. *Royal Commission on Coal, 1871, Committee E,* Appendix Table No. 152.

30. *The Frauds and Abuses of the Coal Dealers Detected and Exposed: in a Letter to an Alderman of London* (1747).

31. ibid.

32. Under 1 and 2, W. IV, C. 76, 1831.

33. *House of Commons, Select Committee on the Coal Trade, 1830.*

34. *House of Lords, Select Committee on the Coal Trade, 1830.*

35. These figures relate to the standard colliery vessel of some 220 tons measurement. For larger ships, the average number of journeys was lower, rarely exceeding seven.

36. See especially the evidence of Thomas Fletcher, Coal Buyer, *House of Commons, Select Committee on the Coal Trade, 1800, Minutes of Evidence.*

37. By 1800 it was estimated that a mere 14 factors and 75 buyers, operating in the Coal Exchange, monopolised the coal trade. They served virtually all the needs of London and the home counties.

38. John Buddle, *House of Lords, Select Committee on the Coal Trade, 1830, Minutes of Evidence.*

39. This despite a large increase in the number of meters employed by the City of London. In 1712 there had been 15 principal meters and 60 assistants; by 1830 there were still 15 principal meters but 158 deputy meters.

40. Thomas Smith, *House of Commons, Select Committee on the Coal Trade, 1800, Minutes of Evidence.*

41. Ingrain comprised one additional chaldron in every score which, by Act of Parliament, was due free of charge to the purchaser. The custom had developed since a 'heaped' vat was used to unload from vessel to lighter. However, no indication was provided of the size of the 'heap' so that to insure against under-measurement it was determined that 21 London chaldrons were to count as a score.

42. See evidence of George Easterby, shipowner, and Thomas Smith, corn distiller, *House of Commons, Select Committee on the Coal Trade, 1800, Minutes of Evidence.*

43. See the testimony of Thomas Hawkes, a first buyer on the Coal Exchange since 1777, *House of Commons, Select Committee on the Coal Trade, 1800, Minutes of Evidence.*

44. T. Telltruth, *A Dark Story: or a brief Development of the Nefarious Conduct of the Black Diamond Mongers, with Regard to the Present System of the Coal Trade* (1815).

45. *Some General Observations on the Present Practice of Carrying on the Coal Trade in the Metropolis, by Persons who are well Acquainted with the Subject here Treated on* (1804); also evidence of George Easterby, *House of Commons, Select Committee on the Coal Trade, 1800, Minutes of Evidence.*

46. In the years immediately after the Napoleonic Wars, the retail value of sales was between 4 and 5 times greater than the value of pit-head output. By the 1830's the value of sales was only about 3 times greater.

47. *House of Commons, Select Committee on the Coal Trade, 1800.*

48. Another estimate has the average price per London chaldron in 1800 rather lower at £2. 12s. 3½d. *(House of Commons, Select Committee on the Coal Trade, 1830).*

Whichever is more accurate, the 'spread' is still remarkable.

49. Marquis of Londonderry, speech delivered in House of Lords, 12th Feb. 1830.

50. *House of Lords, Select Committee on the Coal Trade, 1830, Minutes of Evidence.*

51. Respectively 9 Anne, C.28, and 4 Geo. II, C.30.

52. John Stevenson, *Observations on the Coal Trade in the Port of Newcastle-upon-Tyne with a Comparative View of the Two Bills brought into the House of Commons last Session by the Right Hon. Lord Mulgrave and Sir Matthew White Ridley* (1789).

53. Securing alternative sources of supply was regarded as the principal means of eliminating abuses in the coal trade. To this end, the Committee recommended that existing impediments to canal traffic be removed. These included the high tonnage duties charged by canal owners, heavy tolls and the requirement that coal should not be carried lower than Reading. The arrival of large supplies of inland coal on the London market should not, it was argued, seriously harm the northern trade. Coal from the north was superior in quality and would still be given preference by most consumers provided it was realistically priced.

54. But at the same time, Parliament failed to take any decisive action over the Limitation of the Vend. Hence by repealing previous Acts in so far as they related to combination in the coal trade, Parliament in fact legalised the Vend for the first time since the early 18th century.

55. One hundred and fifty weighers were subsequently appointed to represent both shipmasters and buyers, their cost being met equally by buyers and sellers.

56. These city dues were not finally repealed until 1890.

57. A useful summary of duties charged is provided in Ashton and Sykes, op. cit., Appendix D, pp. 247-8.

58. Granting a monopoly to the Hostmen altered the 1529 Act of Parliament which had conferred upon *all* citizens of Newcastle the exclusive right to trade in coal and all other commodities shipped from the town.

59. The purchase proved a bargain for the State since by the time the tax was abolished the State had not only recovered its initial outlay but earned a surplus approaching £350,000.

60. John Frost, *Cheap Coals: or a Countermine to the Minister and His Three City Members* (1792).

61. Ashton and Sykes, op. cit., p. 248.

62. Advocates of the coastwise trade maintained that besides adversely affecting the coalmining industry and hence employment in the north, such discrimination injured the 'universal nursery of our ships and sailors' which the coastal trade was claimed to be.

63. *Royal Commission on Coal, 1871, Committee E.* Figures do not include bunker coal.

CHAPTER 3

1. P. Deane and W. A. Cole, *British Economic Growth 1688-1959* (1962), pp. 75-9. The index includes the contributions made to output by industry and commerce, agriculture, government and defence and rent and services.

2. Pollard, op. cit., p. 79.

3. The continued importance of water power is emphasised by A. E. Musson, 'Industrial Motive Power in the United Kingdom 1800-1870', *Econ. Hist. Rev.,* Second series, Vol. XXIX (1976), pp. 416-20.

4. Ashton and Sykes, op. cit., pp. 12-13.

5. For instance even by 1800 it is likely that of the total output of 10.1 million tons produced in Britain, over one-half was still used for domestic purposes while the demands of metallurgy accounted for only about 10%.

6. Ashton and Sykes, op. cit., p. 12.

7. ibid.

8. From 1854 statistics were collected by Robert Hunt, Keeper of Mining Records and published in *Mineral Statistics of the United Kingdom of Great Britain and Ireland.* Subsequently the figures were published as Blue Books.

9. Output increased by more than 20 times over the 19th century, rising from 10.1 million to 225.2 million tons.

10. Deane and Cole, op. cit., Tables 15, 17 and 18.

11. Musson, 'Industrial Motive Power in the United Kingdom', pp. 417 and 423-5.

12. C. R. Fay, *Great Britain from Adam Smith to the Present Day* (1928), p. 260.

13. For details see R. H. Campbell, *Carron Company* (1961), pp. 35-7.

14. C. K. Hyde, 'Technological Change in the British Wrought Iron Industry, 1750-1815; A Reinterpretation', *Econ. Hist. Rev.,* Second series, Vol. XXVII (1974), pp. 190-206.

15. *Royal Commission on Coal, 1871, Committee E.*

16. C. K. Hyde, 'The Adoption of the Hot Blast by the British Iron Industry: a Reinterpretation', *Explorations in Economic History,* Vol. 10 (1973), pp. 281-93.

17. Patent of 1769, quoted in Special Act of Parliament (1775), 15 Geo. III, C.61. Watt's patent had been due to expire in 1783 but the Act of 1775 granted to him and his executors the sole privilege of making and selling steam engines in Great Britain and her Colonies for a further 25 years.

18. For details, see N. Von Tunzlemann, 'Technological Diffusion during the Industrial Revolution: the Case of the Cornish Pumping Engine', in R. M. Hartwell (ed.), *The Industrial Revolution* (1970), pp. 77-98.

19. The technology of the steam engine in the first half of the 19th century is ably described by H. W. Dickinson, *A Short History of the Steam Engine* (second edition, 1963); R. L. Hills, *Power in the Industrial Revolution* (1970).

20. N. Rosenberg, 'Factors Affecting the Diffusion of Technology', *Explorations in Economic History,* Vol. 10 (1972), p. 7. There is a large literature on this subject: see among others, J. Jewkes, D. Sawers and R. Stillerman, *The Sources of Invention* (1958); A. E. Musson, 'The Diffusion of Technology in Great Britain during the Industrial Revolution', in Musson (ed.), *Science, Technology and Economic Growth,* pp. 97-114; J. Tann, 'Fuel Savings in the Process Industries during the Industrial Revolution: A study in Technological Diffusion', *Business History,* Vol. XV (1973), pp. 149-59.

21. Musson, 'Industrial Motive Power in the United Kingdom', p. 435.

22. Hyde, 'The Adoption of the Hot Blast', pp. 281-93.

23. B. R. Mitchell, 'The Coming of the Railway and United Kingdom Economic Growth', *Journal of Economic History,* Vol. XXIV (1964), pp. 21-2.

24. *Royal Commission on Coal, 1871, Committee E.*

25. G. R. Hawke, *Railways and Economic Growth in England and Wales, 1840-1870* (1970), pp. 294-5.

26. *Royal Commission on Coal, 1871, Committee B.*

27. For details see Campbell, op. cit., pp. 214-15.

28. Mitchell and Deane, op. cit., pp. 217-18: over the same period the tonnage of sailing ships rose from 2.3 million to 3.8 million.

29. Bagwell, op. cit., p. 70.

30. H. J. Dyos and D. H. Aldcroft, *British Transport: An Economic Survey from the Seventeenth Century to the Twentieth* (1974), p. 258.

31. Mitchell, loc. cit., pp. 21-2; Hawke, op. cit., pp. 213-45.

32. Hawke, op. cit., pp. 296-7.

33. *The Petition of Proprietors of Collieries on the River Wear to the House of Commons with Regard to Coals Carried Inland,* 1816.

34. Government duty on coastwise coal reached a peak of 24% of selling price at the

ship's side in 1810. In that year, duty amounted to 12/6d. and average price to 51/8d. per London chaldron.

35. *House of Commons, Select Committee on the State of the Coal Trade, 1836.*

36. ibid, especially pp. xxxvii-xli.

37. *Watson Collection, Resolutions Passed at the Coal Trade Office, Newcastle-upon-Tyne,* Aug. 1833 (North of England Institute of Mining and Mechanical Engineers).

38. Dunn, *View of the Coal Trade,* p. 203. The 'north' comprised the districts of Tyne, Wear, Tees, Hartley and Blyth.

39. Bagwell, op. cit., p. 114.

40. Hawke, op. cit., pp. 157-81, *passim.* The remainder of this section is drawn from this source.

41. Griffin, op. cit., pp. 49, 106-9.

42. Barriers were necessary to ensure safety where, for instance, there existed the danger of flooding from adjacent abandoned workings or to guard against fire in cases where the seams were liable to spontaneous combustion.

43. See evidence of T. Evans, Inspector of Mines, to Committee C on 'Waste in Working', *Royal Commission on Coal, 1871, General Minutes and Proceedings of Committees A-E,* C. 435-1, 1871.

44. For details of the longwall system and the distinction between longwall retreating and longwall advancing, see H. Stanley Jevons, *The British Coal Trade* (1915, re-published 1969), pp. 202-6 and 208-9.

45. Evidence of G. B. Forster to Committee C, *Royal Commission on Coal, 1871, General Minutes and Proceedings of Committees A-E.*

46. As for instance at the Walker and Hebburn Collieries in the Northern Coalfield. Galloway, op. cit., I, pp. 393-4.

47. K. N. Moss, 'Ventilation of Coal Mines', in Mining Association of Great Britain, *Historical Review of Coalmining;* Galloway, op. cit., I, pp. 389-90.

48. It was for precisely this reason that the tragic explosion at New Hartley Colliery in 1862 cost 204 lives.

49. For details, see Galloway, op. cit., I, p. 418.

50. *The Report of the South Shields Committee* (1843).

51. *Report from the Select Committee of the House of Lords Appointed to Inquire into the Best Means of Preventing the Occurrence of Dangerous Accidents in Coal Mines,* 613, 1849.

52. P. E. H. Hair, 'Mortality from Violence in British Coal-Mines, 1800-80', *Econ. Hist. Rev.,* Second series, Vol. XXI (1968), p. 546.

53. See, for instance, the evidence of Sir H. T. De La Beche, Director of the Museum of Practical Geology in London, *Select Committee of the House of Lords on Accidents in Coal Mines,* 1849.

54. This was the conclusion reached by the *Select Committee of the House of Lords on Accidents in Coal Mines,* 1849. Nonetheless, it strongly emphasised Goldsworthy Gurney's steam-jet, an endorsement reinforced by the 1852 *Select Committee of the House of Commons.* However, experiments on an extensive scale led the *Select Committee of the House of Commons on Accidents in Coal Mines,* 1854 (Fourth Report, 325), to reject this emphasis and to conclude that where coal lay at considerable depth below the surface, the ventilating furnace was the most effective and economical means of providing currents of air in the workings. The Committee also recommended that no colliery should be without some artificial means of ventilation and that this should be legally enforceable.

55. See, for instance, George Stephenson, *A Description of the Safety Lamp Invented by George Stephenson and Now in Use in Killingworth Colliery: to which is added an Account of the Lamp Construction by Sir Humphry Davy* (1817).

56. *SRO, CB/10/15.*

57. Full details of the principles of the safety lamp can be found in Galloway, op. cit., I, pp. 426-39. It was only Stephenson's third design, tried at Killingworth Colliery at the end of November, 1815, that enjoyed moderate success. It appears to have borrowed heavily from the work previously published by Sir Humphry Davy.

58. ibid., p. 435.

59. *Watson Collection, pamphlet issued following a General Meeting of the Coalowners of Tyne and Wear, John Lambton, M.P. in the Chair, Newcastle, 26 Nov., 1817.*

60. *Watson Collection, Letters by William Martin to John Watson.* This and the following extracts in the paragraph are drawn from letters dated 15/12/1823, 10/1/1824 and 23/1/1824.

61. *House of Lords, Select Committee on the Coal Trade, 1830;* see also *House of Commons, Select Committee on the Coal Trade, Minutes of Evidence,* 1830, p. 273.

62. *House of Lords, Select Committee on Accidents in Coal Mines,* 1849; see also *Report of Charles Morton, Inspector of Mines for Yorkshire, Derbyshire, Notts, Leicestershire and Warwickshire, to H.M. Secretary of State,* 1851. Morton reported that in his districts, especially Yorkshire, the Clanny lamp was preferred due to the better light it afforded.

63. On this issue see particularly the evidence of Thomas J. Taylor, viewer in the North of England and mineral agent of the Duke of Northumberland, *House of Commons, Second Report from the Select Committee on Accidents in Coal Mines, Minutes of Evidence,* 258, 1854.

64. Hair, loc. cit., p. 551.

65. Evidence of John Buddle before the *Select Committees of both the Houses of Lords and Commons, 1830.*

66. R. Bald, *A General View of the Coal Trade of Scotland* (1808).

67. *SRO, CB 10/14, R. Bald to James Russell, Correspondence Regarding Inflammable Air and Sir Humphry Davy's Lamp,* 16 Nov. 1816.

68. G. Poole, 'The History and Development of Underground Haulage', in Mining Association of Great Britain, *Historical Review of Coalmining.*

69. Details of the employment of cages and tubs can be found in Galloway, op. cit., I, pp. 482-4.

70. Only by the 20th century, did the pumping engines finally gravitate to the bottom of the shaft, once electric power enabled the volume of water to be raised in one lift.

71. A. and N. L. Clow, 'Lord Dundonald', *Econ. Hist. Rev.,* First series, Vol. XII (1942), pp. 47-58.

72. For the growth and spread of street lighting before the Industrial Revolution, particularly the introduction of oil-burning street lamps, see M. Falkus, 'Lighting in the Dark Ages of English Economic History: Town Streets before the Industrial Revolution', in D. C. Coleman and A. H. John (eds.), *Trade Government and Economy in Pre-Industrial England.* (1976), pp. 248-73.

73. *Bell Collection, May 1805,* North of England Institute of Mining and Mechanical Engineers.

74. Candidus, *Observations on Gas Lights: Being an Impartial Inquiry Concerning the Injurious Effects on the Health of the Community from the Use of Coal for Lighting the Metropolis* (1817).

75. PEP, *Report on the Gas Industry in Great Britain* (1939), p. 41.

76. M. E. Falkus, 'The British Gas Industry before 1850', *Econ. Hist. Rev.,* Second series, Vol. XX (1967), p. 495.

77. C. H. Feinstein, *Capital Accumulation and Economic Growth in Great Britain, 1760-1860.*

78. Measured at constant 1851-60 prices: Feinstein, op. cit., Table 6.

79. Dunn, *History of the Viewers,* p. 17.

Notes

CHAPTER 4

1. *Statistical Tables relating to the Production, Consumption and Imports and Exports of Coal in the British Empire and the Principal Foreign Countries in Each Year 1886-1910,* 284, 1911.

2. Deane and Cole, op. cit., p. 229.

3. D. L. Burn, *The Economic History of Steel Making, 1867-1939* (1940), p. 185.

4. Quoted in D. H. Aldcroft, 'Technical Progress and British Enterprise 1875-1914', *Business History,* Vol. VIII (1966), p. 128.

5. Musson, 'Industrial Motive Power in the United Kingdom', p. 435.

6. *First Census of Production, 1907: Final Report,* Cd. 6320 (1912), pp. 17-18.

7. *House of Commons, Report from the Select Committee on the Causes of the Present Dearness and Scarcity of Coal,* 313, 1873.

8. The average price of coal in London in 1896, at 14/5d. amounted to only 46% of the 31/- per ton fetched in the peak year of 1873.

9. Calculated on the basis of the net national income estimates provided by Deane and Cole, op. cit., pp. 329-31.

10. Jevons, op. cit., p. 676.

11. *House of Commons, Report of the Select Committee on the Present Dearness and Scarcity of Coal,* 1873.

12. These and the figures which follow in this paragraph were calculated from *House of Commons Statement Showing the Coal Production, Consumption, and Number of Persons Employed in the Principal Countries of the World from 1883 to 1893,* 317, 1894; *Statistical Tables Relating to the Production, Consumption etc. of Coal in each Year from 1886 to 1910,* 284, 1911: Gibson, op. cit., pp. 213ff.

13. The countries which contributed to this increase in output were British India, Canada, Australia, New Zealand and South Africa.

14. From an average of 404 million tons in 1885/89 to 1,071 million tons in 1909/13.

15. A. J. Taylor, 'The Coal Industry', in D. H. Aldcroft (ed.), *The Development of British Industry and Foreign Competition 1875-1914* (1968), p. 41.

16. D. A. Thomas, 'The Growth and Direction of our Foreign Trade in Coal during the last Half Century', *Journal of the Royal Statistical Society,* Vol. LXVI (1903), p. 454.

17. Jevons, op. cit., pp. 692-3.

18. For the rapid development of steam coal production in South Wales, see M. J. Daunton, *Coal Metropolis, Cardiff 1870-1914* (1977), pp. 4-5; Jevons, op. cit., p. 750.

19. For instance, minimum royalties affecting price in 1890 were 4d. per ton in West Scotland, South Wales and Yorkshire, 2½d. per ton in Northumberland and Durham, but only 1¾d. in Westphalia, less than 1½d. in Belgium and nil in France. *Final Report of the Royal Commission Appointed to Inquire into the Subject of Mining Royalties,* C. 6980, (1893).

20. *Royal Commission on Mining Royalties, 1893.*

21. D. N. McCloskey, 'International Differences in Productivity? Coal and Steel in America and Britain before World War I', in D. N. McCloskey (ed.), *Essays on a Mature Economy: Britain after 1840* (1971), pp. 289-95.

22. Scottish Home Department, *Scottish Coalfields: Report of the Scottish Coalfield Committee,* Cmd. 6575 (1944), pp. 6-16; A. J. Taylor, 'Labour Productivity and Technological Innovation in the British Coal Industry, 1850-1914', *Econ. Hist. Rev.,* Second series, Vol. XIV (1961), p. 59.

23. Daunton, op. cit., p. 7.

CHAPTER 5

1. *Third Report of the Royal Commission on Mines,* Cd. 5561, 1911.

2. *Report on the Ventilation of Mines by J. Kenyon Blackwell,* HMSO, 1850.

Notes

3. *Fourth Report of the Select Committee on Accidents in Coal Mines,* 325, 1854.

4. *Final Report of HM Commissioners Appointed to Inquire into Accidents in Mines,* C. 4699, 1886 (Hereafter, *Royal Commission on Accidents in Mines, 1886).*

5. This was in response to the disaster at Hartley Colliery. See H. & B. Duckham, *Great Pit Disasters: Great Britain 1700 to the Present Day* (1973), pp. 95-114.

6. *Royal Commission on Accidents in Mines, 1886.*

7. *Royal Commission on Mines, Report of an Inquiry into the Ventilation of Coal Mines and the Methods of Examining for Firedamp made on behalf of the Royal Commission on Mines by John Cadman and E. B. Whalley, Cd. 4551, 1909.*

8. *Second Report of the Royal Commission on Mines,* Cd. 4820, 1909.

9. *Third Report of the Royal Commission on Mines,* Cd. 5561, 1911.

10. See *Final Report of the Royal Commission on Accidents in Mines, 1886* and the *Royal Commission Appointed to Inquire into the Effect of Coal Dust in Originating and Extending Explosions in Mines, 1894.*

11. Quoted in *Final Report of the Royal Commission on Accidents in Mines, 1886.*

12. A full account of the Haswell disaster and of the views of Faraday and Lyell can be found in Galloway, op. cit., II, pp. 181-98.

13. *Second Report of the Royal Commission on Mines,* Cd. 4820, 1909.

14. *Second Report of the Royal Commission on Mines, 1909;* see also *Report of a Committee Appointed by the Royal Commission on Mines to Inquire into the Causes of, and Means of Preventing, Accidents from Falls of Ground, Underground Haulage, and in Shafts,* Cd. 4821, 1909.

15. In 1907, a mere 36 collieries in Scotland operated with safety lamps, 33 with mixed lights and no fewer than 433 with naked lights. Scottish miners opposed the use of safety lamps since they alleged that defects in the roof and sides could be more readily discerned with a naked light.

16. Evidence of Thomas Taylor, viewer and mineral agent of the Duke of Northumberland, *Second Report from the Select Committee on Accidents in Coal Mines, Minutes of Evidence,* 258, 1854.

17. *Royal Commission on Accidents in Mines, 1886.*

18. ibid, appendix 24, pp. 202-19.

19. Griffin, op. cit., p. 120.

20. See R. W. Dron, 'The Lighting of Mines', in Mining Association of Great Britain, *Historical Review of Coal Mining* (1923).

21. *Annual Report of the Secretary for Mines for the Year 1936,* HMSO, 1937.

22. A full account of both Main and Tail and Endless Rope haulage can be found in NCB, *A Short History of the Scottish Coalmining Industry* (1958), pp. 68-71; Jevons, op. cit., pp. 215-18.

23. Home Office, *Report of the Departmental Committee on the Use of Electricity in Mines,* Cd. 1916, 1904.

24. See the evidence of George Blake Walker, managing director of the Wharncliffe Silkstone Collieries near Barnsley, and that of M. H. Habershon, mining engineer of Thorncliffe Collieries near Sheffield, *Minutes of Evidence before the Departmental Committee on the Use of Electricity in Mines,* Cd. 1917, 1904.

25. *Royal Commission on Accidents in Mines, 1886.*

26. E. O. Forster Brown, 'The History of Winding', in Mining Association of Great Britain, *Historical Review of Coalmining.*

27. *Report of the Departmental Committee Appointed to Consider the Working of the Existing Special Rules for the Use of Electricity in Mines,* Cd. 5498, 1911.

28. Further details can be found in D. Hay, 'The Development of Mechanical and Electrical Power in Collieries since 1850', in Mining Association of Great Britain, *Historical Review of Coalmining.*

29. The turbine which replaced the reciprocating piston motor was simple, more durable and required only a moderate consumption of air. It was another example of a British invention migrating across the Atlantic before 1914 since engineering practice in this country was not sufficiently advanced to provide the necessary accuracy. Innovation was rapid in the United States where machine tool practice was much superior to that of Britain.

30. NCB, op. cit., p. 81.

31. *Report of the Departmental Committee on the Use of Electricity in Mines,* Cd. 1916, 1904.

32. *Mines and Quarries, Report of HM Inspector of Mines for the Year 1913 for the Divisions Scotland, Northern, Yorkshire etc,* respectively Cd. 7439 and Cd. 7439 I-VI, 1914.

33. Evidence of Robert Smillie, *Minutes of Evidence Taken before the Departmental Committee on the Working of the Existing Special Rules for the Use of Electricity in Mines,* Cd. 5533, 1911.

34. Taylor, 'Labour Productivity and Technological Innovation', pp. 60-62.

35. N. K. Buxton, 'Entrepreneurial Efficiency in the British Coal Industry between the Wars', *Econ. Hist. Rev.,* Second series, Vol. XXIII (1970), pp. 483-4; G. C. Allen, *British Industries and Their Organisation* (1952), p. 65; R. Walters, 'Labour Productivity in the South Wales Steam-Coal Industry, 1870-1914', *Econ. Hist. Rev.,* Second series, Vol. XXVIII (1975), pp. 296-7.

36. For example, see the evidence of Mr Lloyd Wilson, one of the owners of Flimby and Broughton Moor Colliery in Cumberland, *Minutes of Evidence Taken Before the Departmental Committee on the Use of Electricity in Coal Mines,* 1904.

37. According to the Samuel Commission in 1925 technical economies in coalmining included the more efficient provision of electric power, purchase of supplies, working of repair and maintenance workshops and control over stocks. Commercial economies consisted of a stronger sales organisation, the advantages to be derived from bulk buying, and improved transport and distribution. *Samuel Commission, 1925,* Vol. 1, Report, Cd. 2600 (1926), pp. 49-51.

38. For the importance of the distinction between 'major' and 'minor' innovations in this context, see A. Lamfalussy, *Investment and Growth in Mature Economies* (1961), pp. 74-8.

39. ibid, pp. 79-94.

40. *Samuel Commission, 1925,* Vol. III, p. 175.

41. Taylor, 'Labour Productivity and Technological Innovation', p. 65.

42. *Samuel Commission, 1925,* Vol. I, pp. 111-23.

43 J. W. F. Rowe, *Wages in the Coal Industry* (1923), pp. 126-7.

44. Walters, loc. cit., pp. 288-90.

45. ibid, pp. 291-2.

46. Taylor, loc. cit., p. 54.

47. See also R. A. S. Redmayne, *The Problem of the Coal Mines* (1945), p. 40.

48. For a similar pattern in the regional coalfields, see A. Slaven, 'Earnings and Productivity in the Scottish Coal-Mining Industry during the Nineteenth Century: The Dixon Enterprises', in P. L. Payne (ed.), *Studies in Scottish Business History* (1967), pp. 244-7;, Walters, loc. cit., pp. 283-5.

CHAPTER 6

1. *Queries Concerning the State of the Pitmen on the River Tyne by Sir John Swinburne Bt: Replies thereto by Mr Thomas of Benton Hall,* unpublished manuscript, copied 1807, North of England Institute of Mining and Mechanical Engineers.

2. ibid.

3. *Report of the Commissioner Appointed Under the Provisions of the Act 5 and 6*

Notes

Vict., C.99, to Inquire into the Operation of that Act and into the State of the Population in the Mining Districts, 1850 (Henceforth *Report on Mining Districts, 1850).*

4. ibid.

5. For the position in Scotland during the early 19th century, see B. F. Duckham, *A History of the Scottish Coal Industry, Vol. I, 1700-1815* (1970), pp. 283-4.

6. Evidence of George Elliot, agent of the Marquis of Londonderry, *Second Report of the Select Committee on Accidents in Coal Mines, Minutes of Evidence,* 258, 1854.

7. ibid.

8. See evidence of Thomas Burt, coal-hewer in Northumberland, *Report from the Select Committee Appointed to Inquire into the Operation of the Acts for the Regulation and Inspection of Mines, With Minutes of Evidence,* 431, 1866.

9. ibid. Virtually all the evidence given on the condition of children under 12 years of age was in the same vein. See, for instance, the evidence of B. Owen, a miner from Staffordshire; J. Wilkins, a miner from Nottinghamshire; W. Matthews, proprietor of Corbyns Hall Works, South Staffordshire, and President of the Mining Association of Great Britain. There was general agreement between witnesses that children under 12, or even 14, should not be allowed underground.

10. *Reports on Mining Districts for 1850 and 1855.*

11. *Second Report of the Royal Commission on Mines,* Cd. 4820, 1909.

12. For a discussion, see B. F. Duckham, 'Serfdom in 18th Century Scotland', *History,* Vol. LIV (1969).

13. For details of these measures, see Duckham, op. cit., pp. 294-313.

14. In 1804, 12 to 14 guineas were paid on the Tyne, and 18 guineas on the Wear. Ashton and Sykes, op. cit., p. 94.

15. ibid; see also Duckham, op. cit., p. 310.

16. *Midland Mining Commission, First Report* (1843), p. xxxiv.

17. 57 Geo. III, cap. 122 and 1 and 2 Gul. IV, cap. 37.

18. For details, see B. Lewis, *Coal Mining in the Eighteenth and Nineteenth Centuries* (1971), pp. 56-7; Galloway, op. cit., II, pp. 148-9.

19. *Report of the South Shields Committee Appointed to Investigate the Causes of Accidents in Coal Mines,* 1843.

20. *First Report of the Commissioners for Inquiring into the Conditions of Employment of Children in Mines,* 380, 1842 (Henceforth, *Children's Employment Commission, 1842).* The Commission was established in 1840 with four members and six sub-commissioners. In 1841 the number of sub-commissioners was raised to 12 and later to 20.

21. For discussion of these criticisms see D. Fraser, *The Evolution of the British Welfare State* (1973), pp. 39-40.

22. For vehement opposition to this possibility and outright rejection of 'this . . . method of throwing doubt on the contemporary evidence ot bad social conditions,' see E. J. Hobsbawm, *Labouring Men: Studies in the History of Labour* (1964), pp. 110-11.

23. Hair, loc. cit., p. 555.

24. In this sense the 1842 Commission escaped one of the criticisms commonly made of such bodies: namely that they had little or no effect on subsequent government action. For a discussion of this and other criticisms of commissions and committees see T. J. Cartwright, *Royal Commissions and Departmental Committees in Britain* (1975), pp. 209-15.

25. For full details of bearing in Scotland, see Duckham, op. cit., pp. 94-101; R. R. S. Megaw, 'Women Coal-bearers in Midlothian', *Scottish Studies,* Vol. X (1965).

26. *Children's Employment Commission,* 1842.

27. *Children's Employment Commission: Appendix to First Report of the Commissioners; Mines, Part II, Reports and Evidence from Sub-Commissioners, 1842,* p. 103.

28. ibid., p. 21.

29. ibid, p. 81.

30. ibid, p. 71.

31. 5 and 6 Vict, cap. 99.

32. Lewis, op. cit., pp. 59-60.

33. Galloway, op cit., II, p. 153.

34. H. S. Tremenheere acted as inspector under the provisions of the 1842 Act from 1843 until 1859.

35. 13 and 14 Vict., cap. 100, and 18 and 19 Vict., cap. 108.

36. *House of Commons, Fourth Report from the Select Committee on Accidents in Coal Mines,* 325, 1854.

37. *Report on Mining Districts, 1855.*

38. For the most prominent of these, see D. Spring, 'English Landowners and Nineteenth Century Industrialism', in J. T. Ward and R. G. Wilson (eds.), *Land and Industry: The Landed Estate and the Industrial Revolution* (1971), pp. 31-3.

39. Duckham, op. cit., p. 288, *passim.*

40. *House of Lords, Select Committee on the Coal Trade, 1830.*

41. Evidence of Thomas Taylor, viewer and mineral agent of the Duke of Northumberland, *House of Commons, Second Report from the Select Committee on Accidents in Coal Mines,* 258, 1854.

42. *Watson Collection, North of England Institute of Mining and Mechanical Engineers.*

43. *Queries Concerning the State of the Pitmen on the River Tyne,* op. cit.; see also evidence of John Buddle, *House of Lords, Select Committee on the Coal Trade, 1830.*

44. *Board of Trade, Return of Rates of Wages in the Mines and Quarries in the United Kingdom,* C. 6455, 1891.

45. Evidence of William Matthews, President of the Mining Association of Great Britain, *House of Commons, Select Committee on the Operation of the Acts for the Regulation and Inspection of Mines,* 431, 1866.

46. F. L. M. Thompson, *English Landed Society in the Nineteenth Century* (1963), pp. 265-6; R. W. Sturgess, 'Landowners, Mining and Urban Development in Nineteenth Century Staffordshire', in Ward and Wilson, op. cit., p. 178.

47. Among others, see the opinions of George Hollingworth, appearing on behalf of the National Association of Colliery Managers; William Maurice, Midland Branch of the National Association; and Evan Williams, representing owners in South Wales, *Minutes of Evidence Taken Before the Royal Commission on Mines,* Vol. IV, Cd. 4667, 1909.

48. Evidence of B. Owen, *Minutes of Evidence from the Select Committee Appointed to Inquire into the Operation of the Acts for the Regulation and Inspection of Mines,* 431, 1866. Italics inserted.

49. ibid.

50. *Report from the Select Committee of the House of Commons on the Operation of the Acts for the Regulation and Inspection of Mines,* 496, 1867.

51. 23 and 24 Vict., cap. 11.

52. Lewis, op. cit., p. 64.

53. 35 and 36 Vict., cap. 76.

54. For a detailed discussion of this Petition, see *Report from the Select Committee on the Operation of the Acts for the Regulation and Inspection of Mines,* 1867.

55. A further aspect of the Miners' Petition deploring the lack of facilities to educate miners' children was largely covered by the 1876 Elementary Education Act. Since education became a matter of national concern, the need for 'education clauses' in future

mining legislation was removed.

56. Respectively 50 and 51 Vict., cap. 58 and 59, and 60 Vict., cap. 43.

57. *Second Report of the Royal Commission on Mines,* Cd. 4820, 1909.

58. 8 Edw. VII. cap. 57 and 1 and 2 Geo. V, cap. 50.

59. Hair, loc. cit., pp. 551-2: the statistics used later in the paragraph are derived from the same source.

60. Operating under the Mines Regulation Acts, Employers' Liability Act of 1880 or the Workmen's Compensation Act of 1897.

61. J. Benson, 'English Coal-Miners' Trade-Union Accident Funds, 1850-1900', *Econ. Hist. Rev.,* Second series, Vol. XXVIII (1975), pp. 401-12.

62. *Report from the Select Committee of the House of Lords on Accidents in Coal Mines,* 613, 1849.

63. Nef, op. cit., 11, pp. 195-6.

64. Ashton and Sykes, op. cit., pp. 136-7.

65. *Buddle-Atkinson Collection,* Vol. 8, North of England Institute of Mining and Mechanical Engineers.

66. See the contemporary evidence cited in Ashton and Sykes, op. cit., pp. 147-8.

67. Adam Smith, *The Wealth of Nations* (1908 ed.), Book I, p. 116.

68. Coal output traditionally depended on the domestic demand of such industries as iron, railways, gas and electricity. However, at Govan Collieries in Scotland, earnings were more directly influenced from the 1880's by the vagaries of the export trade. This was due to the rapid growth of overseas shipments and pointed to the fact that wide divergences would in future develop in the fortunes of districts serving the home market and those more heavily committed to foreign sales. Slaven, *Studies in Scottish Business History* (1967), loc. cit., pp. 234-5.

69. *The Scotsman* newspaper, 22.11.1874.

70. G. J. Barnsby, 'The Standard of Living in the Black Country during the Nineteenth Century', *Econ. Hist. Rev.,* Second series, Vol. XXIV (1971), pp. 225 and 238.

71. Griffin, op. cit., p. 79.

72. A. M. Neuman, *Economic Organisation of the British Coal Industry* (1934), p. 321 *passim.*

73. Neuman, op. cit., p. 342; *Final Report of the Royal Commission on Mining Royalties,* C. 6980, 1893; *Report to the Board of Trade on the Relation of Wages in Certain Industries to the Cost of Production,* C. 6535, 1891.

74. Taylor, 'Labour Productivity and Technological Innovation', p. 55; Walters, loc. cit., pp. 286-7.

75. For details of these the reader is directed to J. E. Williams, 'Labour in the Coalfields: A Critical Bibliography', *Bulletin of the Society for the Study of Labour History* (1962), No. 4, and R. G. Neville and J. Benson, 'Labour in the Coalfields II: A Select Critical Bibliography', *Bulletin of the Society for the Study of Labour History* (1975), No. 31.

76. Jevons, op. cit., pp. 447-8.

77. Hobsbawm, op. cit., pp. 7-9.

78. For a good discussion of the relevance of the Combination Acts, see A. E. Musson, *British Trade Unions 1800-1875,* Studies in Economic History (1972), pp. 22-6.

79. *Report of Matthias Dunn, Inspector of Coal Mines for Durham, Northumberland, Cumberland and Scotland to HM Secretary of State,* 1851; Musson, *British Trade Unions,* pp. 27-8.

80. Sidney and Beatrice Webb, *The History of Trade Unionism* (1894, reprinted 1950), p. 181.

81. However there were some successes, notably the policy of restriction of output by the 'darg' or stint which was imposed on employers by miners in Scotland.

82. Miners in Northumberland and Durham went on strike in 1831, refusing to enter into any bond until various grievances had been remedied. At first successful in winning concessions from employers, Hepburn's Union was broken in the following year by the importation of labour from other districts.

83. For discussion of the activities of the Miners' Association see A. J. Taylor, 'The Miners' Association of Great Britain and Northern Ireland, 1842-1848', *Economica*, Vol. XXII (1955); R. Page Arnot, *The Miners* (1949), I. pp. 41-3.

84. Although it continued for a further 30 years in Durham, being replaced in 1872 by a fortnightly agreement.

85. Jevons, op. cit., pp. 472-8; Lewis, op. cit., pp. 73-5.

86. Details of the struggle to secure employers' acceptance of this measure, and of their constant evasions once it had become law, can be found in the Webbs, op. cit., pp. 304-5.

87. R. V. Clements, 'British Trade Unions and Popular Political Economy 1850-1875', *Econ. Hist. Rev.*, Second series, Vol. XIV (1961), p. 101.

88. Quoted in the Webbs, op. cit., p. 256.

89. R. Challinor, *Alexander Macdonald and the Miners*, CPGB, Our History Pamphlet, No. 48 (1967); Lewis, op. cit., pp. 77-8.

90. For details see D. Kynaston, *King Labour: The British Working Class, 1850-1914* (1976), pp. 57-8.

91. J. H. Porter, 'Wage Bargaining under Conciliation Agreements, 1860-1914', *Econ. Hist. Rev.*, Second series, Vol. XXIII (1970), p. 463.

92. ibid., p. 475.

93. Details of the sliding-scales in operation in each district are provided by the Webbs, op. cit., appendix III, pp. 735-6; Jevons, op. cit., pp. 489-519.

94. This objection was first raised by the Northern counties in 1863 when an Eight Hour Bill for boys under 14 was advocated. Over time, it gradually developed into a general objection to legal regulation of the hours of adult men.

95. See, for instance, details of the discussion and vote on this issue at the TUC conference in Liverpool in 1890, *Report on the Strikes and Lock-Outs of 1890 by the Labour Correspondent to the Board of Trade*, c. 6476, 1891.

96. W. R. Garside, *The Durham Miners, 1919-1960* (1971), p. 25.

97. B. McCormick and J. E. Williams, 'The Miners and the Eight-Hour Day, 1863-1910', *Econ. Hist. Rev.*, Second series, Vol. XII (1959), pp. 225-6.

98. The existing scale was formally terminated by the Yorkshire Miners' Association, newly created by the amalgamation of the South and West Yorkshire Associations.

99. Between 1892 and 1894, the average strength of 'new' unionism was 107,000 out of a total TUC membership of 1,555,000. Kynaston, op. cit., p. 144.

100. The South Wales Miners' Federation was formed in 1898 and agreed to abolish the sliding-scale when the existing agreement ended in 1902.

101. The Durham Miners' Association had previously joined the MFGB in 1892 but had been expelled in the following year due to its refusal to join the national strike of 1893. Again in 1896, the Association applied for membership but its contribution to the Federation was returned when it refused to support legislative action to achieve the eight-hour day. Once the 1908 Act had resolved the latter issue, the way was open for affiliation to the MFGB.

102. A. E. P. Duffy, 'New Unionism in Britain, 1889-1890: A Re-Appraisal', *Econ. Hist. Rev.*, Second series, Vol. XIV (1961), p. 308; Page Arnot, op. cit., I, pp. 144-9.

103. R. Davidson, 'Llewellyn Smith, the Labour Department and Government Growth 1886-1909', in G. Sutherland (ed.), *Studies in the Growth of Nineteenth Century Government* (1972), p. 251.

104. The total number of working-days lost through disputes is an aggregate of days lost in the following industries: building, metal, engineering and shipbuilding, textiles, clothing, transport and mining and quarrying. See Mitchell and Deane, op. cit., p. 72.

105. Many miners in South Wales regarded the sliding-scale as a 'starving-scale' and demanded instead a minimum wage policy. After a bitter strike, the employers finally accepted, in theory, the principle of a minimum wage. The South Wales Miners' Federation was formed, specifically opposed to the sliding-scale, and affiliated to the MFGB in 1899.

106. Full details of the early work of the conciliation boards can be found in J. E. Williams, *The Derbyshire Miners* (1962), pp. 344-63. The coal industry passed through distinct phases in the settlement of wages. Arbitration was followed by sliding-scales which, in turn, were superseded by conciliation boards.

107. The strike and its effects are fully analysed in Williams, op. cit., pp. 393-441; Jevons, op. cit., pp. 520-68; Page Arnot, op. cit., II, pp. 90-122.

108. Rowe, op. cit., pp. 102-10; Jevons, op. cit., pp. 602-3.

109. Some 500,000 miners were represented at the Jolimont Congress by more than 40 delegates from Britain, 60 from Belgium, 6 from France, 5 from Germany and 1 from Austria.

110. It proved virtually impossible for British miners to ascertain the eventual destination of their coal. See *Report on Strikes and Lock-Outs by the Labour Correspondent to the Board of Trade,* 1891.

111. For the transformation of mining unions from Liberalism to Labourism see R. Gregory, *The Miners and British Politics, 1906-1914* (1968).

112. Duffy, loc. cit., p. 308; H. Pelling, *History of British Trade Unionism* (1963), p. 108; Musson, *British Trade Unions,* p. 67.

113. Secured by passing the 1906 Trade Disputes Act. For details, see the Webbs, op. cit., pp. 604-8; G. D. H. Cole, *A Short History of the British Working Class Movement* (1947), III, pp. 41-7.

114. For the importance of private pressure groups in prompting mining reforms, see D. Morrah, 'A Historical Outline of Coal Mining Legislation', in Mining Assocation of Great Britain, *Historical Review of Coalmining.*

115. S. Pollard, 'Trade Unions and the Labour Market, 1870-1914', *Yorkshire Bulletin of Econ. & Soc. Research,* Vol. 17 (1965), p. 106.

116. Page Arnot, op. cit., pp. 252-4.

117. Pollard, loc. cit., pp. 109-11. The remainder of the paragraph is drawn largely from this source.

118. Cole, op. cit., II, pp. 190-91.

CHAPTER 7

1. Average f.o.b. prices per ton increased from 13/10d. in 1913 to 30/3d. in 1918 and to 79/11d. in 1920.

2. This loss was partly offset by the recruitment of untrained personnel into the mines, See *Report of the Departmental Committee Appointed by the Board of Trade to Consider the Position of the Coal Trade after the War,* Cd. 9093, 1918.

3. *Coal Mining Organisation Committee, Third General Report of the Departmental Committee on the Conditions Prevailing in the Coal Mining Industry due to the War,* Cd. 8345, 1916.

4. For details, see W. R. Scott and J. Cunison, *The Industries of the Clyde Valley during the War,* Economic and Social History of the World War (1924), pp. 36-7.

5. See the 'margin of difference' between pit-head and f.o.b. export prices during the period of control in Newman, op. cit., p. 39.

6. In 1916, a distinction was made in coal export policy between allies and neutrals. The Board of Trade began in that year to regulate the price of coal and freights charged to France and Italy. Once under complete Government control in 1917, the British mines were periodically issued with schedules of price by class of coal. These stipulated the

prices to be charged to France and Italy but only the minimum chargeable to neutral countries.

7. For details, see Page Arnot, *The Miners: Years of Struggle* (1953), pp. 164-70.

8. G. D. H. Cole, *Labour in the Coal Mining Industry, 1914-1921* (1923), Economic and Social History of the World War, pp. 49-55.

9. *Glasgow Herald Trade Review*, Dec. 1918.

10. By means of the Coal Mines Control Agreement (Confirmation) Act of 1918, the Coal Mines (Emergency) Act of 1919, and the Mining Industry Act of 1920.

11. For example, by March 1920, South Wales was showing a profit of no less than 18/7d. per ton. H. Wilson, *New Deal for Coal* (1945), p. 14, n.1.

12. R. H. Tawney, 'The Abolition of Economic Controls, 1918-21', *Econ. Hist. Rev.,* First series, Vol. XIII (1943), pp. 14-16.

13. *PRO, Power 26/14.* For details of the Interim Reports of the Sankey Commission and of the negotiations surrounding the wage increase of 2/- per shift see Page Arnot, *The Miners: Years of Struggle,* pp. 198-202.

14. *PRO, Power 26/51.*

15. *First Annual Report of the Secretary for Mines for 1921,* HMSO (1922).

16. ibid.

17. *PRO, Power 26/51.*

18. World output in 1913 was 1,237 million tons, of which Britain produced 287 million.

19. W. H. B. Court, 'Problems of the British Coal Industry Between the Wars', *Econ. Hist. Rev.,* First series, Vol. XV (1945), p. 4; H. W. Singer, 'The Coal Question Re-Considered: Effects of Economy and Substitution', *Review of Economic Studies,* Vol. 8, (1940-41), pp. 166-77.

20. Court, loc. cit., p. 4.

21. *Eighteenth Annual Report of the Secretary for Mines for 1938,* HMSO (1940).

22. European output rose from 552.5 million tons in 1909/13 to 604.6 million in 1927 and to 687.0 million in 1937.

23. See I. Svennilson, *Growth and Stagnation in the European Economy* (1954), pp. 252-3.

24. International Labour Office (ILO), *The World Coal-Mining Industry,* I, Economic Conditions (1938), pp. 75-6.

25. League of Nations, *Problem of the Coal Industry,* p. 9.

26. J. H. Jones, G. Cartwright and P. H. Guenault, *The Coal-Mining Industry: An International Study in Planning* (1939), p. 35.

27. Between 1913-28, British exports to France fell from 12.8 million tons to 9.1 million tons, and to Germany from 9.0 million tons to 5.4 million tons.

28. ILO, op. cit., pp. 95-6. The calculation for railways is based on lbs of fuel consumed per transportation unit.

29. ibid., p. 84.

30. *PRO, Power 16, 1931;* A. H. Stockder, *German Trade Associations: the Coal Kartells* (1924), pp. 117-18, 165 *passim;* League of Nations, *Memorandum on Coal,* I, pp. 19 and 31-2.

31. *Samuel Commission, 1925,* p. 6.

32. Mines Dept., *Report of the British Coal Delegation to Sweden, Norway and Denmark,* 13th to 25th Sept., 1930, Cmd. 3702, 1930.

33. ILO, op. cit., p. 201.

34. Although Polish coalfields were about 380 miles from the principal Baltic ports, the preferential treatment given by the State Railways allowed an average rate of 3/5d. per ton to be charged from coalfields to ports. This was less than the rate charged in Britain

Notes

for a haul of 40 miles. *Report of the British Coal Delegation, 1930.* See also *PRO, Power* 16, 1931.

35. *Samuel Commission, 1925,* pp. 96-107; League of Nations, *Memorandum on Coal,* II (1927), p. 18.

36. PEP, *Report on the British Coal Industry* (1936), p. 152.

37. ILO, op. cit., p. 218.

38. Between 1929 and 1936, output per man-shift increased by 46% in Poland, 38% in Belgium, 34% in the state mines of the Netherlands and 29% in Germany (Prussia). In Britain the increase was a mere 9%.

39. ILO, op. cit., I, pp. 213-15.

40. Buxton, loc. cit., pp. 490-91.

41. *Eighteenth Annual Report of the Secretary for Mines for the Year 1938;* ILO, op. cit., I, p. 201. German prices include exports from the Saar from 1935.

42. For details of these arrangements see the *Annual Reports of the Secretary for Mines* during the 1930's; PEP, op. cit., pp. 160-62.

43. Due in part to the inclusion of the Saar in Germany from 1935.

44. N. K. Buxton, 'The Coal Industry', in N. K. Buxton and D. H. Aldcroft (eds.), *British Industry Between the Wars: Instability and Industrial Development, 1919-1939* (Forthcoming).

45. *Iron and Steel Industry: Reports by the British Iron and Steel Federation and the Joint Iron Council to the Minister of Supply,* Cmd. 6811, 1946.

46. From 13.5 thousand to 15.0 thousand cu. ft. PEP, op. cit., p. 108.

47. *Seventeenth and Eighteenth Annual Reports of the Secretary for Mines for the years 1937 and 1938* respectively.

48. This is a revised version of a part of my paper, 'The Coal Industry', in Buxton and Aldcroft (eds.), *British Industry Between the Wars.*

49. Other factors influencing the rate of growth of output per man-shift were, as observed earlier, the organisation and layout of mines, the shift from steam to electric power and the selective reduction of the labour force, so raising the average speed and skill of retained employees.

50. In this context, see particularly the ILO, op. cit., p. 110. The rate of increase is understated in all countries since no account is taken in Table 7 of reductions in the length of working shift between 1913-36.

51. ILO, op. cit., pp. 159-60.

52. Ministry of Fuel & Power, *Coal Mining: Report of the Technical Advisory Committee,* Cd. 6610 (1945), p. 65. (Hereafter referred to as the *Reid Report, 1945.*)

53. For a detailed discussion of the disadvantages of the Endless Rope system of haulage, the most popular method used in Britain, see *Reid Report, 1945,* pp. 67-8.

54. ibid, p. 33.

55. See R. A. S. Redmayne, *The Problem of the Coal Mines,* pp. 28-9. In Durham, both demand-and supply-side factors prevented rapid mechanisation. Depression in local heavy industry created a serious deficiency in demand; at the same time, difficult underground conditions and the fact that several of the pits were virtually worked out made owners reluctant to commit themselves to a programme of heavy capital expenditure.

56. *Reid Report, 1945,* p. 16.

57. See my paper, 'Avoiding the Pitfalls: Entrepreneurial Efficiency in the Coal Industry Again', *Econ. Hist. Rev.,* Second series, Vol. XXV (1972), pp. 669-73.

58. This holds good in all but the two districts mentioned above, Durham and South Wales.

59. For the developments in mechanisation in Scotland and the reasons for them, see N. K. Buxton, 'Entrepreneurial Efficiency in the British Coal Industry', pp. 483-6.

CHAPTER 8

1. The best is probably G. A. Phillips, *The General Strike: the Politics of Industrial Conflict* (1976); see also M. Morris, *The General Strike* (1976); P. Renshaw, *The General Strike* (1975); J. Skelley (ed.), *The General Strike 1926,* (1976); longer-established texts include Page Arnot, *The Miners: Years of Struggle;* G. D. H. Cole, *A Short History of the Working Class Movement, III, 1900-1937* (1937); M. Heinemann, *Britain's Coal* (1944).

2. The South Wales Unofficial Reform Committee, *The Miners' Next Step* (1912).

3. Phillips, op. cit., p. 7.

4. Preamble to Keir Hardie's Nationalisation Bill, 1893, reproduced in Page Arnot, *The Miners: Years of Struggle,* p. 149.

5. *Final Report of the Royal Commission Appointed to Inquire into the Subject of Mining Royalties,* C. 6980, 1893, p. 47.

6. ibid., p. 43.

7. M. Barratt-Brown, 'Coal as a Nationalised Industry', *Economic Studies,* Vol. 4 (1969), pp. 95-6; F. Hodges, *Nationalisation of the Mines* (1920).

8. Quoted in D. Lloyd George (ed.), *Coal and Power: Report of an Enquiry Presided over by David Lloyd George* (1924), pp. 5-6.

9. *Coal Industry Commission, Reports and Evidence,* Cd. 359, 360-1, 1919.

10. Details of the negotiations and areas of dispute are provided by the *First Annual Report of the Secretary for Mines for 1921,* 1922, pp. 9-16.

11. *PRO, Power 16/508/Pt. 1,* letters by the Prime Minister and President of the Board of Trade to Frank Hodges, 12th October 1921 and 29th October 1921 respectively.

12. The 1921 dispute and its aftermath are fully examined in Cole, *Labour in the Coal Mining Industry, 1914-1921,* pp. 162-242.

13. *The Samuel Commission, 1925,* p. 163; for an assessment of the miners' real wage position see Phillips, op. cit., appendix I, pp. 297-300.

14. A discussion of the effects of the General Strike can be found in Phillips, op. cit., pp. 264-95.

15. Morris, op. cit., pp. 276-86.

16. *PRO, Cab. 24/204/176.*

17. Mining Association of Great Britain, *One Hundred Questions and Answers About Coal* (1938), pp. 63-4.

18. *PRO, Cab. 27/395.*

19. *PRO, Cab. 27/395,* submission by Evan Williams on behalf of coalowners.

20. Mining Association of Great Britain, *The Miners' Claims Considered* (1935); *PRO, Premier 1/150.*

21. H. & B. Duckham, op. cit., p. 197.

22. *Royal Commission on Safety in Coal Mines, 1938,* p. 68.

23. In 1907 the proportion relates to Great Britain and in 1924 and 1935 to the United Kingdom. Deane and Cole, op. cit., Tables 40, 41 and 79.

24. N. K. Buxton and D. I. MacKay, *British Employment Statistics: A Guide to Sources and Methods* (1977), pp. 47-84.

25. The aims of the Scheme are outlined in the *Report of the Ministry of Labour* (1928), Cd. 3333, pp. 16-19.

26. *Second Annual Report of the Secretary for Mines for 1922,* HMSO, 1923.

27. The principles of wage-determination before 1921 are outlined in the *Final Report of the Royal Commission on Mining Royalties, 1893.*

28. Profits were assessed over so-called 'ascertainment periods', the length of which

varied according to the preference of each district.

29. Standard wages were defined as the district 'basis rate' existing at end-March 1921, plus the district percentages payable in July 1914, plus, in the case of pieceworkers, the percentage additions which were made consequent upon the reduction of hours from 8 to 7 in 1919.

30. Mining Association, *The Situation in the Coal Industry: Attitude of the Coal Owners* (1923).

31. PEP, op. cit., p. 171.

32. *Report by a Court of Inquiry Concerning the Coal Mining Industry Dispute, 1925,* Cd. 2478, 1925.

33. PEP, op. cit., p. 174.

34. There was one exception to this general rule. In 1937, annual earnings of miners in North Derbyshire and Nottinghamshire marginally exceeded those of Scottish miners.

CHAPTER 9

1. *Samuel Commission, 1925,* pp. 259-65; *Mining Industry Act, 1926: Report by the Board of Trade on the Working of Part I of the Act,* Cd. 3214, 1928.

2. Details of these measures can be found in the *Annual Reports of the Secretary for Mines* and Neuman, op. cit., pp. 244-8.

3. *Samuel Commission, 1925,* p. 223.

4. Although in fact it covered the coal mines of nine counties. Details of the operations of the Scheme can be found in Jones, Cartwright and Guenault, op. cit., pp. 93-107..

5. Mines Dept., *Coal Mines Act 1930: Report by the Board of Trade on the Working of Schemes under Part I of the Act,* Cd. 3982, 1931, and Cd. 4224, 1932.

6. *PRO, Prem. 1/172, Coal Policy: Memorandum by Sir Ernest Gowers,* 1933.

7. Mines Dept., *Coal Mines Act 1930: Report by the Board of Trade,* Cd. 5474, 1938.

8. Part I was extended in 1931 for a one-year period and then extended again by the 1932 Coal Mines Act for a period of five years.

9. Sir Ernest Gowers, 'The Coal Question Today', address given by the chairman of the CMRC to the Dundee Business Club, 1934.

10. Sir Ernest Gowers, Address to the Cardiff Business Club, 1933.

11. Statement by Ernest Brown, Prime Minister's Meeting, Dec. 1933, *PRO, Prem. 1/172.*

12. *PRO, Prem. 1/150.*

13. For details, see *PRO, Coal 12/13.*

14. *Eighteenth Annual Report of the Secretary for Mines for the Year 1938,* HMSO, 1940.

15. *The Reid Report, 1945,* pp. 34-5.

16. *PRO, Prem. 1/172.*

17. *Samuel Commission, 1925,* pp. 241-59.

18. W. A. Lee, *Thirty Years in Coal, 1917-1947* (1954), p. 23.

19. *The Reid Report 1945,* p. 30; see also A. Beacham, 'Efficiency and Organisation of the British Coal Industry', *Economic Journal,* Vol. LV (1945), pp. 207-9.

20. M. W. Kirby, 'Comment' on 'Entrepreneurial Efficiency in the British Coal Industry', *Econ. Hist. Rev.,* Second series, Vol. XXV (1972), pp. 655-7; also his *The British Coalmining Industry 1870-1946: A Political and Economic History* (1977), pp. 236-7. Kirby seems obsessed with the issue of undertakings and apparently accepts that amalgamations of these would have resulted in significant scale economies because the Samuel Commission said so. He does not appear to have considered the nature of the economies to be obtained or to have appreciated that the important technical economies, discussed at length by the Reid Committee, depended by their very nature on enlarging *mine*-size and reorganising underground roads and layouts.

Notes

21. See for instance, *Samuel Commission, 1925,* Vol. I, Table 31, p. 264 and Vol. III, Table 12, Appendix No. 18, p. 196.

22. Neuman, op. cit., pp. 508-23.

23. R. W. Dron, *The Economics of Coal Mining* (1928), pp. 113-14.

24. ibid, pp. 114-18.

25. For evidence of the comparative efficiency of small mines, see Buxton, 'Entrepreneurial Efficiency in the British Coal Industry', pp. 479-82.

26. Board of Trade, *Memorandum on the Production, Distribution and Rationing of Coal,* Cd. 6364, 1942.

27. W. H. B. Court, *Coal,* History of the Second World War Series (1951). pp. 70-75.

28. A useful analysis of the factors responsible for the decline in output between 1939 and 1945 was presented by the *Owners' Side of the Joint National Negotiating Committee, 7.6.45 PRO, Coal, 11/103.*

29. PEP, *The Fuel and Power Industries,* pp. 74-5.

30. See National Coal Board, *Annual Report and Statement of Accounts for the Year Ended 31 December 1946,* 174, 1948, pp. 2-3.

31. For details, see M.P. Jackson, *The Price of Coal,* (1974), pp. 48-51.

32. Exports and bunker coal fell from 46.3 to a mere 7.8 million tons between 1938 and 1945.

33. For details, see PEP, op. cit., pp. 226-8.

34. *Cherwell to PM, 17/1/1945, PRO, Prem. 4/95.*

35. *Coal Budget for Year 1945-6 Presented by the Minister of Fuel and Power to the Lord President's Committee, 9/3/45, PRO, Prem, 4/95.*

36. The War Emergency Supplementary Assistance (or Necessitous Undertakings) Scheme had been first introduced in mid-1941. It was continued by the Coal (Charges) Order of June 1942 under revised conditions.

37. First implemented by the Central Council of Coal Owners under the Coal Mines (War Levy) Scheme at the end of 1940. The Board of Trade converted this, and the Coal Mines Guaranteed Wage Levy, into a lump sum charge in 1942 and passed over responsibility for the operation of the scheme to the new Ministry of Fuel and Power.

38. For details, see Ministry of Fuel and Power, *Financial Position of Coalmining Industry: Coal Charges Account,* Cd. 6617, 1945 (Henceforth, *Coal Charges Account, 1945).*

39. ibid.

40. ibid.

41. These included expenses incurred over special recruitment and training measures, miners' transfer expenses to other collieries, charges under the new Workmen's Compensation Bill and old cases of pneumoconiosis etc.

42. Full details of these awards can be found in Court, op. cit., pp. 219-28 and 251-69.

43. *Coal Charges Account, 1945.*

44. The others were Cumberland, North Wales, Bristol and Somerset, and the Forest of Dean which between them accounted for little more than 2½% of total output.

45. For district costs per ton and recoveries from the CCA, see Court, op. cit., p. 346; *Coal Charges Account, 1945.*

46. The increase in money earnings is shown in Table 1. Between 1939 and 1945, the working-class cost of living index showed an increase of about 30%.

47. *Owners' Case to Joint National Negotiating Committee,* submissions dated 17.2.1945, 15.3.1945 and 7.6.1945, *PRO, Coal 11/103.*

48. Garside, op. cit., p. 390.

49. For instance, *Report of the Scottish Coalfields Committee; Regional Survey of the Coalfields, 1944 North Eastern Coalfield, 1945; The Reid Report, 1945,* p. 138.

50. R. Foot, *A Plan for Coal: Being the Report to the Colliery Owners, Mining Association of Great Britain* (1945).

51. Wilson, op. cit., p. 194.

52. The Coal Industry Nationalisation Act did not nationalise the colliery companies as such, in the sense of transferring their shares to public ownership and depriving them of all their assets. While most of the latter were transferred to public ownership, the companies kept their investments, cash and other liquid assets and where iron and steel works were owned, these were not touched by nationalisation of the mines.

53. Of these, over 400 were classified as 'small mines' owned by the Board but operated by private concerns under licence from the Board. NCB, *Annual Report for 1946,* pp. 10-11.

54. NCB, *Annual Report and Statement of Accounts for 1947,* 175, 1948, pp. 9-10 and 77-84.

55. Quoted in I. Berkovitch, *Coal on the Switchback: The Coal Industry since Nationalisation* (1977), p. 58.

56. The executive of the MFGB was given a mandate at the Annual Conference in 1942 to prepare plans for the reorganisation of the union. On the basis of the proposals subsequently drawn up, the National Union of Mineworkers was established in 1945.

57. Full details of the negotiations and final agreement can be found in NCB, *Annual Report for 1947,* pp. 10-14, and 197-200.

58. In 1947, the average cost of producing a ton of coal was about 4/3d. higher than in 1946, the bulk of this increase being due to the five-day week bonus and increased wages for the lower-paid.

59. NCB, Annual Report for 1947, pp. 68-72.

60. The Treasury issued a new stock, valued at almost £78.5 million to replace that of the Coal Commission and the affairs of the latter body were wound up. See *Coal Commission, Accounts 1946,* 134, 1948.

CHAPTER 10

1. From the end of the war until 1956-7, markets for British coal had existed in Europe had there been sufficient coal to spare. As it was, exports were generally restricted in favour of domestic consumption.

2. In 1947, coal amounted to 93% of primary fuel sources. Balance of payments considerations limited the amount of oil that could be imported, with the result that in the short term the country was heavily dependent on the domestic coal industry.

3. *Report of the Committee on National Policy for the Use of Fuel and Power Resources,* Cd. 8647, 1952, p. 50.

4. *A Programme for Nuclear Power,* Cd. 9389, 1955.

5. The NCB committed itself to a heavy programme of capital expenditure between 1951 and 1959, consisting both of reconstructions and major new projects. Since expenditure had to be committed years before its completion, the peak was not reached until 1959. However after 1957 few new important construction projects were undertaken and capital spending dropped rapidly. E. F. Schumacher, 'Some Aspects of Coal Board Policy 1947-67', *Economic Studies,* Vol. 4, (1969), p. 25; Colliery Guardian, *National Coal Board: the First Ten Years* (1957), pp. 61-4.

6. On this issue see Barratt-Brown, loc. cit., pp. 124-9.

7. Financial details are regularly available in NCB, *Annual Reports and Accounts.*

8. NCB, *Investing in Coal* (1956), p. 10.

9. In the event, this target was wide of the mark by between 60-70 million tons.

10. NCB, *Annual Report and Accounts 1955* (1956), p. 51.

11. Of this total, £520 million was allocated to the collieries, two-thirds of which was to be invested by 1965 simply to prevent a decline in output: *Plan for Coal* (1950).

12. NCB, *Revised Plan for Coal* (1959). p. 15.

13. For a discussion of the financial implications of the Plans see I. Hicks, 'Finance and Investment Policies of the National Coal Board', *Economic Studies,* Vol. 4 (1969), pp. 154-60; E. S. Simpson, *Coal and the Power Industries in Postwar Britain* (1966), pp. 1-32.

14. NCB, *Report of the Advisory Committee on Organisation, 1955* (Referred to as the Fleck Committee.).

15. *National Coal Board: the First Ten Years,* pp. 45-53; NCB, *Annual Reports and Accounts.*

16. Ministry of Fuel and Power, *Fuel Policy,* Cd. 3438, 1967.

17. The CEGB was compensated by the Exchequer for the extra cost of burning coal.

18. Details of these measures can be found in NCB, *Annual Reports and Accounts;* House of Commons, *Select Committee on Nationalised Industries, National Coal Board,* 471, Vol. 1, Report and Proceedings of the Committee, 1969.

19. Between 1970 and end-1973, the average landed costs of crude oil in Britain rose from $14.47 per metric tonne to $86 per metric tonne, this only a few years after the 1967 White Paper had confidently asserted that it was 'right to base fuel policy on the expectation that the regular supplies of oil at competitive prices will continue to be available'. See Berkovitch, op. cit., pp. 177-9.

20. The need to use energy more efficiently because of the oil crisis was emphasised in National Economic Development Office, *The Increased Cost of Energy: Implications for UK Industry,* 1974.

21. Full details of these measures can be found in NCB, *Report and Accounts 1972/3.*

22. Intensive exploration by the NCB culminated in the discovery of the Selby Coalfield where reserves in one seam—the Barnsley seam—are estimated to be sufficient to provide each year about one-quarter of the 42 million tons of new capacity to be created by 1985.

23. Department of Energy, *Coal Industry Examination: Final Report 1974.*

24. Department of Energy, *Coal for the Future: Progress with 'Plan for Coal' and Prospects to the Year 2000, 1977 (a).*

25. Total inland consumption of primary energy increased from 249 to 321 million tons of coal equivalent between 1950 and 1975. Over the same period, GDP at 1970 factor cost rose from £29,080 million to £46,861 million.

26. *Digest of UK Energy Statistics 1975,* HMSO, 1976.

27. See J. Chesshire and C. Buckley, 'Energy Use in UK Industry', *Energy Policy,* Vol. 4, (1976), pp. 237-54.

28. *Digest of UK Energy Statistics, 1975;* see also G. L. Reid, K. Allen and D. J. Harris, *The Nationalised Fuel Industries* (1973), p. 22. Thermal efficiency is defined as the calorific value of energy generated as a percentage of the calorific value of the fuel consumed.

29. For some account of these and a history of the AGR decision in 1965, see H. Rush, G. MacKerron and J. Surrey, 'The Advanced Gas-cooled Reactor: A Case Study in Reactor Choice', *Energy Policy,* Vol. 5, (1977) pp. 95-105.

30. The AGRs were expected by the mid 1970's to operate at only two-thirds of their original electricity-generating capacity. They were derated from 600 megawatt reactors to 400 megawatts.

31. *The Times,* 3.1.78.

32. Berkovitch, op. cit., pp. 125 and 195.

33. For an account of the trials and tribulations of the NCB in the 1960's, see Lord Robens, *Ten Year Stint* (1972).

34. NCB, *Annual Report and Accounts 1975/6.*

35. D. M. Kelly, 'The Process of Mechanisation in British Coalmining since 1945', *Economic Studies,* Vol. 4 (1969), p. 136; *National Coal Board: the First Ten Years,* pp. 39-44.

Notes

36. *First Report from the Select Committee on Nationalised Industries 1974-75: the Purchasing of Powered Roof Supports and Spares by the National Coal Board,* 129, 1974.

37. Details of these are available in NCB, *Annual Reports and Accounts.*

38. *Report of a Court of Inquiry into a Dispute between NCB and the NUM under the Chairmanship of the Rt. Hon. Lord Wilberforce,* Cd. 4903, 1972.

39. J. R. Clynes, Foreword to F. Hodges, *Nationalisation of the Mines,* p. vi.

40. Quoted in C. Robinson, *The Energy 'Crisis' and British Coal.* Institute of Economic Affairs, Hobart Papers, 59 (1974), p. 44.

41. Deficits were incurred in 1947, 1965-6 and 1969-70.

42. See for instance, the Treasury, *Nationalised Industries: A Review of Economic and Financial Objectives,* Cd. 3437, 1967; R. Bates and N. Fraser, *Investment Decisions in the Nationalised Fuel Industries* (1974); C. D. Foster, *Politics, Finance and the Role of Economics: an Essay on the Control of Public Enterprise* (1971).

43. *Nationalised Industries: A Review of Economic and Financial Objectives,* 1967.

44. National Board for Prices and Incomes Report No. 153, *Coal Prices (Second Report),* Cd. 4455, 1970; I. M. D. Little, *The Price of Fuel* (1953); D. L. Bevan, 'The Nationalised Industries', in D. Morris (ed.), *The Economic System in the UK* (1977); M. V. Posner, *Fuel Policy: A Study in Applied Economics* (1973).

45. Posner, op. cit., pp. 33-6; but see the definition of marginal costs in the coal industry in NBPI, *Coal Prices,* op. cit.

46. Price changes had to be ratified, where this was considered necessary, by the NBPI. This body was, however, dissolved in 1971.

47. See C. Wilkinson, 'Recent Developments in European Coal and Steel Community Policies', *The Three Banks Review,* No. 113 (1977), pp. 57-8.

48. During the period 1970-75, Britain accounted for 46% of Community output, Germany 40%, France 10% and Belgium 3%. Statistical Office of the European Community, *Energy Statistics Yearbook, 1970-5* (1976). Britain officially became a full member of the ECSC at the start of 1973.

49. Posner, op. cit., pp. 20-22.

CHAPTER 11

1. These White Papers were respectively Ministry of Fuel and Power, *Fuel Policy,* Cd. 2798, 1965 and Cd. 3438, 1967.

2. It is not possible here to do more than provide a brief outline of the debate. For more comprehensive treatment, see the two White Papers on *Fuel Policy* of 1965 and 1967; *Report of the Select Committee on Nationalised Industries, National Coal Board,* Vols. 1 and 2, 1969; Posner, op. cit., pp. 40-44; C. Robinson, *A Policy for Fuel?,* Institute of Economic Affairs, Occasional Paper 31 (1969), and his *Competition for Fuel,* Supplement to Occasional Paper 31 (1971).

3. Robinson, *The Energy 'Crisis' and British Coal;* P. L. Cook and A. H. Surrey, *Energy Policy: Strategies for Uncertainty* (1977), pp. 80-97.

4. Cook and Surrey. op. cit., pp. 52-3. One million tonnes of petroleum is normally regarded as being equivalent to 1.65 million tons of coal.

INDEX

INDEX